THE ISRAELI CONSTITUTION

The Israeli Constitution

FROM EVOLUTION TO REVOLUTION

Gideon Sapir

OXFORD
UNIVERSITY PRESS

OXFORD
UNIVERSITY PRESS

Oxford University Press is a department of the University of Oxford. It furthers the University's
objective of excellence in research, scholarship, and education by publishing worldwide. Oxford is
a registered trademark of Oxford University Press in the UK and certain other countries.

Published in the United States of America by Oxford University Press
198 Madison Avenue, New York, NY 10016, United States of America.

Library of Congress Cataloging-in-Publication Data
Names: Sapir, Gideon, author.
Title: The Israeli Constitution : from evolution to revolution / Gideon Sapir.
Description: New York : Oxford University Press, 2018. | Includes bibliographical references and index.
Identifiers: LCCN 2017057809 | ISBN 9780190680329 ((hardback) : alk. paper)
Subjects: LCSH: Constitutional law—Israel. | Constitutional history—Israel. | Israel—Politics
    and government.
Classification: LCC KMK1750 .S27 2018 | DDC 342.569402—dc23
LC record available at https://lccn.loc.gov/2017057809

9 8 7 6 5 4 3 2 1

Printed by Sheridan Books, Inc., United States of America

Note to Readers
This publication is designed to provide accurate and authoritative information in regard to the subject
matter covered. It is based upon sources believed to be accurate and reliable and is intended to be current
as of the time it was written. It is sold with the understanding that the publisher is not engaged in rendering
legal, accounting, or other professional services. If legal advice or other expert assistance is required, the
services of a competent professional person should be sought. Also, to confirm that the information has
not been affected or changed by recent developments, traditional legal research techniques should be
used, including checking primary sources where appropriate.

*(Based on the Declaration of Principles jointly adopted by a Committee of the
American Bar Association and a Committee of Publishers and Associations.)*

**You may order this or any other Oxford University Press publication
by visiting the Oxford University Press website at www.oup.com.**

Contents

Acknowledgments

THIS BOOK IS the product of many years of teaching and research at Bar-Ilan University's Faculty of Law. It is my pleasant duty to thank many who assisted me at various stages of its writing.

The Faculty of Law ensured the conditions required for the writing. Aharon Barak, Daphne Barak-Erez, Ariel Bendor, Moshe Cohen-Eliya, Yoav Dotan, Menachem Mautner, Barak Medina, Iddo Porat, and Daniel Statman read portions of the manuscript, and made important and useful comments. Many research assistants helped in various ways, and I am grateful to all of them. My wife, Sarit, and my children Rotem, Ilai, Yuval, Iddo, and Barak patiently attended the prolonged discussions of the issues considered in this book.

My beloved father, Arieh Sapir, bequeathed me a concern for the growth and progress of the State of Israel, and his inspiration led me to deal with the topics discussed here. With love and longing, I dedicate the book to his memory.

INTRODUCTION

AT SOCIAL EVENTS, people often ask, "What do you do?" Outside Israel, I usually keep two answers ready because, after my first answer—"I teach constitutional law"—the almost inevitable sequel is, "How can you teach constitutional law *in Israel* if Israel does not have a constitution?" Dealing with this question requires a strategic decision. I can offer a long and thorough response, concisely describing the constitutional history of Israel from its establishment until today. That, however, would probably detract from my appeal as a small-talk partner, and quickly bring the budding relationship to an end. I can obviously choose the opposite course: provide a brief, matter-of-fact answer, clarifying that Israel has a constitution, indeed one traceable to a particular date, and that the Israeli constitution is enforced, as in other countries, through the institution of judicial review. Yet, this approach too entails some risks, since some people are offended when told they are mistaken. So I usually choose a middle course—first, I note that this is an excellent question, and indeed extremely common whenever I am asked about my work. By then, close to having exhausted my exchange-of-pleasantries quota, I rush to conclude by stating that Israeli reality is complex, and inviting the inquirer (with a smile, of course) to the lecture/course I am about to give on the subject.

The explanation for the limited knowledge about Israeli constitutional law lies in a choice that Technion leaders made, some hundred years ago, when, at the end of an extended polemic, they decided to conduct their academic activity in Hebrew. As a result, only a small segment of the rich judicial and academic activity that takes place in Israel in the field of constitutional law has become known to the international community. This book seeks to make a modest contribution by helping to expose the Israeli constitutional scene to the English-speaking scholarly community.

Israeli constitutional law is a sphere of many contradictions and traditions. Growing from the tradition of British law, which was absorbed by the legal system of Mandatory Palestine, Israeli constitutional law has followed the path of constitutional law based on unwritten constitutional principles. At the same time, inspired by the new arena of post-World War II constitutionalism, as well as the phrasing of Israel's Declaration of Independence, the newly established state did plan to adopt a constitution. To date, this vision has, however, not been finalized due to domestic controversies on the content of the constitution. In the meantime, it has been transformed into the enactment of a series of Basic Laws, which function as Israel's de-facto constitution. This special history and its constitutional outcomes are to be explored in this book.

In order to perform the task, I shall use two complementary methods—a chronological description alongside a thematic review. The first part of the book (Chapters 1 to 4) is devoted to a chronological description of the process of establishing a constitution in Israel. As mentioned, the Israeli case is a fascinating example of a constitution that was not created at a clear point in time, but has resulted from an ongoing process that began with the establishment of the state, and is, in fact, still continuing. The second part of the book (Chapters 5 to 8) is built thematically. Each of the chapters in this part is devoted to the review and evaluation of a major constitutional issue that is also the subject of discussion and research in other countries, with emphasis on the unique characteristics of the Israeli case. Read together, the various chapters that comprise this book present Israeli constitutional law as a living sphere, which reflects the dilemmas faced by the country, as well as the challenges of constitutional theory in general. As such, my hope is that the book will promote the future study and development of Israeli constitutional law, as well as an understanding of the complexities of constitutional systems that still cope with the challenge of nation-building and transition.

The Structure of the Book

Chapter 1 describes the constitutional history of the State of Israel from its establishment until the early 1990s. In this period, Israel had no formal Bill of Rights. The Declaration of Independence had promised a constitution, but a public controversy, which lasted nearly two years, made it clear that drafting a constitution was not yet possible. At that point, the Knesset accepted a compromise solution proposed by MK Yizhar Harari: the constitution would be drawn up in a piecemeal process, in the form of Basic Laws that would be consolidated at its conclusion.

The Harari decision was implemented only partially. Although the Knesset enacted a series of Basic Laws over the years, these mainly addressed the rules of the political game, and hardly the realm of values and basic rights at all. In the absence of a constitutional Bill of Rights, the Supreme Court created alternative mechanisms for the protection of human rights. Despite its activistic approach, however, the Supreme Court endorsed restraint, refusing to nullify legislation that explicitly violated human rights, as long as no constitutional Bill of Rights had been enacted. Several attempts to anchor a Bill of Rights in a Basic Law proved unsuccessful, and no breakthrough seemed in sight.

In 1992, a momentous event took place in Israel, or at least this is how the Israeli Supreme Court interpreted it *ex post factum*. The Knesset enacted two Basic Laws dealing with human rights: the Basic Law: Human Dignity and Liberty, and the Basic Law: Freedom of Occupation (hereinafter: "the new Basic Laws"). **Chapter 2** explores an intriguing question that is yet to receive a satisfactory answer: After forty-four years of failure and inaction, why did the Knesset suddenly decide to anchor a Bill of Rights in a Basic Law? What prepared the ground for the constitutional revolution?

Four theses are presented as possible answers. One thesis states that success followed the exploitation of a "constitutional moment" of heightened distrust between the public and the political powers. At this constitutional moment, everyone understood that a change in the balance of forces was required, strengthening the Supreme Court's powers of review. A second thesis pins the success of the maneuver on the tactic adopted by the proponents of the law. Instead of insisting on the legislation of a full Bill of Rights, they split the Bill and referred to the Knesset only the sections on which agreement could be reached. According to a third thesis, what enabled the enactment of the Basic Laws was a tactic adopted by their proponents to refrain from clearly revealing the full meaning of the maneuver they were leading, thereby lulling its traditional opponents. According to this explanation, the almost-total absence of public constitutional discourse contributed to the misunderstanding, an absence that led to general ignorance regarding the influence and consequences of legislating Basic Laws. According to the fourth thesis, the success of the maneuver resulted from two changes in Israel's political reality. The first was the loss of the Labor party's hegemony and the uncertainty about the coalition's future composition, and the second, the growing strength of marginal elements that threatened the hegemony of the secular-center-veteran sector. The first change weakened the interest of coalition parties in opposing the "constitutionalization" of the political system, and the second neutralized the institutional interest of Knesset members representing the older elite in opposing the constitutional move. Chapter 2 concludes with the claim that the maneuver of March 1992 has more than one single explanation, and all four factors mentioned above contributed to its success. Nevertheless, it is argued that none of them could have turned the Basic Laws into what they are today—a fully-fledged, constitutional Bill of Rights. Completing this task became possible through the combination of a dominant and resolute Supreme Court and a weak and hesitant legislature.

Chapter 3 depicts the main constitutional developments since the beginning of the constitutional revolution in March 1992.

A constitutional consensus that developed in Israel over the years was that only "entrenched" Basic Laws enjoy normative primacy. The concept of "entrenchment" was understood literally, as requiring a special majority as a condition for changing the law. The examination of the new Basic Laws in light of this constitutional consensus should have led to the conclusion that their legislation did not really create a "constitutional revolution." Of the two new Basic Laws, only the Basic Law: Freedom of Occupation includes an entrenchment provision, and therefore, according to the constitutional consensus that prevailed at the time the new Basic Laws were enacted, only the Basic Law: Freedom of Occupation would have acquired the constitutional status allowing for judicial review. The Basic Law: Freedom of Occupation protects only one right. If only this Basic Law enjoys constitutional status, the constitutional revolution is a minor one indeed.

At this point, the Supreme Court entered the picture. Although the Basic Law: Human Dignity and Liberty is not entrenched from change, it does include a "limitation clause" specifying the conditions under which it is permitted to infringe the rights that are embodied in it. The Court stated that this clause constitutes "substantive" entrenchment.

The notion of substantive entrenchment enabled the Court to strengthen the constitutional status of the Basic Law: Human Dignity and Liberty. However, this tool proved limited in its range, since the only entrenched laws are the Basic Law: Freedom of Occupation, and the Basic Law: Human Dignity and Liberty. None of the "old" Basic Laws (except for several provisions of other Basic Laws) are entrenched, either substantively or formally. Even after the judicial widening of the concept of entrenchment, the old Basic Laws remained as they had been, and failed to acquire constitutional status. The Court, nevertheless, decided to broaden entrenchment once again by ruling that all Basic Laws, including those that were not entrenched, would thenceforth enjoy normative primacy.

One explanation for the success of the March 1992 constitutional maneuver was, as noted, the compromise that omitted controversial rights from the new Basic Laws.

The result of this compromise was that important rights, such as freedom of religion, equality, and freedom of expression, remained outside—a reality that the Supreme Court found undesirable. On or about the enactment of the new Basic Laws, some of the Supreme Court justices began to develop an interpretive approach that would enable reading the unenumerated rights into the Basic Law: Human Dignity and Liberty—including rights that had been deliberately excluded from the law as part of the compromise—thereby equating their status to that of the rights explicitly enumerated in the law. This broad reading, which has become the prevalent consensus in the Court over the years, means that no additional Basic Laws are necessary to complete the constitutional enterprise.

The conclusion warranted by the facts presented in this chapter is that the true constitutional revolution did not occur at the time of enacting the new Basic Laws in March 1992. It is, instead, an ongoing revolution, taking place largely within the Supreme Court.

The reality of an extremely dominant Court instituting a constitutional revolution while dramatically changing the rules of the political game invites public reaction. **Chapter 4** is devoted to a description of this reaction. The chapter also deals with the intriguing fact that, in contrast to the critical dimension of the public reaction, legal academia explicitly or implicitly supported the Court's moves almost without exception in the first years after the March 1992 revolution. An interesting trend has emerged over the recent decade: criticism is now extending to include circles that had, at first, supported the Court's moves, and this chapter will outline several explanations for this development.

The rest of Chapter 4 is devoted to a description and evaluation of several proposals raised by opponents of the Court's moves, who have sought to thwart or amend them. Among these proposals was one that called for denying the Supreme Court the authority to engage in judicial review, by instead entrusting it to a special constitutional court; another that sought to enlarge the bench and establish a special procedure and a minimum majority as a condition for rescinding laws; a proposal to change the procedure for electing judges; and one to anchor in the constitution clear limitations on the authority of the Court. As for now, all of these proposals have failed to materialize.

Chapter 5 focuses on the challenge of social rights in the context of Israeli constitutional law. The constitutional status of social rights and their enforceability is an open question in many systems, but even more so in Israel, which lacks explicit recognition of these rights. The debate on the constitutionality of social rights in Israel emerged following the 1992 constitutional revolution. At first, it was not clear *if* social and economic rights are considered protected constitutional rights. However, this debate is largely over. Israeli jurisprudence has gradually but consistently recognized that the basic right to human dignity includes social and economic rights, and they enjoy constitutional protection. The first part of the chapter will be devoted to describing the changes that occurred in the court's position on the matter from 1992 until today.

While most judges view the move with favor, and are even effusive with their obiter dicta supporting additional expansion of social rights, there are judges who have reservations about this trend, and warn of what they see as an unrestrained intrusion on the part of the judicial branch into the other branches of government. I shall describe these two approaches in the second part of the chapter, and see just how much the opposition's concerns are justified.

Another question that occupies writers in the field regards the influence of litigation and judicial intervention on the actual situation on the ground. There are those who argue that the attempt to lead to social change via the court is doomed to failure, and that the effort to bring change should focus on the legislature and public discourse. I shall examine this argument in the last part of the chapter with a test case: s series of rulings—in the field of integrating children with special needs into the regular education system—in which the court revealed quite a bit of activism in enforcing a social right. I will argue that judicial intervention only led to a modest change, and try to discern the reasons for this.

Chapter 6 analyzes the process of constitutional balancing and the various balancing formulas utilized by the Supreme Court. Human rights, important as they are, are not unlimited. Sometimes they clash with each other, at other times they clash with public and private interests, and in all those cases, a balance has to be made between the right and its competitors. Every system of constitutional law has its own balancing mechanisms. In Israel, the accepted approach for many years was that upon a clash between a human right and public interest, a vertical balance should be made between the two, whilst in cases of a clash between rights, the balancing formula was horizontal. Choosing the vertical balancing formula leads to the complete adoption of one party's position and the absolute rejection of the other party's. On the other hand, choosing the horizontal balancing formula requires a compromise between the two parties, in such a way that neither gains full satisfaction, on the one hand, but neither is entirely rejected, on the other hand.

Over the years, judges and academics in Israel criticized the policy of the a priori choice of vertical balancing in cases of confrontation between rights and interests. They asserted that even if the proponents are not of equal status, they still represent two proper, recognized values. Consequently, if they can both be protected by a reasonable waiver on the part of each of them, consideration should at least be given to that possibility, rather than rejecting it outright.

In 1992, with the enactment of the new Basic Laws, said balancing criteria were prima facie abandoned. Both new Basic Laws include a limitation clause that restricts any infringement of constitutional rights "to an extent no greater than required." The Supreme Court interpreted this clause as setting a requirement of proportionality, relying on German and Canadian jurisprudence. Since its entry into Israel, proportionality has become a dominant doctrine in Israel's constitutional law, with a sophisticated body of case law interpreting it.

In this chapter I shall concentrate on a description of several issues that raise special comparative interest. Amongst other things, I shall indicate the fact that the Supreme Court has interpreted the last component of proportionality (proportionality sensu stricto) in such a way as to provide a certain answer to the criticism that was leveled at the old balancing criteria.

Chapter 7 is dedicated to the issue of emergency constitutional powers and other national security-related constitutional matters. Israel offers a unique case study for assessing the constitutional regulation of national security. The special value attached to the Israeli example derives from several factors. First, Israel has experienced continuous existential threats since the time of its establishment. Therefore, in Israel, the constitutional regulation of national security is not merely a matter for the law books; it is the result of a constant challenge to both the existence of the country and the rule of law. Second, Israel presents a working laboratory for one of the constitutional models dealing with national threats—a model based on the power to declare an emergency regime. Against the controversy surrounding this model, Israeli law serves as an example of both its advantages and its weaknesses. Third, the Supreme Court also exercises judicial review in matters related to the military and national security, thereby making the regulation of security matters in Israel a living legal reality.

The analysis in this chapter is aimed at reviewing and evaluating the Israeli case study, taking into consideration its unique traits, as well as its potential contribution to understanding the relative advantages and disadvantages of models for regulating emergency conditions in other systems.

The Jewish religion occupies a prominent place in legislation and public life in Israel. The reasons for this are varied. First, the Jewish religion has an all-encompassing character that leads it to strive to influence public life, as opposed to religions such as Protestantism, whose ambitions are more restrained. Second, the Jewish religious group in Israel is large and dominant, and therefore has greater political power than religious groups in most countries in the West. Finally, even part of the non-religious Jewish group is interested in maintaining a degree of ties to religion, in light of the unique connection in Judaism between religion and nation.

In the first decades of Israel's existence, the relations of religion and state in Israel were anchored in a series of arrangements, which were known as the "status quo." There is a debate regarding the creation circumstances of the status quo. Some claim that most of the arrangements it contains were formed on the eve of the state's founding. In contrast, some claim that the status quo arrangements were formed after the state was founded, during the first years of its existence. Either way, the status quo was preserved for a number of decades, even if its specifics were changed a little here and there. This situation has altered over the last two decades; the status quo is weakening, and many arrangements, which were once considered to be set in stone, have been reopened for discussion.

A number of causes joined together to undermine the status quo, one of them—if not the main one—being the increasing intervention of the Supreme Court in questions of values in general, and in matters of religion and state in particular. In **Chapter 8** I shall describe the customary arrangement regarding three central issues—the draft of yeshiva students into the IDF, marriage and divorce law, and Sabbath—as well as the changes that have taken place over the years in every one of those issues, focusing on the court's role in creating the change.

Constitutional History

1

FROM THE ESTABLISHMENT OF ISRAEL

UNTIL THE REVOLUTION

I. The Declaration of Independence

On May 15, 1948, as the British Mandate was ending, members of the People's Council assembled to proclaim the establishment of the State of Israel. The Declaration of Independence was divided into several parts and addressed many issues. Among others, it promised the new state a constitution:

> We declare that, with effect from the moment of the termination of the Mandate being tonight, the eve of Sabbath, 6 Iyar, 5708 (May 15, 1948), until the establishment of the elected, regular authorities of the state in accordance with the Constitution, which shall be adopted by the Elected Constituent Assembly not later than 1 October 1948, the People's Council shall act as a Provisional Council of State, and its executive organ, the People's Administration, shall be the Provisional Government of the Jewish State, to be called "Israel."[1]

The Declaration traced the course of a constitution-drafting process involving three stages. In the first stage, a "Provisional Council of State" would function as a temporary legislature; in the second stage, and in parallel to the first, elections would be held for a "Constituent Assembly" charged with drafting a constitution, which would dissolve after concluding its task; in the third stage, elections would be held for the legislature (according to the electoral system determined in the constitution) that would replace the Provisional Council of State, leading to the dissolution of the Provisional Council.

How determined were the founders to draft a constitution? Readers of the Declaration of Independence will find that its text closely matches the United Nations' decision on the partition of Palestine.[2] This match was warranted given that the People's Council sought to attain the broadest international consensus for the one-sided step it had adopted—proclaiming the establishment of the State of Israel.[3] Given these circumstances, doubts emerge lest the members of the People's Council had not really intended to draft a constitution, and its mention in the Declaration had merely been meant to ensure international legitimation. Comments by Moshe Sharett (who then served as the Minister of Foreign Affairs) in July 1948 at a discussion in Mapai, the ruling party, seem to confirm this suspicion. Sharett said that founding the regime in Israel on a constitution could help the country attain UN membership.[4] But after Israel had been recognized by many countries and accepted as a UN member in March 1949, "the association that Sharett had pointed out between the drafting of a constitution and the immediate interests of the State of Israel was no longer relevant."[5]

This chapter will tell the story of the constitution that was not drafted.

II. The Attempt to Turn the Declaration of Independence into the Constitution

The ink had barely dried on the Declaration of Independence, and it was already at the center of significant concerns. In three of the first ten cases submitted to the Supreme Court acting as High Court of Justice, the petitioners asked to repeal legislation. In two of these cases, the petitioners relied inter alia on the claim that the legislation in question was incompatible with the Declaration of Independence that, in their view, enjoyed constitutional validity. In the first case, the petitioners contested legislation allowing administrative detentions, claiming that the law that allowed them contradicted the terms of the Declaration.[6] In the second case, the petitioners relied on a similar claim in an attempt to repeal a confiscation decree on their property.[7] In both cases, the Court rejected the attempt to ascribe constitutional status to the Declaration of Independence and to use it in order to void legislation. The justices explained:

We cannot accept the attractive argument of counsel for the petitioner . . . The only object of the Declaration was to affirm the fact of the foundation and establishment of the state for the purpose of its recognition by international law. It gives expression to the vision of the people and their faith, but it contains no element of constitutional law that determines the validity of various ordinances and laws, or their repeal.[8]

Some claim that the Court's refusal to grant constitutional status to the Declaration of Independence was a tactical decision rather than a matter of principle. In their view, at the basis of the refusal was "the Court's estimate that the Knesset would indeed enact a constitution that would be anchored in the principles of the Declaration,"[9] rendering superfluous any urgent need for granting the Declaration constitutional status. Others add to this hypothesis a normative evaluation, viewing the Court's abstention from granting constitutional status to the Declaration as no less than a "missed opportunity of historical dimensions."[10] Supporters of this view seem to ascribe no importance to the way a constitution is enacted. In their view, the end justifies the means: we need a constitution, and the mode of its enactment is therefore entirely irrelevant—through a special procedure and with broad agreement or coerced by the Court.[11]

The factual claim that the Court refrained from granting constitutional status to the Declaration of Independence not on grounds of principle, but because it misjudged the future of the constitutional project, is questionable. A different explanation of the Court's refusal to agree to the petitioners' request could claim that the Court's position was dictated by its self-perception at the time, as one whose role was to enforce the decisions of democratic bodies rather than prevail over them. Underlying the refusal of the Supreme Court's justices to grant constitutional status to the Declaration of Independence was a fundamental principle rather than a tactical consideration. This alternative explanation is supported by the fact that, even after it became clear that the constitutional project would not materialize, the Court persisted in its refusal, and saw the Declaration as, at most, an expression of the people's vision and faith.[12] It is also generally compatible with the Court's approach for over a generation—judicial restraint. Proclaiming that the Declaration of Independence is a constitution is an activist step incompatible with a worldview supporting judicial restraint.[13]

III. The Knesset Debate until the Harari Decision
1. THE DISCUSSION

At its ninth meeting, on July 8, 1948, the Provisional Council of State chose a constitutional committee. The task of this committee was to prepare a proposal for a constitution that the Provisional Council of State or the Constitutional Assembly would vote on.[14] The committee held more than twenty meetings, and dealt mainly with such questions as the structure of the regime, the judicial system, the electoral system, the president, and the government. In the committee's early days, all its members still agreed that enacting a constitution was a desirable aim; however, by the end of 1948, this consensus was gradually eroded, and various participants began to express reservations concerning the need for it.[15]

In January 1949, elections were held for the Constitutional Assembly. The various party platforms dealt with constitutional issues and detailed their views in their regard denoting that, at this stage, drafting a constitution was still viewed as an obvious step.[16]

According to the course determined in the Declaration of Independence, the Provisional Council of State was supposed to serve as the legislator until the election of the ordinary institutions prescribed in the constitution. In 1949, however, the Provisional Council of State enacted the Transition Law, which stated that, when the Constitutional Assembly was convened, the Provisional Council of State would cease to exist, and would transfer its powers to the Assembly.[17] Uri Yadin, who was then a senior officer at the Ministry of Justice, explained the reason for the decision:

> According to the Declaration of Independence, the Provisional Council of State was to continue functioning and operating not only until the election of the Constitutional Assembly, but until the establishment of the new government according to the new constitution. The role of the Constitutional Assembly was to be confined to the preparation and approval of the constitution, and ordinary legislation was to remain in the hands of the Provisional Council of State until the Constitutional Assembly ended its term . . . As long as this program was tied to the date of October 1, 1948, that is, for as long as the intention and the hope were to implement all its stages over four and a half months . . . it was definitely possible to agree to it . . . But now, after all the events that have taken place since the establishment of Israel, the original program can obviously no longer be implemented. We can no longer agree to the existence of the Provisional Council of State together with the Constitutional Assembly and, consequently, we must assign to the Constitutional Assembly all the roles of the Council of State.[18]

The Transition Law then granted the Constitutional Assembly the role of an ordinary legislator, in addition to its original role as a body that was meant to draft a constitution.[19] The meeting of the Provisional Council of State that discussed the Transition Law addressed the issue of whether to compel the Constitutional Assembly, by law, to draft a constitution. Although the majority of the Constitution Committee supported this motion, the minority view (which was also the government's view) that refused to impose this obligation was the one ultimately accepted.[20]

Once elected, the Constitutional Assembly—which then changed its name to the "First Knesset"[21]—dealt in its Constitution, Law, and Justice Committee with a matter of principle: Was it at all proper to enact a written constitution to be accepted as one unit by the First Knesset? Or would it be better to postpone the enactment of the constitution for a few years and, in the interim, regulate the action of government institutions through ordinary primary legislation? For a year—from May 1949 until June 1950—the Knesset engaged in a fiery debate between the constitution's supporters and its opponents.[22] The ongoing discussion and the inability to reach consensus concerning the contents, the form, and even the very need for a constitution, finally led to the adoption of a compromise formula proposed by MK Yitzhak Harari:[23]

> The First Knesset assigns to the Constitution, Law, and Justice Committee the task of preparing a constitution proposal for the country. The constitution will be made up of chapters so that each one is a separate basic law onto itself. The chapters will be submitted to the Knesset as the Committee completes its work, and all the chapters together will be collected into the constitution of the country.[24]

The Harari decision thus determined that the process of drafting a constitution would take place in stages, in the form of basic laws that would only be compiled when the process was completed.

2. REASONS FOR THE LACK OF SUCCESS

Why was no constitution enacted immediately following the establishment of the State of Israel? Some point to the religious camp as zealously opposing a constitution as a matter of principle, and view it as responsible for the failure.[25] The claim appears not only in writings *about* the religious, but also in writings *by* the religious.[26]

The historical evidence, however, refutes the claim placing the onus of responsibility on the religious. In the course of the discussions surrounding the constitution, disputes emerged concerning part of its contents, some of them addressing religion and state.[27] This is very different, however, from presenting the religious, or problems related to the status of religion, as the sole or main "guilty party" for the thwarting of the constitutional project. First, as has been correctly pointed out, "the majority of religious politicians, as well as many rabbis . . . never objected in principle to enacting a constitution, and even agreed to the idea at certain stages."[28] Second, and more important, opposition to the constitution was not confined to the religious. Many in the governing party, Mapai, also expressed their opposition. The lines more or less overlapped those of coalition-opposition.[29] Mapai leader and Israel's first prime minister, David Ben-Gurion, expressed several times his strong opposition to the enactment of a constitution enjoying normative primacy. In a discussion in the Constitution, Law, and Justice Committee of the Knesset in the summer of 1949, Ben-Gurion spoke at length about the constitution and detailed his reasons for opposing it,[30] henceforth leading the opposition to this project within his party. Given Mapai's standing and Ben-Gurion's dominance within it at the time, it seems that he had a crucial part in the hindering of the constitution.[31]

The division between supporters and opponents of the constitution according to coalition-opposition lines continued to characterize the political system in Israel at later periods as well. As Negbi notes, the constitution's supporters were usually from the opposition, but tended to change their views when they came to govern.[32] The reasons for that are obvious. In a parliamentary democracy, coalition parties rule the legislature. A constitution limits the legislators' powers, and therefore the ruling parties have a stake in avoiding the enactment of a constitution.

Indeed, not only the coalition parties, but also the legislature as a whole, including those in opposition benches, has an interest in preventing the adoption of a constitution. Jon Elster, who studied constitution-making processes in various countries, notes that various interests may play a role in them. One such is the "institutional interest," and one of the interested institutions is the legislature. The legislators' built-in interest does not relate to a specific content they would like to make part of the constitution, but on their opposition in principle to a Bill of Rights that would considerably limit their powers. Elster suggests a way of overcoming this problem: that the constitution be adopted by a body set up ad hoc that would disperse after completing its task. Such a body, Elster argues, would have no institutional interests.[33]

Elster's thesis provides another possible explanation for the failure to draft a constitution when Israel was established. The course presented in the Declaration of Independence, as noted, included elections for a Constitutional Assembly that would draft a constitution, and thereby conclude its role; elections would then be held for the legislature based on the arrangement determined in the constitution. This course is compatible with Elster's recommendation that the constitution be drafted by a body specifically set up for this purpose, which would then disperse. Reality, however, was different. The Provisional Council of State disbanded itself and transferred its powers to the Constitutional Assembly. Once the Assembly turned into a legislature, a built-in interest emerged within it against the adoption of a constitution. Therefore, the transformation of the Constitutional Assembly into the First Knesset provides an additional explanation for the failure of this Knesset, as well as those that followed, to draft a constitution.

3. THE HARARI DECISION: OPEN QUESTIONS

The Harari decision, as noted, stated that the constitution would be drafted in stages, in the form of Basic Laws that would be joined together at the end of the process, but this decision was not fully implemented either. Typically, constitutions include two kinds of issues: the structure of the regime, and the system's fundamental values. In the years following the Harari decision, the Knesset did enact a series of Basic Laws, but these laws focused on the structural aspect, and hardly addressed the area of fundamental values.[34] Nor was the status of these Basic Laws clear: Do these laws enjoy constitutional status as soon as they are enacted, or would such status be assigned to them only when compiled in a single document? In Ruth Gavison's terms, "the question of the constitution's rigidity and primacy remained open and the decision on it was postponed, without specifying whether it was until the compilation of the Basic Laws into a constitution or by applying different arrangements to the various Basic Laws along the way."[35]

Another question to which the answer is unclear concerns the seriousness that accompanied the Harari decision. Did the legislators who supported this decision really intend to use the course that was determined in it for gradually moving forward in the task of drafting the constitution? Or did they support it merely because they wanted to remove the constitution issue from the agenda? Two indications strengthen doubts in this regard. First, soon after the enactment of the Harari decision, the Knesset passed several laws of "constitutional" content—such as the Law of Return, 5710-1950, and the Law of Equal Rights for Women, 5711-1951—without referring to them as "Basic Laws." As Gavison notes, anchoring these constitutional issues in ordinary legislation hardly fits the formal commitment to draft a constitution chapter by chapter.[36] Second, as noted, the Knesset did enact a number of Basic Laws regulating the structural realm over the years, but the pace of their legislation was extremely slow. Eight years elapsed from the Harari decision until the Knesset enacted the first Basic Law—Basic Law: The Knesset. Even after the first Basic Law was enacted, the enterprise of legislating Basic Laws proceeded extremely slowly. These findings support the conclusion that the Harari decision, at least for some of its supporters, was merely an excuse to remove a troublesome item from the agenda.[37]

IV. The Status of the Basic Laws

The Harari decision, as noted, failed to clarify what would be the status of the Basic Laws until their compilation in a single document. This issue has been examined both directly and indirectly in the case law, and the answer has been shaped in the course of time, through a combination of the judicial decisions and their scholarly interpretations. Several rulings that have become part of the narrative on this question are reviewed below. It should be noted at the outset, though, that the selection of these rulings as particularly important for determining the status of the Basic Laws was not a decision of the court judges, but rather of the legal academia. Moreover, the scholarship itself did not always view them as uniquely important close to the time of their issuance, and some were marked as significant only long after.

1. THE *BERGMAN* RULING

The Sixth Knesset legislated the Knesset and Local Authorities Elections Law (Financing, Limits on Expenditures and Control) 5729-1969 (henceforth Financing Law), which determined that only political parties that had been represented in this Knesset would receive financing toward the elections in the Seventh Knesset. Bergman claimed that this arrangement contradicted the provision in section 4 of Basic Law: The Knesset, which states: "The Knesset shall be elected by . . . equal . . . elections." Section 46 of the Basic Law states that an absolute majority of Knesset members is required for changing section 4. Given that the Financing Law had not been passed by an absolute majority, the petitioner argued that the Minister of Finance must refrain from allocating funds on its basis.[38]

Considering Bergman's claim required the Court to decide on factual questions: Does the Financing Law violate the principle of equal elections stated in section 4? If so, should this violation be viewed as a change of section 4? But before it addressed these factual issues, the Court had to decide on two preliminary questions:

1. Is the Court authorized to examine a claim that a Knesset law is invalid?
2. Do Basic Laws have a special status so that, when a contradiction is found between a provision in a Basic Law and a later provision in an ordinary law, the provision in the Basic Law overrides it?

The Court did mention these two questions, but explained that it saw no need to decide on them because the Attorney General had agreed to assume, for the sake of the discussion (and without deciding), that the answer to both would be affirmative.[39] Scholars who analyzed the decision, however, found in it more than the Court had claimed it contains. According to David Kretzmer:

> That the Court avoided a decision on the first question . . . cannot cover up for the actual decision. Had the Court concluded that the Financing Law involved no flaw, its determination that it need not decide whether it was authorized to repeal the law had it found it was flawed would have been understandable. In *Bergman*, however, the Court found that the Financing Law was flawed. It issued a court order against the Minister of Finance, forbidding him to act according to section 6 of said law for as long as this flaw was not corrected. One can thus hardly relate seriously to the claim that this ruling does not create a precedent regarding the Court's authority in principle to review primary legislation.[40]

2. THE THREE POSSIBLE READINGS OF *BERGMAN*

Kretzmer argues that the Court actually decided on the first question and assumed it had the authority to examine a claim stating that a Knesset law is invalid. And yet, as he notes, the Court's answer to the second question is not as clear. The Court forbade the Knesset to act according to the law, and set two options before it: either to amend the law by removing the violation of equality, or to pass the law again with the required majority. Kretzmer explains that at least three options are available for interpreting this decision. According to the first and most far-reaching one, the Court answered the second question in the affirmative: the law was repealed because it contradicted a Basic Law, relying on the assumption that Basic Laws enjoy primacy over primary legislation. According to the second option, the Court answered the question in the affirmative but with reservations: the only Basic Laws that would enjoy primacy are those in which the Knesset had explicitly stated its intention to grant them this prerogative, as manifested in their entrenchment. According to this option, the primacy of section 4 in Basic Law: The Knesset followed from a combination of two indicators—its being part of a Basic Law and its being entrenched. According to the third option, the Court did not answer the question at all. It did repeal the Financing Law, as this law failed to meet the absolute majority requirement that was a condition for changing the equality principle stated in section 4 of the Basic Law, but section 4 being part of a Basic Law made no difference in this regard. Section 4 would have enjoyed preference even if it had been part of an ordinary law. According to this option, the Court preferred section 4 because it believed that the Knesset has the authority to limit itself (as well as subsequent legislatures) through ordinary primary legislation, too. The determination that the Knesset has the authority to limit itself is not a trivial matter, and its correctness can definitely be questioned,[41] but the decision on this matter is not directly connected to the status of the Basic Laws.

3. *NEGEV*: REJECTING OPTION 1 (ALL BASIC LAWS ENJOY PRIMACY)

The *Negev* decision limited the range of options for understanding *Bergman*.[42] The appellant had been convicted of selling fuel of a lower octane than that set in the standard. In its defense, it claimed that the standard (considered a regulation) it was accused of having transgressed was invalid, because the civil servant who had determined it—after the power had been delegated to him by the minister—had not been authorized to do so. The appellant based his claim on section 31(b) of Basic Law: The Government, which states that a minister authorized to make regulations cannot delegate this authority. To decide on the appellant's claim, the Court needed to determine the relationship between said section 31b, which prohibited the delegation of authority, and section 21 of the Law of Standards 5713-1953, which stated a contrary provision, allowing the minister to delegate authority to the civil servant in charge. The Court decided on this contradiction between the two laws in favor of the Law of Standards, relying on the usual interpretation principle that a special law overrides a general law. In its decision, the Court granted no weight at all to the fact that section 31(b) was part of a Basic Law. This approach precludes the first option for understanding the ruling in *Bergman*, whereby all Basic Laws enjoy primacy. Had that been the case, the Court should have favored the provision in Basic Law: The Government (that enjoys normative primacy) over the provision in the Law of Standards. And yet, the ruling in *Negev* did not deny the second option for interpreting the ruling in *Bergman*, whereby only entrenched elements in the Basic Laws enjoy constitutional status, given that section 31(b) in Basic Law: The Government had not been entrenched.

4. *KANIEL*—REJECTING OPTION 2? (PRIMACY FOR ENTRENCHED BASIC LAWS)

Another ruling relevant to the understanding of *Bergman* is *Kaniel*.[43] Kaniel petitioned against the law on the distribution of excess votes (Knesset Elections Law [Amendment No. 4], 5733-1973), proposed by MKs Yohanan Bader from the Gahal party and Abraham Ofer from the Labor party (henceforth: Bader-Ofer law). He claimed that the law granted prominent advantages to the large factions at the expense of the small ones, and thereby failed to meet the equality demand stated in section 4 of Basic Law: The Knesset. The Bader-Ofer law passed with a majority of more than sixty-one MKs, as required by section 46 of the Basic Law, but the petitioners claimed that it should still be repealed because it was not called a "Basic Law." Basic Law: The Knesset did not explicitly state that its amendment required a Basic Law, but the petitioners argued that such a demand was warranted. If Basic Laws have constitutional status, their amendment is only possible through a document of equal status.

The Court rejected the petitioners' claim, and determined: "The claim that amendments according to section 46 require the legislation of a Basic Law or a special law is not supported by the wording of the Basic Law. In our view, it can also be done through ordinary Knesset legislation, as in the amendment of the law discussed here."[44]

On the face of it, the Court's decision dismisses not only the first option for understanding the ruling in *Bergman*, whereby all Basic Laws enjoy normative primacy, but also the second option, whereby primacy accrues only to those components of the Basic Law that are entrenched. If the entrenchment of a section in a Basic Law grants it constitutional status, and if the Bader-Ofer law "amends" section 4 of Basic Law: The Knesset, which is entrenched, then Kaniel's claim is legally correct: just as primary legislation cannot be amended through secondary legislation, whose status is lower, a constitution cannot be amended through primary legislation. The Court's refusal to add (as a condition for justifying the amendment of an entrenched provision) the demand that the amendment be passed in a Basic Law, ostensibly voids the second interpretation of the *Bergman* ruling as well. All that is left, then, is the third option of interpretation: enforcing the entrenchment in *Bergman* did not follow from its inclusion in a Basic Law, but from the assumption that the Knesset is allowed to limit itself through an ordinary law too. If this is the correct reading of the Court's position, the Court's view is that the Basic Laws do not enjoy special status, even when entrenched.

5. THE VIEW THAT WAS ACCEPTED

The *Negev* and *Kaniel* rulings together seem to suggest that the Court dismissed the first and second options for interpreting *Bergman*, which grant constitutional status to the Basic Laws, or at least to their entrenched components. The only way to understand the *Bergman* decision, then, is to adopt the third option, stating that the Knesset is allowed to limit itself and, on this matter, a Basic Law is in no way different from an ordinary law.[45] Nevertheless, the view that gradually became dominant in academic circles is that in *Bergman*—and in three other cases where the Court also repealed legal provisions on the grounds that they contradicted section 4 of Basic Law: The Knesset[46]—the Court had endorsed the second interpretation of the *Bergman* ruling. According to this interpretation, as noted, entrenched components of Basic Laws enjoy constitutional status.[47] This view was also the one adopted in later Supreme Court rulings. Thus, for instance, referring to *Bergman* and its implications, President Barak notes: "It is clear that the Court recognized the normative primacy of the entrenched Basic Laws."[48] The endorsement of this view also explains Justice Zamir's determination: "The constitutional revolution did not begin now, with the enactment of the Basic Laws on human rights. It began a generation ago, with the *Bergman* decision."[49] Justice Zamir even referred to *Bergman* as the Israeli *Marbury v. Madison*.[50] However, Zamir's claim is justified only if we assume that the repeal of the Financing Law in *Bergman* was not based on the Knesset's choice to limit itself, but on the constitutional status of section 4 of Basic Law: The Knesset.

If Justice Zamir is correct, and if the ruling in *Bergman* was the first case in Israel's constitutional history where the Court repealed primary legislation after ruling that at least some of the Basic Laws enjoy primacy, a considerable measure of irony is involved. The justice who wrote the main decision in *Bergman*—Moshe Landau, who served in the Supreme Court for many years, acted briefly as its President, and is viewed to this day as one of its prominent figures—was known, over his many years on the bench, as a supporter of judicial restraint.[51] In his academic writing, too, Landau supported a conservative position. In a classic article he published in 1971, he supported a "thin constitution" that would only deal with the structure of the regime. He voiced a vigorous and well-argued opposition to the inclusion of values and basic rights in the constitution because he held, inter alia, that such an inclusion would compel the Court to rule on value issues, a step he considered illegitimate and dangerous.[52] Out of all the judges in the history of the Israeli Supreme Court, would the conservative Justice Landau be the one to raise the banner of a constitutional revolution in the realm of civil rights?[53]

V. Civil Rights in the Absence of a Constitution

Despite some limited progress in the institutional arena, in the area of civil rights the constitutional project did not move forward at all. More than four decades elapsed since the promise recorded in the Declaration of Independence to draft a constitution, and not even a single Basic Law was enacted in the area of civil rights. This situation, however, did not prevent the Court from acting to protect individual rights, even without a constitution. The Court's endeavor in this regard is particularly impressive because its foundations were set in Israel's early years, which were also the early years of the Court's existence—years of a centralized one-party government, when the public consciousness favored the collective good and the good of the state over the good of the individual. Great courage was required back then to stand up to the government and fight the human rights war, and to do so without a written Bill of Rights.[54] The Court's comprehensive involvement in the protection of human rights has rightfully led Israeli scholars to take pride in this unique Israeli phenomenon: effective protection of human rights even without a constitution.[55]

The Court developed various means for protecting human rights. First, it determined that human rights have constitutional status in Israeli law, even if they are not anchored in a written constitution or even in an ordinary law. Second, the Court relied on the "interpretive presumption" that (primary and secondary) legislation must be interpreted in ways compatible with human rights, and assumed that government authorities are also compelled to protect these rights. Third, the Court stated that explicit (rather than general) legislative authorization would be required to allow the executive to violate human rights. Finally, the Court did not hesitate to review and occasionally void executive decisions that violated human rights, when it concluded that the violation had been unjustified. The Court's use of each of these tools in the protection of human rights is illustrated below.

I. RECOGNIZING RIGHTS AND DEMANDING EXPLICIT AUTHORIZATION AS A PRECONDITION FOR THEIR VIOLATION

Bejerano and his colleagues had acted as "fixers" at the Licensing Bureau until the Ministry of Transport ordered that they should not be allowed to engage in this occupation any further. Bejerano and his colleagues petitioned the Supreme Court (sitting as High Court of Justice) against the Ministry of Transport, which responded by noting that the petitioners were the ones who should show on what basis did they claim a right to go on doing what they had done so far, and, barring any source for this right, their petition should be dismissed. Supreme Court Justice Shneor Zalman Cheshin reversed the process. He determined that "the natural right of every person is to seek sources of sustenance and to find work able to support him."[56] In other words, Cheshin stated that freedom of occupation is everyone's prerogative and is based on "natural law" and, therefore, it needs not rely on legislation.

After proclaiming the existence of the right, Cheshin proceeded to the question of whether this right can be violated. On this matter, Cheshin is less clear. He determined that the right can only be limited by law,[57] but whether he intended primary or secondary legislation remains ambiguous, as is the required level of explicitness. A later ruling sharpened these parameters. The *Miterani* ruling, issued thirty years after *Bejerano*, dealt with similar factual circumstances. On a similar question that emerged in this case, (then) Justice Shamgar stated:

> A basic right cannot be denied or limited except by explicit primary leg-
> islation and, insofar as no Basic Law determines otherwise, even by sec-
> ondary legislation that has been authorized for this purpose by primary
> legislation . . . Authorization in this case means, in my view, "explicit authori-
> zation," and I intend by that only a case where the primary legislation clearly
> and explicitly states that it authorizes secondary legislation to issue regulations
> prohibiting or limiting work in a specific profession.[58]

In Shamgar's view, the executive is allowed to violate human rights only if explicitly authorized by the legislature. Barring such explicit authorization, the violation of rights will be dismissed outright.[59]

2. A RESTRICTIVE READING OF LAWS

The Shtreits got married in Romania in a civil ceremony. The marriage failed. The husband wanted a divorce, but the wife refused. The Penal Law Amendment (Bigamy) Law, 5719 (1959) prohibits polygamy, but exempts from the bigamy offense a Jewish man who is granted a marriage license following the final decision of a rabbinic court upheld by the two Chief Rabbis.[60] Mr. Shtreit asked the Rabbinic Court for a marriage license, which he was granted. Before the Chief Rabbis upheld the ruling, the wife petitioned the High Court of Justice to forbid them from doing so.[61]

The High Court of Justice considered several questions. The important one for the current discussion touched on the relationship between the exemption from the bigamy offense that the law grants Jewish men, and the exemption it grants to members of other religious denominations. Section 5 of the law deals with Jews, and allows the Rabbinate to grant a married man a marriage license without limiting the causes for such action. Section 6 of the law discusses members of others religious denominations, and is far less liberal. This section restricts the authority to grant a marriage license to two instances: the partner's mental illness, which precludes the possibility of obtaining agreement to a divorce; or the partner's absence for a period of at least seven years, which makes death a plausible assumption. The Court determined that section 5, which deals with Jews, should be read in light of section 6, which deals with members of other religious denominations, so that Jews would also be allowed to marry a second wife only in the same circumstances that allow members of other denominations to do so. The Court explained that its main reason for endorsing a restrictive interpretation of section 5 is that a broad interpretation of that section would violate the principle of religious equality—as anchored in the Declaration of Independence and in the Universal Declaration of Human Rights—granting Jews an unjustified "advantage" over members of other religious denominations. The Court relied on the presumption that the legislators could not have intended to violate basic rights—in this case the right to equality.[62]

The interpretation of section 5 suggested by the Court is strained. Had legislators meant to apply an equal arrangement to Jews and non-Jews, why did they dedicate a separate section to each group? Why did they choose a laconic formulation for the section applying to Jews, without setting any limitation on the Rabbis' authority to grant a marriage license, while clearly confining the circumstances allowing the granting of a license in the section applying to non-Jews? The Court tries to overcome this difficulty and argues that the reason for the duplication and for the clear difference in the wording reflects the fact that Halacha already limits the license to the special circumstances enumerated in section 6, making their mention redundant. Non-Jews, by contrast, had no such tradition, requiring prior definition of the reasons justifying the granting of a marriage license.[63] This explanation, however, is insufficient. This example, then, is an excellent illustration of the Court's readiness to deviate from the clear meaning of the law and to stretch its interpretation to the utmost, all to make it compatible with the protection of human rights.

3. EXAMINING ADMINISTRATIVE DISCRETION

Three tools created by the Court to protect human rights have been presented so far: the Court acknowledged the rights and their constitutional status, even though they had not been anchored in a constitution or in primary legislation (*Bejerano*); it required the legislator's explicit authorization as a condition for violation of rights by the executive (*Miterani*); it tried to interpret legislation viewed as violating them in a way that would remove the violation (*Shtreit*). But the Court was ready to go even further to protect human rights. It viewed itself as authorized to examine the government's discretion when it exercised the powers it had been granted by law. The Court was ready to void decisions of the executive if it found they had unjustifiably violated a basic right. One of the first and most famous cases that show the Court adopting this course is *Kol Ha'am*.

The High Court of Justice discussed a petition against the suspension of the Communist newspaper "*Kol Ha'am*", which condemned the government's pro-American policy in the Korean War and denunciated it as "speculating in the blood of Israeli youth." The Minister of Interior ordered the suspension of the newspaper, relying on the administrative authority it had been granted during the Mandate period—the authority to suspend newspapers likely to endanger "public peace." The Court intervened and annulled the suspension.

The decision comprises four chapters:[64] In the first chapter, Justice Agranat—who would eventually become President of the Supreme Court—reinforced two important fundamental principles: recognizing the existence of freedom of expression, perceiving it as a precondition for the realization of almost all other rights, and recognizing the democratic character of the regime, which inspires and fosters other rights derived from the country's democratic character.

In the second chapter, Agranat stated that, despite its importance, the principle of freedom of expression is not an isolated concern in the legal system. At times, it clashes with other values and principles, then leading to a need for balancing conflicting values.

In the third chapter, Agranat proceeded to suggest a balancing test appropriate to the limitation of freedom of expression. In the case at stake, the discussion focused on section 19 of the Press Ordinance, which grants the Minister of Interior the power to suspend the publication of a newspaper when "the publication is likely, in the opinion of the Minister of Interior, to endanger public peace." Agranat argued that the term "likely" points to the existence of a causal connection between the publication and the danger to public peace, but does not specify the precise connection, and leaves room for the Court's discretion in its definition. Recourse to a remote causal link would increase the minister's power, whereas recourse to a close causal link would increase the freedom of the press. Agranat examined two tests—the "bad tendency" test, stating that it suffices for an expression to show a slight or even remote tendency to endanger the public peace to justify its limitation, and the "close probability" test, which requires a causal link of close probability as a condition for limiting the expression. After discussing the two tests, Agranat chose the close probability formula, thereby fixating a high standard of protection for freedom of expression.

In the fourth chapter, Agranat applied the close probability test to the publications discussed in the petition and concluded that, in the circumstances of the case, there was no close probability that public peace would be disturbed were the newspaper to continue publication. On these grounds, he accepted the newspaper's petition and dismissed the suspension decision.

Balancing between rights and interests, and annulling administrative decisions that fail to do so properly, are now a day-to-day concern for the Israeli Supreme Court. Someone reading the *Kol Ha'am* ruling today may not find it particularly impressive, but such a perception would be a grave injustice to this decision. The *Kol Ha'am* ruling set the analytical structure for balancing rights and public interests, and the possibility of voiding a government decision that fails to set a proper balance between them. The ruling voiding the Minister of Interior's decision was issued, as noted, in a period entirely different from the one we live in today, when the collective good was set above the individual good, when broad powers were concentrated in the government, and criticism of its discretionary decisions was perceived as almost seditious. Intellectual power and public courage were thus required to write the trailblazing opinion in the *Kol Ha'am* ruling.

4. SETTING THE LIMIT: REFUSING TO REPEAL LAWS

Over the years, then, the Supreme Court built an impressive system for protecting human rights.[65] It recognized their existence, interpreted Knesset legislation in their light, demanded the legislature's explicit authorization for all violations of rights by the executive, and did not hesitate to examine and dismiss the executive's discretion when it considered such violations unjustified. Nevertheless, even though it was pressured to do so, the Court refused to take one step: it refused to void primary legislation that violates human rights, even if it found the violation unjustified. The Court stated, "If the Knesset has issued an explicit provision that leaves no room for doubt, it must be followed even if it is incompatible with the principles of the Declaration of Independence."[66]

VI. Failed Attempts and Lost Patience

Over the years, many attempts were made to anchor a Bill of Rights in a Basic Law, but these attempts failed.[67] The failure need not surprise us. As Elster showed, constitutions are usually passed in conditions of crisis, which compel the discussion of fundamental questions and lead rival factions to show greater flexibility and willingness to compromise.[68] The window of opportunity that opened up at the time the State of Israel was established closed without bringing about a constitution. In the years since, the gaps between various segments of Israeli society have only widened, thus further lessening the chances of enacting a constitution.[69]

But the absence of a constitution, as noted, did not prevent the Court from effectively protecting individual rights. And yet, new winds blowing in the Supreme Court attested that its last word in the area of human rights was yet to be said.

In 1989, a retroactive amendment to the Financing Law was on the agenda, raising the allocation for each Knesset seat. The petitioner—the "La'or" movement—claimed that a retroactive raise violates the equality principle in section 4 of Basic Law: The Knesset, which is entrenched with a requirement of an absolute majority.[70] Although all the parties would enjoy a raise on an equal basis, the large parties had planned their expenses and, during the election campaign, spent far more than the budget allocated to them according to the law. The smaller parties, which had been unaware of the envisaged reform, planned the election campaign according to the budget at their disposal and, therefore, the value of the increase they received after the election was extremely limited.

Section 4 of Basic Law: The Knesset is indeed entrenched with the requirement of an absolute majority, but the Financing Law did pass with an absolute majority in all three hearings, seemingly overcoming the hurdle set in the Basic Law. Yet the petitioners still tried. The law discussed in the petition was tabled by Knesset members, not by the government. The three hearings were therefore preceded by a preliminary hearing (as required by the Knesset Rules of Procedure). The petitioners claimed that the absolute majority requirement applies to the preliminary hearing as well, and since the motion failed to pass this hearing with an absolute majority, the amendment should be annulled. Justices Elon and Maltz accepted the petition, and decided to void the law. By contrast, Justice Barak rejected the petition after stating that the demand of absolute majority concerns only the three hearings but not the preliminary one.

Had proceedings stopped here, *La'or* would have sunk into oblivion and would not have become part of the corpus of important decisions. The petitioners, however, had a further claim. They argued that, in addition to violating the equality principle formulated in section 4 of the Basic Law, the Financing Law violates the general principle of equality, which they claimed to be fundamental to our legal system. They requested the Court to determine that a law opposed to this principle is legally invalid, even if it is passed with a special majority in the Knesset.

Justice Elon rejected this claim outright, and stated, "The very essence of our democratic regime, with its three branches of government, is that we do not question the parliament's legislative endeavor."[71] By contrast, Justice Barak held that this was an important claim. Barak discussed the claim at length and, in the summary, stated as follows:

> Three conclusions are warranted: one, that the court in a democratic society may in principle declare void a law opposed to the system's fundamental principles. Even if these fundamental principles are not part of a rigid constitution or an entrenched Basic Law, the view that a law's contents cannot be grounds for declaring it void is in no way self-evident ... The second, that according to our accepted social and legal approach, the Court does not assume for itself the authority to declare void a law opposed to the basic principles of our system. This approach ... reflects Israel's social consensus and is supported by the enlightened public ... The third, that in light of the social-legal views

widespread in Israel and in light of the Court's consistent case law over the years, it would be improper for us to deviate from an approach that reflects our legal-political tradition. It would be improper for us to adopt a new approach that recognizes the Court's power to declare void a law that does not contradict a provision entrenched in a Basic Law but is opposed to fundamental principles of the system. Were we to do so, we would appear to the public as deviating from the social consensus on the role and the power of a judge in Israeli society, whose perception of the judicial role is incompatible with this far-reaching decision. I believe that, in the public's view, such a deep and important decision should be made—at this stage of our national life—by the people and their elected representatives.[72]

Latent in Barak's comments is a far-reaching innovation. Barak determined that, in principle, the Court is authorized to void a law that violates human rights *despite the absence of a written constitution that would allow this.* In this statement, Barak clearly indicates his future intentions to the Knesset. Barak, as it were, told the legislators: if you persist in your refusal, if you do not enact a Bill of Rights in the near future, we judges will act and will allow, even in the absence of a written document, the voiding of primary legislation that violates human rights unjustifiably. We will thereby make the need for a legislated Bill of Rights redundant, and we will render you, the legislators, irrelevant.

The innovation latent in Barak's comments goes even further. The basic principle of equality in elections discussed in *La'or* had been anchored in a Basic Law, and the amendment of the law had met the requirements set in this constitutional document. The petitioners, then, had not asked the Court to void the law *in the absence of a constitution*, but to void the law even though the constitution had legitimized it. Barak's readiness to consider voiding the law, then, established an *additional innovation*, stating that, if a provision constitutes a grave violation of the system's fundamental values, *the Court has a right to act according to a more rigorous standard than the one established in the constitution*, voiding a law even though it meets the constitutional standard.[73]

Ultimately, Justice Barak did not void the amendment of the Financing Law, and these two innovations were thus suggested merely as *dicta*. Yet, this was not the first time that Barak downplayed a vastly significant innovation in an obiter dictum, only to use it later as the basis of a ruling.[74] A seasoned observer of Barak's working methods, then, could have understood the drift of his remarks.[75]

2

THE CONSTITUTIONAL REVOLUTION: HOW DID IT HAPPEN?

I. Introduction

From its establishment foundation in 1948 and until the early 1990s, the State of Israel had no formal Bill of Rights. Although the Declaration of Independence had promised a constitution, a public debate that continued for almost two years clarified that keeping this promise would not be possible. Many obstacles stood in the way of this initiative, among them the failure of attempts to bridge deep value disputes; the reservations of the ruling party, Mapai, about endorsing a constitution that would limit the government's power, and, possibly, the transformation of the Constitutional Assembly into the First Knesset, a move that weakened its interest in drafting a constitution. The result was the acceptance of the resolution proposed by MK Yizhar Harari: the constitution-drafting process would proceed in stages, in the shape of Basic Laws that would be joined together at its end.

The Harari decision was only partly implemented. The Knesset did enact a series of Basic Laws, but all of them focused on structural aspects, without touching on basic freedoms. The status of these laws was not clear either. In the absence of a constitutional Bill of Rights, the Supreme Court created alternative mechanisms to protect human rights, and Israeli scholars, with good reason, have conveyed their pride for the Israeli phenomenon of effective protection for human rights even without a constitution. Despite its activism, in the absence of a constitution, the Court showed self-restraint and refused to void primary legislation that violates human rights. Over the years, several attempts to anchor a Bill of Rights in a Basic Law failed, and the Court began to lose patience. In the *La'or* ruling, issued in 1989, Justice Barak hinted to the Knesset that it was running out of time, and that unless it enacted a Bill of Rights soon, the Court would assume authority for voiding primary legislation even in its absence.

A momentous event took place in 1992. The Knesset enacted two Basic Laws dealing with human rights: Basic Law: Human Dignity and Liberty, and Basic Law: Freedom of Occupation (henceforth: the new Basic Laws).[1] As its name attests, Basic Law: Freedom of Occupation deals with one right only, freedom of occupation. Basic Law: Human Dignity and Liberty regulates several rights—preservation of life and body, property, movement from and to Israel, liberty, dignity, and privacy. Absent from the list of rights protected in these two laws are several important human rights such as equality, freedom of expression, and freedom of religion. The omission of these rights, as shown below, was a deliberate act rather than an unintended mistake. Besides prohibiting the violation of the enumerated rights, both laws include a limitation clause posing four cumulative conditions that, if met, legitimize the violation of the rights and preclude the voidance of this act.[2]

The Supreme Court has used the new Basic Laws as a platform for creating a full-fledged constitution, and academics have contributed their share to this expeditious process. At first, the scholarly discourse focused on general questions such as the legitimacy of the move,[3] or the contents of the "values of the State of Israel as a Jewish and democratic state"[4] that, according to the sections describing the aims of the new Basic Laws, these laws are meant to protect. In no time, however, the academics shifted into a detailed discussion of the constitutional innovations and their influence on various areas of Israeli law.[5]

In Chapter 3 below, I describe the constitutional developments since March 1992 that, as noted, have originated mostly in the Court. Before proceeding to this description, I wish to deal with one intriguing question that has yet to be considered: after forty-four years of failures and parliamentary paralysis, how did the Knesset suddenly anchor a Bill of Rights in a Basic Law? What prepared the ground for what many had thought impossible?[6] Four possible answers to this question are presented in this chapter. All, or at least some of them, may together have created a powerful drive that set in motion what has been called the "constitutional revolution."

One thesis attributes the success of the constitutional revolution to the exploitation of a "constitutional moment" that emerged from an acute crisis of trust between the public and the political establishment. At this constitutional moment, all those involved understood the need for changing the balance of power and strengthening the Court's powers of review. A second thesis ascribes the move's success to the tactic adopted by its proponents who, rather than insist on the ratification of a full-fledged Bill of Rights, chose to split it into sub-units, and enact only those sections on which consensus could be reached. They also adopted a conciliatory tone that succeeded in bridging divergent views. According to a third thesis, what enabled the enactment of these laws was a tactic adopted by their sponsors, who did not clearly expose the full import of the move they had been leading, thereby lulling the traditional opponents of this move. The fourth and last explanation attributes the move's success to two shifts in Israel's political reality. The first was the Labor Party's loss of hegemony and the ensuing uncertainty about the identity of future coalitions, and the second was the growing strength of marginal elements that threatened the secular-centralized-veteran hegemony in Israeli society. The first shift weakened the resistance of the coalition parties to the "constitutionalization" of the political system, whereas the second neutralized the institutional interest of MKs representing the old elite in opposing the constitutional move. Each of these explanations will be discussed below.

II. A Historical Moment

Bruce Ackerman proposes dividing the history of the democratic game into two types of periods.[7] At most times, the normal "political game" prevails. For brief periods, however, the public becomes sharply aware of the crucial significance attached to the constitutional question on the agenda. At such times, voting patterns do not express the concerns of day-to-day politics, but rather the public's judicious position on the constitutional issue. Through this distinction, Ackerman attempts to explain and justify, from a democratic perspective, several constitutional changes in American society that came about without anchor in a formal constitutional amendment. The most striking was the U.S. Supreme Court's reversal concerning initiatives led by President Roosevelt in the 1930s, in response to the grave economic crisis. For a number of years, the U.S. Supreme Court curbed these initiatives, repealing a series of laws designed to implement them. Then, at some point soon after the 1936 presidential elections in which Roosevelt was elected for a second term, the Court suddenly changed its stance and ratified legislation identical to that it had repealed only a short time earlier. One explanation that has been suggested for this reversal was the Court's fear of interference with its independence, given the president's attempt to expand it and appoint justices who would agree to authorize the legislative initiatives.

Ackerman explains the change differently. He does not view it as judicial capitulation, but as the Court's recognition of the constitutional change that had taken place in the United States.[8] Ackerman holds that the presidential elections of 1936 were conducted at a moment of "constitutional politics," when the public was conscious of the importance attached to the dispute between the president and the Supreme Court, and of the reasons underlying their respective conceptions. The massive public support for the president in the 1936 elections conveyed a constitutional verdict. The Court honored this constitutional decision, and therefore changed its view.[9]

Ackerman's theory is descriptive, but has a normative dimension as well. It not only explains the change in the Supreme Court's approach, but also justifies it. The Court's involvement in fashioning the Constitution is problematic, and becomes all the more so given that the Constitution sets a clear mechanism for its change.[10] Ackerman's claim that the constitutional change is not a product of a judicial, but rather of a public decision, solves at least part of the problem.[11]

Ackerman's theory does not fit the facts of Israeli reality in all its details. Contrary to the American example, constitutional change in Israel was not the result of a conflict between the Court and the political system, nor did it evolve after the public expressed its view through elections. Nonetheless, the principle underlying Ackerman's theory may also provide an explanation of developments in the Israeli context at both the factual and normative levels. The factual question was posed above—how did the Knesset succeed in overcoming all the obstacles and, against overwhelming odds, enact a constitution? The normative question pertains to the legitimacy of the constitutional move. One question that the Israeli Supreme Court discussed several years after the enactment of the new Basic Laws was the source of the Knesset's authority to enact a constitution. The justices proposed several formal answers to this question,[12] but they failed to contend with the normative perplexity that accompanied it. The new Basic Laws, as will be shown, were enacted quite in passing. Even if the Knesset was authorized, on formal grounds, to enact a constitution, the way the new Basic Laws were enacted would not seem to be the proper course to follow concerning such a significant event.[13] Ackerman's approach, however, could help to neutralize this value-based criticism. If, in Israel as well, constitutional change occurred at a moment of constitutional politics and reflecting an informed and deliberate public decision, this might answer not only the factual, but also the normative question.

An explanation in the spirit of Ackerman's theory could be formulated as follows. Several problematic moves at the end of the 1980s and early 1990s brought public distrust in the Israeli political system to new heights. Broad public consensus emerged concerning the need for a systemic revamping of the political system as a precondition for solving the crisis, leading to two far-reaching changes. One affected the relationship between the legislative and executive branches, with the transition from a model of parliamentary democracy to a hybrid model that adopted features of the presidential model, in an attempt to strengthen the standing of the government and its leader.[14] The other change related to the relationship between the legislature and the Court, with the adoption of Basic Laws that allowed the Supreme Court to review the value-based decisions of the legislators. According to this line of argument, the new Basic Laws were not a random event, but a direct result of the crisis that beset Israel's political system, and of the public recognition that such change was imperative.[15]

Ackerman's theory is complex, and involves more than a moment of constitutional politics. It describes a mechanism of constitutional change in four stages.[16] At the first stage, one branch of government proposes constitutional change. At the second stage, another branch of government obstructs the move. The third stage involves a decision-making procedure with the participation of the public. The public's stance will determine whether the attempt at constitutional change will succeed or fail. If the public supports the change, the government branch that opposes it will withdraw its opposition, and if the public does not support the change, the initiative will fail, and the prevalent constitutional arrangement will remain in place.

This complex mechanism is significant both factually and normatively. The frontal collision between the Court and the political system is a crucial factor in the creation of public awareness. Elections conducted in the shadow of a focused confrontation provide normative justification for constitutional change. The four-stage mechanism need not be replicated precisely in this order to attest to public involvement and justify the ensuing change, but barring such a mechanism, the existence of a constitutional moment and of public support for the process of change requires some definite indication. It is hard to find clear evidence of a constitutional moment in Israel before the adoption of the Basic Laws and of marked public support for their enactment in the spirit of Ackerman's theory. The claim arguing that a crisis of trust prevailed between the public and the political system during the relevant period appears to be substantiated.[17] No evidence, however, supports the claim stating that the significance of the constitutional revolution was presented to, discussed, and broadly supported by the public prior to the Knesset vote on the adoption of the new Basic Laws. The issue received minimal media coverage at the time, both before and after the enactment of the Basic Laws. As Amnon Rubinstein notes:

> Most of the media never even reported on the legislative process, and the television entirely ignored it. When the law passed the second and third readings, journalists reported it but some editors did not consider it newsworthy. Most of the media never told their readers that the Knesset had passed a law as revolutionary as Basic Law: Human Dignity and Liberty.[18]

The political echelons were not involved in any special preparations that could point to special awareness of the issue's importance. Most members of the Knesset were not even present at the time of the vote on the Basic Laws.[19] Ruth Gavison notes: "The new Basic Laws … began to acquire their high profile with a series of articles and lectures by Justice Barak, who also has a copyright on the labeling of the 1992 legislation as 'the constitutional revolution.'"[20] Rather than pointing to a historical moment, these data suggest that this was an entirely ordinary political moment. As Aharon Barak indicates, "the constitutional revolution took place quietly, almost clandestinely."[21]

The argument about the adoption of the constitution at a "banal" moment has been raised in the past, in the context of the debate on the normative justification of the constitutional revolution.[22] Insofar as this is true, however, it denies the relevance of Ackerman's theory in the factual context as well. If the enactment of the Basic Laws was not the outcome of a broad wave of public support in them during a crisis of trust in the political system, the question arises anew: How did proponents of these laws manage to overcome the obstacles that had precluded their adoption for a generation?

III. Compromise

One major obstacle preventing the drafting of a constitution at the time of Israel's establishment was that various sectors of the Israeli society disagreed about its contents. The Harari decision sought to overcome this difficulty by splitting the constitutional endeavor into segments: if reaching consensus on a comprehensive document proved impossible, an attempt could be made to proceed gradually, each time anchoring partial agreements. Some legislators involved in the process of enacting the new Basic Laws argue that their reliance on this method may be one of the explanations for the 1992 success. Instead of insisting on a complete Bill of Rights, they opted for gradual progress: to anchor, at the first stage, the rights they had reached agreement on, and to defer the continuation of the process for a later stage.[23] Less problematic rights—such as human dignity, property rights, freedom of movement, freedom of occupation, and liberty—were included in the Basic Laws. Rights that were more problematic and politically contested in the Israeli context—such as freedom of religion, freedom of expression, and equality—were omitted or removed from the Basic Laws during the negotiation stages. In addition to agreement on the temporary omission of some of these rights, these scholars also point to several other elements of compromise meant to placate the religious front, which had traditionally opposed the entrenchment of human rights in a Basic Law. In this context, they mention, for example, the inclusion of a "validity of laws" section in Basic

Law: Human Dignity and Liberty, and the omission of a determination (which had originally been included in this section) stating that provisions of laws extant prior to the enactment of the Basic Law would be interpreted "in the spirit of this Basic Law."[24] The validity of laws section, ensuring that existing laws will not be affected by the enactment of the Basic Law, was meant to placate those who feared that a Basic Law would dramatically change arrangements that had been in force in Israel prior to its legislation. Deleting the obligation to interpret extant legislation in the spirit of the Basic Law was meant to prevent the option of changing this legislation, rather than by repealing it, by reinterpreting it "in the spirit" of the Basic Law.[25]

But even taking into account the elements of the "compromise," the reasons for the change in the stance of the religious camp remain unclear. The key factor that thwarted the constitutional project in Israel's early years, as noted, was not the religious front, but the ruling party, Mapai, and its leader, David Ben-Gurion.[26] And yet, in the period since the establishment of Israel in 1948 and up to 1992, the religious camp consistently opposed the adoption of a constitutional Bill of Rights, with good reason. Their main concern was the fear that upgrading human rights would grant the Court legitimacy to intervene in the legislature's decisions on controversial matters, and particularly on matters of religion and state. As long as the Court was limited in its ability to intervene in the Knesset's legislation, the religious sector succeeded in protecting its interests through the ordinary political game. The composition of the Court does not favor the religious interest, and the spirit of its opinions on religion and state matters, as will be shown below, was incompatible with the traditional religious position.[27] From these circumstances, the observer should have understood that the Court, if and when capable of expanding its involvement in the decisions of the political system, would not support the religious interest. What reason could have brought religious MKs to renounce the relative security of their position, and grant the Court additional power, enabling it to intervene in legislative decisions on religion and state?

In order to explain the surprising softening in the stance of the religious, some have added the inclusion of another compromise element in the Basic Laws: the anchoring of the Jewish character of the State of Israel in its dual definition as Jewish and democratic.[28] According to this claim, the religious camp saw the constitutional anchoring of Israel's Jewish identity as a significant achievement that would prevent erosion of this dimension.[29] But even if we were to agree that the anchoring of Israel's Jewish character played a role in reducing religious opposition, we are still left wondering why they agreed to the law. Did they not understand that empowering the court would provide the judges with a weapon that could be used against their interests? Indeed, in *ex post factum* comments, some of the opponents gave a different explanation of what had happened. It is to this explanation that we now turn.

IV. Deception

According to a third thesis, the success of the 1992 initiative was the result of mistake and deception.[30] According to this explanation, the two Basic Laws faced no serious resistance because their traditional opponents mistakenly believed—due to the deceptions of the laws' proponents—that the Basic Laws would not enjoy primacy, and would not allow the Court to review primary legislation.

The strongest evidence for the deception claim are the words of MK Uriel Lynn, Chairman of the Constitution, Law, and Justice Committee when submitting Basic Law: Human Dignity and Liberty to the plenum for a second reading: "We are not shifting the weight to the Supreme Court. We are not adopting what was proposed in Basic Law: Legislation or Basic Law: Human Rights, which were submitted in the past. No constitutional court is being established . . . with special power to repeal laws."[31] MK Lynn then added:

> The power has not shifted to the judiciary. The power remains in this house. And if, heaven forbid, experience with this law were to show that we erred and that the interpretation given to this law does not overlap the legislator's genuine intention, the Knesset can change the law . . . I oppose the establishment of a constitutional court because I think that it gives extraordinary power to a limited group of judges, whose interpretation will be the one to determine the annulment of laws in Israel.[32]

The deception thesis, however true, challenges the actual validity of the new Basic Laws. The challenge is not posed by the moral problem tied to the deception, but by its consequences: What could be the validity of a document that calls itself a "constitution" if it was adopted when many of its supporters did not understand that they were actually voting for a constitution? To the best of my knowledge, no precedent exists in any democratic country for a move in which the Court determines *ex post factum* that a constitution was adopted, when large numbers of the participants in the process had never intended to draft a constitution.[33] But the deception thesis is marred by a certain weakness. Even if the legislation's proponents attempted to camouflage the real meaning of this move, how could its traditional opponents fail to see through the smokescreen? And even assuming that the average Israeli politician is far busier with survival than with parliamentary work requiring knowledge and understanding, the starting point of this discussion still was that previous attempts to anchor a Bill of Rights in a Basic Law had failed precisely because the opponents understood its far-reaching implications. The notion that the Knesset of 1992 was so unsophisticated as to "buy" what could not be sold to its predecessors seems hardly acceptable.

In the past, I offered a partial answer to this flaw in the argument: opponents to the anchoring of a Bill of Rights in the constitution may have been negligent, but even if they had been more thorough, they still would have had reasonable grounds for accepting the claims of the legislation's backers, at least regarding Basic Law: Human Dignity and Liberty.[34] A constitutional truism that had gained increasing currency in Israel over the years is that Basic Laws do not enjoy normative primacy, except for their entrenched components.[35] Moreover, the concept of "entrenchment" was understood literally, as a requirement of form (and perhaps of procedure), as a condition for changing the law. Basic Law: Freedom of Occupation is entrenched, but Basic Law: Human Dignity and Liberty is not. Hence, according to the constitutional doctrine that prevailed when the Basic Laws were enacted, only Basic Law: Freedom of Occupation was supposed to enjoy constitutional status, and enable judicial review of primary legislation.[36] As Judith Karp noted, "Prima facie, Basic Law: Human Dignity and Liberty lacks any accepted and recognizable sign that might attest to the legislator's intention to turn it into it a meta-law enjoying preferential constitutional status, which enables it to determine the validity of laws that contravene it."[37]

Scholars who from a purely academic perspective analyzed the Basic Laws soon after their adoption determined that Basic Law: Human Dignity and Liberty does not enable judicial review.[38] Even Aharon Barak, who addressed the status of Basic Law: Human Dignity and Liberty in his academic work, left the question unresolved.[39] Anyone familiar with Justice Barak's use of his academic work as an auxiliary tool used to substantiate controversial judicial innovations he was planning to introduce in the future could easily have anticipated what was to come.[40] Yet, Barak's recourse to this interim period, on his way to substantiating the constitutional status of the Basic Law, attests that the move he was leading was indeed problematic.

The end of the story is well known. The Court changed the doctrine. It first added the idea of "substantive entrenchment," which granted primacy to Basic Law: Human Dignity and Liberty, and then annulled the entrenchment requirement altogether as a condition for primacy, and invested all Basic Laws with constitutional status.[41] According to the doctrine prevalent at the time the two new Basic Laws were enacted, only Basic Law: Freedom of Occupation, which entrenches one specific right, enjoyed constitutional status. Basic Law: Human Dignity and Liberty became a constitutional law only at a later stage, in the *Bank Mizrahi* ruling, where the Court changed the constitutional doctrine. If the constitutional revolution did not occur with the enactment of the Basic Laws but later, and if it did not take place in the Knesset but in the Supreme Court, it is no longer necessary to explain how their proponents prevailed over the traditional opposition in the Knesset. The legislators did not oppose the constitution because, in their understanding, no constitution was on the agenda.

The deception claim is tempting, but not free of flaws. In an article that Amnon Rubinstein, who had proposed the law, wrote several years after the enactment of Basic Law: Human Dignity and Liberty, he adamantly refuted not only the deception claim, but also the mistake claim. Rubinstein insisted that MKs were clearly aware of its constitutional status before they voted on Basic Law: Human Dignity and Liberty, and the move's success did not result from deception or mistake but from compromise.[42] Although Rubinstein's statements cannot be reconciled with those of MK Lynn quoted above, some of the evidence he adduces to support his claim cannot be easily dismissed. For instance, Rubinstein quotes MK Yitzhak Levi, then the leader of the National Religious Party, who explained in a newspaper interview that he himself had proposed including the principles of the Declaration of Independence in the Basic Laws to block the possibility of the Court repealing the Law of Return (1950).[43] This quote appears to give the impression that the NRP leader, who, according to Rubinstein's testimony, "helped the writer, through his legal erudition and his sincere desire to make a change, to reach several trailblazing compromises,"[44] understood the law's potential.[45] Rubinstein argues that the deception thesis is also incompatible with the persistent struggle that representatives of the religious parties waged over the content of the rights to be included in the law, and the wording of the section on the validity of laws. This claim, too, sounds very persuasive. If Rubinstein is right, not only was there no deception, but not even any mistake.

The attempt to pin the religious bloc's agreement to soften their approach concerning Basic Law: Human Dignity and Liberty on the fact that the law lacks entrenchment, which justified assuming it has no constitutional validity, is problematic. The law's original version had included an entrenchment section, which was omitted from the Basic Law only on the second reading. The demand of MKs Ravitz and Halpert from United Torah Judaism to eliminate this section passed by a majority of one.[46] MK Levi, who supported the law, announced that he would vote in favor of omitting the entrenchment section. Ostensibly, this matter could be claimed to be evidence showing that religious MKs understood the crucial importance of the entrenchment issue, thereby strengthening the proposed explanation, but it could also lead us to a different conclusion. If religious MKs indeed understood that the status of the Basic Law would be determined on the basis of the entrenchment question, and if they never intended to grant powers of judicial review to the Court, why did MK Levi support the bill in the first reading, and why did he not resolutely oppose it as long as the entrenchment section remained? How did ultra-Orthodox

MKs, who were senior partners in the government coalition, allow the bill to reach a second reading without using all the political means at their disposal to foil it at an earlier stage?

The mistake/deception claim in its strong version stumbles upon certain factual difficulties, but a somewhat toned-down version of it might prove more persuasive. To some extent, the weakness of the mistake claim follows from a reading of the 1992 events in the perspective of today's reality. However, we must beware of such anachronisms. Things that are now obvious to any law student, and perhaps even to the public, were unknown in 1992. As Yoav Dotan notes, until 1992,

> Israeli case law was dominated by the principle of parliamentary primacy, and the course on constitutional law in law faculties was essentially a general introduction to the course on public law. A cursory examination of the most famous academic textbook on Israeli constitutional law—*The Constitutional Law of the State of Israel* by Prof. Amnon Rubinstein in its 1980 third edition—will attest to it. Of the book's many chapters, only one addresses the Knesset's constitutional standing, and this chapter too is largely a historical survey. Judicial review of the constitutionality of laws occupies about five pages, and at its center is the reference to the well-known *Bergman* ruling. The possibility that the courts would deviate from the narrow path set in this ruling and would systematically review Knesset legislation—even when it infringes entrenched sections of Basic Laws—is mentioned as a "speculation" that contradicts a dominant principle: the principle of parliamentary sovereignty.[47]

The current awareness in Israel of the possibility of judicial review stems from the Court's use of the powers it granted itself and from the sharp public response to the Court's moves. Had MK Levi and his colleagues known then what they know today, they would probably have resolutely opposed the enactment of the Basic Laws. In that sense, MK Levi's support in the Basic Laws may be defined as a mistake. Only this understanding can help clarifying some of his statements, such as the following reference to the meaning of the limitation clause proposed in Basic Law: Freedom of Occupation:

> The question is how one understands this section. One interpretation could be that a law is a law, and this Basic Law is not meant to limit any other law . . . Another possibility is to say that . . . here we are qualifying other laws, and saying that we will examine the laws and, insofar as they contain elements that are not in the public interest, the Basic Law will prevail . . . My *understanding is that this Basic Law does not purport to cancel any other law.*[48]

The deception claim can also be formulated in a milder version. Prior to the enactment of the Basic Laws, constitutional experts held a significant advantage over their colleagues who were not versed in the law in general and in constitutional law in particular. Jurists such as MKs Rubinstein and Lynn knew and understood a great deal more than other MKs who had no legal training, such as Levi, Ravitz, and Halpert, who represented religious parties. In these circumstances, the cited statements by MK Lynn, who was then chairman of the Constitution, Justice, and Law Committee, might have been accepted at face value and percolated down into the consciousness of the law's traditional opponents. Rubinstein argues that Lynn never referred to the question of whether the Court would be authorized to engage in judicial review and repeal primary legislation. In his view, acquiring the authority to engage in judicial review was obvious, and he suggests interpreting Lynn's statements as dealing with the question of the model that would be chosen for performing judicial review: a constitutional court or the existing judiciary.[49] Lynn, too, when he realized several years after the adoption of the Basic Laws that his statements had provided a basis for the deception claim, was quick to refute it in the spirit of Rubinstein's explanation.[50] On reading Lynn's account, however, I find the explanation contrived and entirely unacceptable.[51] The explanation—that Lynn had intended his remarks to be about the constitutional model to be chosen, rather than about the question of whether judicial review would be possible—seems even less plausible when taking into account that Lynn made these statements in 1992. Sophisticated constitutional discourse was then just beginning in Israel, and the question of whether to adopt a centralized or decentralized mechanism of judicial review had yet to be discussed in earnest. In these circumstances, to assume that listeners were relating literally to Lynn's comments as negating the Court's authority to engage in judicial review appears far more plausible.

The milder version of the deception claim—stating that proponents of this move did not really "deceive" their colleagues, but presented it in vague terms, exploiting the lack of awareness, knowledge, and sophistication typical of the constitutional Israeli discourse at the time—may find further support in jurists' statements after the enactment of the Basic Laws. In the *Bank Mizrahi* landmark ruling, described in the next chapter, which was issued long after Chief Justice Barak and others had begun enlisting support for the constitutional revolution idea, Justice Cheshin forcefully stated that the Basic Laws lacked constitutional validity.[52] Similar views were also conveyed by the former deputy chief justice of the Supreme Court, Menachem Elon,[53] by former chief justice Moshe Landau,[54] and by Ruth Gavison.[55] Even Chief Justice Barak conceded that "until the *Bank Mizrahi* ruling, it was possible to claim . . . that the Basic Laws on human rights had not triggered any constitutional revolution, neither in the parameters of existing law nor in the parameters of the desirable law."[56] There are no grounds for assuming that religious MKs were aware of these jurists' positions prior to the enactment of the Basic Laws. Yet, the continued adherence of these legal experts to the view that this was not a constitutional revolution lends support to the claim that, in the deliberations that preceded the enactment of the Basic Laws, MKs could certainly have construed them as not empowering the Court to repeal primary legislation.

The milder version of the deception thesis can also rely on the pattern that characterized the reception of the Basic Laws in the Knesset itself, in the media, and in the public at large. Rubinstein and Lynn assert that all the members of the Constitution, Law, and Justice Committee clearly understood the far-reaching implications of the new Basic Laws. Yet, they too would probably find it hard to explain the indifference that these two laws encountered in the Knesset plenum and in the media. In the third reading of Basic Law: Human Dignity and Liberty, only fifty-four MKs participated. Whatever our view on the functioning of the Knesset, it seems illogical that such a small number of MKs participated in such a crucial vote.[57] In the days before, during, and after the enactment of the Basic Laws, we find no echo of them in the media. Whatever our view of the Israeli media is, it makes no sense that it would pass up a scoop as significant as a constitutional revolution. Even if we were to accept Rubinstein's and Lynn's claims that neither of them deliberately deceived Knesset members, the data on vote participation and the silence of the media at least lend credence to the claim that neither of them made a special effort to explain the historic significance of the occasion to the MKs and to the public at large. They certainly substantiate MK Shevah Weiss' definition of the move as "a semi-clandestine, semi-legitimate smuggling of a constitution into the agenda of the State of Israel,"[58] or the explanation of Claude Klein, who ascribes the success of the initiative to a "sophisticated exploitation of the 'end of season' atmosphere that prevails in the final days of a Knesset term."[59]

The deception/mistake thesis needs to be tempered not only because the conduct of the religious MKs is incompatible with its extreme version, but also because of the need to consider an additional factor, the influence of which on the constitutional revolution I have so far mentioned only incidentally. By this I refer to the Court. In his academic work, Barak claimed that "the revolutionary body that made the revolution was the Knesset itself. The revolution was made according to the rules and laws that set the rules of the revolution. This was a constitutional 'constitutional revolution.' "[60] However, even according to Barak, the Knesset action was a necessary but not a sufficient condition for the revolution to occur: "The constitutional revolution became possible in 1992 by dint of the cooperation between the constituent and judicial branches. Neither one of them could have made this revolution on its own. Only by joining forces did the Knesset and the Court bring about the constitutional revolution."[61]

For my purposes, even if the success of Rubinstein, Lynn, and their colleagues was helped by their failure to explain the full revolutionary potential of their initiative, they could not have reached their goal without the Court's close cooperation. Given their professional and personal familiarity with its members, the law's proponents may have anticipated the cooperation of the justices,[62] but even they do not seem to have imagined how close this cooperation would be. The next chapter describes at length the Court's endeavor in the writing and development of the constitution in a way that made any further legislation superfluous. The Supreme Court found a way, for example, to smuggle into the Basic Laws the rights that their proponents had been forced to waive. The Court also determined that the enactment of the two Basic Laws led to the upgrading of all the old Basic Laws, those that past rulings had stated did not enjoy normative primacy. Did the proponents of the law ever imagine that the Court would make use of the new Basic Laws for this purpose? Did they ever imagine that the Court would use this opportunity to design an entire constitution? Presumably, the answer to these questions is negative. Hence, even if the law's proponents had engaged in "proper disclosure," they would have been able to reveal only a trace of what today is known to all.

V. A Joint Project of Old Elites

We have thus far focused on the question of how supporters of a Bill of Rights anchored in the constitution overcame the traditional opposition of the religious bloc. The formulation of the question in these terms, however, is not sufficiently precise. Opposition to a constitution in Israel's early years was not confined to the religious, and included, as noted, the ruling party, Mapai. Furthermore, according to Elster's thesis as presented above, once the Constituent Assembly became the First Knesset, its members (including representatives of the opposition) became less interested in adopting a constitution. Assuming that the institutional interest had not disappeared, and that the division along coalition-opposition lines had not changed, the 1992 success required overcoming not only elements that opposed the project in principle, but also the ingrained interests of the coalition forces, and, to a certain extent, even of the Knesset as a whole, against the anchoring of a Bill of Rights in the constitution. What changed, then?

The triumph over the coalition parties' built-in opposition to a constitution that would curtail their powers could be explained as resulting from the change in the balance of power in Israel from the end of the 1970s. Until then, the Israeli political system had enjoyed stability. The identity of the ruling party had been known in advance, and even its partners in the government coalition had been more or less fixed. Since the 1977 elections to the Ninth Knesset, however, the political system has been characterized by volatility. The government keeps changing hands, and no party reaching power can be sure it will remain there for long.[63] A ruling party firmly established in power will not support the weakening of the parliament it controls. By contrast, a ruling party with a high probability of becoming an opposition party in the near future has no strong interest in resisting the adoption of a constitution.[64]

The instability of Israeli governments largely neutralized the interest of the coalition parties in opposing a constitution. But what of the legislature's institutional interest against a constitution that would limit its power? This interest, as noted, is common to all political parties, whatever their status, and did not change when the balance of power between the various parties shifted at the end of the 1970s. This is where the fourth explanation enters the picture. According to this explanation, the Knesset's institutional interest did not disappear, but specific circumstances I shall discuss immediately below led a considerable number of MKs to act against their own institutional interest, and strengthen the power of the Court.

In the past few decades, Israel's political system has been characterized not only by fluctuations in the identity of the ruling parties, but also by the erosion of the "center," as well as by the growing strength of elements that had once been located in the periphery. This trend is evident in the weakening of the veteran parties, and in the growth and buildup of sectorial parties.[65] The hegemony of the secular-Jewish-veteran center, comprising a moderate left and right, is in jeopardy. Members of this group fear the prospect of a dramatic change in the character of the country, which will occur as elements whose value systems differ from those of the secular center take control of the political power centers. With emerging concern about an "alien" takeover of the legislature, a conflict erupts between the legislators' institutional interest and their sectorial value-based interest. If the Knesset is no longer firmly controlled by supporters of the old values, legislators wishing to ensure the continued dominance of these values might look elsewhere for protection, even at the cost of harming the interest of the Knesset to which they belong.

In Israel, such protection can be found in the Supreme Court. The mechanism for selecting justices in Israel is unique, in that it grants incumbent Supreme Court justices unparalleled power to select those who join their ranks.[66] In the past, the composition of the Supreme Court had traditionally reflected the values of the old elite. For as long as the mechanism for selecting justices remains unchanged, this elite can be sure of its values' persistent hegemony.[67] From the perspective of the elite's representatives in the legislature, who fear a "hostile takeover," bolstering the Court's power and entrusting it with the authority to review the legislature's decisions has a compelling logic, even if it means harming their own institutional interest.[68]

This explanation for the constitutional revolution in Israel was presented, inter alia, by Ran Hirschl in a series of articles, as part of a general theory aiming to explain self-weakening acts performed in various parliaments, a move that ostensibly defies logic.[69] This explanation, as noted, is persuasive in the Israeli context, because of Israel's unique and exceptional system of judicial appointments. By contrast, Hirschl's attempt to turn a local explanation into a general theory explaining parallel processes in other countries is less convincing. The weakness of the explanation as a general theory lies in its failure to take into account the mechanisms of judicial selection common in most countries that grant influence, if not control, to the political system over the judicial product. When the political system controls the selection mechanism, transferring authority to the Court serves the threatened elites only for a brief period—as soon as the elite loses control of the political system, it will also lose control of the courts. Hence, only in Israel (where the Court is and will continue to be controlled by the old elites) is it logical for the elites to shift the center of gravity to the courts. In other countries, where control of the courts is largely in the hands of whoever controls the other branches of government, it is entirely illogical for the legislature to concede some of its rights.[70]

VI. Summary

This chapter presented four possible explanations for the surprising adoption of Basic Laws concerning human rights in March 1992. Each of these explanations has both strengths and weaknesses. The historical moment argument is borne out by the reality that had prevailed in Israel prior to the adoption of the Basic Laws, and by the public, extra-parliamentary pressure for the enactment of a constitution that crystallized at the time. Yet, this explanation is incompatible with the indifference (and this is an understatement) that accompanied the enactment of the Basic Laws in the Knesset, and in the public at large. The compromise argument is consistent with the wording of the Basic Laws and with the evidence of negotiations and compromises in the course of the legislative process. Yet, questions remain regarding the unexpected toning-down of the resistance to these laws among their opponents, though *ex post factum*, some of them explicitly denied that this was the case.

The deception/mistake argument explains, better than the compromise argument, the surprising agreement of the traditional opponents, and the total silence that accompanied the adoption of the Basic Laws. This argument is further supported by the comments of the laws' proponents and interpreters prior to and immediately after their enactment. This argument, however, is strongly denied by the laws' proponents, and is in some tension with statements by Yitzhak Levi, an MK representing a religious party. The argument of a joint move by the old elites explains the disappearance of the coalition's interests, and those of the legislature as a whole, against the transfer of authority to the Court, but does not pretend to explain the success in overriding the contrary religious interest.

Which of these explanations is correct? The available evidence does not allow a conclusive answer to this question. Even if we were equipped to offer a definitive opinion, I am not sure that one correct answer could be isolated, and the claim that all four factors contributed to the success of the legislation is compelling. The crisis of public faith in the political system generated public pressure on the Knesset, leading the legislators themselves to appreciate the need for change. The tactics of splitting the Bill of Rights into separate components, and the willingness to negotiate, tempered the stance of its traditional opponents. The deliberate ambiguity and the ambivalent statements of the Basic Laws' proponents were aided by the vagueness of constitutional doctrines, and by the lack of awareness concerning constitutional matters then prevalent in the public in general and among MKs in particular. All these factors blurred the revolutionary potential of the Basic Laws and lulled their opponents. Finally, the fears of the old elites for their hegemony, and the volatility that has characterized the government since the end of the 1970s, neutralized the legislature's institutional interest and the interest of those holding the reins of power against the transfer of the power focus to the Court. They also strengthened a sense of urgency among the laws' proponents. All these elements came together and led to the legislation of the Basic Laws. And yet, all these could not have turned the new Basic Laws into what they are today—a fully-fledged, constitutional Bill of Rights. To complete this task, a dominant and determined Court paired off with a weak and hesitant legislature. This tale will be told in the next chapter.

THE REVOLUTION AFTER THE REVOLUTION

I. Introduction

The previous chapter examined several possible explanations for the surprising breakthrough of March 1992. The various explanations were not claimed to be mutually exclusive, and all were plausibly assumed to have contributed to the move's success. Yet the chapter ended with the claim that, without detracting from the importance of the Knesset's legislative endeavor, the constitutional revolution is an ongoing enterprise that, both then and now, is driven mainly by the Supreme Court. The legislators provided the platform, but the impressive structure standing on that platform today is the creation of the Supreme Court. In order to obtain a full picture of the constitutional revolution from its dawn until the present, and even more so, in order to evaluate this revolution, the story that needs to be told is that of the Supreme Court's achievement in transforming the missing Basic Laws into a full constitution. This chapter is devoted to this task.

II. Upgrading Basic Law: Human Dignity and Liberty

The accepted convention that developed in Israel over the years, as noted in previous chapters, had been that the Knesset is authorized to legislate laws with constitutional status, and that it exercises this authority only when it entrenches a clause in a Basic Law. Basic Laws that are not entrenched do not enjoy constitutional validity, and their status equals that of ordinary primary legislation. Moreover, the concept of "entrenchment" was understood literally, as requiring a special majority as a condition for amending the law.[1] Since a decisive majority of the clauses in the old Basic Laws had not been entrenched, the statement concerning the constitutional status of entrenched clauses was of limited validity only.

The examination of Basic Law: Freedom of Occupation and Basic Law: Human Dignity and Liberty (henceforth: the new Basic Laws) in light of this constitutional convention should lead to the conclusion that their legislation did not create a genuine "constitutional revolution." Only Basic Law: Freedom of Occupation includes an entrenchment clause, stating that amending the law is possible only through a Basic Law enacted with an absolute majority, while Basic Law: Human Dignity and Liberty is not entrenched. According to the constitutional convention in force at the time the new Basic Laws were enacted, only Basic Law: Freedom of Occupation should have acquired constitutional status, enabling judicial review of primary legislation. Scholars, as noted, did indeed assume this literal understanding as self-evident when discussing the issue soon after the enactment of the new Basic Laws. They stated simply that Basic Law: Human Dignity and Liberty does not have primacy, and therefore does not enable judicial review of primary legislation. Basic Law: Freedom of Occupation protects only one right, which is not even the "queen of rights." If only this Basic Law enjoys constitutional status, then the constitutional revolution is a mini-revolution at best.

Here, however, is where President Barak enters the picture. Soon after the enactment of the new Basic Laws, Barak published an article where he first raised the possibility that this law too, though unentrenched, would have primacy. More precisely, Barak argued that the concept of "entrenchment" should be interpreted broadly, so that Basic Law: Human Dignity and Liberty would also be entrenched. The Basic Law is indeed not entrenched from amendment, but does include a clause, called the "limitation clause," stating under what conditions the rights enshrined in it could be infringed. This clause, as noted, deals with the conditions for infringing rights rather than with the conditions for amending the law. Barak proposed viewing this clause as a kind of "substantive" entrenchment that grants the Basic Law normative primacy, as opposed to the entrenchment that had been known thus far, to which he refers as "formal entrenchment." Barak left the issue "for further consideration," and expressed hope that the Knesset would soon act and add "formal entrenchment" to the Basic Law, thereby removing any doubts as to its status.[2]

The Knesset did not fulfill Barak's wish and did not add "formal entrenchment" to Basic Law: Human Dignity and Liberty.[3] Barak then donned his other cap, the judicial one, turning his academic-conceptual view into a compelling doctrine, in his opinion in the longest decision ever issued by the Supreme Court—the decision on the Gal statute.

During the 1980s and early 1990s, the agricultural sector in Israel stumbled into a crisis. After incurring huge debts, it was on the verge of collapse, and the government took a number of steps in order to save it. Through primary legislation, the Knesset put in place mechanisms for restructuring and waiving part of the sector's debts to the banks. One of the laws, dealing with the debts of cooperative settlements [moshavim], became known as the "Gal statute," named after the then Chairman of the Finance Committee, Gedaliyah Gal, who was a member of such a settlement.[4] The banks, who were the main injured party in the arrangement, attacked the law in court. The original lawsuit, demanding full payment of the debt, was submitted to the District Court by Mizrahi Bank against several moshavim. After the moshavim responded that part of the debt had been legally waived, the bank asked the Court to declare the law invalid because of its unjustifiable infringement of the bank's property right, a right enshrined in Basic Law: Human Dignity and Liberty. Heniya Stein, the District Court Registrar dealing with the case, accepted the bank's position and declared the law void. The moshavim appealed, and the case moved to the Supreme Court.

A principle widely accepted in jurisprudential literature throughout the world, which in the past had also been accepted in Israel, is that judges confine themselves to the discussion of issues required for deciding the case at hand, and endeavor to justify their verdict relying on the minimum required for decision. Questions that need not be discussed are postponed for the time they become vital for a decision. Since the early 1980s, the Israeli Supreme Court has been eroding this principle and writing long opinions, including extensive theoretical discussions that are not required for deciding the case. The decision on *Bank Mizrahi* involves an extremely bold departure from this principle, bringing some to claim that the Court has buried this principle forever.[5] A scholar who submitted the monumental decision on the Gal statute to rigorous examination found that 90 percent of it deals with issues that are not required for the matter at hand.[6]

One question that the Supreme Court justices considered at length was the status of Basic Law: Human Dignity and Liberty. The decision on this question was not necessary for deciding on the appeal, given that the Supreme Court overturned the District Court's decision. All the justices agreed that, even if the law under attack violated the banks' property right enshrined in the Basic Law, the violation was within the terms of the "limitation clause," which states under what conditions a law can be considered valid even when it violates a human right. If the violation of the property right is justified, answering the question of whether the Basic Law enjoys the normative primacy that would grant the Court authority to void primary legislation contradicting it is entirely irrelevant to a decision on the case. Nevertheless, as noted, the justices discussed the status of Basic Law: Human Dignity and Liberty at great length. Barak repeated the argument he had raised when wearing his scholarly cap, whereby Basic Law: Human Dignity and Liberty is substantively entrenched, and therefore enjoys normative primacy. Unlike the view he had expressed as a scholar, however, this time Barak issued a compelling judicial opinion.[7]

III. Upgrading All the Old Basic Laws

The notion of substantive entrenchment allowed President of the Supreme Court Barak to bolster the constitutional status of Basic Law: Human Dignity and Liberty. The scope of this device was limited, however, since Basic Law: Human Dignity and Liberty and Basic Law: Freedom of Occupation are the only ones substantively entrenched. All the "old" Basic Laws—except for a few clauses in Basic Law: The Knesset—were not entrenched, either formally or substantively. Even after the judicial expansion of the entrenchment concept, then, the old Basic Laws seemingly remained in their previous status, and failed to acquire constitutional standing. This was not Barak's view. In *Bank Mizrahi*, he stated as follows:

> Most Basic Laws do not include limitation clauses . . . the absence of a limitation clause does not detract from the normative status of the Basic Law as a superior norm in the Israeli legal system. The absence of a limitation clause negates the rigidity of the Basic Law in relation to other Basic Laws, and permits its amendment or infringement by a Basic Law enacted later by a regular majority. The absence of a limitation clause does not lower the status of the Basic Law to the level of regular law. A non-rigid Basic Law is still a Basic Law. It is not a "regular" law and it cannot be amended by regular legislation.[8]

In *Bank Mizrahi*, Barak erases in one stroke a long-serving and accepted constitutional convention, well established in both the jurisprudence and the literature, stating that entrenchment is required as an indication of the legislator's intention to grant a Basic Law constitutional status. Henceforth, according to Barak, all Basic Laws, old and new, have normative primacy.[9]

In the past, as noted, the Court had tried to avoid discussion of issues that were not required for a decision in the case at hand, and even concerning required issues, it had tried to minimize arguments and limit itself to those sufficient for the decision. Matters that are not necessary for the decision are known in professional parlance as obiter dictum, in order to distinguish them from elements vital to the decision, known as ratio decidendi. One of the skills that law students acquire at the start of their legal training is to distinguish ratio from obiter. This distinction is particularly important because only the ratio sets a compelling precedent to the courts whereas the obiter does not, and judges are indeed allowed to disregard it altogether. Although good lawyers try to include obiter dicta in their arguments if these assist their clients, they know that their value is limited. Judges too can refer to obiter dicta from previous rulings, but they will also be aware of the need for a distinction between rulings that are compelling and obiter dicta that are not. As long as the judicial profession adhered to cost-effective working methods, distinguishing between ratio and obiter was easy, and the importance of the distinction was clear. Once Israeli Supreme Court justices began to take license with this distinction and to devote a considerable part of their opinions to questions that were not at all required, or to complementary arguments that could have been done without, the factual distinction between ratio and obiter became more difficult, and the legal distinction between them became questionable as well. The logic is obvious: if justices devote so much effort and room to the discussion of obiter dicta, they obviously ascribe great importance to them, and their stance will influence the views of lower instance lawyers and judges in their regard.

But although the Court has blurred the border between ratio and obiter, the distinction between them is still valid. According to this distinction, both statements by Barak and his colleagues in *Bank Mizrahi*—the statement that Basic Law: Human Dignity and Liberty is substantively entrenched and thus enjoys primacy, and the statement that all Basic Laws, including those that are not entrenched at all, are upgraded and assume constitutional status—were not required for the decision in the case at hand, and therefore lack compelling validity. In decisions issued several years after *Bank Mizrahi*, these two obiters became ratio. In fact, the second obiter (which upgraded all Basic Laws) made the first obiter (which had granted constitutional status to Basic Laws including "substantive entrenchment") redundant. A ruling that in one stroke turned the second obiter into ratio, and thereby upgraded all Basic Laws—those in existence and those to be legislated in the future—is described briefly below.

The Herut-National Jewish Movement list, headed by Michael Kleiner, ran in the elections for the Sixteenth Knesset. In the time it was allotted for election propaganda, this list tried to broadcast a jingle of *"Biladi"* (a Palestinian patriotic song), showing in the background a flag of Israel that, in the course of the song, changes into a Palestinian flag. Mishael Cheshin, a Supreme Court justice who officiated as chairman of the Central Elections Committee, decided to disqualify the broadcast. Herut, in response, petitioned the High Court of Justice. The attorney for the

Central Elections Committee argued that the Supreme Court has no authority to review the discretion of the Elections Committee chairman, and therefore asked the Court to reject the petition out of hand. He rested his claim on section 137 of the Knesset Elections Law [combined version] 5729-1969 (henceforth: Elections Law), stating that:

> Any complaint concerning acts of commission or omission according to this law is within the exclusive purview of the Central Committee; no court will deal with petitions for relief concerning such acts of commission or omission or requests for a decision or an instruction of the Central Committee, of the Chairman of the Committee and its deputies, of a regional committee or a ballot station committee.

The petitioners argued in return that their right to petition the Court is enshrined in section 15 of Basic Law: The Judiciary. According to this law, when sitting as a High Court of Justice, the Supreme Court is vested with unlimited authority to grant petitioners relief against any state authority, for the sake of justice. The Court was required to choose between the two seemingly contradictory legislations. It accepted the petitioners' request and stated as follows:

> The decisions cited by the State Attorney in support of its arguments were handed down before our *Bank Mizrahi* judgment, and they are inconsistent with it. Therefore, section 137 of the Elections Law does not have the power to negate the authority of the High Court. Thus, inasmuch as section 137 of the Elections Law—which states that "no court" shall grant the remedies there stated—can be interpreted as negating the authority of the High Court of Justice, it is unconstitutional, and thus void regarding its application to the High Court of Justice.[10]

Basic Law: The Judiciary is not entrenched, either formally or substantively. Nevertheless, the Court preferred it to the Elections Law, claiming it enjoys constitutional status. The Court thereby upgraded its ruling in *Bank Mizrahi* (stating that all Basic Laws enjoy constitutional status) from obiter to ratio.

IV. The Judicial Creation of a Basic Law: Legislation

Every constitution needs an "operating system," dealing with its mode of acceptance, with its amendments, and with infringements of the principles included in it.[11] The

Supreme Court's upgrade of all Basic Laws created a problem because most Basic Laws are not entrenched, either through a formal entrenchment (stating how they can be amended) or through a substantive entrenchment (stating how the principles set in them can be infringed). A Basic Law regulating this matter could obviously be legislated, but the odds of the Knesset legislating such a Basic Law in the near future are slim.

The reason for the low plausibility is simple: immediately after the legislation of the new Basic Laws, or, more precisely, after the Supreme Court headed by Barak began speaking of the "constitutional revolution" that it claimed had occurred with the legislation of the new Basic Laws, the traditional opponents of a constitution understood the mistake that (from their perspective) they had made. Henceforth, all attempts to exploit the momentum that was created in March 1992 and complete the project of drafting a constitution met with suspicion and resistance. Some said half-jokingly that, given the Court's moves, they would henceforth oppose any attempt to complete the constitution, even if they were asked to enshrine the Ten Commandments in it.[12] It then transpired, however, that the Court no longer needed the Knesset's help in order to proceed. As will be shown below, the Court interprets the Basic Laws as it wishes, and includes in them whatever it pleases. Hence, it does not need to "thicken" the constitution with additional contents through the legislation of new Basic Laws. Nevertheless, the Court is definitely interested in obtaining the legislator's *ex post factum* approval for the moves it performs. The Court will be able to obtain the authorization it is so badly lacking if, for instance, the Knesset was to legislate a Basic Law recognizing the constitutional status of all the Basic Laws, and establishing avenues for amending them and infringing them. If the legislation of a Basic Law regulating the question of amendment and infringement were indeed to serve the interests of the Supreme Court by legitimizing the steps it has taken since March 1992, opponents of the Court and of the constitutional project it leads will never agree to it.

The slim chance that the Knesset will agree to legislate a Basic Law determining the ways of amending and infringing Basic Laws that are silent on these issues explains an additional series of obiter dicta in *Bank Mizrahi*, which deal with these questions. The justices, mainly Barak and Shamgar, discuss at great length the conditions required for amending and infringing Basic Laws. Both determine that, given the decision that all Basic Laws enjoy constitutional status, it will henceforth not be possible to amend them except through another Basic Law.[13]

Adding the condition that a Basic Law can only be amended through another Basic Law is problematic, inter alia because it is incompatible with the explicit wording of section 4 of Basic Law: The Knesset. Contrary to other Basic Laws, which do not deal at all with the question of whether they can be amended and how, this section states: "This section shall not be varied save by a majority of the members of the Knesset." It does not require that the amendment be performed through a Basic Law. Adding a requirement to a Basic Law on a matter that is specifically discussed in it without including it is more problematic than adding a condition on a matter that is not discussed in it at all. Following is Barak's answer to this bewilderment:

> I suggest that we determine that this provision relates to infringement of the electoral system—similar to infringement of the principle of equality in the *Bergman* case and its offshoots—and not to changing the electoral system itself. It is clear that if the subject were a change in the electoral system—such as a change from proportional representation to regional elections—then not only would a Basic Law be required, but also a "majority of the members of Knesset" as set forth in s. 4 of Basic Law: The Knesset.[14]

Section 4 of Basic Law: The Knesset specifically notes the condition required for its *variation*. This fact, however, does not deter Barak from suggesting that this section be interpreted as dealing with *infringement*.

I have so far described how Barak and Shamgar dealt with the question of how to *vary* a Basic Law. They also dealt in detail, however, with the question of how the values protected by these laws can be *infringed*. Both draw a distinction between Basic Laws that regulate the issue of infringement and Basic Laws that are silent on this question. The two new Basic Laws—Basic Law: Freedom of Occupation and Basic Law: Human Dignity and Liberty—include a "limitation clause" setting conditions that, if present, will enable the legitimation of a law or an administrative act infringing values protected by these Basic Laws. Clearly, then, the way to infringe an instruction set in these Basic Laws is the way set in the limitation clause, and Shamgar and Barak indeed state so. The other Basic Laws are silent on the question of their infringement. Once all Basic Laws are upgraded, it must be determined whether and how it is possible to infringe the values protected in silent Basic Laws. Shamgar offers several options for solving this problem. According to the first option, the values protected in silent Basic Laws can be infringed through a regular law, without any special procedure. According to the second option, a silent Basic Law can be infringed through ordinary primary legislation, but the Knesset must explicitly clarify in this legislation its intention to infringe the Basic Law. According to the third option, the one that Shamgar chooses, "a variation or infringement outside the framework of the limitation clause, which too forms a part of the Basic Law, may only be carried out by a law of equal status, i.e. by means of a Basic Law or on the basis of an authorization in a Basic Law."[15]

President Barak is less decisive than Shamgar concerning the infringement of a silent Basic Law. At first, Barak explains the logic of the second option raised by Shamgar:

> The Court could have concluded that in the absence of an entrenchment provision, the provisions of a Basic Law may be infringed by regular legislation, but only where that infringement is explicit. It would therefore have been possible to continue to emphasize the superior normative status of the Basic Law, while at the same time maintaining the appropriate distinction between a Basic Law providing for entrenchment and a Basic Law that is silent in this regard.[16]

Ultimately, however, Barak proposes reserving this issue "for further consideration, since Basic Law: Human Dignity and Liberty contains an entrenchment provision ... [that] is substantive, permitting infringement by means of regular legislation only if the regular legislation meets the substantive requirements."[17]

Barak's reason for refraining from ruling on the infringement of provisions in a silent Basic Law—no need to decide on this question in the ruling—seems persuasive. According to the logic of this argument, however, he should have refrained from ruling on the issue long before. He should not have upgraded all the Basic Laws, because the question at hand touched only on Basic Law: Human Dignity and Liberty. He should not have ruled on the status of Basic Law: Human Dignity and Liberty, which lacks formal entrenchment, because in any event he held that the infringement of the right to property that the Basic Law protects is justified in the circumstances of the case. According to his view, then, the result of the appeal was not at all affected by the status of the Basic Law. Why, then, did Barak choose to halt precisely at the question of whether a silent Basic Law can be infringed, and how?

What Barak had left "for further consideration" in *Bank Mizrahi*, he decides upon in *Herut*. He joins Shamgar's stance in *Bank Mizrahi* and states: "a regular law does not have the power to infringe the provisions of a Basic Law, unless such is allowed by the limitation clauses that are part of the Basic Laws themselves."[18] In other words, if the Basic Law does not include a limitation clause stating conditions for infringing it, its provisions should not be infringed, but only amended, through a Basic Law.[19] In his opinion in *Herut*, Barak also argues that this decision does not set a precedent, and relies on previous jurisprudence.[20] This claim is incorrect. In *Bank Mizrahi*, as noted, Barak had left the issue "for further consideration," and had even toyed with an option different from the one he eventually chose in *Herut*, whereby "arrangements in a non-entrenched (silent) Basic Law may be infringed through regular legislation."[21]

Ostensibly, the Court appears to have reached a decision regarding the infringement of a silent Basic Law; however, on further scrutiny, we find that the last word on the subject is yet to be said. In *Hofnung*, whose circumstances are irrelevant to our concern here, Justice Zamir raised another, fourth possibility, for solving the question of infringing a silent Basic Law. According to Zamir's proposal, the limitation clause in the two new Basic Laws should apply to silent Basic Laws as well. Infringement of provisions in a silent Basic Law is thus legitimate if it meets the test of the limitation clause.[22] Justice Barak, who presided in the *Hofnung* panel, showed interest in Zamir's proposal, but did not decide on it, and wrote as follows:

> My colleague's suggestion develops, as it were, a judicial limitation clause when the Basic Law makes no explicit determination on the question. A similar approach was adopted by the Supreme Court of the United States. The American Bill of Rights includes several rights—such as freedom of speech and freedom of religion—that are defined in absolute terms and include no limitation clause. The Supreme Court did not hesitate to develop judicial limitation clauses, and thereby turned absolute rights into relative rights.[23]

V. The Myth about Justice Cheshin

The previous sections reviewed a series of obiter dicta in *Bank Mizrahi*, and described how at least some of these statements eventually became compelling rules, turning the minor move of legislating new Basic Laws into a major revolution. The Court granted normative primacy to all Basic Laws, old and new, and set stringent conditions for their variation and for the infringement of the principles enshrined in them. The Court did so while changing constitutional doctrines that had been established in the past, and ignoring the wording of the Basic Laws.

Two justices did not join the majority view in *Bank Mizrahi*. One, Zvi Tal, refused to broaden the context beyond what was required for deciding on the case.[24] The other, Mishael Cheshin, wrote a long, forceful, and substantiated opinion, explaining why he was unwilling to join his colleagues and grant constitutional status to the new Basic Laws. Cheshin raised many claims against his colleagues' position, but the focus of his critique is on what he describes as an attempt to sneak a constitution into Israel's agenda. Addressing what, in his view, is the proper way of issuing a constitution, Cheshin says as follows:

> But it should be performed in the way of all the nations. Let a constitution be drafted and submitted for a referendum. Let the constitution be adopted

in a process of six readings spread out over the two Knessets. Let any act be done, provided that it involves a substantial deviation from regular legislative proceedings, and provided that the people are involved in the enactment of the constitution. All of these are legitimate acts, and we will acquiesce to them and cherish them. But with all my might I will oppose our recognition of the Knesset's authority to enact a constitution *by force of a judicial ruling*, via a legal analysis of a document dating back forty seven years, in reliance on disputed conceptions which have no firm roots in Israeli society. And where is the people? Should we not ask its opinion? On the contrary, let us call the people and consult them . . . If the people and its leaders desire a constitution, the means will be found for adopting one. And, if they don't want one, then the constitution will not be enacted. But I cannot agree to enacting a constitution *without consulting the people . . . Has today's nation* conferred upon its Knesset representatives the power to limit the tomorrow's, even if only on constitutional matters? And if they tell me: Yes, indeed, forty-seven years ago, then I too will respond that our concern is with the *people of today.* Did it grant its delegates in the Knesset today the power to frame a constitution? When did the people give a mandate to its Knesset delegates to enact a rigid constitution for Israel?[25]

Seemingly, we are looking at an incisive and courageous dissenting opinion, opposed to the incidental framing of a constitution, and on these grounds, refusing to grant normative primacy to the new (as well as the old) Basic Laws.[26] After the dust settles, however, two facts become clear:

(1) Cheshin's outlook is no different from that of the other justices. Despite his opposition to the idea of granting constitutional status to the Basic Laws, Cheshin agrees to respect various forms of limitation that the Knesset imposes on itself. He is willing to enforce a requirement whereby changes in a Basic Law be performed through another Basic Law,[27] or a requirement that variations of a law—regardless of whether it is a Basic Law or a regular law—be enacted by a special majority, as long as the required special majority is no greater than an absolute majority (sixty-one in the Knesset).[28] Cheshin is even willing to accept, to some extent, the "substantive entrenchment" of Basic Law: Human Dignity and Liberty:

Our opinion is therefore that Basic Law: Human Dignity and Liberty can only be violated or varied by force of an explicit provision to that effect in a later law; an implicit variation or implicit violation in the later law will not suffice. In the event of classic rules of interpretation being inadequate for reconciling a provision in the Basic Law with a later provision, i.e. we find that the two provisions are indeed contradictory, and assuming that the later provision does not expressly repeal the provision of the Basic Law, we may conclude that despite it being the earlier provision, the Basic Law's provision nonetheless shall prevail.[29]

Finally, Cheshin does not outright reject the proposal of his colleagues demanding that variations of all Basic Laws, old and new, be done through a Basic Law, even though the Basic Laws do not pose such a requirement:

Indeed, holding that a Basic Law can be varied or violated only by another Basic Law has a persuasive ring. But I nevertheless ask myself whether we can add a requirement to the statute that was not expressly established by the statute itself. However, I do not regard this as a cardinal question.[30]

Cheshin's hesitation on the last point is particularly problematic. The requirement that variations or infringements of a Basic Law be performed solely through another Basic Law, even if the Basic Law is silent in this regard, could be understandable only if we assume that the Basic Law enjoys supremacy. This rationale, as recalled, was precisely the one that Kaniel adduced in his petition against the Bader-Ofer law.[31] Cheshin, however, explicitly states that the Basic Laws do not have constitutional status. What, then, could be the basis for his statement that a silent Basic Law cannot be amended, except through another Basic Law? Cheshin's readiness to consider the addition of such a condition means that, in practical terms, his stance on the question of the constitution is extremely similar to that of his colleagues, and, moreover, also inconsistent.

(2) Cheshin's opposition swiftly collapses. Despite Cheshin's series of concessions, as described above, some differences do remain between his view and that of his colleagues. For instance, Cheshin legitimizes violations of a provision in Basic Law: Human Dignity and Liberty even if it fails to pass the tests of the limitation clause, if the Knesset clearly and explicitly expresses its intention to infringe the right. Besides practical differences between Cheshin's view and that of his colleagues, there is also some weight to his insistent claim that framing a constitution, which upgrades certain values and entrenches them from amendment and infringement, should be conducted through a special democratic procedure attesting to public awareness of, and involvement in, the process. Cheshin is not bashful when conveying his reservations in *Bank Mizrahi*, doing so at length and putting his rhetorical talent to full use.

Given his weighty critique of his fellow judges and the length of his opinion, Cheshin could have been expected to go on voicing his unique stance after *Bank Mizrahi* as well. Such persistence would have been particularly warranted, because all the points of controversy between Cheshin and his colleagues were discussed in

Bank Mizrahi only incidentally, as it were, and were never decided. And yet, this is not what happened.[32] After *Bank Mizrahi*, Cheshin relinquished his dissenting stance on the question of the Court's proper role in the process of framing a constitution, and joined the majority justices.[33] Below is a brief description of the evidence attesting to this.

Tsemah[34] questioned the constitutionality of section 237A(a) of the Military Law 5715-1955, which states: "A disciplinary officer who is a military policeman can issue a detention order for any soldier for a period of up to 96 hours." The petitioners, from the military defense, claimed that such a long period of detention prior to the detainee's appearance before a judge violates the right to freedom enshrined in section 3 of Basic Law: Human Dignity and Liberty, and fails to meet the requirements of the limitation clause. The Court, sitting in an expanded panel of nine justices, accepted the petition and repealed this section. Justice Zamir wrote the main opinion in the case, but Justice Cheshin was among the judges who agreed with it. Concerning *Bank Mizrahi*, as noted, Cheshin had held that the Knesset could override the limitation clause in Basic Law: Human Dignity and Liberty if it simply clarified its intention to do so—for instance, by adding a prefatory comment such as "regardless of" at the beginning of the infringing passage. According to Cheshin's method, then, section 237A(a) could have become acceptable if the Knesset were to add a clarification stating it was aware that this section violates a right and still chose to legislate it. Cheshin, however, does not bother to mention this possibility in his opinion, and confines himself to stating, "I agree." It could be argued that Cheshin need not suggest to the state its available options for making the current situation acceptable. And yet, if we add to the zeal of Cheshin's claim in *Bank Mizrahi* his usual habit of making considerable additions to the main decision written by his colleagues, even when he completely agrees with them,[35] his silence in *Tsemah* is puzzling.

Cheshin's silence in *Tsemah* is not a one-time event. In decisions on constitutional matters that he issued after *Bank Mizrahi*, he never referred again to his view that the old and new Basic Laws lack constitutional status.[36] Furthermore, in his opinion in *Commitment to Peace and Social Justice v. Minister of Finance*, which considered the constitutionality of a law that had reduced income supplement benefits, Cheshin seems to join his colleagues in the majority opinion in *Bank Mizrahi*, and states the following:

Prior to the commencement of the two Basic Laws of 5752-1992—the Basic Law: Human Dignity and Liberty and the Basic Law: Freedom of Occupation—the court did not have jurisdiction to order the legal voidance of a provision in a statute of the Knesset . . . The power that the court acquired in these two new Basic Laws—the power to declare a provision in a statute of the Knesset void—once again raised questions that were once critical questions.[37]

The change in Cheshin's view could perhaps be explained as adherence to what Yoram Shahar called the tradition of precedential loyalty prevalent among Supreme Court justices, whereby "once the Supreme Court has issued its view, in any panel composition, even the dissenters are committed to it."[38] According to Shahar, this strategy stems from the justices' moral commitment, and from their wish to help the Supreme Court preserve and expand its power. Shahar holds that the justices' awareness of the contribution of unity and cohesion to the buttressing of the Court's power affected not only the majority of the justices, who ab initio set up for themselves "a quiet channel within the collective and downplayed their individual voice,"[39] but also the minority, who set themselves up as dissenters. Shahar notes that, "time told that ultimately, after making their mark and having their say, they too took on the burden of the collective and did not question its scheme of power."[40]

And yet, even after bringing Shahar's findings into the equation, Cheshin's approach still requires an explanation. First, even if a justice toes the line on grounds of cooperation and a desire to strengthen the Court's standing, he is at least allowed to hint at his displeasure with the majority view, particularly when such an essential issue is at stake, and certainly if the majority view he dissented from was merely obiter dictum, as was indeed the case in *Bank Mizrahi*.[41] Second, the "falling in line" thesis cannot explain the zeal that Cheshin enlisted in his support for the majority decision. Cheshin refrained from repeating his stance in *Bank Mizrahi*, whereby Israel does not yet have a constitution, and he even offers formulations that place him on the side of the majority. Moreover, in later decisions he even takes a lead in his readiness to consider the voiding of primary legislation. As described in Chapter 1, Justice Barak had claimed in *La'or* that the Court is in principle allowed to void primary legislation that infringes human rights even in the absence of a constitution. Moreover, Barak's statement in *La'or* entailed an implication even more far-reaching: even if a constitution does exist, the Court is allowed to set a higher threshold than that set in the constitution, and in its light, void legislation that may have passed the constitutional threshold. These two statements, as noted, entail a huge change.[42] And yet, we find Cheshin, purportedly a conservative, willing to go just as far as Barak. In *Rubinstein*, the Court presided over by Barak canceled the arrangement deferring military service for yeshiva students who engage in full-time religious study, an arrangement that had been in force for many years.[43] Barak founded his decision on the claim that the Minister of Defense who had granted the deferment had not been authorized by law to make a decision in principle concerning all yeshiva students, but only to grant exemptions on an individual basis. Barak's interpretation of the law relied on the interpretive presumption that primary arrangements of this kind should properly be reached through the legislative branch.[44] Barak returned the question of the yeshiva students' enlistment to the legislators, without stating whether a Knesset decision to leave the current arrangement in place while enshrining it in primary legislation could pass the test of constitutional review.

Cheshin joined Barak, but also chose to add:

> With respect to the future, administrative regulations cannot, in the normative sense, provide Yeshiva students with an exemption from military service. We all agree on this point. Personally, I will not decide the issue (on which we were not asked to decide) of whether legislation passed by the Knesset could exempt Yeshiva students from military service. There are those who would argue (and I will not elaborate) that even a Knesset statute would not be sufficient. It could further be argued that even a Basic Law would not be sufficient.[45]

Cheshin intimates that, insofar as it depends on him, even if the current arrangement were to be enshrined in primary legislation, it would not pass the test of the High Court of Justice. In support of his position, Cheshin directs the reader to his opinion in *Bank Mizrahi*, but does not clarify what exactly is the argument he is relying upon. Hence, we can only hypothesize as to his intention. Two options come to mind for understanding Cheshin's stance. One is that, in his view, enshrining in law a sweeping exemption to all yeshiva students would violate the principle of equality (assuming that this principle is enshrined in the Basic Law), and such a law would therefore be voided. If this was Cheshin's intention, this is a further instance of his disregard of the stance he had presented in *Bank Mizrahi*, where he had argued that the provisions in Basic Law: Human Dignity and Liberty can be overridden through explicit reference to the Basic Law in the violating law. The second option is that Cheshin does not justify the possibility of voiding a law enshrining the deferral of service on the contradiction between this law and the Basic Law, but rather on the contradiction between this law and a general principle of equality. According to this option, Cheshin agrees with the view first presented by Barak in *La'or*, whereby primary legislation may be voided even in the absence of a written constitution. If Cheshin does indeed join Barak's stance in *La'or*, their positions are still significantly different. Whereas Barak explains at length the grounds for his far-reaching view, Cheshin slips this view into a laconic incidental remark without even trying to clarify it. Be that as it may, Cheshin's statements in *Rubinstein* bear no trace of the conservative view he had presented so forcefully in *Bank Mizrahi*.

Whatever had remained obscure in Cheshin's opinion in *Rubinstein*, he clarifies in a later case dealing with the validity of the law legislated in the wake of the

Rubinstein decision, which enshrined in primary legislation the exemption granted to yeshiva students following the recommendations of a committee headed by former justice Zvi Tal. Cheshin, in a dissenting opinion, held that the law should be voided. In his view, the law

> is in appalling contradiction to all the basic principles woven into our life, to all the truths, to all the aspirations, to all the hopes upon which the renewed State of Israel is built. And I am not talking only of the principles of Basic Law: Human Dignity and Liberty. I go back to the principles that the very state is built upon, to those values that breathe life into Knesset legislation—from the Basic Laws and up to regular laws: up to the fundamental principle telling us that the absolutely first condition for all the other rights is the state's very existence; up to the recognition that without a state there are no rights and we are in a vacuum; up to the fundamental principle of existence and survival, a principle on which and from which man and nation begin; up to the fundamental principle of equality—equality in a Jewish and democratic state—the fundamental principle that gave rise to the equality principle in Basic Law: Human Dignity and Liberty, a principle on which my colleague the President builds his opinion. And when I bring all these together, my one and only conclusion is that the Law of Service Deferral is stillborn.[46]

Barak, actually the first to have formulated the possibility of voiding primary legislation in the absence of a constitution, wishes to qualify Cheshin's determined statement:

> In my view, we need not decide on these questions in the petitions before us, and this for two reasons. First, we must strongly endeavor to decide on the constitutional questions of a law opposed to basic values in the context of a decision about the constitutionality of a law vis-à-vis a Basic Law. Israel is now at the height of a constitutional move that is taking place by means of Basic Laws. We must make every interpretive effort to decide on the constitutionality of the law in the context of the arrangements set in the Basic Laws . . . Second, even if there is a narrow realm in the context of which the constitutionality of a law can be examined without reference to the Basic Laws, the case before us does not fall in this category.[47]

To the outside observer, Cheshin appears to have shifted over the years from being a critic of the constitutional revolution to being its most devoted defender. Take, for instance, the threat "to cut off the hand that will be raised against the Court," which Cheshin voiced against Minister of Justice Daniel Friedmann.[48] Indeed, Cheshin's position at the forefront of the battle for the Court is not in *direct* contradiction with his positions on the proper role of the Court in the constitution-framing project. And yet, someone who in *Bank Mizrahi* rallied to a rearguard battle against his colleagues' attempt to create a constitution ex nihilo without the agreement or even the participation of the people, is not supposed to enlist in a heroic defense of the Court against an attempt to slightly restrain it.

Against the background of these facts, we cannot but wonder at Cheshin's later statements at a gathering in his honor:

> My opinion has not changed at all, nor have I heard any proper answers to the questions I have raised ... In the granting of constitutional powers to the Knesset in *Bank Mizrahi*, I saw, and see to this day, a kind of sleight of hand, alchemy at its best, a creation *ex nihilo*.[49]

VI. Expanding the Range of Unenumerated Rights

One explanation for the success of the March 1992 constitutional maneuver was that it reflected a compromise that led to the omission of controversial rights from the new Basic Laws. The result of the compromise was that the Basic Laws were indeed enacted, but important rights such as freedom of religion, equality, and freedom of speech remained outside. In the new reality, two groups of fundamental rights were created—one group of rights that was upgraded since it was included in the new Basic Laws, and another group that was not. The rights that were not upgraded did continue to enjoy the constitutional status that the Court had granted them even before the legislation of the new Basic Laws, but since they had not been included in the Basic Laws, they enjoyed only partial protection. The Court can void actions of the executive that infringe these rights without justification, but it is prevented from intervening in unjustifiable infringements of these rights through primary legislation.

This division of human rights into two groups—some receiving full protection and some only partial—was intolerable to the Supreme Court. Soon after the legislation of the new Basic Laws, some of the justices began inserting obiter dicta in their decisions, suggesting that Basic Law: Human Dignity and Liberty should be interpreted so as to allow reading the unenumerated rights as part of it, thereby equating the status of these rights to that of rights explicitly enumerated in the Basic Law.[50] The justices suggested several interpretive tactics in order to achieve this aim,[51] and the main one among them was the use of the right to dignity enshrined in sections 2 and 4 of Basic Law: Human Dignity and Liberty.[52] They explained that the right to dignity should not be read only in its plain sense, as a specific right forbidding humiliation, but as an "overarching right" serving as a "pass-key" to all human rights, including the unenumerated ones. The stance of the "expanding" justices merited surprising support from Judith Karp, who was the representative of the State Attorney's office in the process of legislating the Basic Laws and accompanied it throughout. Karp admitted that the rights that had not been included in the Basic Law had been deliberately omitted,[53] but argued that once the Basic Law had been published it had a life of its own, which allowed a reading opposed to that of the drafters' intentions.[54]

Despite the united front that the Supreme Court justices tried to present, judges and a few academics nonetheless pointed out the problem attached to the expanded interpretation of the right to dignity. Opponents relied on the context, on the legislative history, and on the traditional meaning that had been attached to the concept of "dignity" on the eve of the Basic Law's legislation. I will succinctly present some of these counterclaims.[55]

The Context. The limiting interpretation of sections 2 and 4 of the Basic Law, whereby dignity is a particular right, is the natural linguistic interpretation of the right. The right to dignity appears in these two sections next to the preservation of life and body. Had the right to dignity been an overarching right that includes all the unenumerated rights, it would have been proper to classify it in a separate operative section. Moreover, if the right to dignity included all other rights, it would have sufficed to enshrine it in the Basic Law without adding any others. The inclusion of other rights in the Basic Law shows that the right to dignity serves in the Basic Law as a particular right, rather than as an overarching one.

The Legislative History. The restrictive interpretation of the right to dignity is compatible with legislative history, since it fits the nature of the Basic Law, as ultimately the product of a compromise between different desires and aspirations. An expanded reading of the right to dignity as including such rights as equality, freedom of speech, and freedom of religion brings in through the window what the Knesset took out through the front door, blatantly ignoring the legislators' intention.[56] Opponents of the expansion also added that the Court's glaring obliviousness to the legislators' intention would work as a double-edged sword, jeopardizing the trust between the Knesset and the Court, precluding any possible cooperation between the two bodies in the constitutional realm, strengthening criticism of the Court, and ultimately leading the legislature to weaken it.

The Traditional Meaning. The right to dignity preceded the legislation of Basic Law: Human Dignity and Liberty. The Court acknowledged this right as a basic right long before the Basic Law, and even used it several times to void decisions of the executive branch. In all these cases, the meaning assigned to the right to dignity had been the restricted one—dignity in the sense of absence of humiliation.[57] Barring contradictory evidence, one may plausibly assume that when legislators decided to include the right to dignity in the Basic Law, they intended to read this right in the denotation that had been attached to it prior to the legislation of the Basic Laws.

Among the Supreme Court justices as well, some had reservations about the judicial expansion of the rights included in the Basic Laws. Justice Dorner, for instance, whose term of office in the Supreme Court had actually been characterized by extensive activism, had reservations about the inclusion of the right to equality and freedom of speech in the right to human dignity.[58] She explained this reluctance by arguing that the expansive interpretation contradicts the original intention of the Basic Law's sponsors, and it is therefore questionable whether it is possible—and even if possible, whether it is proper—to endorse it. Over the years, however, judges supporting the expansive reading became increasingly dominant.

For a long time, the Supreme Court refrained from voiding legislation that was found to contradict a right not enumerated in a Basic Law. The expansive interpretation was mentioned in dicta, and did not become a compelling decision. [59] In February 2012, however, the Supreme Court did eventually take the last step in the incorporation of unenumerated rights into the Basic Law, in a decision that nullified a law exempting ultra-Orthodox Jews from military service.[60] The Court held that this exemption infringed on the (unenumerated) right to equality of the citizens who must serve in the army, and that this infringement could not be saved under the limitation clause.[61]

The willingness of the Supreme Court to expand the list of rights included in the Basic Laws did not stop at civil and political rights not explicitly enumerated in the Basic Laws, but rather, over the years, has also expanded to the family of social laws, which were also deliberately omitted from the Basic Laws. I shall describe the main developments in status of social rights below, and dedicate Chapter 5 to an in-depth description and evaluation of this topic.

In his book *Constitutional Interpretation*, which was published in 1994, soon after the passing of Basic Law: Human Dignity and Freedom, Aharon Barak dealt with unenumerated rights as part of his discussion on the interpretation of the right to dignity, and presented three possible approaches. The first, limiting approach, interprets the right to dignity as denoting the absence of humiliation. A second, expanding approach, interprets the right as including all human rights: civil and political, as well as social. A third, which Barak calls "an intermediate approach," interprets the right to dignity as including all civil and political rights, but not social rights. Of the three, Barak chose the intermediate one, arguing that an interpretation of the Basic Law as including social rights is too expansive.[62]

In the years following the "constitutional revolution," the Israeli academic discourse on human rights has conveyed objections to what the critics referred to as the Supreme Court's tendency to protect the rights of the rich and ignore the rights of the weak. The claim was that Supreme Court justices adhere to a libertarian worldview, a right-wing social doctrine, as reflected in their decisions.[63] Barak's proposal to include in the right to dignity civil and political rights, but not social rights to some extent, supported this critique. Respecting social rights will compel the state to tax the public and create a system for transferring wealth from the rich to the poor. It will also require expanding the administration and increasing the state's involvement in the economy. These steps are not popular among free market enthusiasts. If the Court is indeed identified with a right-wing socioeconomic outlook, it will obviously be uninterested in enshrining social rights in the constitution.

The strong criticism leveled against the Court may have affected Barak, or perhaps he simply re-examined the entire issue, but sometime toward the end of the 1990s, he changed his mind on this question. In a series of decisions, he expressed in obiter dictum the view that certain social rights are also included in the right to dignity. The main right that Barak upgraded was the right to minimal sustenance.[64] Barak indeed explained that the scope of social rights included in the right to dignity is more restricted than what it would have been had these rights been included in the constitution as independent rights,[65] but this caveat cannot blur the clear change in his stance concerning these rights' status.[66]

Did the change in Barak's position also result in actual changes in the Court's decisions? Some have responded in the negative, bringing proof for their position from the fact that despite the recognition of the constitutional status of social rights, the Court has, in practice, avoided ruling in favor of appellants in a series of cases that argued unjustified governmental harm to these rights. However, in recent years there have been signs of a new development, in which the Court not only reads social rights into the Basic Laws, but also grants this reading practical meaning. A clear example of this can be seen in the *Hassan* case from 2012, in which the Supreme Court repealed primary legislation after having found that it unjustifiably harms a social right. The appellants argued against the constitutionality of an article in Israel's Income Supplement Law, which stated that those who own or use a vehicle are considered to have income at the level of the income supplement, and are therefore denied eligibility to this stipend. The Court held that the law unjustifiably violates the right to *human subsistence,* derived from the basic right to human dignity.[67]

VII. De-facto Abolition of the Preservation of Laws Section

Basic Law: Human Dignity and Freedom contains a "validity of laws" clause, stating that it "shall not affect the validity of any law that existed prior to the inception of the Basic Law." As explained in Chapter 2 above, this clause was part of the political compromise that allowed the Basic Laws to be passed in the first place.[68] A number of rulings have recently been handed down, which points to the intent of the Court to bypass and perhaps even annul the validity of laws clause.

In a relatively brief ruling given at the end of August 2017, the request of same sex couples to marry in a civil ceremony in the State of Israel was rejected.[69] Marriage and divorce in Israel is arranged according to religious law, and in the case of Jews—according to Jewish Halacha.[70] The Court was asked by the appellants to rule that the law, which grants religious law a monopoly in matters of marriage, is invalid, as it discriminates against same-sex couples, or at least to interpret it so that it does not apply to marriages of members of the same sex. The Court did not accept the request, with the main reason being that the law in question was passed before the legislation of the Basic Laws, and is therefore immune from being struck down. Deputy Supreme Court President Rubinstein quoted the words of then Knesset Constitutional Committee Chairman, Uriel Lynn, in discussions prior to the passing of Basic Law: Human Dignity and Freedom, in which he explicitly referred to the connection between the preservation of laws section and the desire to shield the religious monopoly in matters of marriage from being repealed:

> There are a number of reservations [proposals to change the formulation of the law proposal], and I want to address them. One proposal . . . says: "That which is stated in this law and implied by it shall not harm the Marriage and Divorce Law or other laws and regulations which come to anchor the heritage of Israel, which exist today." We came to the conclusion that this is not necessary, as there is a general instruction, which states that the law harms no existing law.[71]

So far, this is a simple, even trivial ruling. However, here one of the justices of the panel, Justice Baron, added the following:

> The validity of laws section was a kind of political compromise, which allowed the start of the constitutional revolution in Israel. However, it is not out of the realm of possibility that the time will come when the strength of the preservation of laws will not suffice to block constitutional processes, and especially an examination of the adapting of the laws of personal status to today's reality[72]

In other words, Justice Baron is saying that the compromise that led to the Basic Laws is acceptable in her eyes, because it allowed the "start of the revolution," but now that the coup has been completed, the price paid to arrive at that compromise can be tossed aside, and the validity of laws clause can be repealed.

The gun that Justice Baron placed on the table in the first act has since been fired, in a ruling handed down two weeks later. The Arab residents of East Jerusalem enjoy the status of permanent residents. A number of said residents were elected to the Palestinian Parliament in 2006 on a Hamas-affiliated candidate list. Section 11(b) to the Entry Into Israel Law states that the Minister of Interior is authorized to revoke residency "according to his judgment."[73] The Minister of Interior decided to make use of his authority and revoke the residency of those Hamas members. This is an old law from 1952, and it therefore enjoys the protection of the validity of laws section.

Justice Fogelman, who wrote the primary opinion, found a way to bypass this constitutional obstacle, stating that: "In my view, in our matter the balance between the various purposes leads to the conclusion that the phrase 'according to his judgment' does not grant the Minister of Interior the authority to revoke the license for permanent residency of residents of East Jerusalem due to breach of trust."[74]

The operative conclusion of this ruling is that if the state wishes to revoke the residency of Hamas members, it must now pass a new law, which explicitly authorizes the Minister to do so. Ostensibly, this is a minor ruling, which throws the ball back into the legislature's court. In fact, the Court's ruling effectively empties the existing law of meaning, with the aim of bypassing the validity of laws clause. If the validity of laws clause prevents the Court from directly repealing old legislation, then it can be overcome with an "interpretation" that denies the meaning of the words of the law. Such an interpretation will necessarily force the legislators to pass a new law, and this law, when passed, will be vulnerable to repeal by the Court, as it will not enjoy the protection of the validity of laws clause.

Indeed, this is not conspiratorial theorizing. Justice Hendel, in his minority opinion, understood matters precisely in this way:

Section 11(a) to the Entry Law is old legislation that authorizes the minister, in a clear manner, to revoke residency licenses. As old legislation, its validity should not be harmed, and it should be interpreted in the spirit of the Basic Laws. An instruction according to which the Knesset must rearrange the matter, in the event it is adopted, will lead to the new arrangement not being an old law, but a new law exposed to the more stringent tests of the limitation clause. Yet, after all, the preservation of laws paragraph is as its name suggests. The law must be preserved. The protected law must not be ordered invalid—but here, too, this is the practical consequence that derives from the approach of my colleague. I believe that there is no room for creating a mechanism of transferring the track in a way ruling that an old law is de facto invalid, and all that is left is to pass a new law.[75]

VIII. Supreme Principles Overriding the Basic Laws

One of the primary formal characteristics of a constitution is that it is rigid. Usually, the rigidity is relative, in the sense that the constitution can be changed even if the conditions for this are not easy to attain. However, there are constitutions that entrench certain components absolutely, in the sense that they explicitly determine that these components cannot be changed or repealed.[76] Absolute entrenchment arouses quite a bit of difficulty, since it prevents the next generations from changing the rule established by their predecessors. Either way, an even more far-reaching position is being presented in the discourse of international constitutional theory, according to which even if the constitutional text does not explicitly include the absolute entrenchment of a given component of the constitution, there are elements in the constitution that cannot be changed. The doctrine in question is called the "unconstitutional constitutional amendment" (hereinafter: the doctrine), and those who support it propose to see the limits it sets as implicitly deriving from the constitutional text or from constitutional supreme principles.[77]

Echoes of the approach, which place at the top of the norms pyramid principles that cannot be harmed, even with a constitution, can also be found in the ruling of the Supreme Court. The story begins with the *La'or* case, in which Justice Barak (in a minority opinion) was willing, in principle, to strike down a law, based on unwritten fundamental principles, even though it met the requirements laid down in Basic Law: The Knesset.[78] Barak repeated this position in the *Mitrael* case, where he recognized the possibility of striking down a law in principle, even if it met the requirements of the "override" clause, included in section 8 of Basic Law: Human Dignity and Freedom.[79] True, in both cases a clash between the supreme principles and the Basic Law was not on the agenda, but rather a clash between these principles and a regular law, but the fact that Barak was willing in both cases to strike down the law, even though it met the requirements of the Basic Law, show that as far as he is concerned, the supreme principles stand above the Basic Law. Such a determination logically leads to the conclusion that supreme principles will win out in the event they directly clash with the constitution. And indeed, Barak explicitly stated such a position in the *Bank Mizrahi* case, when he noted that "It is accepted and known that courts examine the constitutionality of constitutional amendments. More than once, a constitutional amendment has been invalidated due to being unconstitutional, and this not just because of matters of 'form' . . . but also in matters of essence."[80]

Justice Cheshin also arrived at this conclusion, in the *Movement for Quality of Government in Israel* case, and in the *Rubinstein* case before it, which were both discussed in Section IV above. In the *Movement* case, the Court was asked to repeal a law that arranged the draft of yeshiva students into the IDF. President Barak, who wrote the primary opinion in the case, ruled that an examination of the effect of the arrangement established in law on reality showed that it unjustifiably harmed the right to equality (which he read into the right to dignity, included in Basic Law: Human Dignity and Freedom), but in the end he decided not to repeal the law, but to wait and see what the law's long-term effects would be. Cheshin's position was more conservative than Barak on the one hand, but it was far more radical on the other. Cheshin ruled that the law does not harm the right to equality included in the Basic Law, but despite this, he suggested (in a minority opinion) to nullify the law on the grounds that it contradicts the basic principles of the Israeli system. So far, this was "only" an implementation of the doctrine developed by Barak in the two previous rulings. But now the words of Cheshin in the *Movement* case must be joined with what he said in the *Rubinstein* case dealing with the same subject, according to which even if the existing arrangement is anchored in the future in a Basic Law, it is worthy of being disqualified, due to its clash with the basic principles of the system.

The next step in the undermining of the supreme status of the constitution was registered in the *Bar-On* affair. Section 3(a)(2) of Basic Law: The State Economy states that "The Budget will be for one year."[81] In 2009, in the face of the global economic crisis and the need for fiscal certainty, the Ministry of Finance proposed that the budget of 2009–2010 be passed as a biannual one. This arrangement could have been anchored in regular primary legislation. However, due to the fear that the court would strike down the law, on the grounds that it contradicts the Basic Law, it was decided to anchor the arrangement in the Basic Law by amending it—but with its validity being limited to just two years. Therefore, Basic Law: The State Economy for the years of 2009 and 2010 (Special Instructions)(Temporary Provision)(Amendment) was passed, and in section 1(a)(1) it was stated that the budget for those years would be biannual. Later on, the government wished, again, to pass a biannual budget, as a test-run for examining the possibility that the budget be passed biannually on a regular basis. Once again, the appropriate Basic Law was passed for this purpose.[82]

In the *Bar-On* case, the appellants requested that the Court declare the invalidity of the temporary provision. The appellants claimed, among other things, that the use of a temporary provision in the context of Basic Laws that enjoy a constitutional status amounted to "misuse" of the tool of Basic Laws, in the sense that this is not really an amendment of the constitution, but an attempt to bypass its instructions. The Court rejected the appeal, but still accepted the argument that, in extreme cases, misuse of the heading Basic Law will make the repeal of the law unavoidable.

After the *Bar-On* ruling, the Knesset used the tool of the temporary provision three more times, for the purpose of legitimizing three biannual budgets. The Court decided to intervene with the last one. The ruling in the *College of Law and Business* case—decided in September 2017—did not see the Court repeal the Basic Law, but it did issue a "notice of invalidity" stating that if the Knesset used this mechanism one more time, the Basic Law would be struck down.[83]

Did the Court use the doctrine of the unconstitutional constitutional amendment here? Ostensibly, the answer is no. True, the two doctrines—that of the unconstitutional constitutional amendment and that of misuse of a Basic Law— lead to the same result of striking down a Basic Law, but the reasons are different. A constitutional amendment becomes unconstitutional for substantive reasons while the striking down of a Basic Law due to misuse of the constitutional tool was determined, in our case, for the "technical" reason of the invalid combination of the Basic Law and the temporary provision. However, even if this distinction is formally valid, a look at the various opinions written on the case creates the impression that at least some of the judges do not consider the difference between the two doctrines to be that great. This impression is based on two things. First, in describing the doctrine of misuse of the Basic Law, the Court stressed that such use includes not only attempts to bypass the constitution by way of a temporary provision, but also cases in which "Legislation that wears the garb of basic legislation penetrates the constitutional fabric for reasons which are beside the point."[84] In other words, the doctrine of misuse includes not only technical flaws, but also essential ones. Second, some of the justices discussed the doctrine of the unconstitutional constitutional amendment favorably and at length, alongside their discussion of the doctrine of misuse, and the justice who wrote the primary opinion, Deputy Supreme Court President Rubinstein, mixed the two without really separating them.[85]

The *College* ruling is interesting not just due to the precedent-setting use of the tool of striking down a Basic Law, but also due to the reproachful rhetoric used by some of the justices, especially Justice Rubinstein. Rubinstein pegs the practice of misuse of the Basic Law to a broader fallacy: in his view, this amounts to a "devaluation in the status of the Basic Laws, constitutional texts," which even finds expression both in the problematic combination of a Basic Law and a temporary provision, "and—in the broader context—in the non-completion of the constitution of the state, in accordance with the Harari decision of 1950."[86]

Rubinstein's claim that the Knesset is "unserious" demonstrates an enormous lack of self-awareness. As was described in the previous chapter, the circumstances of the passing of the Basic Laws of 1992 are far from meeting the acceptable standards of the formation of a constitution. However, even those who claim that this process was free of flaws will have difficulty denying the emerging picture in the two-and-a-half decades that have passed since then, according to which the constitution in Israel is primarily being written by the Court. The Court updated the status of the "old" Basic Laws on its say-so, after having treated them like regular laws in the past. The Court has consistently expanded the scope of the constitution, via the "interpretation" of Basic Laws in a matter clearly contrary to the intent of its formulators, and now it turns out that the top of the pyramid is occupied by supreme principles, which the Court may someday use to strike down Basic Laws. If the Knesset is being disrespectful of the constitution, this is to a large degree due to the fact that they had (and still have) a good teacher for it.

4

BACK TO THE FUTURE

I. Reactions

Chapters 2 and 3 described the progression from the legislation of Basic Law: Freedom of Occupation and Basic Law: Human Dignity and Liberty (henceforth the new Basic Laws) up to the Court's use of these two laws to draft a written constitution of its own creation.

The Court's activist stance could have expected resistance from various groups. First, the religious public, who had opposed the constitutional project. Over the years, the religious bloc's opposition to the initiatives to draft a constitution had derived, as noted, from the fear that shifting the center from the legislative to the judicial power would harm religious interests. Below, I shall briefly illustrate how the Court has indeed violated the status quo in matters of religion and state relying on the constitutional revolution claim. For the religious public, then, it is logical not to brush aside the change brought about by the Court and to seek ways of opposing it. In particular, opposition is to be expected if one accepts the second and third hypotheses suggested in Chapter 2 above in an attempt to explain the success of the 1992 maneuver. If the new Basic Laws were the product of a compromise between supporters and opponents of the constitution, and if the Court disregarded the compromise, upset the arrangement, and used the constitution to promote an agenda of its own, those who feel affected by the breach of this compromise will probably be embittered. If the legislation's success involved misrepresentation on the part of its sponsors, which led the religious bloc to be mistaken concerning the true meaning of the Basic Laws, then the anger of those who were mistaken and misled is even more expected and understandable.

Another party injured by the maneuver led by the Court is the legislature, as well as the political system in general. In Chapter 2, when attempting to explain the success of the March 1992 maneuver, I claimed that some of the legislators may have toned down their opposition and supported the enactment of a constitution, even though they did understand that the Knesset would be weakened as a result. I explained that the readiness of Knesset members belonging to the old elites to operate against their own institutional interest followed from their fear of losing control of the Knesset. If the Knesset can drop into the lap of groups supporting "problematic" world views, and if, by contrast, the old elites' control of the Court is assured for the time being, it seems prudent to seek to strengthen it. However, once the Court began using the Basic Laws, and particularly when this use exceeded everyone's expectations, even those of the very sponsors of this legislation, at least some MKs could be expected to resist the Court's involvement in Knesset decisions. Critics would first come from the ranks of opponents to the views imposed by the Court, but even supporters of the Court's decisions in principle may feel threatened and criticize its activism.

Another party that we could have assumed would be critical of the Court's activism is the legal academia. The proper balance between the power of the Court and the power of the political system is a matter of intense concern for public law scholars in the world in general, and in the United States in particular. The institution of judicial review, including the annulment of primary legislation when the Court holds it to be incompatible with constitutional provisions, is controversial. Some oppose judicial review altogether, and claim that it clashes with the foundations of democracy. Others justify judicial review in principle, but propose qualifying it in various ways. In recent decades, Israel's legal academia has been influenced by moods and ideas resonating in the American discourse—inter alia because many of its members have acquired their legal education at American universities.[1] Given these circumstances, we might plausibly assume that at least some Israeli jurists would have internalized these critical approaches and applied them to the Israeli context.

This assumption is further strengthened when we take into account the course that the Israeli Supreme Court has followed. The situation in Israel differs from that in the United States in several significant ways. No one in the United States questions the supreme status of the U.S. Constitution, as well as the Court's authority to use it as a criterion for examining political decisions. The controversy in the

United States touches only on questions such as determining the proper way of interpreting the Constitution or the proper extent of its use. In Israel, by contrast, the dispute begins with far more preliminary questions, and concerns basic issues, such as the Knesset's very authority to draft a constitution; whether the Knesset intended to draft a constitution; what is the proper way of drafting a constitution, even if the Knesset does have the authority to do this; and whether the Court's boundless creativity in constructing a huge structure on the modest platform that the Knesset had provided for its use is legitimate. These questions are discussed at greater length further in this chapter; however, already at this stage, it should be noted that they are largely specific to Israel. I know of no other Western country where so much doubt has been cast on the legal and moral legitimacy of enacting a constitution and on the Supreme Court's use of it. In these circumstances, some academics could have been expected to criticize the conduct of the new Basic Laws' sponsors and of the Supreme Court. In this chapter I shall examine the responses of various parties—the religious, the political, and the academic—to the actions of the Supreme Court.

I. THE RELIGIOUS

Several differences prevail between the two new Basic Laws. Basic Law: Freedom of Occupation deals with only one right, whereas Basic Law: Human Dignity and Liberty deals with several rights; Basic Law: Freedom of Occupation is formally entrenched, whereas Basic Law: Human Dignity and Liberty is not entrenched; Basic Law: Freedom of Occupation has no "validity of laws" (preservation of validity of old laws) clause, whereas Basic Law: Human Dignity and Liberty has such a clause. The two laws were also enacted in different circumstances. The rate of MKs participating in the voting on both these laws was very low, but Basic Law: Freedom of Occupation was enacted without opposition, whereas Basic Law: Human Dignity and Liberty barely passed. These differences stem from one source: establishing freedom of occupation was a matter of broad consensus, whereas establishing the other rights was controversial. The explanation for the fact that opponents of the constitution within the religious parties agreed to support, or at least did not vigorously oppose, a separate and entrenched Basic Law protecting the right to freedom of occupation, and that right only, is that they never imagined any tension between the right to work and make a living and the arrangements set out in the status quo on religion and state.[2]

Shortly after the enactment of Basic Law: Freedom of Occupation, religious MKs realized they had been mistaken (obviously, from their perspective). Ever since its enactment, Basic Law: Freedom of Occupation has been used by the Supreme Court to undermine the religious status quo in all its key areas. Below is one example of the Court's use of freedom of occupation as a tool for rejecting the status quo, an example that brought in its wake an interesting constitutional development.

Since Israel's establishment, the import of frozen meat had been an exclusive state prerogative exercised through the Government Trade Administration. The reason adduced for the nationalization of this market was that Israel is under a state of emergency, and the regular supply of basic commodities must therefore be ensured while preventing speculation. This arrangement implied that the state only imported kosher meat, an arrangement that simplifies the problem, since everyone can consume it. In 1992, the government decided to privatize the area of meat imports, and stated that, henceforth, imports would take place through private and commercial agencies. According to the government's decision, a committee comprising the director generals of several ministries was established in order to issue directives for its implementation. The committee made recommendations and the government began discussing them, but then postponed their implementation without stating a date. Mitrael, a company that wished to import meat into Israel, submitted a petition in this regard. The Supreme Court upheld the petition and ruled that, subject to the government's authority to make another decision, "the government must implement the said decisions within a reasonable time, which we state is a period of four months."[3]

Shas, an ultra-Orthodox party that was a partner in the government coalition, opposed the granting of unsupervised import permits. Shas argued that granting these permits would violate the status quo and flood the market with non-kosher meat, which is cheaper. The government discussed the matter several times, and ultimately decided to regulate the privatization of meat imports through legislation. Until the completion of the legislation process, the situation would remain unchanged, that is, the government would be the sole importer of meat. Behind the change in the government's decision, as noted, was the concern that, barring any constraining legislation, privatization would encourage the large-scale import of non-kosher meat, in contradiction to the prevailing status quo, as well as to the coalition's commitment to Shas in this regard.

Mitrael petitioned the High Court of Justice once again.[4] The Supreme Court stated that the government had changed its decision due to "religious considerations," which are unrelated and alien to the authority to grant import permits. Hence, the Court upheld the petition, and ordered the state to grant import permits to Mitrael. Justice Orr, who wrote the main opinion on the case, added that the refusal to grant import permits violates Mitrael's freedom of occupation, and, incidentally, stated that this violation would not pass the test of the limitation clause (which states conditions allowing infringements of the right).[5]

As explained in Chapter 1, the Court had protected human rights before the 1992 revolution as well, and had not hesitated to void executive decisions that, in its view, had violated rights unjustifiably. In the absence of a written constitution, however, the Court had refused to take the further step of voiding primary legislation. Had the frozen meat affair erupted before the legislation of Basic Law: Freedom of Occupation, the government could have overridden the Court's decision by turning the government monopoly into law, or by adding a provision to the law, stating that granting meat import permits is contingent on the Rabbinate's approval. After the enactment of the new Basic Laws, however, the Court assumed authority to void primary legislation that, in its view, contradicts these Laws, so that turning the current arrangement into law could no longer ensure the arrangement's immunity.

According to the arrangement set in the two Basic Laws, a law or an administrative act that infringes rights protected in the Basic Laws need not always be voided. The limitation clause states that an arrangement infringing a right will not be voided if it was enacted for a proper purpose and to an extent no greater than required.[6] The government could therefore try to turn the current arrangement into law, hoping that the Court would determine that the law meets the terms of the limitation clause. As noted, however, Justice Orr had incidentally stated that the prohibition on importing non-kosher meat would not pass the limitation clause test. Given Justice Orr's stance, attempting to turn the status quo into law would have been pointless.

The Court's ruling in *Mitrael* led to a frenzy of activity in the coalition. Shas, which understood that the usual political tools would not help in this case, targeted Basic Law: Freedom of Occupation for attack. Members of other religious factions in the Knesset woke up from their slumber to an understanding of the damage the Basic Law inflicts on their interests. The political crisis became more acute, posing a danger to the Basic Law. At this stage, Justice Barak entered the picture. Barak proposed a compromise solution, whereby the Basic Law would be amended and a "notwithstanding" clause would be added.[7] The notwithstanding clause would state that a law that violates freedom of occupation and does not pass the test of the limitation clause would nevertheless be of effect if it was passed by a majority of Knesset members and if it explicitly stated that it had been enacted notwithstanding the provisions of Basic Law: Freedom of Occupation. A law complying with the terms of this notwithstanding clause would be valid for four years at most, and then expire. Barak drew inspiration for the compromise proposal from the Canadian Charter of Rights and Freedoms, which contains a similar formulation.[8] Barak's intervention in the political crisis probably stemmed from his desire to protect Basic Law: Freedom of Occupation, as well as his entire legal endeavor of Basic Laws. From his perspective, it was better to slightly weaken Basic Law: Freedom of Occupation than to endanger its very existence.

The government adopted Barak's compromise solution, and in its wake, so did the Knesset. Several MKs did express their opposition to the proposed amendment, claiming that it was tantamount to rescinding the Basic Law's constitutional character,[9] but a majority supported the motion, be it because they hoped that its adoption would bring back political composure, or because they agreed with Barak that it was preferable to sacrifice a "pawn" in order to save the "queen." After the amendment of Basic Law: Freedom of Occupation, the Knesset enacted in 1994 a law on the import of frozen meat. The law, which was enacted with a majority greater than half of the MKs, and stated that it is valid notwithstanding what the Basic Law determines, stated that "no one will import meat unless in possession of a kosher certificate."[10]

On the surface, adding a notwithstanding mechanism to Basic Law: Freedom of Occupation not only ended the crisis revolving around the import of frozen meat, but also turned back the process more generally, by creating an effective mechanism for protecting the status quo from possible threats by the Supreme Court. And yet, for several reasons detailed below, this is actually not the case. One reason is the Court's decision on a further petition by Mitrael, whereas the others lie in the conditions of the notwithstanding clause.

After the enactment of the law on the import of frozen meat, Mitrael again petitioned the High Court of Justice.[11] This time, it stated two claims. One was that "the notwithstanding clause was intended and could indeed help the legislator to deviate, for the purpose of solving various temporary constraints, from a specific constitutional provision (that is, section 4 of Basic Law: Freedom of Occupation), but does not allow it to collapse the frame altogether."[12] The petitioners claimed that the law on the import of frozen meat collapses the frame and must therefore be voided, even though it complies with the conditions of the notwithstanding clause. President Barak discussed the petitioners' claim sympathetically, but finally stated he need not decide on it:

Indeed, even if we assumed—without deciding on the matter—that there are aims and basic principles that a deviant law cannot violate, these are certainly the basic principles and aims that our entire constitutional structure, including the Basic Laws themselves, rests upon, and whose violation is serious and substantive ... Were it not so, the notwithstanding clause is emptied of its essential meaning. This is not the case before us. The infringement of freedom of occupation is minimal, since the petitioners do have an option of importing kosher meat without any need for import permits, contrary to the circumstances before the change in the government's policy. However much violation of property, of freedom of conscience, and of equality might be hidden in this law, it does not affect the foundations of our constitutional regime. On these grounds, the petitioners' first claim must be rejected.[13]

Barak's argument is actually a transmutation of his obiter in *La'or*.[14] In *La'or*, as noted, the discussion had hinged on a law that infringed the right to equality entrenched in section 4 of Basic Law: The Knesset. The law was enacted with the majority required by the Basic Law as a condition for changing the section. Nevertheless, Barak was, in principle, ready to consider voiding the attacked law after stating that the Court may set a threshold higher than that set in the constitution.[15] In *Mitrael*, Barak reiterated the same rationale, this time using it as a possible basis for overriding the notwithstanding clause. Barak agreed with the petitioners' stance that the use of the notwithstanding clause is not the end, in the sense that it does not grant a law complying with its conditions assured immunity, but requires first an examination of whether the right's infringement is not too severe. Were this innovation of Barak to be accepted, the result would be that even when the Knesset uses the notwithstanding clause in order to entrench some components of the status quo from intervention by the High Court of Justice, the validity of the legislation would still depend on the Court's ratification.

Even without the qualification that Barak added to the validity of the notwithstanding clause, the notwithstanding mechanism does not return us to the situation that had prevailed prior to the legislation of Basic Law: Freedom of Occupation, because of the conditions attached to its use and due to its limited relevance. In order to protect an arrangement that violates freedom of occupation from the intervention of the High Court of Justice, the support of at least sixty-one MKs must be attained. These MKs are required to declare that they support the law, yet are aware that they are thereby infringing freedom of occupation unjustifiably. Attaining an absolute majority is quite hard; extracting a confession from MKs admitting that they are deliberately breaching constitutional provisions is even harder, and all this in order to ensure quiet for four years at most, after which the arrangement will again be exposed to judicial review. Therefore, adding a notwithstanding mechanism to the Basic Law cannot ensure protection for the status quo arrangement.

The Court's decision concerning the import of frozen meat was only one in a series of decisions issued since the "constitutional revolution" wherein the Court intervened in the status quo. The Court also intervened, for example, in the sale of pork. According to the law, a local authority is authorized to issue a bylaw forbidding or limiting the sale of pork within its limits.[16] For years, many local authorities had enacted such bylaws, and the Court had not intervened in their discretion. Several years ago, however, the Court, presided over by Justice Barak decided that, since these bylaws violate freedom of occupation, limitations should be set on the restraints they are allowed to place on the sale of pork.[17] In brief, the Court determined that the sale of pork can be limited only in areas with a high concentration of observant population. In principle, the decision of the Court compelled the amendment of many bylaws inconsistent with this determination.

The status quo in the realm of dietary laws was eroded even further. The Law Forbidding Fraud Concerning Dietary Laws 1982-5743 forbids manufacturers and eatery owners to present in writing a product or an establishment as abiding by Jewish dietary laws unless they have been granted a certificate to that effect by the Rabbinate. The law grants the authority to issue such certificates to the Chief Rabbinate, to a rabbi appointed by it, or to a local rabbi, and limits the discretion of the authorized bodies when it determines that, "in granting a certificate, the rabbi will only consider the dietary laws."[18] In the guiding opinion on this issue in *Raskin*, the Court interpreted this limitation as compelling the relevant agencies to consider "only the core of the dietary laws."[19] This determination severely restricted the Rabbinate's discretion, but granted a kind of immunity to decisions that were within the range of this discretion. Another decision represents a trend expanding the scope of the Court's intervention in the Rabbinate's decisions in a way that not only limits the type of considerations the Rabbinate may take into account, but also enables intervention in the latter's discretion, even when it had only taken into account legitimate considerations. In this decision, the Court stated that, since the refusal to grant a certificate infringes the petitioner's freedom of occupation, a lenient halakhic stance that enables granting a certificate should be preferred to a stringent stance that does not.[20]

The Court bases its increasing involvement in religion and state matters not only on the right to freedom of occupation. In recent decades in general, and since the enactment of the new Basic Laws in particular, the Court has been using a spectrum of values and rights in order to become involved in the political decisions on these matters. This action has marked the Court in general, and Justice Barak who led this trend in particular, as enemies of the ultra-Orthodox bloc, and, to some extent, of the religious-national bloc as well.[21] Contributing to the growing hostility toward the Court is also its image as representing left-wing positions on defense and foreign affairs. In recent decades, some overlap has emerged between the observant bloc and the bloc supporting hawkish positions on defense and foreign affairs.[22] The accepted view, stating that the Court uses its power in order to tilt the balance in favor of the Left, has strengthened the feeling in the observant bloc that the Court has ceased to serve as a neutral arbiter, and has instead become an active player in the political game. Justifying the Court's decisions on normative-constitutional grounds, pinning these grounds on the new Basic Laws, and granting these laws constitutional status while interpreting them in extremely broad terms, strongly hinders any option of overturning the Court's decisions. All these circumstances strengthen the sense of the religious right-wing bloc that the rules of the game have been breached, and that the political game has become unfair.[23]

The frustration of the observant bloc became prominently evident in a demonstration in front of the Supreme Court building in February 1999. Between 250,000 and 400,000 people took part in that demonstration, where the Court was harshly attacked.[24] Many public figures, including religious ones, did condemn the frontal attack on the Court. Some of them, however, emphasized that, although they deplored the intensity and the ad hominem style of the attack, they agreed with the critique of the Court.[25]

The sense of frustration within the religious and right-wing public was corroborated and supported by academics who are not suspected of a pro-religious bias. Menachem Mautner, for example, said the following:

> Both through its sweeping activism and through its attempt to participate in the determination of the country's normative profile, the Supreme Court has assumed an active role in the post-hegemonic struggle over the shape of Israel, which began in the late 1980s. The Court has "taken sides". It has acted in a way clearly identified with the secular group that wishes to preserve and strengthen Israel's affiliation with Western liberalism.[26]

The right-wing observant public presently seems to relate with great skepticism to Menachem Begin's celebrated statement of several decades ago: "There are judges in Jerusalem."[27]

2. THE POLITICAL SYSTEM

Drafting a constitution, as noted, strengthens the Court's status at the expense of the two other powers, which could perhaps explain the first Knesset's resolve to abstain from drafting one. I suggested above that, when the Constitutional Assembly turned into the First Knesset, it became its interest to prevent the enactment of a constitution. If this assumption is correct, I would have to explain how the sponsors of the new Basic Laws handled this matter on their way to success. I explained that the Knesset is a majoritarian institution, and, consequently, the threat of new forces to the dominance of the old elites could eventually be reflected in the Knesset's balance of power. By contrast, the Supreme Court is not a majoritarian institution, because the mechanism for selecting its justices grants the officiating justices preferred status in determining who will join their ranks. Hence, if the Supreme Court had in the past been controlled by the old elites, their dominance could be preserved even if the balance of power within Israeli society changes against them. I therefore suggested that at least some Knesset members chose to act against their own institutional interest, and weaken the Knesset in order to protect their value system, whose dominance had been jeopardized.

The Knesset did vote for the two new Basic Laws, but most MKs were entirely unaware of their far-reaching significance. The age of innocence soon passed, however, when the Court proclaimed the constitutional revolution and embarked in a flurry of activity relying on the new Basic Laws as a source of legitimation. Among many MKs, this sobering up was accompanied by serious criticism of the Court's judicial activism, evident in its intensive involvement in political decisions. This criticism also targeted the problematic enactment of the two new Basic Laws, on which the Court pinned the "constitutional revolution." The following statements by Haim Ramon, in the Knesset plenum, illustrate this type of criticism:

> I wish to remind the members of the Knesset how we enacted the Basic Laws towards the end of the twelfth Knesset's term. I was then chairman of the Labor faction . . . Not even MK Amnon Rubinstein, and certainly not I, imagined an interpretation such as the one that the Court has endorsed . . . I call this constitutional revolution an accidental constitutional revolution, because the legislators did not intend it.[28]

The criticism did cross political boundaries, but was still voiced with greater frequency and intensity in right-wing circles, due to their sense that the Supreme Court leans toward the left wing of the political map. Many Supreme Court decisions could be pointed out to justify this feeling, but one of the most prominent is the decision on petitions against the Law on the Implementation of the Disengagement Plan, 5765-2005, which provided the legal basis for the evacuation of Jews living in the Gaza Strip. The petition was heard by an expanded panel of eleven justices. The Court wrote a long and fully argued opinion, which rejected the vast majority of the petitioners' claims.[29] The justices split into two groups, one including ten justices and the other only one, Justice Edmond Levi. The majority justices agreed and signed one opinion, which was anonymous.

In the United States, when value-loaded cases are considered, justices often split in their views, and decisions are often made in a majority of one, with each of the justices painstakingly arguing their decision at length.[30] In Israel, by contrast, decisions in most of these cases are unanimous or almost unanimous.[31] Usually, one justice writes a detailed opinion, and all others join without making further additions. Although the unanimous decision of the majority on the disengagement is therefore not exceptional, this decision included at least two unique components that do merit attention.

One unique component of the majority decision is that, unlike other unanimous decisions where one justice wrote and signed the opinion and all others concurred, this decision was signed by all the justices, without any one of them assuming responsibility for its writing. In fact, a detailed analysis of the decision's style shows that it was written by several justices. This practice, to the best of my knowledge, is not in use in the Israeli Supreme Court. There is apparently one good reason for it, at least in "common law" countries. In this system, the court is not supposed to function as one unit. The judges may consult with one another, and even make compromises in the course of dealing with the case, but ultimately, each judge is required to think and express his or her own opinion.[32] A reality where only one judge writes an opinion in a complex case, and particularly in an expanded panel, is implausible, because it is hard to assume that no dispute—even a minor one—would emerge within such a large group. But a reality where several justices cooperate in the writing of a verdict, when the product is assigned anonymously to all, without the writer of each section assuming responsibility for what that person wrote, is even more problematic. The only possible explanation for this unique practice of group anonymous writing is the will of the majority justices to present a unified, solid front in order to convey a political message: the conclusion of the Supreme Court is so clear and consensual that there could be no basis for appeal.[33]

The verdict on the disengagement has another unique characteristic. The Court is in two minds about it. The majority justices state several times that the question at stake is political, and therefore they do not see themselves as authorized to intervene in the discretion of the political system.[34] The political question doctrine is part of the non-judiciability rationale that the Court uses in order to filter petitions and reject outright any petition it does not wish to hear. In its first decades, the Court made widespread use of this doctrine. From the early 1980s onward, the doctrine was abandoned and the Court almost stopped using it, but in recent years we see signs of its return.[35] Hence, the Court's use of the non-judiciability doctrine does not pose a problem in principle. The problem lies in the fact that, although the Court declares it will not examine the legislature's discretion, it states several times in the opinion that there are no flaws in the legislature's decision.[36] Such a determination is not possible unless the decision is examined in-depth, but this is precisely what the Court says it will not do. The interesting phenomenon of the Court declaring it will not enter the issue, together with a sweeping legitimation of the Knesset's decision that would be impossible without considering the details, is consistent with the decision to write one anonymous opinion. The Court tries to provide the political system with the public-moral legitimation it requires, but without a rigorous examination of the value claims, because a rigorous examination of that kind would clearly paint the Court in political colors, a price that the Court is seeking to avoid.

The displeasure of some MKs at the Court's increasing intervention in the Knesset's decisions has often led to a crisis in the relationship between the Court and the Knesset. One such crisis moment in the relationship occurred during Reuven Rivlin's first term as Knesset Chairman. Rivlin strongly condemned the readiness of the judiciary, led by the Supreme Court, to void primary legislation, as well as the Supreme Court's general attitude toward the Knesset that, in his view, conveyed disrespect for the Knesset and its sovereignty.[37] One catalyst for Rivlin's statement was a decision by a judge in a local affairs court to void a Knesset law.[38] Rivlin said that Knesset laws had not been enacted in order to be trampled upon by any judge who so wishes. As interpersonal and inter-institutional tensions increased, attempts were made to settle disputes.[39] Generally, however, the last two decades have been characterized by tension between some Knesset members and the Knesset as an institution on the one hand, and the Supreme Court on the other.[40]

The aforementioned tension did not escape the Court's notice, and in a ruling in 2011, Justice Elyakim Rubinstein pointed to the fact that since the *Bank Mizrahi* ruling, the Knesset had imposed on itself "an operative constitutional silence"— which it did not in other legislative issues. Rubinstein proposed that the reason for this lay in the fact that some of the legislators "are not too happy with the constitutional powers of this court, and fear that additional constitutional texts might only empower it further." Rubinstein tried to allay these fears. He argued that the Court used its authority to strike down primary legislation "cautiously and sparingly," and that in any event, a careful examination of the cases in which the Court struck down primary legislation would reveal that these were matters "that generally do not concern the troubled parties."[41]

Rubinstein's statement attests to either a misunderstanding or an unwillingness on the part of some of the Supreme Court justices to understand the central reason for the political and public criticism being hurled at them. For the critics, the problem lies not in the scope of the judicial review or its content in this or that case; the problem is much more profound and fundamental. From their perspective, the Court is the one that declared, unilaterally, that a constitutional revolution had occurred; it is the one that stated that all the Basic Laws enjoy supremacy, and granted itself the authority to strike down primary legislation based on the Basic Laws; and today it consistently ignores the compromises that accompanied their passing, and shapes their content as it wishes. The legislation of additional Basic Laws will thus serve as legitimation of the Court's moves thus far, and give it a green light to continue on the path it set for itself. Precisely because of this, the Court's critics do not simply adopt an approach of constitutional silence, but as I will show later in the chapter, they are also trying to restrict the Court's moves in various ways.

3. ACADEMIA

Beside the criticism of the Supreme Court by some MKs, as well as by the religious bloc considered at the opening of this chapter, some criticism could also have been expected from the legal academia concerning the way the Court interprets and uses the Basic Laws. As noted, the constitutional interpretation adopted by the Supreme Court disregards the original meaning of the Basic Laws and the original intentions of their sponsors. This disregard could have been expected to evoke criticism among academics, who are probably aware of the controversy surrounding the proper interpretation of the constitution. Criticism could have focused on a more basic issue—the very proclamation that the March 1992 events marked a constitutional revolution. I know of no parallel to the Israeli reality of a constitutional revolution carried out by individuals, none of whom is aware of having done so. In other countries, when a public dispute involves constitutional questions, the dispute touches on the interpretation of the constitution and on its mode of implementation in concrete circumstances.[42] In no other country besides Israel does controversy prevail on the question of whether or not a constitution exists in the first place.

A review of the legal literature covering the first few years after the March 1992 events and the proclamation of the constitutional revolution does reveal a vast output of academic writing, which increases over time. Some of the writers dealt not only with the contents of the Basic Laws and with the change they effected, but also conveyed views on the move and its circumstances. Some academics welcomed the constitutional revolution and expressed support for the Court's moves.[43] Almost entirely missing from the legal journals, however, is any writing criticizing the Court for its involvement in the creation of the constitution or questioning the legitimacy of this involvement. Two main writers are the exceptions that prove the rule: Ruth Gavison, and former Supreme Court president, Justice Moshe Landau. In 1997 Gavison published a comprehensive critical article entitled "The Constitutional Revolution: Reality or Self-Fulfilling Prophecy."[44] In this article, later published as a book, Gavison reviewed the developments since March 1992, and examined them against the background of concepts from the realm of constitutional theory. Gavison was highly critical of the Court's moves, pointed out their normative failures, and turned attention to their risks. Landau, too, attacked Barak, who had been his rival ever since they had both served together for a brief period in the Supreme Court. Landau's articles, though shorter and less comprehensive than Gavison's, are extremely sharp. He blamed the Court for deceit and illegitimate conduct.[45]

How can we explain the abstention of the legal academia from criticizing the Court's moves? In my view, the answer is clear. The legal academia in Israel identifies mostly with the liberal group, whose hegemony has been jeopardized in recent decades. This is precisely the group that, as noted, had sponsored the enactment of the Basic Laws to preserve at least part of its power. This is also the group that gained the most from the constitutional revolution performed by the Court, using the Basic Laws as an excuse and as a platform. Seeing beyond one's group interest while preserving intellectual integrity requires enormous mental resources.[46] Even Gavison, who, as noted, was among the few who criticized the Court, opened her critical article with a long and convoluted attempt to justify her decision to voice her critique in public.[47] This apology is understandable, given Gavison's membership in the former hegemonic group, leading to her need to justify herself to its members.[48]

4. CHANGING TRENDS IN THE PUBLIC ATTITUDE

The public reaction to the Court's decisions, as reported so far, was mixed—the religious and right-wing bloc sharply criticized these moves, whereas legal scholars refrained from criticism, and even protected the Court. All this, however, happened only in the first years after the enactment of the Basic Laws. More recently, a change has begun to surface in the public attitude to the Court. The critics' ranks have expanded,[49] and now include voices from the academia as well,[50] among them some who had explicitly or implicitly supported the Court's moves at the beginning, but later changed their minds and joined the critics. The most prominent among those joining the critics' ranks at a later stage is Menachem Mautner, prominent in this regard for two reasons. First, he ranks among the most respected legal academics in Israel, and his critique is therefore highly significant. Second, Mautner did not merely shift from the silent to the critical bloc, but completely reversed his position, from explicit support to criticism of the Court. From the early 1990s and until the early 2000s, Mautner had been one of the Court's most fervent backers. He concluded his famous article, "The Decline of Formalism and the Rise of Values in Israeli Law," with a description of Israel as characterized by a polarized reality, where a war is being waged between liberal forces, led by the Supreme Court, and clerical, anti-liberal forces. Mautner called on everyone who yearns for progress and light to support the Court's struggle,[51] and he reiterated this idea on several occasions. For example, in an article he published in 2003, Mautner said the following:

> We learn from Prof. Gavison's writings elsewhere that the very fact that the Supreme Court's normative conceptions are in dispute must necessarily restrict the scope of their application . . . I question this. The normative conceptions

imbued in the decisions of the Supreme Court and of the other courts in the country are an important element in the creation and preservation of Israeli liberalism. Those committed to the preservation and development of a cultural and political liberal regime in Israel must persist in their struggle for the role of the courts' normative conceptions in Israel's public life, even if some groups seek to restrict them or dismiss them.[52]

Mautner's approach in these articles located him at the forefront of the camp supporting the Court's moves. In recent years, however, several profiles of Mautner appeared in the press, presenting him as one of the Court's most severe critics and counting him among the leaders of the struggle against it.[53] A review of Mautner's latest writing does indeed suggest a change in his views.[54]

In recent years, Daniel Friedmann, a renowned law professor and the former Minister of Justice, has been the leading figure in the struggle against the Supreme Court's dominance. Friedmann made several suggestions for reform in the judiciary in general, and regarding constitutional issues in particular.[55] The addition of individuals such as Mautner and Friedmann to the camp of the Court's critics endows this criticism with a certain legitimation, including for those who, in principle, belong to the political-normative camp the Court is identified with. Henceforth, even if you are not observant or right wing, you may legitimately criticize the Court's involvement in the enactment of the constitution in Israel.[56]

What might explain the current change in the former hegemons' camp? In a recent book, Mautner discusses this issue. In his view, a new situation has emerged—the strongest critiques of the Court are not voiced by religious individuals, but rather by members of the social group that, since the end of the 1970s, had lent unqualified support to the Court's moves. Mautner states: "This change in the political behavior of the liberal former hegemons is *nothing less than dramatic* and demands an explanation."[57] Mautner offers three possible explanations for this change. Since his own views have changed, his explanations may also shed light on the change in his position.

According to the first explanation, the critique follows from a reduced sense of anxiety among the liberal former hegemons: "As the years passed, the LFH's feeling that they were facing rising religious-nationalist forces and that the Supreme Court was the last stronghold that would protect them from a takeover by these forces weakened, and the post-hegemonic situation became part of the country's normal, ongoing daily reality."[58] According to the second explanation, the criticism reflects the declining public trust in the Court, including among the former hegemons:

In the first generation after the decline of the hegemony...the LFH insistently emphasized the protection of liberal-democratic values against what they perceived as a threat . . . As the years passed and their anxiety over the harm to these values waned, the LFH could make room . . . for other important values, such as integrity. Over the years, when that value was applied to the conduct of the Supreme Court, the Court did not appear to fully meet the test.

According to the third explanation, the spreading criticism denotes that the positions of the conservative, right-wing bloc have percolated down to the ranks of the former hegemons' ranks.

II. Proposals for Change

Friedmann was not the only one to make proposals for change and reform. In the course of the years since the 1992 revolution, many proposals concerning the Court and the institution of judicial review were tabled in the Knesset and submitted to the public, including transferring the authority for performing judicial review from the Supreme Court to a special constitutional court, changing the justices' selection procedures in an attempt to strengthen the democratic aspect of the Court's decisions, anchoring clear limitations on the Court's powers in the constitution, and several others. These proposals confronted strong opposition from many jurists and politicians, who steadfastly supported the Court. For the time being, the defensive struggle appears to have succeeded, and most of these initiatives are no longer on the agenda. The proposals, however, still deserve thorough examination, and some of them are briefly described and evaluated below.

1. SHIFTING TO A CENTRALIZED MODEL OF JUDICIAL REVIEW

One proposal, in several variations, is to entrust the authority for judicial review to one single court. Some have suggested concentrating this authority in the Supreme Court, and some have proposed entrusting it to a special court erected for this purpose.[59] The official logic behind the first version is to maintain the Knesset's honor. Supporters of this proposal hold that granting all courts the option of voiding Knesset laws debases the Knesset and shows contempt for its laws, and this authority should be limited to the Supreme Court.[60] Barak supported this claim in a lecture he delivered in June 2003. Reviewing the considerations in favor of centralized and decentralized versions, he concluded that one consideration tilts the scales in favor of the centralized model:

This consideration derives from the constitutional culture of our legal system. According to this consideration, the transition from a parliamentary democracy to a parliamentary-constitutional democracy would be too sharp were every court authorized to void laws . . . and society must indeed be educated on the essence of a constitution and of judicial review to acknowledge the court's authority to determine . . . the constitutionality of the law. So long as this notion has not deeply penetrated public consciousness, judicial review should preferably be confined to the Supreme Court.[61]

Specifically, then, Barak does not hold that granting all courts the authority to void laws debases the Knesset, but does agree that today, because the broad public is not properly familiar with the institution of judicial review, this is the impression that could be created. He therefore proposes endorsing a centralized model, for the time being.

The logic underlying the suggestion to establish a special constitutional court is more complex. One reason for supporting it could rely on the claim that a decision on constitutional matters is not a legal decision in the professional sense of the word, but is related to a normative consideration of political character. Hence, in order to preserve the apolitical character of the judiciary, limiting the authority to perform judicial review to one court is not enough, and the court dealing with these matters must be separated from the customary system.[62] Another reason for the proposal to concentrate authority in a special court is the current composition of the Israeli Supreme Court. The usual argument, as noted, is that the Supreme Court is biased in a specific political-normative direction, and given the current procedure for judicial appointments in Israel, changes in this trend are hard to envisage in the near future. Anyone who disagrees with the Court's values has a good reason for opposing the notion of entrusting the Court with the task of judicial review. In other words, the proposal to establish a special constitutional court could reflect a desire to ensure that the body entrusted with the task of judicial review will be balanced in its composition, and convey the range of views prevalent in the Israeli public without granting any of these views a priori, unbending advantage.[63]

Constitutional theory discourse distinguishes between a centralized and a decentralized model of judicial review.[64] In the centralized model, which originates in Austria, only one court is authorized to engage in judicial review, whereas in the decentralized model, all courts are authorized to do so. Whereas the centralized model prevails in continental countries, the decentralized model is more frequent in common law countries. Proposals made in Israel to confine the authority for judicial review to one single court, be it a special court or the Supreme Court, imply endorsement of the centralized model. When examining the advantages and disadvantages of this proposal in the Israeli context, the arguments that led continental countries to endorse this model merit examination.

The usual claim is that the choice of the centralized method rests on a perception of judicial review as, fundamentally, a political act of legislative character that infringes the legislators' exclusive authority to enact laws. To grant proper weight to the separation-of-powers principle, we should refrain from authorizing the judiciary as a whole to perform the review, and confine it instead to one tribunal.[65] Not by chance is centralization far more widespread in continental Europe, where the judges' role is perceived as restricted and far less central and authoritative than in common law countries. The legal system in continental countries rests on legislation rather than on common law judicial decisions. Furthermore, judicial decisions are built more as mathematical or geometrical proofs, when the conclusion is described as deriving directly from the law. Arguments familiar in common law countries—such as policy considerations, balances, and so forth—are missing from the typical continental decision. This perception of the judge's role is incompatible with the option of granting authority to the courts to decide on important value questions.

Choosing the centralized model is appropriate to continental countries for a further reason. These countries did not adopt the principle of stare decisis. Every decision is limited to the case at hand, and does not compel future ones. Moreover, the judiciary in continental countries is split into several separate systems. Germany, for instance, has five separate judicial systems, each one in charge of a particular area. Each one has a Supreme Court of its own, and there is no overarching Supreme Court. Granting authority to perform judicial review to all the courts would invite contradictions between the decisions of various instances on constitutional matters, creating lack of clarity concerning the status of certain laws.[66]

Most of the countries that adopted the centralized model went beyond the centralization of authority for conducting judicial review in one specific court, and established a special court for this purpose. This step, too, is particularly appropriate to continental philosophy. If judicial review is a legislative-political act, assigning one court to perform it will not suffice in order to preserve the separation of powers—a separate institution detached from the customary judicial system must be established for this purpose. Another advantage of centralizing authority on constitutional issues in one special court is that recognizing the political character of this court's decisions will justify adopting a political mechanism for selecting its judges. Such an approach would answer the critique about the tension between judicial review and the democratic principle,[67] a point discussed further below.

Confining authority to a special tribunal detached from the judicial system is appropriate not only to continental philosophy, but also to the reality of continental countries.[68] First, continental courts are large, bureaucratic institutions, which would be hard-pressed to meet the challenge of delivering a quick decision on burning constitutional issues. Second, supreme courts in continental countries lack the authority to filter the cases that reach them. Their caseload is thus enormous, and they might find it difficult to face weighty constitutional cases. Third, and most crucial, judges in the continental system are career judges, who begin their professional lives immediately after graduation, and gain promotion mainly because of seniority. These judges are "educated" to perceive their role as legal administrators required to apply legislative rulings to concrete cases, in technical fashion and without involvement in the shaping of policy. The constitutional field is strewn with questions of policy and balances, and decisions in their regard require abilities that the continental judge has neither been trained nor "educated" to develop. For all these reasons, it is evident why an ordinary court and ordinary judges would not succeed at the task of judicial review.

Most of the considerations described above—which have brought continental countries to adopt the centralized model, and to establish a special tribunal for judicial review with judges selected by the political system—are irrelevant in the Israeli context. Israeli judges are not career judges, but rather jurists who served several years as attorneys before their judicial appointment. The basis of Israel's legal system was laid down by the British Mandate authorities, and therefore, in principle, Israel belongs to the family of common law countries. Judges in the various judicial instances are well versed in the application of strong discretion in ordinary (non-constitutional) cases, a pattern accepted as legitimate and noncontroversial. The Supreme Court is indeed extremely busy, since, in addition to its role as High Court of Justice, it serves as an appeal court for civil and criminal cases, many of them first appeals granted by right. This problem, however, could be solved with relative ease. The authority of magistrate courts could be broadened, turning district courts into appeal courts. Such a change would considerably reduce the mass of cases that the Supreme Court is forced to hear, enabling it to devote most of its time to questions of precedent in the area of civil and criminal law, and also, obviously, to constitutional questions.[69] Incidentally, this is the case in the United States. On most issues, the U.S. Supreme Court sits as a third instance, and has the authority to hear or to reject a case outright.

The question that remains open is the political nature of constitutional adjudication. The general understanding, even in common law countries, is that constitutional deliberations and decisions are political. In fact, the consensual view is that the Court, even if it had wished so, could not have avoided resorting to value-political considerations in its decisions. However, awareness of the political character of judicial review has not prevented common law countries, such as Canada and the United States, from endorsing the decentralized model. It does lead these countries, however, to adopt a judge-appointing mechanism that grants the political system control of the Court's composition.[70] The combination of these two elements—recognition of the political character of constitutional proceedings, and hence the adoption of a political mechanism of appointments—has a liberating effect. It enables the Court to acknowledge the value considerations it takes into account without resorting to futile claims such as "we remain 'neutral.'" In sum, if the centralized model is adopted for fear of politicizing the judiciary, this problem can also be solved within the decentralized model.

I have so far explained why the centralized model is not required in common law countries. Yet, this model also has several flaws that cast doubt on the wisdom of its adoption in the first place: first, the centralized model does not offer a suitable answer to the main problem it pretends to solve; and second, even if it does solve the problem, it exacts an extremely high price, raising the question of whether costs do not exceed benefits.

Adopting the centralized model had been meant to ensure that the judiciary stays outside what is essentially a political discourse, but this goal remains elusive, for several reasons. According to the centralized model, constitutional questions can reach the constitutional court through several channels.[71] One of those channels is by referral. When a claim of unconstitutionality is raised, the court dealing with the case stops proceedings and directs the matter for decision, as an abstract question, to the constitutional court. In all the countries where such a mechanism exists, however, the referring court retains quite a significant role. The referring court must determine—as a prerequisite for referral—that the constitutional argument concerning the attacked law is sufficiently strong. In order to make this determination, the referring court must use strong discretion[72]—precisely the discretion that supporters of the centralized model seek to avoid.

In recent decades, exterior factors have also played a role in continental countries, adding a decentralized dimension to constitutional adjudication. For instance, the legal system of the European Union assumes preeminence over the internal legislation of individual countries, meaning that, were a contradiction to arise between the laws of the Union and internal legislation, the former would prevail. The Italian constitutional court determined that a contradiction between the two legal systems is considered an indirect breach of the Italian constitution.[73] Since Italy adopted the centralized model, the result of this determination by the Italian court is that only the Italian constitutional court is allowed to consider a claim about a contradiction between the Union's law and internal Italian law, thus preserving the centralized dimension of judicial review. The European Court of Justice (ECJ), however, rejected this determination, and clarified that all Italian courts are authorized to void a local law contradicting the laws of the Union.[74] This decision created a strange situation: ordinary courts in Italy are not authorized to void internal legislation that contradicts the Italian constitution, but they are authorized to void it if it is opposed to the Union's laws. This ECJ decision adds a decentralized dimension to constitutional judicial review in Italy, and strengthens my claim that the choice of the centralized model does not deprive ordinary courts from the option—indeed, the duty—to discuss constitutional questions. The decentralized model, then, is inevitable.

The addition of a decentralized dimension to centralized systems originates not only in European Union law, but in other international schemes as well, such as the European Convention of Human Rights. The Convention does not grant the European Court of Human Rights, residing in Strasbourg, the authority to void primary legislation in countries that are signatories to the Convention. In some of these countries, however, conventions enjoy a status that is superior to that of primary legislation, and courts are asked to ignore primary legislation opposing conventions' provisions. The result is that, in these countries, beside the centralized model of judicial review touching on the internal constitution, a decentralized model has emerged regarding international conventions.

Adopting a centralized model, then, becomes less and less possible. Nevertheless, serious thought should be given to its merits because, contrary to this model's adduced benefits, the price of endorsing it is extremely high. Let us assume, for the purposes of the current discussion, that the reason for drafting a constitution is the desire to protect fundamental values. One course for engaging in the examination of a law claimed to contradict the constitution is, as noted, referral. But this is a very cumbersome path, as it compels the court dealing with a case to stop proceedings and refer the question to the constitutional court. The referral obviously delays closure, and judges might prefer to reject the claim of unconstitutionality if only to avoid delays and reach a quick decision. Ordinary judges are required, as noted, to examine the constitutional question as a preliminary condition for referring it to the constitutional court. But as long as they lack the authority to decide on constitutional questions, their awareness of constitutional aspects will at best be limited, and they might merely due to ignorance reject outright claims deserving a hearing. If the constitution's aim is to protect fundamental values, adopting a centralized mechanism could prejudice attainment of this aim.

Several claims against adoption of the centralized model have been raised so far: it is unnecessary for achieving the aims for whose sake it was chosen, it is not at all clear whether it can be used, and its costs might exceed its benefits. In concluding the discussion of this model, an additional element bearing on the Israeli context deserves emphasis—Israel has not adopted the centralized model, but does not operate according to the decentralized model either. Currently in use in Israel is an intermediate model, with both centralized and decentralized components. The decentralized model allows all judicial instances to consider claims against the constitutionality of primary legislation, but this is not the case in Israel. All ordinary courts in Israel are indeed authorized to void a law, and the Israeli model thereby resembles the decentralized model. The authority of all courts to do so, however, is acquired incidentally, in the course of hearing and deciding another matter within their purview.[75] In light of the incidental character of constitutionality discussions in ordinary courts, their decisions on this matter compel only the parties involved, and do not determine a ruling that is generally valid.[76] The only court in Israel authorized to deal directly with a claim questioning the constitutionality of a law, and the only one whose decisions turn into a compelling ruling precluding use of the abrogated law, is the Supreme Court, when sitting as High Court of Justice. Hence, if the reason for preferring the centralized model is the concern about contempt for the Knesset, it can be disregarded, because the model currently in use in Israel does not affront the Knesset's honor.[77]

2. EXPANDING THE PANEL, DETERMINING A PROCEDURE, AND THE MAJORITY REQUIREMENT

A second proposal that appears in several bills is to set a minimum number of justices or to determine the precise size of the panel of justices authorized to consider and void primary legislation.[78] Attached to this proposal are usually two more: to add procedural components,[79] and to require a solid majority of the justices in the panel[80] as conditions for voiding a law. The first two proposals are warranted. As for the third, there are arguments for and against.

At present, the Court can consider the validity of laws in a panel of only three justices, but in some circumstances, the President of the Supreme Court, the Deputy President, or the panel that began hearing the case can decide to broaden the panel to include a higher, odd number of justices.[81] The President of the Supreme Court is also authorized to determine who will be the justices on the panel, and whether it will be an ordinary panel or a broadened one. In recent years, the President's authority has been challenged on both these issues, particularly concerning the authority to determine the panel's composition.[82] On the assumption that justices differ from one another in their views on different issues, and on the assumption that their views affect their decisions, the authority to determine who will be the justices on the panel enables the President to influence the contents of the decision—a patently illegitimate option. In 2001, a conference was held at Bar-Ilan University dealing with institutional aspects in the activity of the Supreme Court. The conference was concluded with a lecture by the then President of the Supreme Court, Justice Aharon Barak. He discussed this issue in his lecture, and claimed he hardly ever intervenes in the determination of the panels, and that the panels and the cases referred to each are determined at random. Nevertheless, Barak noted that he does intervene in the determination of the panel in some cases, and, for instance, in cases touching on religion and state issues, he tries to ensure that the Court's religious justice will be a member of the panel.[83]

Not only is this account not reassuring, it is even worrisome. In a large majority of the cases heard by the Court, the question of who are the justices is obviously not particularly significant. The few cases where the justices' identity is significant are the politically and normatively sensitive cases, where justices cannot but be influenced by their worldview, and it is precisely in such cases that Barak admits that he intervenes in the determination of the panel.[84]

Barak's example illustrates the problem. I have claimed in the past that three general characteristics are evident in the Supreme Court's case law on freedom of religion.[85] First, almost all the petitions submitted to the Court claiming violations of freedom of religion are rejected.[86] Second, in the few cases where the Court was sympathetic to petitioners adducing freedom of religion arguments, the petitions dealt with the interests of non-Orthodox Jewish groups.[87] Third, one may cautiously discern a trend pointing to a split between religious and secular justices in freedom of religion cases. When a Jewish-religious-Orthodox interest is at stake, Orthodox justices tend to accept the claim about violation of freedom of religion,[88] and secular judges tend to reject it; when at stake is a Jewish-religious Conservative or Reform interest, the trend is reversed: Orthodox justices tend to reject it,[89] while secular justices tend to accept it.[90] The last two points are interrelated since, given the balance of power within the Supreme Court, if secular justices hold that non-Orthodox religious movements require greater protection, most Orthodox petitions are bound to be rejected.[91]

Barak's admission that he had intervened in the determination of the justices on the panel in religion and state cases is thus worrisome, but the problem is not contingent on whether the President of the Supreme Court actively intervenes in deciding the panels that will consider specific cases. The problem lies in the very authority invested in him to intervene, and would exist even if the President consistently refrained from exercising it. The very existence of this prerogative threatens the Court's reputation as an impartial body.

If we agree that assigning justices to a case could determine the fate of a petition, the problem does not begin with the authority vested in the President to determine the justices on the panel. Rather, the problem is more fundamental, and lies in the panels system in use in Israel. If the justice's worldview influences his or her decisions, and if one panel of three justices can reach a decision different from that of another, the petitioners depend on luck—who will be the justices in their case. Furthermore, not only does the fate of the specific petition depend on fate (or on the Court's

President), but so does the question of principle raised by the petition. The reason is related to an interesting phenomenon discussed by Yoram Shahar, whereby even though the Supreme Court is not bound by its previous decisions and is allowed to reverse them or deviate from them,[92] a tradition of conformity prevails among Supreme Court justices. Justices who were not part of a panel considering a particular issue accept its decision as compelling, and even justices who had dissented on a particular matter tend to fall in line with the majority in their later decisions.[93] Consequently, the panel assigned to a case on any question of principle determines the line the Court will henceforth follow.

To sum up this point, the panels system is problematic because it entrusts the fate of the case to chance. Furthermore, given the tendency to conformity among Supreme Court justices, the panels system also entrusts to chance the fate of the issue of principle raised by the petition. Finally, if the Supreme Court President is authorized to determine the panels and the cases that will be referred to them, he can intervene to make the randomness deliberate. The solution to these grave problems is quite clear— expanding the panels and creating a situation whereby all the justices in the Court or a large majority of them are part of the panel, at least on issues of principle. This requirement is certainly imperative in cases with a potential for voiding a law. The main obstacle in this course is the further workload it imposes on the justices, a workload that is already unbearable. But this problem has a simple solution, as noted above—turning the Supreme Court into a third instance, able to filter the cases it will hear.

The demand to broaden the panels does not require a formal arrangement in legislation, since this is actually the practice in use today. As Guy Zeidman showed, the Court has often set up expanded panels in recent decades, particularly in cases of principle.[94] But although broader panels have become an almost fixed practice, it would still not be redundant to turn this practice into a compelling legal procedure. The authority vested in the President to refer a case to a specific justice, even if properly implemented, is improper as long as it depends on the Court's goodwill. The question of whether to adjudicate in a panel of three or expand the panel, and if so, how many justices to include in it, should not depend on the discretion of the Court or of any of its justices, but should be compellingly determined by law.

The demand to compel the Court by law to establish a larger panel seems justified. By contrast, deciding whether it is proper to demand a special majority of justices as a condition for voiding a law is harder. The advantage of requiring such a majority is clear—the voiding of a law challenges the political system, so everything possible should be done to confer legitimation on such a step. One way to strengthen the legitimation of the voiding is to require that it be supported by a clear majority of the justices. Israel's Supreme Court would also appear to operate on the assumption of a direct correlation between the size of the majority and the public legitimation of the decision. Proof is that, unlike in the United States, where decisions on controversial matters of principle are often decided on a majority of one,[95] in Israel, most of the recent important decisions considered by broader panels have been either unanimous or supported by a decisive majority. These interesting findings could be ascribed to the relative homogeneity of Supreme Court justices in Israel. Nevertheless, the central constitutional decisions of the last two decades, in expanded panels and with a clear majority, reflect the wishes of the Supreme Court to ensure legitimation to these decisions.

However, the requirement of a clear majority as a condition for voiding a law has a disadvantage, too. Imagine a situation where most Supreme Court justices hold that a particular law is unconstitutional, but the majority is not sufficiently large to void the law. How will such a law be perceived by the public? What will be its legitimation? The Court can ensure legitimation of a law's invalidation not only through the requirement of a clear majority, but through other means as well. In the end, then, leaving things as they are without requiring a clear majority as a condition for voiding a law seems like a preferable option.

3. CHANGING THE SELECTION MECHANISM

Basic Law: The Judiciary states:

1. A judge will be appointed by the President of the state upon election by a Judicial Appointments Committee.
2. The Committee will consist of nine members: the President of the Supreme Court, two other judges of the Supreme Court elected by the body of judges thereof, the Minister of Justice and another minister designated by the Government, two members of the Knesset elected by the Knesset,[96] and two representatives of the Bar elected by its national council. The Minister of Justice will chair the Committee.

Mordechai Haller harshly condemned the Israeli system of judicial appointments, claiming as follows:

In Israel . . . judges are selected by—themselves . . . The four politicians all represent diffuse interests. By tradition, one of the Knesset members represents the government and the other the opposition, which means the two are more likely than not to disagree when matters of ideology are at stake. The justice minister is the single member of the government *least* appropriate for representing popular interests against the views of the justices, since he is usually a lawyer himself, advised by the judicial establishment and often beholden to it; he is therefore likely to disagree with the other government minister, whose principal loyalty is to the government and to the values of the electorate that put that government in power. The five representatives of the legal establishment, however, have their interests neatly lined up: The three justices will naturally become a single voting bloc, protecting the interests and prevailing views of the Supreme Court itself. Moreover, it is safe to assume that the selection of the two junior justices to the committee will have been heavily influenced, if not dictated, by the court president, himself a member of the committee. As for the representatives of the Bar Association, they are seen within their own fields as inferiors in the legal hierarchy, of which the judges are the apex, and it is they who will pay a price for failing to represent the very same values that the judges are defending.[97]

Haller was not the only one puzzled by the selection mechanism in use in Israel,[98] and the critique gains further support when Israel's selection mechanism is compared with those in use in other countries. In a comparative perspective, the Israeli mechanism is revealed as unique and without parallel in any other Western country. In all Western countries, judicial appointments are controlled by the political system.[99] By contrast, Israel grants its Supreme Court justices a decisive role in determining who will join their ranks. Given the critics' arguments and the comparative data, it is only natural that proposals have been tabled for changing the system, seeking to make appointment procedures more democratic, and the Court's role in them less influential. Suggestions for change have been raised in various forums, including the Knesset.[100]

On January 18, 2000, the Judicial Appointments Committee nominated Supreme Court Justice Yitzhak Zamir as head of a commission charged with examining the current arrangements for selecting justices and with suggesting ways for their improvement. In April 2002, the commission—whose members included MK Amnon Rubinstein, a professor of constitutional law who had promoted the enactment of the new Basic Laws, and Attorney Yori Guy-Ron as representative of the Bar—submitted its conclusions. The commission rejected outright the claims against the judicial appointments mechanism and the proposals for its change. The commission stated that the Israeli system "has been widely praised outside Israel," and that "it is one of the best systems in the world for appointing judges."[101] No evidence was attached in support of these claims.[102] The commission concluded its discussions on this matter as follows:

The commission is aware of judicial appointments methods in use in other countries. On the basis of the comparative material, the views that were submitted to the commission, the considerations touching on the matter, and the cumulative experience, the commission holds that the system currently in use in Israel for selecting judges, including the composition of the Judicial Appointments' Committee, is preferable to the systems used in other countries. Hence, this commission does not recommend trying another system, which will necessarily involve the risks of a decline in the judges' professional standard and a violation of the judiciary's vital autonomy, and possibly an erosion of public trust. In sum, the commission recommends leaving the composition of the Judicial Appointments Committee, as determined by the law, without change.[103]

The commission's stance against increased involvement of the political system in judicial appointments does not rely on evidence, as noted, and is also opposed to views generally accepted among comparative law specialists who deal with the judiciary. For example, John Bell notes in his book *Judiciaries within Europe* that political involvement in the procedures of appointment is definitely required:

In a divided society, there are different views about the way in which society should go. Having judges who . . . reflect together a variety of tendencies in society may be one way in which judicial decisions can come to terms with the political dimensions of decisions . . . these are reasons why most systems include politicians in the judicial appointments process.[104]

Bell rejects outright the claim that the involvement of politicians in the selection procedures will make the selection process, and in its wake the judicial process, political. In his view, political involvement in judicial decisions is a fact, and denying it is pointless. The only question is what political stance will triumph:

Banishing politicians from the process does not banish political issues. They will surface in debates about the composition of the judiciary, and might be reflected in a role for associations of like-minded judges and lawyers who will seek to secure representation of their ideas in the judiciary through membership in the judicial appointments commission.[105]

Bell's claims seem so logical that one can hardly understand how the Zamir commission failed to see reality in this fashion.[106] The commission's persistence may reflect its deep commitment to the Supreme Court in its current composition. This commitment could also explain the commission's denial of facts known to any citizen interested in Israel: "A claim has been raised that the three judges of the Supreme Court who serve in the Judicial Appointments Committee see themselves committed to vote according to the decision of all the judges in the Supreme Court, and that they accordingly vote unanimously. *Factually, however, this claim is incorrect.*[107] The Zamir commission does not point to its evidence for this claim. An examination of the data shows that this claim is definitely correct. It is a well-known fact that Supreme Court justices hold preliminary consultations before every meeting of the Judicial Appointments Committee, and their representatives consistently vote according to their members' previous agreement.[108] Only once in recent years did a Supreme Court justice who was a member of the Committee decide to adopt an independent stance. After doing so, he was strongly condemned by his colleagues, and refrained from doing so again.[109] The Knesset did indeed attempt in 2004 to eradicate the practice of unanimous voting by the Supreme Court representatives in the Committee, and added to the Law of the Courts [Combined Version] 5744-1984 a provision stating that "each member of the committee will vote according to his own discretion and will not be compelled by the decisions of the body he represents in the committee."[110] It is not clear, however, whether this legislation has attained its aim.

The discussion so far indicates that the justices' selection mechanism used in Israel is an exception in the democratic landscape. The arguments in its favor are not supported by evidence, and contradicting views widely prevalent in this regard in Western countries.

4. RESTRICTING THE COURT'S AUTHORITY IN THE CONSTITUTION

A fourth type of change suggested in the various proposals calls for explicitly excluding certain questions from the Supreme Court's purview, and assigning them to the political system for regulation. This course, for instance, is the one recommended by the Israel Democracy Institute in its proposal for a constitution, regarding several religion and state questions.[111] The two relevant sections are:

163. Constitutional justiciability

(a) The Supreme Court . . . may rule that a law is not valid because it is unconstitutional.

164. Constitutional Non-Justiciability

(a) Article 163 shall not apply with respect to a piece of legislation which concerns any of the topics enumerated in Subarticle (c).

(b) . . .

(c) The topics are as follows:

    (a) Joining a religion, including conversion, belonging to a religion or renouncing it;

(b) The authority of the religious tribunals at the time of establishing this Constitution, conducting marriages and divorces according to religious law, creating partnerships and their dissolution in accordance with the law, and the application of religious law to issues of personal status, which at the establishment of the Constitution are adjudicated pursuant to personal law of the parties;

(c) The Jewish character of the Sabbath and Jewish Holidays in the public domain;

(d) Maintaining Jewish dietary laws in governmental institutions;

(e) Granting Israeli citizenship to relatives of one eligible to immigrate to Israel.[112]

What is the logic underlying this proposal? The explanation provided is that "the special nature of these subjects necessitates that they be determined by the Legislative Branch, as in the past, while neutralizing the influence of the Constitution. Therefore, the constitutional arrangement negates the power of the courts to repeal a piece of legislation on these issues."[113] But why declare certain issues non-justiciable in the Supreme Court, thereby preventing the Court from using the constitution to decide on them, rather than to simply abstain from dealing with them in the constitution? Because the Supreme Court, as described at length above, does not feel obliged to abide by the compromises agreed upon by the constitution's drafters, and allows itself to interpret the constitution and implement it against their intentions. Therefore, excluding certain issues from the constitution cannot guarantee that the Court will abstain from using the constitution to decide on them, and they must be explicitly excluded from the Court's jurisdiction as well.

Is this proposal advisable? Answering this question requires close examination of several normative and practical questions. At the normative level, we will first have to answer questions such as: What is the purpose of drafting a constitution? What should be the role of the Court in employing a constitutional strategy? At the practical level, we must figure out whether and to what extent will the Court feel compelled by the explicit exclusion of certain matters from its purview: Will it be possible to prevent the Court from disregarding this explicit negation of its authority? Answers to these questions are beyond the scope of this book.

III. Summary

Several proposals for change have been reviewed so far, most of them formulated in response to the Court's moves. What happened to these proposals? The Court's

Presidents, first Aharon Barak and then Dorit Beinisch, who was appointed after his retirement, together with their supporters in the political system, in the academia, and in the Court's ranks, enlisted in a serious effort to repeal the various proposals, particularly those of Minister of Justice Daniel Friedmann.[114] As of today, the holding battle has been successful: all attempts to introduce change have been dismissed.

Ostensibly, the Court and its supporters should be pleased with the current status quo. The constitution was not adopted as is usual in other countries, but that is precisely what enables the Court to shape it according to its own worldview with relative ease, without the painful compromises that would have been required had the constitution been adopted following proper procedure. Furthermore, as time passes, the controversial innovations introduced by the Court gain more and more legitimacy,[115] increasing the chances that legislators will ultimately give their consent to the entire move *ex post factum*. And yet, despite the appearance of growing success, the Court and the camp it represents confront a lurking danger that has only worsened over the years.

The recent decades have indeed marked the Court's growing strength and its success in imposing its values on the Israeli public, but this success is only a matter of appearance. The Court has so far succeeded in repelling all of the attacks, but its public standing has been undermined. Studies conducted in the early 1990s, before the "constitutional revolution," found that the Supreme Court had enjoyed high levels of public trust, in comparison to the trust enjoyed by the other two branches of government, but also in absolute terms.[116] Similar studies conducted in recent years show that the Court is still at the top of the public trust scale, but trust levels are far lower than those recorded before the revolution.[117] The dramatic decline of public trust in the Court is not surprising. It had been clearly envisaged by Justice Landau in an article he wrote in the early 1970s. Landau warned that the Court's involvement in value controversies would mar its public image as a neutral arbiter.[118] Landau could not have foreseen the flimsy basis that the Court would rely upon to justify its involvement. Had he taken into account this datum as well, his forecast would probably have been even gloomier.

The sharp decline of the public's trust in the Court must trouble its supporters as well as its opponents. The courts in general and the Supreme Court in particular can make a significant contribution to the strength of the society and the political system. The Court, which is perceived as an independent and impartial body, can be an effective instrument for resolving differences and easing personal and public tensions. Once the Court has lost its neutral image and is identified, justifiably or not, with one party to the conflict, or once it is perceived as an entity seeking to expand its power at the expense of the other branches of government, it can no longer serve as a consensual arbiter, and society loses a precious preservation tool. We can safely assume that the camp currently in power in the Court also fears for the stability of Israel. They, too, understand that this stability depends, inter alia, on the public trust in the Court,[119] and they must therefore understand the danger attendant in acting one-sidedly for so long. They must understand the need to find a way of regaining the prestige and the trust that the Court had enjoyed until not long ago.[120]

Some hold that the way to restore the Court's standing is to create mechanisms that will slightly weaken it and bring it down to its "natural size." This was the motivation behind some of the proposals discussed above. But although a certain logic underlies some of these proposals, one main problem characterizes the conduct of the current constitutional discourse in Israel. The discussion unfolds in response to the Court's moves, when at least some of those involved view the Court as the "enemy." This thinking actually perpetuates the Court's supremacy. The Knesset does not set an agenda, but wrangles with the Court and reacts to its moves. The Knesset must take back the lead in drafting a constitution, and for this purpose, it must initiate rather than react.

Constitutional Challenges

5

SOCIAL RIGHTS

I. Introduction

In the international discourse of human rights, rights are usually divided into two groups. One group includes civil and political rights, such as freedom of expression, religion, and the right to property, and a second group includes social rights, or to be more precise: rights related to social welfare, such as housing, health, and education.

The latter group of rights is relatively new in the rights discourse. Many countries do not include these rights in their constitutions.[1] However, since the end of World War II, they have become the lot of at least some of the liberal democracies.[2] Nevertheless, even those countries that include welfare-related rights in their constitutions usually distinguish between these rights and civil and political rights. While civil an–d political rights are clearly spelled out in the constitution, and anyone who suffers an infringement of these rights can appeal to the court for help, social rights are usually formulated as an ultimate and general goal, and in some cases are not enforceable at the individual level, but rather implemented by the legislature or the executive branch, after having been anchored in an appropriate budgetary framework.[3]

A similar distinction between the two groups can be seen in international human rights documents. Here, they are divided among two different covenants: the covenant on civil and political rights, and the covenant on social, economic, and cultural rights.[4] The covenant on civil rights includes an enforcement mechanism in the protocol, which allows victims of the violations of human rights to file complaints against signatories to the protocol who violated their rights.[5]

By contrast, the covenant dealing with social rights lacks teeth, and primarily includes mechanisms of periodic reports examining the state of affairs in countries signed on to the protocol.[6] Moreover, while the covenant on civil rights imposes an immediate obligation on member states to "respect and ensure" human rights for all,[7] the very obligation of states signed onto the covenants on social rights is subject to two reservations: it is conditioned on the amount of resources at the country's disposal, and its implementation is meant to be gradual. In addition, the covenant leaves it up to the member states to decide how to proceed toward fulfilling the goals of the covenant.[8]

The difference between the two groups of rights can be attributed to two possible reasons. According to one explanation, there is no essential difference between the two groups. The inferior status of social rights derives solely from the fact that they are newer to the international rights discourse.[9] If this explanation is accurate, we should assume that the coming years will witness the strengthening of these rights, which will be expressed in the increased readiness of the Court to intervene and enforce their implementation.

According to the other explanation, the reason social rights are not included in some of the constitutions, and are not enforced in the same manner and to the same extent as civil and political rights, is a principled one, deriving from the essential difference between the two groups of rights. In this context, arguments are made regarding both the degree to which social interests fit into the framework of rights or constitutional rights,[10] and the degree to which it is appropriate or legitimate that they be enforced by the judicial system.[11] In our discussion here, we will not lay out all the arguments and counterarguments on the question of whether the two groups of rights should be made equal. I will, instead, suffice with a description of the developments that have occurred over the years regarding the approach of the Israeli Supreme Court on the matter (Section II of this chapter), and a (cautious) attempt to try and predict the future (Section III).

Another question that occupies writers in the field regards the influence of litigation and judicial intervention on the actual situation in reality. There are those who argue that the attempt to lead to social changes via the Court is doomed to failure, and that the effort to bring change should focus on the legislature and public discourse. This is an empirical question, and to answer it would require an extensive comparative study, with due attention to institutional and cultural differences between the legal systems surveyed and the rapid development of the legal and judicial involvement in the field.

Here, too, I will suffice with a modest contribution. In Section IV of this chapter, I will present a test case: a series of rulings—in the field of integrating children with special needs into the regular education system—in which the Court revealed quite a bit of activism in enforcing a social right. I will argue that judicial intervention only led to a modest change, and we will propose a number of explanations for this.

II. A Move in Three Stages

Social rights are not enumerated in the written legal corpus in Israel, despite repeated attempts to anchor them in the constitution.[12] However, as described in Chapter 3 above, there are also a number of civil and political rights that are not enumerated in this corpus, and this did not prevent the Supreme Court from proposing to read them into the Basic Laws through interpretation, as a derivation of the right to dignity included in Basic Law: Human Dignity and Freedom. What is the position of the Supreme Court on social rights? Below, I will describe a number of central milestones in the formation of the Supreme Court's approach to the matter, from 1992 until today.

1. FIRST STAGE—REFUSAL TO RECOGNIZE THE CONSTITUTIONAL STATUS OF SOCIAL RIGHTS

In his book *Constitutional Interpretation,* which was published in 1994, soon after the passing of Basic Law: Human Dignity and Freedom, Aharon Barak discussed, as an academic, the question of non-enumerated rights, as part of his discussion of the right to dignity.

Barak presented three possible approaches. The first, a limiting approach, interprets the right to dignity in the sense of absence of humiliation. A second, an expanding approach, interprets the right as including all human rights: civil and political, as well as social. A third approach, which Barak calls an "intermediate approach," interprets the right to dignity as including all the civil and political rights, but not the social rights. Of the three, Barak chose the intermediate route. His justification for this was that interpreting the Basic Law as including social rights would be too expansive.[13]

Calling an approach that includes all civil and political rights within the right to dignity—including rights deliberately omitted from the Basic Law—an "intermediate option" is odd. This is a daring and far-reaching interpretation, which would be better described as a "very expansive interpretation."

Some would argue that Barak's decision to call this approach "intermediate" derives from a strategic consideration. One way to hide the radicalism of this approach and present it as moderate is to propose and reject an even more expansive interpretation, which includes social rights within the right to dignity. In other words, it may be that Barak was not seriously considering interpreting the Basic Law as including social rights, but only raised the option in order to justify the inclusion of the missing civil and political rights in the Basic Law. Either way, Barak's reservations about reading social rights into the right to dignity affected the rulings of his fellow judges. A good example of this is the opinion of Justice Theodor Orr in the ruling regarding *Friends of GILAT*.

The Friends of GILAT association operated an educational enrichment program, which focused on children diagnosed as normal, who were born into a family situation involving serious economic difficulties. The aim of the program was to bring the children to a point where they could normally integrate into society, both socially and intellectually. For a number of years, the state supported the association's activity. At a certain point, the state decided to withdraw its support, and the association petitioned the Supreme Court against the decision. The petitioners argued, inter alia, that the state's decision seriously infringes the basic right to education of the children belonging to this group, and they wished to anchor this right in a number of sources, including Basic Law: Human Dignity and Freedom.

Justice Orr—who wrote the primary opinion in the case—noted that "education is a social tool the importance of which cannot be exaggerated," but stated that "this does not require the conclusion that Israeli law includes a constitutional right to education." Orr explained that "a constitutional right requires constitutional anchoring. Basic Law: Human Dignity and Freedom does not explicitly anchor the right to education. The argument, according to which the framework of the human right to dignity includes the right to education, assumes a 'broad model' in the interpretation of the right to dignity, which leads to significant difficulty . . . Therefore, we cannot derive the existence of a constitutional right to education from the right of people to dignity."[14] The two other members of the panel, Justices Tal and Dorner, explained that the conduct of the Ministry of Education met the threshold of reasonableness, and they therefore did not see a need to make a determination on the question of the right to education.[15]

Justice Orr's opinion has been subject to academic criticism. The criticism focused less on the very refusal to read the right to education into the Basic Law, and more on the unjustified connection made by Justice Orr between the question of its anchoring in the Basic Law and the question of the right's constitutional status.[16] The critics argued, justifiably, that certain rights enjoyed a constitutional status even before the passing of the Basic Laws, and this status is preserved even if they were not enshrined in them.

As I explain in Chapter 3, the difference between rights included in the Basic Laws and unenumerated rights has to do mainly with the possibility of attacking primary legislation. However, as the critics noted, primary legislation was not under discussion in this case, but rather an administrative decision. To repeal it, the petitioners had no need to anchor the right to education in any Basic Law.

2. SECOND STAGE—RECOGNITION WITHOUT "TEETH"

Israeli academic discourse on human rights has voiced criticism of the post-Constitutional Revolution Supreme Court's tendency to protect the rights of the rich and ignore the rights of the poor, at least per the critics. They argue that Supreme Court justices adhere to a libertarian worldview, and that this can be seen in their rulings.[17]

Barak's proposal in his book to include civil and political rights in Basic Law: Human Dignity and Freedom, but not social rights, provided a degree of support for this criticism. Respecting social rights would require the state to put its hand into the citizens' pockets and create a system of transfer payments from rich to poor. This would also require the expansion of the administrative mechanism and the increased intervention of the state in economic life. These steps are not favored by advocates of the free market, located on the right wing of the social-economic map. If the court is indeed identified with a right-wing socioeconomic view, it will obviously not be interested in anchoring social rights in the constitution.

It may be that this fierce criticism influenced the Court,[18] and it may be that it was simply the result of a re-examination of the issue, but at a certain point, sometime at the end of the 1990s, Barak changed his opinion on the matter. In a series of rulings, he expressed his opinion in a number of obiter dicta that certain social rights are included in the right to dignity. The primary right that Barak upgraded was the right to minimal living conditions.[19] Barak did explain that the extent of the social rights included in the right to dignity is more limited than it could be if the rights were included in the constitution as independent rights,[20] but this reservation cannot hide the clear change in Barak's position on the question of the status of these rights.[21]

Did the change in Barak's position also lead to a practical change in the Court's rulings? Some have responded in the negative, presenting as evidence the way the Court handled a series of appeals against various stipend cuts carried out by the political system. In the *Manor* case, the petitioners argued against the decision to cut old-age stipends. The argument was that the cut would lead some of the elderly to drop below the threshold of minimal living conditions. The Court rejected the appeal. It did assume that the right to minimal living conditions enjoys constitutional status, but stated that the test of whether any cut harms the right to minimal living conditions should be carried out after all the existing transfer mechanisms are taken into account, especially the income supplement stipend—a stipend the declared purpose of which is to ensure every citizen makes a minimal amount. Since the petitioners did not calculate all the relevant elements, they also did not prove their argument that cutting old-age stipends harms the right to minimal living conditions.[22]

The social organizations got the message. The next petition filed on the issue, by Commitment to Social Peace and Justice, was aimed at an amendment to the National Insurance Law, which significantly cut the income supplement stipend. In response to the petition, the state recognized the constitutionality of the right to minimal living conditions, but argued that the right was not harmed under those circumstances. The original panel that deliberated on the petition was headed by Justice Dalia Dorner. Dorner issued a show cause order instructing the state to explain the level of overall income required to respect the right at the time of the petition.[23]

The injunction led to a great deal of uproar in the political system. It was argued that the Court was overstepping its boundaries and intervening without authority in matters given to the judgment of the political system. A week after the injunction was handed down, the Knesset held a discussion on the matter, sending out the following message: "The Knesset views with great concern the slide of the court into areas which are clearly within the authority of the executive and legislative branches ... [The Knesset] warns of the continuation of this trend, which may develop into a constitutional crisis in Israel."[24]

While the petition was still pending, Justice Dorner retired and was replaced by Justice Barak on the case. Barak "climbed down" the ladder Dorner had ascended, exempted the state from the obligation to get down to numbers, and rejected the petition. In the ruling, which was given in an expanded panel of seven justices, Barak repeated his principled recognition of the constitutional status of the right to minimal living conditions. He also repeated the principle he laid down in the previous affair, that is, the argument that the claim of harm to the right must be based on a detailed and exacting examination of the specific petitioner's sources of income. Barak also stated that the petitioners once again did not bring enough evidence to establish their argument, even though the petition was aimed at the income supplement stipend, entitlement to which is supposed to be established after factoring in the recipient's sources of income.[25]

The significance of the requirement of this "concrete" proof was that every case would be judged on its own merits, and all petitioners must prove that they themselves, personally, were so badly harmed that they cannot live with dignity. Some claimed that Barak thus emptied the right of any meaning.[26] The demand placed procedural barriers before petitioners, as they were now obligated to lay out their life stories, their income and expenses, efforts to find work, and so on, even before the Court discussed their petition. The demand for concrete proof also possibly implied that even if the petitioners overcame all these obstacles and proved harm to their ability to live with dignity—it would still be doubtful if the Court could repeal a law because of this individual case, or will, at most, provide succor for the individual petitioner and no more.

The criticism launched at the Court was therefore that although it recognized the constitutional status of the rights to minimal and dignified living standards in principle, it effectively became the wrong address for protecting that right, in light of the detailed path laid down to prove harm to that right. Indeed, despite President Barak's invitation at the end of his ruling for additional petitions regarding the issue of income supplements for retired citizens,[27] such petitions were not actually filed.

3. THIRD STAGE—ENFORCING THE RIGHT TO MINIMAL LIVING STANDARDS

In the previous section, we described how the Supreme Court began to adopt a rhetoric of recognition of the importance of social rights at the end of the 1990s and onward, declaring their inclusion in basic Right: Human Dignity and Freedom. However, it still wasn't clear how much this was an expression of real commitment on the Court's part to enforce such rights.[28] Recent years have seen the first signs of a new development, in which the Supreme Court is not just establishing the constitutional status of social rights, but also giving them practical expression in its rulings. Below we will describe the ruling in the *Hassan* case, which marks out this trend.[29]

In the *Hassan* case, the Income Supplement Law was once again on the agenda.[30] This time, the petitioners argued against the constitutionality of an article in the law, which stated that those who own or use a vehicle are considered to have income at the level of the income supplement, and they and their family are therefore denied eligibility to this stipend. The central argument of the petitioners was that the pre-emptory judgment made by the article constituted unconstitutional harm to the right to live with dignity.

In response to the appeal, the state made two central arguments:

1. The aforementioned article constitutes "pure" socioeconomic policy by the legislator, and therefore does not at all fall under the limited parameters of the right to live with dignity.

2. Constitutional analysis should distinguish between civil-political rights and social rights, and in regard to the latter—the proportionality test should be limited to the first sub-test, which examines if there is a rational connection between means and goals.

The Court rejected both arguments. It stated that the state attributes "narrow and limited significance to the right," and therefore rejected the state's interpretation. As for the respondents' argument regarding the distinction between social rights and civil and political rights, the Court further stated that the very fact that the right to live with dignity is a social right does not justify applying a different judicial model for constitutional review.

In light of this statement, the Court applied the right to dignity based on the two-stage constitutional model of examination, used regarding all rights, stressing that the place for consideration of budgetary requirements was at the second stage of the constitutional examination. In the framework of this constitutional analysis, the Court arrived at the conclusion that the aforementioned article does not meet the second test of proportionality, and therefore a tool that causes less harm to the right must be used. The Court explained the difficulty in that the rule established by the article is preemptory, leading to the complete denial of the stipend from anyone who owns or uses a car.[31]

The primary innovation in the ruling is that this is the first time in which the Supreme Court repealed primary legislation after having found that it unjustifiably harms a social right. The Court did so by fundamentally changing its approach in the matter of *Commitment* noted above, according to which proof of harm to dignity must be focused solely on specific, individual cases.[32] In addition to the innovation in the "bottom line," the ruling has a number of significant statements regarding the importance of the right to a minimum of dignified human existence, at the center of which is the statement that it should not be seen as a right derived from the right to human dignity, but rather "it should be seen as a right which constitutes *a tangible expression* human dignity," and that this right "is embedded deep inside the core of the constitutional right to dignity."[33]

Since the decision of the Court in the *Hassan* case, there was another case where the Court demonstrated readiness to provide operative succor in the name of protection of social rights.[34] In the case of *Kav La'Oved*, the petition revolved around the health insurance arrangements of work migrants living in Israel for long periods of time.

In general, the entitlement of work migrants to health insurance is handled separately from the arrangement applying to Israel's citizens and residents by force of the National Insurance Law. The order issued by force of the designated law on the issue determines the extent of the "health basket" granted to a work migrant, which will be provided to him as part of the insurance that the employer must purchase for them.

This "health basket" is different from the legally established arrangement for Israel's citizens and residents in two main respects: the arrangement is private, and based on the purchase of insurance from the employer, and in addition—the basket itself is smaller. The Supreme Court accepted the petition and ordered the state to provide a more beneficial arrangement for this group, among the rest, because the partial coverage harms the right to health, which derives from the right to human dignity.[35]

Despite the importance of this ruling in the matter of *Kav La'Oved*, it seems that its innovation is limited in scope in comparison to the *Hassan* ruling, for two main reasons: First, while the court repealed a Knesset law in the *Hassan* case, the *Kav La'Oved* case involved secondary legislation. Second, while the *Hassan* case involved the Court imposing an obligation on the state, in the matter of *Kav La'Oved* it left the issue of whether to impose the insurance obligation and subsequent costs on the state or the employers up to the judgment of the authorities.[36]

III. Quo Vadis?

So far, we've described the process of the Supreme Court from refusal—or at least hesitation—to grant social rights a constitutional status, to a state of readiness to grant them such a status at the declarative level, without giving such a statement "teeth," and ending with the repeal of primary legislation, after finding that it unjustifiably harms the right for minimal living standards.

However, while most judges view the move favorably, and are even effusive with their obiter dicta supporting additional expansion of social rights, there are judges who have reservations about this trend, and warn of what they see as an unrestrained intrusion on the part of the judicial branch into the other branches of government. We will describe these two approaches below, and then see just how much the opposition's concerns are justified.

I. THE FAVORABLE VIEW

As noted, the Supreme Court recognized the constitutional status of minimal living standards as the derivative of the right to dignity enumerated in Basic Law: Human Dignity and Freedom, and even repealed an article in a law after it found it caused unjustifiable harm to this right. However, the question to be asked is the extent of this constitutional derivative right. Many judges interpret this right expansively, in two ways: placing the threshold for minimal and dignified living at a relatively high level, and interpreting the right as including additional components, each representing additional social rights. There is a plethora of obiter dicta on this matter. We will try and focus on the most important of these below.

A limiting interpretation of the right to a minimal standard of living in the area of nutrition would suffice with preventing hunger or malnutrition. However, a number of obiter dicta have offered a more expansive interpretation, aiming to ensure that the individual "can realize their freedom as a human being."[37]

This interpretation requires all individuals to have enough food so as not to be regularly concerned about where they will find their next meal, as those who are occupied with securing the conditions of their survival cannot be free to choose additional goals and work to achieve them. By the way, it can be that the difference between the two aforementioned interpretations of the right to minimal living standards is based on a different understanding of the right to dignity, from which the right to minimal living standards is derived: the limiting interpretation sees dignity as the reverse of humiliation, while the more expanding one sees it as being connected to freedom of choice and autonomy.

In many obiter dicta, judges include not just food supply in minimal living standards, but also other basic human needs, and they also propose an expansive interpretation of those needs beyond the necessary minimum. For instance, it is suggested that the right to minimal living standards includes the right to housing, with an emphasis on this not meaning just a roof over one's head, but also a residence in which the individual can "realize their privacy and family life."[38] The same passage mentions the right to health, which is interpreted not just as the right to receive "medical care in emergency cases,"[39] but the reception of health services "to the extent that they fall under the definition of the necessary minimum level for minimal human existence in society."[40] In short, the interpretation adopted by the Court regarding all the components included in the right to a minimal dignified existence is relatively expansive, and it wishes to ensure a standard of living for an individual, which "would enable them to make their choices and realize their freedoms."[41]

Even if the right to a dignified minimal existence includes many components in addition to the nutritional one, such as housing and medical treatment, it is not clear that all members of the family of social rights can be included in this framework.[42] The favor most judges express toward the idea of granting a constitutional status for social rights is therefore expressed in the readiness to derive social rights from the right to dignity directly, and not just by including them in the right to dignified minimal existence. Particularly prominent in this context is the right to education, the attitude to which underwent a change, perhaps even a revolution, since Justice Orr's reservations in the *Friends of GILAT* case.[43]

2. THE CRITICAL STANCE

While Supreme Court justices tend toward raising social rights to the level of civil and political rights, as well as the extent of judicial review in their regard to that applied in the case of civil and social rights, there are Supreme Court justices who take a more critical view. This position was, for instance, adopted by Supreme Court President Asher Grunis in his ruling in the *Rubinstein* case.[44] In this case, the petitioners wished to repeal the Unique Cultural Educational Institutions Law, which allowed the state to grant private Haredi educational institutions 60 percent of standard state high school funding without conditioning it on learning a core curriculum in their studies. The Court rejected the petition for various reasons. For our purposes, what's important is certain parts of Justice Grunis's ruling.

Grunis explained that "we are dealing with the obligation imposed on the state, per the petitioners, to enforce a core curriculum on the Haredi student in these classes, in order to prevent future harm to the dignity of the student. This is a 'positive' aspect of the right to education or the right to dignity, as it involves imposing an obligation on the governmental authorities to take active steps 'in favor' of the individual."[45] Grunis believed that the Court should show a great deal of restraint in applying judicial review involving harm to a positive right—beyond the usual restraint shown by the Court regarding judicial review of primary legislation—offering a number of justifications for this position, as follows:

> First, obligating the governmental authority to protect a positive right takes an accompanying active action, usually, in imposing a budgetary burden on the state. Considerations of budgetary policy, which often involve matters of economic expertise and broad social budgetary policies, are a matter given to the legislative and executive branches, and judicial intervention therein should be restrained ... Second, often judicial review done due to the claim of harm to social rights, involves social and even political considerations, which would be better left to the decision of the legislator ... Third, it seems that there is usually a difference in the extent of judicial intervention, between a case in which the court orders an authority to avoid carrying out a particular activity (or stop carrying it out), and a case in which the court orders an authority to carry out a particular activity. In general, we can say that granting a judicial injunction in which a governmental authority is obligated to take an active step, limits

the authority's freedom of action to a greater degree than a judicial injunction prohibiting it from taking a specific action.[46]

3. ARE THERE GROUNDS FOR THE CRITICS' FEARS?

The fears raised by President Grunis echo some of the common arguments in academic and political discourse among opponents regarding the equation of social rights to civil and political rights.[47] As noted above, this chapter focuses on describing the situation in Israel, and does not get into the global debate on the principled issues. Therefore, I shall not address Grunis's concerns at the principled level below, and instead suffice with their examination in relation to Israeli reality. I shall argue that even if these fears are grounded in reality, their relevance in the Israeli context is mistaken. This is because, despite the favorable statements made by judgments regarding social rights, the effective extent of the Court's intervention in the actions of the other branches of government in their name is quite minimal.

Let's take a look at the *Hassan* case, for instance. As noted, this case is considered a breakthrough compared to the previous *Commitment* case, in the sense that in *Hassan*, a component of the Income Supplement Law was repealed, something that the Court refused to do in the previous case. However, taking a closer look, we will see that the difference in the Court's handling of the two cases is not so clear-cut. In the *Commitment* case, the petitioners and the state disagreed as to where the proper level of minimum income should be placed, which determined entitlement to the income supplement stipend, and the Court avoided intervening in the dispute. By contrast, in the *Hassan* case, there was no real dispute between the petitioners and the state regarding the extent of the right, so much as on the question of the legitimacy of imposing a preemptory rule according to which use of a vehicle, including partial use, denies the right to a stipend, as it serves as an indication that the user's economic condition is better than what that person's dry income data would suggest.

All the Court did in *Hassan* was to repeal the aforementioned rule. Indeed, in its attempt to reject the petition, the state argued that use of a car is in and of itself a form of luxury, which places the user above the bottom threshold, and this argument was rejected by the Court,[48] but nowhere in the ruling did the Court deal directly with the question of the scope of the right to minimal, dignified living, or state any findings on the matter. This means that to the extent that President Grunis's concern regarding the expansion of recognition of the constitutional status of social rights is based on a fear that this could lead to judicial intervention in determining economic policy, the Supreme Court ruling in *Hassan* does not provide a real basis for that fear.

This impression becomes stronger when one compares the conduct of the Court, this time in the Commitment to Social Peace and Justice case, with the parallel conduct of the German Federal Constitutional Court in a similar case, in which the constitutionality of a stipend cut was discussed (this stipend being the equivalent of Israel's income supplement). The German court disqualified the cut after finding that the procedure that led to the decision on cutting the stipends was flawed, in the sense that the collection of information, which served as the basis for setting the minimal level of existence, was deficient.[49]

The procedural review track, which the German court decided to use, is modest in terms of judicial intervention in the decisions of the political system compared to the essential review track. The demand raised by Justice Dorner toward the state, in the early stages of deliberations in the *Commitment* case, to clarify why a clear standard should not be established for the purpose of maintaining minimal living standards, was similar to that of the German court, in that it focused on the procedural level. The fact that the panel headed by President Barak decided to retreat from the demand raised by Dorner, despite its procedural character, strengthens the impression that the Supreme Court is averse toward intervening in matters of social rights.[50]

Another reason that the danger (from Grunis's perspective) of judicial intervention in setting economic policy is not significant has to do with the commonly accepted socioeconomic approach in Israel. From the time the state was established until the political upheaval in 1977, Israel was governed by a party with a left-wing worldview regarding socioeconomic affairs. Accordingly, Israeli legislation regarding matters of welfare took on a clearly socialist character, in the spirit of the dominant party. To ensure a minimum of living standard for all citizens of the state, including those who cannot make enough for a living, the state established a mechanism of social security, which was anchored in law.[51] In addition, Israeli citizens enjoyed health and education services funded almost entirely by the government.[52] In a state where entitlement to minimal living standards is anchored in primary legislation, the possibility of the "danger" that the Court will use the constitutional weapon to intervene in the state's policy is dependent on the Court's readiness to raise the constitutional threshold beyond the standard of ensuring minimum living standards, already anchored in law.

The likelihood that the Court will demonstrate such readiness is not high. We can see this in the dispute that emerged between the majority and minority positions in the *Commitment* case. Justice Edmund Levi, in a minority opinion, proposed accepting the petition, adopting an interpretation according to which every citizen has the right to *suitable* living standards.[53] The majority opinion led by Justice Barak rejected Levi's proposal, stating that the right, which derives from the right to dignity, grants an entitlement to *minimal* living standards only. President Barak explained that it's true that the refusal to accept the expanding approach is not a principled one, but rather one embedded in the fact that Israel has not anchored social rights in the constitution in an explicit manner, and instead established them as derivatives of the right to dignity, a fact that requires taking a relatively narrow view of those rights.[54] However, the important thing for our purpose is not the reason for the Court's refusal to adopt an expansive interpretation of social rights, but (primarily) the fact that as a result of this refusal, the likelihood that the Court will intervene in distributionist decisions made by the political system is narrowed.

Some may argue that despite the advanced social legislation in Israel, the "danger" of judicial intervention in economic matters is not negligible due to the process characterizing the Israeli economy in the past few decades of cutting the level of basic social services provided by the state.[55] Alongside this cut, a free market of services offered at full price has emerged in certain fields, and these services complement those granted by the government.[56] The cut in social services provided by the State of Israel to its citizens is accompanied (and perhaps also caused by) a process in which the state delegates responsibility for the provision of services it once gave directly to private parties, an action known as "outsourcing."[57] Prima facie, the handing over of responsibility to private parties to provide such services does not have to mean any cut in services or the passing-on of the cost of the services to the citizens. However, in practice, these are common side effects of outsourcing. Some argue that the cut in social services and the handing over of responsibility for some of them to private hands deepens economic gaps in the country, and may lead the living standard of some of its citizens to deteriorate below the minimal threshold of living conditions. If they are right, this may invite judicial intervention using social rights as the tool, even with a relatively narrow interpretation thereof.

In my estimation, the likelihood that this scenario will happen is not high. As explained earlier, in the *Commitment* case, the Court avoided intervening in the decisions of the political system to cut the income supplement stipend, retreating from the injunction issued by Justice Dorner during the first stage of deliberations, which obligated the state to spell out the standard for minimal existence obligated by the Basic Law. The Court's avoidance in the *Commitment* case of even demanding that the state clarify its assumptions for its decision to cut the income supplement income attests to the excessive caution adopted by the Court when coming to deal in practice with the right to minimal living standards, and places a real obstacle before anyone who wishes to petition to the Court on any similar future cut.

If the Court was truly interested in preventing the erosion in social services provided by the state, or in transferring the economic burden involved in receiving them to the citizens, it could have done so by applying judicial review on the transfer of responsibility to provide these services to private hands, by imposing limitations on the sorts of services that can be outsourced, among other things. However, at least so far, the Court has tended not to intervene in outsourcing, and has avoided setting limits in this area.[58] Moreover, the one time the Court did repeal legislation concerning outsourcing, it did so in a case where there were good grounds to think that in this particular field, outsourcing would have improved social welfare rather than harming it.[59]

It should be noted that I am not taking a stand here on whether it is proper for the courts—in general and in Israel in particular—to intervene in the economic policy adopted by the other branches of government. All I am arguing is that despite the reams of obiter dicta written by Israeli Supreme Court justices in praise of social rights, the Court's conduct thus far does not point to activism in the socioeconomic arena. If I am right, it is reasonable to assume that the "danger" of real judicial intervention in setting Israel's socioeconomic agenda is not about to happen soon.

IV. Will Judicial Intervention Make a Difference?

So far, I have examined the attitude of the Israeli Supreme Court toward social rights, with the assumption being that judicial recognition of their constitutional status and the Court's readiness to force the state to honor those rights will significantly advance the protection of said rights. In this section I will question the correctness of this assumption. In his classic book *The Hollow Hope*, Gerald Rosenberg casts doubt on the effectiveness of judicial intervention in the field of rights in general, either civil or social.[60]

I will examine a more moderate stance, according to which even if judicial intervention in the field of *civil rights* might be effective, the odds of intervention in the field of *social rights* being successful are fairly limited.[61] First, we will examine a test case: a series of petitions in which the Supreme Court was asked to intervene and enforce the right of children with disabilities to integrate into regular educational frameworks. I will argue that despite the readiness of the Court to intervene, the actual result is far from being satisfactory. Afterward, I will propose two explanations for the relative failure of the struggle to secure the right via the Court, and argue that they are related to the positive character of the right in question.

1. THE HISTORY OF THE STRUGGLE TO INTEGRATE CHILDREN WITH DISABILITIES

The Special Education Law was passed in 1988, in the wake of an initiative of parents of disabled children, who were inspired by a similar existing law in the United

States.[62] Article 4(a) of the Israeli law states that "the state is responsible for providing free special education according to this law," whereas Article 7 states that when placing children with disabilities in educational institutions, preference will be given for their integration in regular educational frameworks over their placement in a school for special education (henceforth: integration).

Over time it turned out that the Ministry of Education, which was tasked with encouraging integration, was not funding the related expenses, and the burden subsequently fell on the parents. As a result, parents unable to bear those costs were forced to move their children, who were found fit to be integrated, to special needs schools. A petition to the Supreme Court was filed against this policy. It argued, inter alia, that the policy in question harmed the right of the children with disabilities to an education.

In its response to the petition, the state argued that the right to free special education, established in Article 4 of the law, can be realized only in a special needs school, while the extent of aid to children with special needs who were integrated into regular educational frameworks is an issue subject to discretion. The Court rejected the state's position, and stated that the correct interpretation of the law demonstrates that the right to free special education also applies to disabled children integrated into regular educational frameworks. The Court based this interpretation on the recognition of the right to education as a basic right, among other things.[63]

The ruling was handed down on August 14, 2002. On November 13, 2002, the Special Education law was amended in a manner that absorbed the Court's ruling, and obligated the state to also fund aid to disabled children integrated in the general education system.[64] The amendment was accepted even though the Knesset foresaw—as the law proposal itself even noted—that its implementation would be costly.[65] The Ministry of Finance asked to postpone the implementation of the amendment due to its costs, but the Knesset rejected the request.

It very quickly became apparent that despite the Court's ruling and legislative developments, the state had no intention of transferring the needed budgetary addition to implement the amendment. As such, a petition was filed to the Supreme Court, asking it to instruct the state to immediately fund the education of the children.[66] In its response to the petition, the state argued that the law allows the Minister of Finance to decide not to allocate the money needed to implement integration, as part of his budgetary discretion. The Court rejected the state's argument, inter alia, because this interpretation did not honor the right of disabled children to education. However, the Court limited its argument, and stated that in light of the additional cost of special education, the law only obligates the funding of aid whose absence would make it utterly impossible for the student to be integrated. Beyond this threshold, the state has the discretion to decide on the extent of the aid given based on educational-professional criteria.[67]

Was the goal achieved this time? Not really. The main cost incurred in the integration of disabled children in regular classrooms involves the employment of personal assistants. This was the basis for the decision, made by the Ministry of Education, to take the authority to allocate paid hours for assistants away from the school, and hand it over to a committee in the Ministry of Education. This decision was also petitioned, this time the argument being that the aforementioned policy effectively denies parents the option of integration if they cannot fund assistants privately.[68] The Court accepted the petition, and as a result, the regulations in the Ministry of Education were changed, so that the degree of entitlement to assistance ceased to be subject to budgetary considerations, and the authority to decide on the matter was returned to the integrating school.

Judicial involvement in the matter did not end there. In July 2007, another petition was filed, where it was argued that the state was violating the rulings of the Court that obligated it to devote an appropriate budget for integration.[69] The petition was rejected. The Court stated, as a factual finding, that the state gradually increased the budget allocated to integration, and that if this additional budget was not enough to fully implement integration, it allowed the gradual expansion of the extent of the services given, as well as the number of those entitled to them. Thus, the Court stated, the state met the minimal threshold established by the Court in the previous affair.[70]

Toward the end of the ruling, the Court added the following:

The determined public struggle of the petitioners is worthy of admiration. Their dedicated activity led to a process that brought about the legislation of the integration chapter in the Special Education Law, and the transfer of significant budgets for its implementation. Their struggle aided in raising the awareness of parents regarding the advantages of the integration program, and it brought the complex issue to the attention of decision makers. Later on, their work was one of the main reasons for the appointment [of a public committee], in which a reexamination was carried out on the manner of operation of the special education system and the distribution of the special education budget. This examination is not yet at an end, and the petitioners' journey is not over. This is a long and complex process, requiring the allocation of significant budgets that may lead to a real change in the structure of the special education system as a whole. It is worth noting that the implementation of such a change needs to be examined carefully and be carried out with the required caution.[71]

In pointing to the achievements produced by the petitioners' struggle, even if the full goal was not reached, the Court tried to appease the petitioners, and justify its refusal to grant their appeal. However, an impartial examination of the actual situation shows a different picture than that described by the Court.

In the annual report submitted by the State Comptroller in May 2013, a special chapter was devoted to "Integration of Students with Special Needs in the Regular Education Institutions." The report stated, among other things, that until 2012, some ten years after the amendment was passed, not only did the number of special needs children integrated in regular schools not increase, it actually declined from 66 percent to 54 percent. The Comptroller also found that the emphasis placed in 2002 on the value of integration in law and court rulings was not expressed in an increase in the resources devoted by the Ministry of Education to integrate children with special needs into the regular education system, in the sense that the relative portion devoted in the budget to special education by the Ministry in 2011 remained the same it had been a decade before. As a result, the financial burden of integration continued to fall largely on the parents of those special needs children.[72]

2. POSSIBLE EXPLANATIONS FOR THE (RELATIVE) FAILURE OF THE STRUGGLE

We have before us a case in which the Court intervened, time and again, in favor of the petitioners wishing to realize their children's right to education. Moreover, the right that the Court tried to enforce is enshrined in primary legislation, and the constitutional right to education serves only as a consideration in interpreting the law. Despite all this, at the end of the day, the right was either not realized or only very partially implemented. How can we explain this?

It seems that this has to do with the positive character of the law. Take note: the argument regarding the positive character of social rights is raised as part of the debate on the question of whether they should be equated to civil rights. Those who support doing so reject the attempt to distinguish between them on this basis, and argue that both types of rights impose limits on the state (negative demands) alongside positive obligations (positive demands).[73]

I need not decide the matter here, as the explanation I will propose for the relative failure of the judicial intervention in realizing the right of education for children with special needs is not based on the debate regarding the existence of a difference between civil rights and social rights, but rather on the argument regarding the ability of the Court to determine the extent of the obligation and enforce it when it comes to a negative aspect of a right, and its ability to do so regarding a positive aspect, regardless of the question of whether the right is a civil or social one.

Even if the explanation I offer for the failure of the struggle to realize the right will not focus on its belonging to the family of social rights, but rather that its realization required the state to take positive action, it will point to a certain connection between the two, and this for the following reason: even if the two types of rights— civil and social—have a positive dimension alongside a negative one, it seems clear that the frequency and weight of the positive dimension is significantly higher when it comes to realizing social rights as opposed to the demand for realizing civil and political ones.[74] If it is harder to determine the extent of the obligation and enforce it when it comes to positive rights, this will have a stronger effect in the field of social rights as opposed to civil rights.

As to the extent of the obligation, some argue that it is harder to define the extent of the obligation imposed by force of positive rights as opposed to defining the obligation imposed by force of negative rights. This is due to the fact that while the prohibition imposed on the state is clear in the case of negative rights, it is unclear how much the state is supposed to act to implement its positive obligations.[75]

Those who support imposing positive rights on the state may reject this distinction, and argue that the ambiguity of positive rights derives only (or primarily) from the lack of judicial deliberation on the matter. However, even if this argument is correct, and there is no inherent difficulty in determining a clear threshold for fulfilling a positive obligation, it appears that there is another difficulty in determining a clear threshold in the case of a positive right, regarding the ability to calculate the consequences that setting such a threshold will have.

Imposing a positive obligation has a budgetary significance, and on the assumption that the overall budget is not unlimited, every such decision will have lateral consequences for various needs (including additional positive rights), whose realization is also dependent on the existence of an appropriate budget. Of course, the imposition of negative obligations also has lateral effects; however, their extent is usually clearly defined, thus making it easier to calculate their effect. The aforementioned difficulty, so the argument goes, makes positive rights less appropriate for judicial enforcement.[76]

Whether the argument regarding a unique difficulty in calculating the consequences in enforcing social rights is analytically correct or not, it is, at the very least, clear that it is what stood at the basis of the Court's ruling in the *Alut* case. As noted, the Court's decision to reject the petition was based primarily on the determination that the state met the bottom threshold to which it was obligated. However, the Court excused its avoidance from intervening with another argument, according to which accepting the petition would lead to "a significant increase in the annual budgetary spending, which would necessarily come at the expense of other components in the state budget that are not subject to the court's review, and of which it is not even aware."[77] The Court explained that this work of balancing is given over—primarily—to the legislative and executive branches.

Thus far, we have proposed that the relative failure to realize the right of children with disabilities to an education was due to the hesitation of the Court to "go all the way," a hesitation derived from the positive character of the right. It is interesting to note that a similar thesis was proposed regarding the effective implementation of the right to housing, anchored in the constitution of South Africa.

In the famous *Grootboom* decision, the South African Constitutional Court held that the political branches in South Africa had violated the constitution by failing to develop a housing plan that would meet the immediate needs of the poorest people most in need of assistance, like the plaintiff. But the Court refused to order an individualized remedy for the plaintiff, such as an order that the state provide her with housing. Instead, the Court merely stated that the political branches had the obligation to "devise and implement a coherent, coordinated programme" and that a "reasonable" part of the total housing budget had to be reserved for those in desperate, immediate need of housing.[78]

The *Grootroom* ruling was enthusiastically adopted by many legal scholars. Mark Tushnet wrote that the Court constituted a new kind of judicial review, "weak form review," which allowed courts to judicially enforce these rights without involving them in complex public policy decisions or letting them run roughshod over the legislature.[79] However, a large group of scholars pointed out that this weak-form enforcement did not work: the legislature did not produce the plan that the Court ordered, and the case did virtually nothing to actually advance the right to housing.[80] More specifically, the claimant in the *Grootboom* case died homeless and penniless, some eight years after winning the case.[81]

The relative failure in realizing the right of disabled children, which was described above, can be attributed not only to the hesitation of the Court to give detailed and operative succor with regard to a positive right, but also because of the difficulty in enforcing that operative succor if and when the Court orders it. The implementation of a negative right requires the state not to act. By contrast, the realization of a positive right requires action, and it therefore suffers from the known limitations of the bureaucratic system. The fact that the aforementioned realization involved a substantial financial expense only adds additional incentive to avoid action, which derives from the desire (welcome in and of itself) of those charged with the public purse to reduce costs.

One of the explanations, proposed by Rosenberg in his book, for the limited success of the Court in advancing social goals, is the "lack of proactive tools required to order significant reform."[82] As we explained, the need for means to actively intervene is particularly relevant in enforcing decisions regarding positive rights. If the lack of such means weakens the effectiveness of judicial decisions in the field of human rights in general, this is particularly true regarding positive rights.

3. WHAT IS THE CONCLUSION?

So far, I offered two reasons for the relative failure of the struggle to enforce the right to education via the Court, arguing that both reasons are related to the positive nature of the claimed right. I also argued that positive rights are far more frequent in the social rights group than they are in the group of civil rights, and that therefore the odds that social rights will be realizable via the Court are lower compared to the odds of realizing civil rights. Even if we are correct, this does not mean that there is no point in using the Court to realize social goals, but that expectations from this venue should be lowered. Even if the Court granted social rights a constitutional status (which the Israeli Court did, in part), and even if it agrees to give them teeth (which it also did, in a limited manner), we should assume (and perhaps understand) the reticence of the Court to give the state precise operative instructions, and take into account that even those instructions it does give will only be partially implemented by the state bureaucracy.

6

BALANCING AND PROPORTIONALITY

I. The Old Balancing System and Its Deficiencies

The heart and soul of the constitutional legal procedure is the balancing stage. Human rights, important as they are, are not unlimited.[1] They sometimes conflict with one another, sometimes they conflict with public and private interests, and in all cases the right must be balanced against competing values. Every legal system has its balancing mechanisms. In Israel, the approach used to be that in a conflict between a human right and a public interest, a vertical balance must be struck between the two,[2] while in the case of a clash between rights, the balancing formula is horizontal.[3] A description of the two balancing formulas was presented by Supreme Court President Barak in *Dayan v. The Police Commissioner of Jerusalem*:

> In the "vertical balance", the one value—which clashes with the other value—has the upper hand. However, this superiority emerges only if the requirements of the balancing formula for the probability of harm to the superior value and its degree are met ... In the "horizontal" balance, the two clashing values are equal in status. The balancing formula examines the degree of mutual concession of each one of the rights.[4]

The importance of the choice between the two possible balancing formulas cannot be exaggerated. A choice of the vertical formula leads to the complete adoption of one party, and the wholesale rejection of the other. By contrast, the horizontal formula requires a compromise between the two parties, where neither party receives full satisfaction, while on the other hand neither is entirely rejected.

In a past article, I argued that the a priori adoption of vertical balance in cases of conflict between rights and interests is problematic. I argued that even if the two sides do not have equal status, they still represent two worthy values. It is therefore hard to understand why compromise is ruled out when a right clashes with an interest, and where one party (usually the right, rather than the interest) simply defeats the other. Why doesn't the court seek the path of compromise, even in cases of a conflict between a right and an interest, so that neither side is forced to entirely concede?

A similar critique on the a priori division between vertical and horizontal balancing was made by Professor Yitzhak Zamir, who wondered whether it is "possible and proper to draw a line between two types of values that overcome each other, and types of values that must concede to one another. Ostensibly, in any conflict between two values recognized by law, even if they are different in weight, an effort must first and foremost be made to ensure the coexistence of the two values alongside one another. The question regarding the preference of one of the values over the other arises only if the efforts for the coexistence of the two values do not succeed."[5] It is interesting to note that even President (ret.) Barak—who is largely responsible for creating the distinction between vertical and horizontal balancing—accepted Zamir's approach, at least in one ruling. In the *Reem* case, which discussed the conflict between freedom of expression and the interest of preserving the Hebrew language, Barak said as follows:

> Sometimes the conflicting values are not of equal status. The court must determine ... the extent to which the superior value was harmed and what the probability of that harm is, which would justify the preference of the one over the other ("vertical balancing"). Here, too, we must make every effort to prevent the direct clash, while determining the required mutual concessions. But lacking any possibility of reconciling the conflicting values, there is no avoiding granting preference ... to the one value over the other.[6]

II. The New Balancing System

The two Basic Laws adopted in Israel in 1992—Basic Law: Human Dignity and Freedom, and Basic Law: Freedom of Occupation—include a limitation clause that sets conditions that must be met to allow harm to the rights enumerated in them. In the framework of the limitation clause, a new, balancing formula was adopted: *proportionality*, which was interpreted by the Court as including three subtests, as is common in other countries:[7] the *suitability* or *appropriateness* (rational connection) test, according to which the means that harm the right be appropriate for the promotion of the purpose of the offending norm; the *least restrictive means* (necessity) test, according to which it will be seen whether there is another means available to promote the purpose, which harms the right to a lesser degree; and the *proportional result* (proportionality sensu stricto) test, which requires an adequate congruence between the harm to the right and the benefit in promoting the purpose.[8]

Ostensibly, the test of proportionality applies only to those rights included in the framework of the Basic Laws, but the Court expanded their application and applied them to unenumerated rights as well.[9] Moreover, in a number of obiter dicta, the Court proposed applying the limitation clause (including the proportionality tests) to the instructions in the Basic Laws that do not explicitly refer to the limitation clause.[10] It can therefore be said that the tests of proportionality have replaced—or at least were supposed to replace—the old balancing formulas.

In an article where I pointed out the deficiencies of the old balancing formulas, I pointed to the fact that these deficiencies can be solved with a correct interpretation of the three tests of proportionality. I argued that one can read the proportionality tests as encouraging compromise, and this as part of the requirement, included in the second test of proportionality—that of least restrictive means—to examine various alternatives to realizing the proper purpose. I based my argument on the assumption that in the overwhelming majority of cases, the various alternatives for realizing the purpose will be distinct from each other not only in the degree to which they harm the protected right, but also in the degree to which each of them will realize the purpose. I proposed softening the necessity test and allowing the evaluation of such alternatives within its framework, despite the difference between them in their effectiveness in realizing the purpose. If this proposal is adopted, the necessity test would be read as a demand for balancing between the benefit component and the harm component contained within each of the alternatives, with the aim of choosing the alternative that best balances between the two. That way, the necessity test would become a compromise formula.

I justified this proposed interpretation of the necessity test not just based on the logic of including an element of compromise, but also based on the internal logic of the tests of proportionality. I argued that the necessity test would be meaningless unless *both* the component harming the right and the component realizing the purpose are treated as variables. This is because there are very few cases in which there would be different alternatives that would promote the purpose to precisely the same extent, and be distinguished from one another only by how much harm they cause the right. Moreover, even if there are entirely equal alternatives in terms of how they realize the purpose, the petitioners will usually not be able to prove that equivalence.[11] If the necessity test allows a comparison just between alternatives that realize the purpose equally, the result will be that the alternative chosen by the state will almost always pass this test of proportionality. The only way to therefore fill the necessity test with content is to examine within its framework alternatives that are distinguished not only by the degree to which they harm the right, but also the extent to which they realize the purpose.[12]

At first glance, one could argue that adopting the proposed interpretation for the second test of proportionality makes it the equivalent of the old horizontal balancing test described above, in which a compromise between the conflicting values *must* be found. However, there is, in fact, a clear difference between the proportionality tests and horizontal balancing. While horizontal balancing *requires* compromise, proportionality tests offer a more sophisticated and flexible approach, which *allows* the judge to compromise, but also leaves the door open for him to rule in favor of the right. The option of deciding is located in the third proportionality test—the proportional result test—which requires the court to consider the very legitimacy in harming the right, even according to the optimal compromise formula. In other words, the proportional result test allows the court to rule that even after the optimal compromise formula has been found, the degree of the realization of the interest, legitimate in and of itself, cannot be justified in light of the cost it exacts in terms of harm to the right, and therefore the right should be given full preference in the circumstances of the case. The location of the decisive result option at the end of the inquiry, rather than at its beginning, and its transformation from an a priori obligation (as it was with the vertical balancing) into merely an option, strengthen the odds that a judicial decisive result in the framework of proportionality tests will be better informed than the old vertical balance.[13]

The aforementioned proposal to include a component of compromise as part of the proportionality tests was adopted by the Israeli Supreme Court in a number of rulings, but with one change: the compromise component was not included in the second proportionality test, but in the third one. The Court did so in the *Beit Sourik* case—in which the Supreme Court disqualified most of the route of the separation barrier north of Jerusalem, after stating that in determining the route, the army commander did not properly balance between the contribution of this route to national security and the harm to the Palestinian residents in the area.[14] Another such case was the *Adala* case—in which Supreme Court President Barak (dissenting) disqualified the amendment to the Citizenship and Entry to Israel Law, which prevented the granting of citizenship to residents of the territories who married Arab citizens of Israel, due to it disproportionately harming the right to a family life and the principle of equality between Jews and Arabs.[15]

In both cases, security needs and human rights were balanced against each other. In both cases, Barak chose to disqualify the arrangement after stating that the state could have chosen a means that would significantly reduce the harm to rights, at the cost of minimal reduction in the realization of the purpose.[16] In both cases Barak preferred compromise, but he rejected the arrangement chosen by the military commander (in the first case) and the Knesset (in the second case), on the grounds that they did not choose a proper compromise. Yet, in both cases Barak placed the evaluation of various compromise options in the framework of the third subtest of proportionality, and not as part of the second test.

Supreme Court President Barak's choice, to use the proportional result test as the arena for checking compromise options, charged this test with two separate functions. The first function is a test in which the court accepts a certain alternative as a given, and *decides* whether to accept or reject it on the basis of a ranking of conflicting values. An example of the use of this function of the proportional result test can be found in *Adala v. Minister of Interior Affairs*,[17] where the Supreme Court nullified an article in the law, which stated that the state is not responsible for damage caused in a conflict zone due to any action taken by the security forces, including non-combatant actions. Regarding the third test of proportionality, the Court stated that the benefit to the public interest from denying the state's responsibility for harm committed by a non-"war action" is not proportionate to the harm caused those affected by it.

The second function, which Supreme Court President Barak added in both rulings, is that of "relative examination." According to this approach, the government's action is examined compared to a possible alternative, the effectiveness of which in advancing the purpose would be somewhat lesser. The government action will be considered disproportionate, according to this test, if this decline in the benefit gained from the action, by adopting the alternative approach, ensures a significant reduction in the harm caused by the government action.[18] For instance, in *The Association for Civil Rights in Israel v. The Central District Commander*,[19] the Court stated that the army may not destroy a terrorist's home for purposes of deterrence without first giving those who dwell there the right to petition against the demolition, but must instead suffice with sealing the house, even though this action somewhat harms the purpose of deterrence, as opposed to the immediate demolition thereof. This is a test that looks at many alternatives, and strives to find the option that reconciles the two conflicting values in the most effective manner.

Some have argued that Barak's interpretation of the proportional result test is a clear deviation from the principled approach of the Israeli Court, or indeed any other court.[20] Whether or not this argument is correct, those familiar with Barak's academic writing could have seen this coming. In a book that was published long before the rulings in question, Barak proposed including the two components in the third subtest:

> The harm is not required, despite the adaption of the means and its lesser harm, if the harm to a protected human right is severe, and the main aims of the proper purpose—even if not all of them—can be achieved with means whose harm to the protected human right is significantly lesser. If we can significantly avoid the severity of the harm, by making an insignificant concession in the realization of the proper purpose, this should be done.[21]

Barak's choice to place the evaluation of compromise possibilities within the framework of the third proportionality test has become the accepted approach in Supreme Court rulings. However, in recent years, there have been cases where judges preferred the second proportionality test as the place to examine compromise options. Such a case was the ruling of Justice Arbel in *Adam*.[22] As part of the government efforts to deal with the problem of the unprecedented infiltration of migrants from Africa into Israel, the Knesset amended the Law to Prevent Infiltration (Crimes and Punishment, in 2012, adding article 30a,[23] which allowed the holding of infiltrators who were issued an expulsion order in custody for a period of up to three years.

In the *Adam* ruling, the Supreme Court unanimously declared this article invalid, after stating that it harms the right to freedom and dignity, and that the means chosen to realize the purpose is not proportionate. Justice Arbel stated that the imprisonment of the infiltrators is not justified, since there is an alternative means for realizing the purpose, which harms human rights less—establishing a fence, which "may significantly aid the reduction of the infiltration phenomenon." In her ruling, Arbel referred to the possibility that erecting the fence would not realize the goal to the same extent as the means taken by the Knesset, but she noted that "in a situation in which the harm to freedom is so severe, the second sub-test requires that the state exhaust and examine a more reasonable and less harmful option, even if there is no certainty in its ability to achieve that goal to the same extent."[24] The other judges agreed with the result Arbel reached, but preferred to include a compromise option evaluation in the framework of the third test of proportionality.[25]

III. Compromise—Where Is It Preferred?

There are two possibilities for the placement of the compromise options evaluation in the framework of the proportionality tests. It can be placed within the framework of the least restrictive means test, or within the proportional result test. Is it important where this evaluation is placed, or does none of this matter, so long as the compromise options are ultimately looked at?

Guy Davidov holds that the compromise options examination should be placed within the framework of the third test.[26] This way, the distinction between the first two tests, which are formal in essence, and the third test, in which the court applies a value judgment, will be preserved.[27] In this manner, it is clear to the observer why the policy was struck down—whether it was a disqualification on the technical grounds of a mismatch between means to ends (as part of the first proportionality test), the technical reason of choosing a means that harms the right beyond what is necessary to realize the purpose to the extent desired by the political system (as part of the second proportionality test), or due to the court's rejection of the value decision made by the legislature or the executive authority (as part of the third proportionality test).

According to Davidov, the transference of the compromise component to the second test blurs the value element, in the sense that it creates the appearance that the policy was disqualified due to harm to a right beyond what was needed to realize the purpose—a technical decision in character—while the real reason is that the court believes that the balance between the two values needs to be a different one, so that while the purpose will be advanced somewhat less, the right will also suffer less harm—a value decision for all intents and purposes.

Moshe Cohen-Eliya prefers the second proportionality test as the proper arena for examining compromise options, even if this means turning this test from a formal one into a value-laden one. Cohen-Eliya notes that there is a significant difference, in terms of the amount of discretion given to the court, between a ruling that places the compromise between competing values at a difference point than the one chosen by the political system, and a ruling that is absolutely in favor of one value against the position of the political system. It is important to sharpen the difference between the two types of judicial intervention, by separating them into two different tests in the framework of proportionality: the intervention that moves the balancing point between conflicting values within the framework of the necessity test, and decisive intervention in favor of one of them within the framework of the proportionality sensu stricto test.

A second argument that was mentioned above in favor of placing the compromise options examination in the framework of the second subtest is that there are few cases where there are two alternatives that will equally advance the purpose, and even if they exist, it is very hard to prove this equivalence. Therefore, the insistence on referring to the dimension of the purpose in the framework of the necessity test as a constant will empty this test of meaning. Indeed, a survey of Israeli Supreme Court rulings—which, as noted, aside from some obiter dicta, interpreted the necessity test restrictively, as requiring a comparison only of those alternatives that realize the purpose in a manner equal to the arrangement chosen—teaches that this test almost never serves to disqualify laws or administrative actions.

A good example for the weakness of the second proportionality test—only including alternatives equal in effectiveness to the one chosen by the state—can be seen in the series of rulings given in the petitions against various parts of the route of the separation barrier. As noted above, in the *Beit Sourik* case, the Court disqualified the route taken, after finding that it does not meet the "relative examination," which President Barak read into the third test of proportionality. However, in that case, as well as the overwhelming majority of other petitions filed against the route of the fence, it was stated that the route taken by the military commander crosses the threshold set by the necessity test. As Gershon Gontovnick notes, this result was almost inevitable, as when the petitioners presented alternatives to the route of the barrier that harmed human rights less, the problem of institutional competence made it hard for the Court to determine whether these realize the purpose to the same degree as the alternative chosen.[28]

Moreover, even in the few cases in which the Court declared the disqualification of arrangements on the grounds that they fail the necessity test, it would seem that this was due to the "unofficial" adoption of the expansive interpretation of this test— in which alternatives that realize the purpose to a lesser extent than the arrangement chosen by the state are also examined—in the sense that the examination of the alternative whose existence led the Court to disqualify the chosen arrangement leads one to question whether the adoption of this alternative would truly have realized the purpose to the same extent.[29]

For instance, in the *Israel Investment Managers Association* case, the Court examined the constitutionality of a law that imposed a license obligation for those involved in managing investment portfolios.[30] The law set a number of conditions for receiving a license, including passing a number of tests, and only exempted investment managers with a seniority of more than seven years at the time the law was passed. The Supreme Court stated that the purpose of the law—protecting the investing public—is proper, but that an exemption based on seven years' seniority did not meet the necessity test, as the purpose of the law could also have been realized with a lower threshold for an exemption. However, it can be speculated whether the alternative to an exam based on shorter work experience would necessarily realize the purpose of the law to the same extent.

Another example of this trend can be seen in the *Adala* case, in which the Supreme Court nullified a law that exempted the state from responsibility for damages caused in a conflict zone, even when they were not the result of war-related activity.[31] The Supreme Court stated that the purpose of this arrangement—removing the damages caused during combat from the normal purview of civilian torts—is proper. Nevertheless, the Court held that the arrangement does not pass the necessity test, since its purpose could have been realized even if the state had exempted itself only from damages caused by war-related activities. It is doubtful that the aforementioned alternative would have realized the purpose of the law to the same extent, as it would require that each and every case be examined to see if it falls under the definition of war-related activity, something that the Court itself admitted creates "problems of proof."[32]

A third reason for the preference of the proposal to place the compromise options examination in the framework of the second subtest lies in the importance of both the questions asked as part of the balancing, and the order in which they are asked. It is important that variations of compromise options between the right and the purpose be examined before the decisive option is looked at. The refusal to pay any price in terms of harm to a right is far more convincing after the various concrete costs of compromise proposals have already been looked at. Tying the examination of compromise options to the examination of the decisive option in the third test raises the fear that the examination itself will go awry. A separation between the two, and the placement of the examination of compromise as part of the second subtest, before examining the possibility of a decisive result in the framework of the third subtest, ensures that the evaluation will be carried out in the proper order.

A last argument in favor of preferring the second proportionality test to the third, as the place for the compromise options evaluation, is that it will make the proportionality tests appropriate for examining conflicts between a right and an interest, as well as conflicts between rights.

As discussed at the beginning of this chapter, the need to balance between conflicting values awakens not only in cases where interests are pitted against rights, but also in those in which rights stand in tension with each other. A common example of this is the conflict between freedom of expression and the press, and the right to privacy and human dignity (such as in the context of the publishing of the names of criminal suspects). The position presented by some of the Supreme Court justices on the matter is that the limitation clause, with its proportionality tests, does not apply in the case of a conflict between rights, only in a conflict between rights and interests.[33]

Justices Barak and Dorner, who expressed this position, did not clearly explain their reasons.[34] It appears that there is at least one textual reason for the restrictive interpretation, which lies in the requirement included in the second proportionality test to ensure that the harm to the right not be more than what is needed to realize the goal. This requirement is understandable when right and interest collide, as then the will to prevent excessive harm to a right is obvious. However, when two conflicting rights are on the agenda, the requirement for lesser harm ostensibly grants preference to one right over the other, without real justification. The mismatch between the test formula, which ostensibly points to a difference between conflicting rights, and the reality of two rights of equal value, is what apparently led Justices Barak and Dorner to reject the proportionality tests as an appropriate balancing formula for the conflict between the two rights.

A similar formulation of the dilemma can be found in the words of Prof. Dieter Grimm, a retired justice of the German Federal Constitutional Court:

> Private law relationships . . . are symmetrical: both individuals have fundamental rights. Private law legislation therefore will often require a reconciliation of two competing private interests, both of which are protected by fundamental rights. This means that the protection of the endangered right can be ensured only by a limitation of other constitutionally protected rights. In such a situation, the question posed in step 2, whether a limitation of a fundamental right went too far, cannot be answered without asking whether the protection given to the endangered right was sufficient.[35]

According to Grimm, Germany solved the problem by skipping over the second subtest and moving directly to the third.[36] In this manner, the need to grant preference to one of the conflicting rights ostensibly deriving from the language of the second test was bypassed. However, this is not the only way to adapt the proportionality tests to situations of clashes between rights. One can also overcome the problematic equation of the second proportionality test in the manner proposed here, by adopting a flexible interpretation of the test, which makes it into one of complete compromise. If the framework of the necessity test will involve the examination not just of options that entirely realize the right defined as a purpose, and which are distinguished from one another only in the harm they cause the other right, but also those that realize the purpose to a lesser degree, the result will be that this framework will also see the two values as having relative weight, without either being given precedence.[37]

IV. A Revival of the Old System?

The proposal to read the proportionality tests as including not only a component of a decisive result, but also the evaluation of a compromise option, has become part of the binding rules in Israel. In light of this fact, one could expect the Supreme Court justices from here on out, in cases of conflicts between rights and interests, to avoid applying the vertical balancing formula, which required them to decide between conflicting values, even if they ultimately conclude that there is no avoiding a decisive result. However, as will be shown below, at least some of the Supreme Court justices continue to use the vertical balancing test, using it to justify their decision in favor of the right and against the conflicting interest, without at all examining any way to reconcile the two based on mutual concessions. This approach was taken in one of two ways: alternating and unexplained use of the vertical balancing test alongside the use of the proportionality test, and absorption of the vertical balancing test into the proper purpose test included in the limitation clause. I will demonstrate the use of each of these methods below.

I. ALTERNATING AND UNEXPLAINED USE OF THE VERTICAL BALANCING TEST

In *Horev*,[38] the Court examined the decision of the Transportation Supervisor to close a transportation artery that goes through the heart of a Haredi neighborhood at prayer times on Sabbath and the Jewish Holidays. Supreme Court President Barak, who led the majority in the case, stated that the conflicting values were the freedom of movement of the secular residents of the area on the one hand—a value that enjoys constitutional status in Israel—and the religious feelings of the Haredi residents of the area on the other hand—a value that the Court, in previous rulings, refused to grant the status of a human right, but nevertheless recognized as an interest worthy of protection. According to the old balancing formulas, the vertical balancing test would be appropriate here, which would lead to a definite decision between right and interest. But in his ruling in *Horev*, Barak explained that the moment the Basic Laws were passed, the dilemma should be decided with the proportionality tests. The use of proportionality tests allowed Barak to justify the Transportation Supervisor's decision in principle, after finding that it expresses a proper compromise between the two conflicting values, in the sense that on the one hand the roads are left open most of the day (thus respecting freedom of movement), while on the other hand ordering their closure during prayer hours (thus respecting religious feelings).

It is interesting to compare Barak's approach on *Horev* to one taken in a similar case, *Gur-Aryeh*.[39] In this case, the Supreme Court discussed the petition of the residents of a religious town against the screening, which was to take place during the Sabbath, of a documentary about them. The Second Authority for Television and Radio, which ordered the film and was about to air it, refused the request of the petitioners to move the broadcast time to a weekday. President Barak, writing the majority opinion in the case, stated that this is a conflict between the respondent's freedom of expression, which is a constitutional right, and the religious feelings of the petitioners, which, as noted, were recognized in jurisprudence as an interest worthy of protection, but not as a constitutional right.

Barak explained that since this is a conflict between a right and an interest, he must use the vertical balancing test, which requires deciding between values. From here on out, it was a foregone result. Barak directed to previous rulings, which stated that freedom of expression must be given priority over feelings, except for cases in which the harm to feelings is particularly severe, and after stating that the harm to feelings does not, in this case, meet the necessary threshold of severity, he rejected the petition.

The difference in Barak's approach in each one of these cases is problematic. The problem does not lie in the different result the Court had reached in both cases, as this might be based on a distinction between the two rights—the right to freedom of movement under discussion in *Horev* and the right to freedom of expression in *Gur-Aryeh*. The problem also does not lie in the very decision in *Gur-Aryeh* to prefer one value over the other. As I explained above, despite the preference of compromise to a decisive result, there may be cases where a decisive result should be adopted even if compromise is possible. The problem lies in the presentation of the rejection of compromise in the *Gur-Aryeh* case as a dictated limitation.

If *Gur-Aryeh* were examined on its own, the only flaw one could attribute to the Court's decision would be the mechanical use of the vertical balancing formula, which requires the Court to decide between conflicting values without allowing the justices the option to examine the possibility of reconciling them. However, a comparison of the ruling in *Gur-Aryeh* to *Horev* raises another, more serious flaw. Barak's parallel use of both balancing mechanisms without any explanation—vertical balance in one case, and proportionality tests in the other—adds a manipulative dimension to his conduct. In the past, the flaw inherent in the mechanical balancing formula, which obligated the Court to decide between values, also bound the justice who created it: if a right and an interest were on the agenda, they would indeed have to choose in a binary fashion. Now, after the proportionality tests have been established, the Court does not really have to decide between rights and interests, and can also reconcile the two. If despite this, the court Continues to selectively use the vertical balancing formula alongside the proportionality tests, presenting the decision in favor of one of the values as forced on it, it is not telling the truth.

2. ABSORBING THE VERTICAL BALANCING FORMULA INTO THE PROPER PURPOSE TEST

An interesting fact is that in Canada, the overwhelming majority of nullifications of primary legislation or the decisions of the executive branch occur in the framework of the second proportionality test.[40] Peter Hogg claims that the minimal use of the third test derives from the fact that this test effectively returns to the preliminary test of "proper purpose." If the purpose is proper, asks Hogg, how then can we reject the action carried out to realize it?[41] This fact led Hogg to argue that the third test is, in fact, superfluous.

Hogg's argument is not convincing. There is no logical or practical necessity that accepting the purpose the state wishes to advance ultimately requires support for the action taken to realize that purpose. The purpose can be proper, and still the action taken to realize it be struck down, at the end of a process of inquiry, after the extent of the harm the action causes to a right are revealed.[42]

Even if Hogg's analytical argument is incorrect, it would appear that his approach, which assigns a significant amount of the work to the purpose examination stage, has supporters among the justices of the Israeli Supreme Court. In a number of obiter dicta, some of the justices went a long way toward raising the threshold of the proper purpose.[43] To be able to move on to the questions of proportionality, it is not enough that the purpose of the law be "to realize social goals that align with the values of the state in general"; the state must also ensure that the goals of the law be "sensitive to the place of human rights in the overall social framework,"[44] and according to one opinion, even "sensitive to the right harmed precisely as it is revealed in the circumstances under examination."[45] The Court also ruled that the greater the harm caused to a right, the greater the need of "pressing essential or social goal" to be advanced by the law, and all this so that it can be considered to have a proper purpose.[46]

Another way to strengthen the status of the requirement of the proper purpose, which arises from a number of obiter dicta, is an integration of the vertical balancing test as part of the proper purpose test. Thus, for instance, in the *Stein* case, which discussed an order to close a café due to the security danger arising from the operation of the business, President Barak stated that:

> A purpose is proper if it maintains the proper balance between the public interest and human rights. For our purposes, the proper balance includes a probability test of "near certainty" ... The requirement of a proper purpose requires the existence of a danger, which is reflected by the very activity in the place which is subject to the closure order ... What is the level of danger and what is its probability? It is not enough to just have some sort of danger. In light of the special character of this means, we can use it only if there is clear and convincing administrative proof that if the means of closing the place is not adopted, then there is near certainty that it will present a real danger to the safety of the public.[47]

However, if the requirement of the proper purpose also includes the vertical balancing test, which leads to the victory of one of the sides of the equation, what room is left, then, for tests of proportionality? The answer would appear to be as follows: if the vertical balance orders the preference of the right over the interest, this means that the purpose is not proper, which leads to the nullification of the governmental act, without the need arising to subject it to proportionality tests. These tests become relevant only in the event that vertical balancing orders the preference of the interest over the right. In the past, in cases where an interest overcame a right, the result of the vertical balance was the confirmation of the governmental act under review. However, according to this approach, after adopting the tests of proportionality, preferring the interest over the right as part of the vertical balance, now included in the proper purpose test, is not the end of the discussion, and the governmental act should be subject to the three tests of proportionality to try and minimize the extent of harm to the right, even if this involves the cost of lesser protection of the interest.

This reading of the requirement of the proper purpose is problematic. It does not align with the language of the limitation clause, as the latter distinguishes between the question of purpose and the question of the means taken to realize it (proportionality). It confuses the goal the law was meant to promote and the obligation to consider the human rights that might be harmed by the means used to realize that goal. "Sensitivity to human rights" is not the goal of the law, but rather a value-based reservation that the mechanisms laid down by the law must meet. More specifically, according to the proportionality tests, the binary method of deciding entirely in favor of one side or the other is deferred to the third proportionality test—proportional result—*after* the various alternatives and their costs have been examined. An attempt to add a prior stage of decisive preference for the right, whether by raising the threshold of the proper purpose or by entirely integrating the vertical balance within the framework of the proper purpose test, makes the proportional result test entirely unnecessary.

But beyond the linguistic and conceptual mismatch, the move in question seems undesirable. Due to our commitments to protecting human rights, there may be cases where the harm to the right will be rejected even if the harm is moderate, and even if the goal in the name of which the right is harmed is legitimate and even desirable. The question is where to place the threshold that will ensure the right is preferred in these cases. One option is to place it as early as the proper purpose stage, and another is to put it off to the end of the process, as part of the third proportionality test, after all the compromise options have been properly examined. The second option seems more appropriate to me.[48]

Let's take the tension between religious sensitivities and freedom of speech, which stood at the center of the discussion in the *Gur-Aryeh* case, as an example. One possibility is to reconcile the two values. However, let us assume that the judge presiding over the case believes that compromise is illegitimate here, since he thinks that the protection of feelings that are not mortally wounded cannot justify even the slightest restriction of freedom of expression, even if the offensive statement was as condemnable as it gets. Even such a judge would derive benefit from deferring the decisive statement to the end of the process of inquiry, after he seriously considered all the alternatives. Then, both his decision and the critique thereof will be far better informed and intelligent than if he had decided in favor of the right in the preliminary stage, without at all trying to reconcile the values.

What can explain this insistence of some of the Supreme Court justices on reviving the vertical balancing test by anchoring it in the proper purpose test? Why are they unwilling to suffice with examining the option of a decisive result in favor of the right within the framework of the third proportionality test? It may be that this derives from a fear that putting off the possibility of a decisive result to the end of the process, after various options to balance the conflicting values were examined in-depth, will increase the number of cases in which the Court will be willing to authorize harm to human rights.

This fear is not baseless. The odds that the Court will reach the conclusion that the harm to the right is not justified, after examining a number of alternatives and trying to minimize the harm to the right from protecting the interest, are smaller than when the Court is required to address only two possible options—a complete preference for the right, at the cost of protecting the interest, or a complete preference for the interest, at the cost of any protection for the right.

However, even if this fear is founded, it is not sufficient to justify raising the threshold at the stage of the proper purpose test, and especially not sufficient to justify raising it by including the vertical balancing test within the framework of the proper purpose requirement. Human rights require strong protection, but at the same time, human rights may sometimes be required to concede to realize other important values. There is, therefore, nothing illegitimate in a process in which the option of preferring some value over a human right or reconciling the values with some harm to the right are examined. The insistence of placing a high threshold already at the beginning of the process derives from excessive "nervousness." More than an expression of a commitment to human rights, it reflects a lack of faith in the ability of judges and elected representatives to properly consider the possibilities on the agenda, without abandoning the obligation to grant human rights the protection they deserve.[49]

V. Proportionality and Probability

In the previous section, I explained why the attempt to bring back the vertical balancing test through the back door is neither proper nor desirable. However, the vertical balancing test contains a very important component that should be retained—the component of probability.[50] As noted, as part of the vertical balancing test, preference for the interest over the right was made conditional on the interest meeting a dual threshold—intensity and probability. For instance, national security was preferred to freedom of expression, but only in the event where preference for the right to express oneself would lead, at a probability level of near certainty, to tangible harm to the security of the country. Including the component of probability in the framework of balancing between the conflicting values is logical and called for, as it fits the manner in which the severity of dangers tends to be evaluated: as a multiple (or another cumulated ratio) of the intensity of the expected harm, and the degree of its probability. The severity of the danger of harm at a lower intensity increases in our eyes as the likelihood of it occurring increases, while at the same time, the lower the probability of an occurrence of the danger, the lesser our evaluation of its severity, even if the expected harm would be of a high intensity.

Consideration of the probability component within the framework of proportionality tests is therefore called for. However, the use of this component needs to be different, in two major ways, from the way it has been used within the framework of the vertical balancing test. First, as part of the vertical balancing, the existence of a probability at some level served as a necessary condition for the post-facto legalization of harm to a right. By contrast, the status of probability is simply one item in a collection of factors worthy of consideration when searching for the proper balance between conflicting values. Second, the probability question was asked as part of the vertical balancing test only in reference to an interest one wishes to protect, while the right way to treat probability is to also address it in relation to the right about to be harmed, with the Court examining the probability that the right will be harmed should the action actually be carried out. Of course, in a significant number of cases, the harm to the right is certain and not merely probable; however, there may very well be cases in which harm is not certain, and in these instances, an examination of the probability that this harm will take place is called for.

For instance, a few years ago, the Court nullified a law that laid the groundwork for a pilot program for privately managed jails.[51] Justice Procaccia based her decision on the fear that the private party would not grant the appropriate weight to its obligation to protect the dignity and relative freedom of the prisoners during their sentences, which would lead to unjustified harm to these rights. Other members of the panel criticized her, and argued that the evaluation privatization must only consider facts known to the Court during the deliberations, and must not rely on speculations regarding the future.[52] In my opinion, the consideration raised by Procaccia is not only legitimate, but even called for. If it is important to protect human rights from unjustified harm, then it would be proper to calculate, as part of the balancing process between rights and other worthy values, not only guaranteed harm to rights, which will occur if the steps under discussion are carried out, but also probable harm, while giving appropriate weight to the level of probability that such harm will occur.

The limitation clause tests, which replaced the vertical balancing formulas, do not include explicit referral to the probability component. They do refer to the component of intensity of harm to the right and the interest—both as part of the second subtest, which requires choosing the option that will protect the interest at the lowest cost in terms of harm to the right, and as part of the third proportionality test, which requires considering gain, in terms of realizing the interest, as opposed to loss, in terms of harm to the right—however, there is no trace of the probability component there. If we wish to read the probability question into the limitation clause tests, we must therefore use the tools of interpretation.

Where can the probability test be placed, and where *should* it be placed? In the rulings of the Supreme Court, one can find hints for three options: as part of the proper purpose test, and as part of the first or third proportionality tests. I will demonstrate and examine each one of these options.

Probability in the framework of the proper purpose test: as noted in the previous section, in *Stein*, where the constitutionality of an order to shut down a café was discussed, issued on the grounds of a security risk emanating from the activity there, President Barak proposed reading the vertical balancing test into the proper purpose test. Accordingly, Barak stated that the closure order will pass the proper purpose test only if it turns out that there are convincing administrative proofs that if the place is not shut down, "there is near certainty that a significant danger will emanate from it to the safety of the public."[53]

Above, I argued that Barak's proposal to include the vertical balancing test with both its components—intensity of expected harm to the interest, and the degree of its probability—at this stage of the discussion is undesirable, due to it largely rendering the proportional result test as superfluous. However, it seems that this counterargument loses some of its validity if the proper purpose test does not include the two components of the vertical balancing test, only the probability one. The counterargument will be further weakened if the probability consideration, as part of the proper purpose test, is treated not as a rigid threshold (as it serves when used for the vertical balancing test), but rather as one of the factors calculated when examining the appropriateness of the purpose.

However, even if the abovementioned modifications are made, it would seem that the proper purpose test is not the natural place for an examination of probability. This is for the following reason: as was explained, probability should be examined not just in reference to the interest whose protection serves as our desire to act, but also in reference to the right that may be harmed if the act is carried out. As its name attests, the proper purpose test focuses on the purpose only, and as such, the probability of harm to the right cannot therefore be examined within the framework of this test.[54] A separation between the two questions of probability, and testing the probability of harm to the interest before testing the probability of harm to the right, will strengthen the danger that the possibility of compromise between the conflicting values, based on reference to the costs and benefits, will be summarily rejected without being thoroughly considered.

Probability in the framework of the first test of proportionality (appropriateness)—in the *Israel Investment Managers* case, described at length in Chapter 3,[55] the Court disqualified some of the minimal requirements imposed by law on veteran investment managers as a condition for them to continue to work. Justice Dorner explained in her opinion that meeting the requirement of a rational connection between the means used and the ends desired "does not require absolute certainty that the means will achieve its goal. Suffice for there to be a significant probability of realizing the purpose via the means that harms the right."[56]

The use Dorner made of probability considerations in *Israel Investment Managers* is sound. Quite often, certain steps are taken without the certainty that they will produce the desired result, whether because there is no way of figuring out the issue for sure, or because the way to do so involved heavy financial costs or unreasonable efforts. Setting a requirement for certainty in realizing the goal as the precondition for approving actions that harm human rights will lead to the disqualification of quite a few reasonable arrangements. On the other hand, it should be kept in mind that the cost involved here is harm to human rights, and it is therefore inconceivable that experimental actions with a low probability of success should be allowed to do so. There is logic in setting a probability threshold—whose precise location will be set according to the interests and rights on the agenda—the meeting of which will be a condition for meeting the requirement of the proof of a rational connection between the means taken and the goal aimed at.

However, even if the inclusion of the probability element within the framework of the appropriateness test is sound, this does not mean that this test is appropriate as a home for probability considerations in the sense we discussed. Two uses of probability are involved here: The use of probability considerations proposed by Justice Dorner was meant to try to figure out the likelihood that using a particular means will realize the interest being defended. On the other hand, probability considerations of the sort we are talking about were meant to help determine the degree of danger to the interest if the action on the agenda is *not* taken, and what would be the severity of the danger to the right if the action in question *is* taken. Including both types of usages of probability in the framework of a single test may lead to analytical confusion, and should therefore be avoided. Another reason for the inappropriateness of the first proportionality test for an examination of the probability of harm to one of the values being weighed is that, much like the proper purpose test, the appropriateness test focuses on the interest, not the right, and therefore the probability of harm to the right cannot be examined within its framework, but rather only the probability of harm to the other value. As already noted, such separation is undesirable.

Probability in the framework of the third proportionality test (proportionality sensu stricto): in one of the prominent rulings of the Supreme Court in recent years, the majority of the Court accepted a petition against the refusal of the army to let women into the pilot training program at the Israeli Air Force flight academy.[57] The army justified its refusal on the grounds that because of instructions of the law meant to protect women, and because of their biological functions, the amount of time the army will be able to benefit from the service of female pilots will be significantly shorter than that of men, reducing the worthwhileness of their training, and harming the planning options for manpower. Justice Dorner, one of the justices in the majority, held that the army's policy failed the third proportionality test, in the sense that the harm in closing the pilot training program to women was greater than the benefit in terms of planning and money. In addition, Justice Dorner explained that the army's claim of planning difficulties was not based "on any tangible factual basis, but only on an assumption the correctness of which is not obvious."[58] A connection of these two sentences may tell us that Justice Dorner believed that when comparing costs and benefits within the framework of the third proportionality test, one must also consider issues of probability.

The possible inclusion of probability considerations in the framework of the proportionality sensu stricto test seems appropriate. After all, in this framework, the gain (in terms of protection of the interest) is measured against the loss (in terms of harm to the right). If an examination of the probability of harm to the right and to the interest is vital for an evaluation of the gain and the loss, the inclusion of an examination of probability within the framework of this test is called for. Another advantage in adding probability considerations to the proportionality sensu stricto test is that as opposed to the proper purpose test and the appropriateness test, which focus only on the purpose side of the equation, the proportionality sensu stricto test examines both sides, and it will therefore be possible to examine their probability within the framework of this test.

In recent years, support has been expressed for this proposal in the *Avneri* ruling, which discussed a petition against the Law to Prevent Harm to the State of Israel by Boycott, 2011. This law imposes tort responsibility, and establishes various administrative limitations on those who knowingly call publicly to boycott the State of Israel. Justice Amit said the following:

> In coming to examine the proportionality of the harm to the right (*stricto sensu*), we balance the benefit that emerges from the realization of the purpose of the law against the harm, which derives from the law's harm to the right. On the favorable side of the scales, we place the degree of benefit and the probability of its realization, and on the damning side of the scales, we place the importance of the right, the intensity of the harm and its probability.[59]

VI. Summary

The vertical balancing test, which was accepted in Israel until the passing of Basic Law: Human Dignity and Freedom and Basic Law: Freedom of Occupation, obligated the judges to choose between conflicting rights and interests, and prefer one over the other decisively. In this chapter I argued that the court should also be allowed to examine options for compromise, even if it ultimately prefers a decisive result. I showed that the limitation clause may provide an answer to the fallacy in the vertical balancing test, and add a component of possible compromise to balance between rights and interests. I further argued that the compromise element should be read into the second proportionality test (necessity).

The Supreme Court has adopted this position in part. It added a component of evaluating compromise options, but it chose to place this component in the third proportionality test of proportionality sensu stricto. I explained why I believe that it would be more correct to place the compromise options evaluation in the framework of the second subtest. However, I argued that the question of location is secondary, and what is really important is that the compromise options evaluation be a necessary component in the balance between rights and interests.

In this context, I pointed to two disturbing developments—hinted at in a number of obiter dicta of the Supreme Court—that the compromise options evaluation is not carried out in every case of a clash between a worthy public interest and a protected right, but only after it is first determined that the right should not win a priori. The adoption of this approach will make the proper purpose into the home of a partial vertical balancing test, which will allow for the categorical preference of rights over worthy public purposes.

Another trend, which has a basis in previous rulings, is of alternating between two balancing formulas, with the court sometimes using the vertical balancing test and sometimes the proportionality test. I explained that the recent practice is not just undesirable but simply illegitimate, since the use thereof allows the court to reach whatever result it desires, without being forced to justify its preferences. It would be better for the court to abandon these two trends, and instead continue to develop the proportionality tests so that a compromise options evaluation will be not only *possible* but also *necessary* in every encounter between human rights and legitimate public interests.

Finally, I argued that it would be proper to include a probability test within the framework of the limitation clause tests in relation to the two components of the equation—the purpose and the harmed right—and that the most appropriate stage for calculating the probability component is the third proportionality test. However, the court must ensure that the addition of probability calculations for balancing costs and benefits does not harm the ad hoc character of the balancing, which examines and decides according to the circumstances of every case, and avoids categorical characterizations. Therefore, the probability considerations should be used not as a rigid threshold—as has been done in the framework of the vertical balancing test—but only as one of the factors to be considered in the framework of calculating cost and benefit.

7

EMERGENCY POWERS

I. Introduction

In many countries, the constitution includes a reference to circumstances in which the country will be in a state of emergency, requiring a change from the normal legal arrangement.[1] It is customary to describe a state of emergency as an isolated event or a series of events related to an abnormal situation that threatens the existence or integrity of the country. Clear examples of states of emergency are war, rebellion, an economic crisis, or a natural disaster.[2] In these situations, the authorities may need to have increased powers, along with limitations of individual rights, in order for the state to be able to deal with the abnormal situation. The basic assumption is that the state of emergency is a fundamentally temporary affair, and that the country will return to its normal regime of peacetime once it is over. The legal picture in Israel on this issue does not fit this paradigm, in the sense that much like quite a few other liberal democracies,[3] the state of emergency in Israel is not temporary. From its establishment until today, the state has operated under the regular and unrepealed declaration of a state of emergency. At first, the basis for this was section 9 of the Law and Administration Ordinance—passed immediately after the state was declared—which stated as follows:

> If it will seem appropriate to the Provisional Council of State, it may declare that a state of emergency exists in the country.[4]

On May 19, shortly after passing the ordinance, the Provisional Council of State[5] declared a state of emergency, and has never repealed it since. In 1992, the Knesset passed Basic Law: The Government, which went into effect in 1996.[6] The Basic Law repealed section 9 of the Law and Administration Ordinance, but replaced it with section 38 of the Basic Law, which authorizes the Knesset to declare the existence of a state of emergency, with each such declaration lasting for a period of no more than one year, with the possibility of declaring it anew.

The move from a declaration mechanism that is not time-limited to a mechanism that limits the validity of the state of emergency to one year did not change anything on the ground, as the Knesset has annually redeclared the existence of a state of emergency from that time until today. In 1999, the Association for Civil Rights in Israel petitioned to the Supreme Court, and asked it to declare the end of the state of emergency, on the grounds that the continued existence of a state of emergency for such a long period of time is unreasonable. The deliberation on the petition took place over the course of thirteen years, with the Court ultimately issuing a ruling on May 8, 2012, rejecting the petition.[7]

In the first fifty years of Israel's existence, the declaration of the state of emergency served as the formal and essential basis for emergency legislation in the country. Formally, the validity of a significant portion of emergency legislation was conditional on the declaration of the existence of a state of emergency. Essentially, the state of emergency served as "justification" for strengthening the executive branch at the expense of the legislature, and securing its wholesale approval to act while limiting human rights, even regarding legislation the validity of which was not made formally conditional on the declaration of a state of emergency.[8] From the beginning of the twenty-first century, a change has become apparent in the manner of arranging emergency laws in Israel, in three main aspects: the center of gravity is moving over to primary legislation by the Knesset, legislation now goes into details and no longer suffices with nothing more than the general delegation of power to the executive, and legislation is no longer conditional on the existence of a state of emergency.

In this chapter, I will describe the structure of emergency laws in Israel, and the changes that took place within that structure over the years, with a focus on emergency laws dealing with security threats, both external and internal.[9] In addition, I will describe the Supreme Court's contribution to shaping the emergency laws, and the subsequent change in how the legislative and executive branches handle the issue, examining just how much the constitutional revolution influenced these changes.

II. The First Fifty Years

Israeli emergency legislation used to be divided into three basic frameworks:[10]

1. Defense (Emergency) Regulations, 5705-1945 (Mandatory legislation).[11]
2. Emergency legislation enacted by government ministers for a period of three months, according to sections 38–39 to Basic Law: the Government (administrative legislation).
3. Emergency legislation of the Knesset, which may be limited in time or conditional on the continued existence of a state of emergency (primary legislation).

Below, I will describe the three frameworks and the ways in which they developed.

1. DEFENSE REGULATIONS (EMERGENCY PERIOD), 1945

The Defense Regulations are an inheritance from the time of the British Mandate, and are the oldest emergency laws in our legal system. They were enacted in 1945 against the background of the British Mandatory government's weakening hold on the Land of Israel. In an attempt to restore control, the British government passed a detailed code granting the Mandatory authorities far-reaching powers.[12]

There was a general outcry of protest in Palestine when the Regulations were adopted. The Jewish Bar Association of Palestine publicly denounced them, stating that the "granting of such wide powers to the authorities without judicial control is a serious breach of the fundamentals of any orderly regime and undermines the very existence of the regime itself."[13]

Despite their Mandatory origin and the sharp criticism by the Jewish community in Palestine of these regulations at the time, upon the establishment of the State of Israel those regulations were recognized as primary legislation and an integral part of the Israeli legal system. This was by force of the continuity instructions laid down in section 11 of the Law and Administration Ordinance, which was immediately passed after the state was established. The section reads as follows:

The law that existed in the Land of Israel on the fifth of Iyar 5708 (May 14, 1948) will remain in force, to the extent that it does not contradict this ordinance or other laws given by the Provisional Council of State, or emanating from it, and subject to changes deriving from the establishment of the state and its authorities.

The Mandatory Defense Regulations have yet to be repealed, and law proposals aiming at doing so in light of some improvement in the security situation, raised from time to time, have all been rejected.[14] The regulations grant the executive authority, and especially military commanders, far-reaching powers. The authority of the military commander is implemented via orders, which, according to another Mandatory ordinance still in force,[15] are superior to law, including Knesset legislation. In other words, army officers have the authority to cause serious harm to individual rights even if it involves violation of Knesset law.

Over the years, a reform was introduced in some of the emergency powers included in the Defense Regulations in their original formulation.[16] One significant reform had to do with Emergency Powers Law (Detention), 5739-1979.[17] The need for this reform was clear to all,[18] but its implementation at that particular point in time can be largely attributed to the personal background of the Minister of Justice at the time, Shmuel Tamir, who in the pre-state years was a member of the Etzel, one of the underground organizations against whom the British used the Defense Regulations; Tamir was even sent into extended administrative detention based on those regulations.[19] The Detention Law led to a better balance between security needs and the obligation to protect human rights.[20] For instance, regulation 111 of the Defense Regulations, which granted authority to the military commander to declare an administrative detention, was repealed. The new legislation now granted this authority solely to the Minister of Defense.[21] In addition, the period of administrative detention was set at no more than six months, during which judicial review would take place after three months. This change in the extent of administrative detention authority saw another significant innovation added to the Detention Law: Section 1 of the law stated that the law only applies so long as the declaration that the country is in a state of emergency is in force.[22]

The most significant reform of the Defense Regulations was carried out in 2016, with the passage of the Combatting Terrorism Law.[23] This law was meant to replace most of the laws and ordinances that regulated the work of the Ministry of Defense in fighting terror. With its passage, many sections in the Defense Regulations were repealed, belonging to three categories: regulations that have a satisfactory alternative in Israeli legislation, even if the repealed regulation was broader and more sweeping than the alternative arrangement;[24] regulations that grant powers that have not been used for many years, and there is therefore no justification to preserve them,[25] or arrangements unworthy of a democratic regime, even if there are no alternatives to them;[26] and regulations dealing with matters that were regulated differently in the Combatting Terrorism Law.[27] After this reform, what remained were mainly regulations that grant authority or determine criminal prohibitions that do not yet have an alternative in Israeli law, and that still serve an essential need.[28]

The validity of the Defense Regulations was first questioned shortly after the founding of the state, in *Lion v. Gubernick*.[29] Lion petitioned to the Supreme Court against the decision (based on the Defense Regulations) to commandeer an apartment he owned for the sake of housing a senior official in the new State of Israel. This action was meant to allow the position holder to live in Tel Aviv and become integrated in the governmental center there. Lion was not meant to receive any compensation for his apartment being seized.

As noted above, section 11 of the Law and Administration Ordinance, 1948, states that the legal regime in the State of Israel will be based on continuity. However, the absorption of existing law was subjected to the following condition: "to the extent that it does not contradict this ordinance or other laws given by the Provisional Council of State, or emanating from it and subject to changes deriving from the establishment of the state and its authorities." Given this condition, it was argued in the *Lion* case that the Mandatory Defense Regulations have no validity in the State of Israel, as required from the changes deriving from the establishment of the state and its authorities, due to their being "of a dictatorial, maybe even anti-Jewish character to the extent that they were directed at strangling the Yishuv, the development of the country by Jews, and the halting of Jewish immigration to the country."[30] According to this argument, the regulations could not be part of Israeli law, "since the State of Israel is a democratic state and a Hebrew state."

The panel of justices that presided over the petition—President Smoira, Deputy President Olshan, and Justice Asaf—recognized this argument as a respectable one, but in the end they rejected it. The primary approach of the justices was that essential changes in the legal situation, as opposed to technical corrections required by the establishment of the state, need to be left in the hands of the legislators. As they put it:

> In light of this argument, the court would need to determine first that a change has emerged due to the establishment of the state, what that change is, and consider whether this change requires the repeal of a particular law, and all this would require the court to do so in a ruling declaring that the law is no longer valid. This is precisely the role of the legislator, and we should not assume in any way that the Israeli legislator in mentioning the words "and changes etc." meant to hand over part of his role to the courts.[31]

Accordingly, the justices' conclusion was that the "changes" the ordinance refers to are only "such technical changes without which it is impossible to apply the law after the establishment of the state and its new authorities," of the sort "which do not require special judgment." The Court pointed to other sections in the Ordinance, which it sought to use to support its chosen, narrow interpretation. However, a reading of the entirety of the ruling shows clearly that this reference was but a technical justification for a principled decision made by the Court—not based on the legislation before it: the Court believed that its ruling was necessary by force of the separation of powers, which they must insist on precisely in the young State of Israel.[32]

Although the Court refused to invalidate the Defense Regulations in *Lion*, it agreed to oversee their implementation. This oversight was done at two levels: the formal and the substantive. In the first years of the state the court sufficed with formal oversight,[33] but over the years it also began to apply substantive judicial review,[34] a development that has reached full formation in 1989, in the *Schnitzer* case.

In this case, the Court overturned a decision of the Chief Military Censor—by force of the authority granted it in regulation 87(1) of the Defense Regulations—to disqualify a section expressing criticism of the performance of the head of the Mossad. Justice Barak, who wrote the main opinion, stated, inter alia, that the interpretation that should be given to the Defense Regulations in the State of Israel is not the same as that given to them in the time of the Mandate:

> The Defense Regulations are today part of the laws of a democratic state. They need to be interpreted against the background of the basic principles of the Israeli legal system ... True, the Defense Regulations deal with state security. This fact has an effect on the manner in which the basic principles of the system are implemented. This fact has no influence on the very applicability of the basic principles. Indeed, every piece of legislation—whether originating in the time of the mandate or having an Israeli origin, whether involving state security or dealing with a matter that is not state security—is interpreted in light of the basic principles of the system. State security and public order do not push aside and do not negate the applicability of the basic values. They are weaved into them, affect their formation, and are balanced within their framework.[35]

2. EMERGENCY PERIOD REGULATIONS

As opposed to the Defense Regulations, which originated in the Mandatory primary legislation and are not limited in time, Emergency Regulations are enacted by the secondary legislators, and are limited to a brief period—no more than three months.

The authority to enact emergency regulations was first established in section 9 of the Law and Administration Ordinance. This section authorized the legislators to declare the existence of a state of emergency, and stated that with this declaration, the government was granted the authority to enact emergency regulations, which can suspend or change primary legislation, for a period of no more than three months. In 1992, the Knesset passed Basic Law: The Government, which included an extensive reform of the Israeli system of government: a move from the parliamentary regime, which was in force in Israel until then, to a semi-presidential regime, in which the prime minister was chosen by direct elections.[36] Alongside this reform, the Basic Law contained additional innovations, including the repeal of section 9 of the Law and Administration Ordinance. However, the Basic Law then reintroduced the existing arrangement with certain changes. Section 38 of the Basic Law, in its present version from 2001, grants the Knesset the authority to declare the existence of a state of emergency, but this is limited to a period of no more than one year. The authority of the government to enact emergency regulations was also anchored anew, and it appears in section 39 of the Basic Law.

Section 39(a) states that "during a state of emergency the Government may make emergency regulations for the defense of the State, public security and the maintenance of supplies and essential services," and Section 39(c) states that "emergency regulations may alter any law temporarily suspend its effect or introduce conditions, and may also impose or increase taxes or other compulsory payments unless there be another provision by law." Section 39(f) adds the factor of the time limitation on emergency regulations, stating that "the force of emergency regulations shall expire three months after the day of their enactment unless their force is extended by law, or they are revoked by the Knesset by law, or pursuant to a decision of a majority of the members of Knesset."

Even though the authority to enact emergency regulations was re-anchored in a Basic Law, a number of limitations were established, which did not appear in the Law and Administration Ordinance. Section 39(e) of the Basic Law states that emergency regulations would not be enacted, and arrangements, means, and authorities not be used by their force, except to the extent that the state of emergency requires it. Section 39(d) of the Basic Law states that emergency regulations could not prevent petitioning to the courts, punish ex post facto, or harm human dignity. These limitations are aligned with limitations customarily included in international human rights covenants, which regulate the issue of emergency powers.[37]

Ostensibly, emergency regulations are short-term instructions, and therefore cause relatively little harm, but matters are different in practice. Section 39(f) of the Basic Law authorizes the Knesset to lengthen the period of emergency regulations—for a specific time or until the emergency period ends—by way of primary legislation, which mentions the regulations in their original formulation or in an amended version. Over time, the Knesset has made much use of this authority.[38]

Over the years, the Supreme Court has addressed the regulatory authority of emergency regulations, but it was only in the 1990s that it began to set significant limits. Among other things, the Court established that the authority to enact emergency regulations was not meant to allow the government to bypass the normal process of legislation in the Knesset, and can therefore only be used where the matter cannot be handled via the usual route. Below, I will describe two central rulings where the Court established this limitation.

At the beginning of the 1990s, Israel found itself suffering from a housing crisis in the wake of the absorption of a large wave of immigrants from the former Soviet Union. To deal with the problem, the Minister of Housing and Construction enacted Emergency Regulations (Plan for Building Housing Units), 1990, which established an expedited mechanism for approving city construction plans. At the same time, the Knesset began an expedited process of legislation meant to solve that problem, but despite the appeals of the Knesset Interior Committee Chairman to the Minister of Housing and Construction that he avoid enacting the regulations in light of the legislation process, the Minister went ahead with the regulations anyway. The law went into force a week after the regulations were passed.

A petition against the regulations by MK Avraham Poraz was accepted. The Court stated that "where there is an option of orderly and speedy legislation by the Knesset, the legislative authority of the executive branch must withdraw from it, as in principle the authority of emergency period legislation must only be used when there is no possibility of waiting for the existence of legislative processes in the Knesset."[39]

The Poraz rule was strengthened in the Paritzky affair, in which the petitioner asked the Supreme Court to declare the invalidity of the emergency regulations that introduced means of identification in addition to those established by law, which a person will be allowed to present in voting for local elections. Adding these means was necessary due to sanctions taken by workers of the Ministry of Interior, which could have prevented hundreds of thousands of eligible voters from exercising their right to vote. The Court criticized the government for avoiding trying to carry out an expedited process of amending the election law, even though it had only four days to do so. However, in light of the fact that the deliberation in the Court took place only two days before the elections, the majority justices, Barak and Dorner, decided not to repeal the regulations.[40]

3. INDEPENDENT EMERGENCY LAWS

In addition to the two categories mentioned so far, matters related to the state of emergency are also regulated in Israel by way of Knesset primary legislation, the validity of which is conditional on the existence of a state of emergency. This primary legislation can be divided into three types, as follows.

1. Laws Extending Emergency Period Regulations

Quantitatively, most of the Knesset emergency legislation extends the validity of emergency regulations at the end of the regulations' three months (or after they have expired).[41] In the country's first years, this practice was used without any formal basis in legislation, and a petition that sought to question the status of extension laws as primary legislation was rejected by the Supreme Court.[42] As noted above, in 1992, the aforementioned authority was anchored in an explicit section in Basic Law: the Government.

2. Original Knesset Emergency Legislation

This legislation is primary legislation for all intents and purposes (and not merely extended emergency regulations); however, the validity of the entire law is conditional on the declaration of a state of emergency. This kind of Knesset emergency legislation has two main patterns. One such pattern is a detailed arrangement of an area of defense. An example of such a law is the Emergency Powers Law (Detention), mentioned above, which regulates the issue of administrative detention of suspects of security crimes in Israel. The other pattern is a framework law, which authorizes the executive branch to enact regulations and publish warrants of execution under the conditions laid down by the law. The most prominent example of such a law is the Supervision of Commodities and Services Law, 5718-1957, which grants government ministers the authority to regulate the provision of products and services, seriously harming Freedom of Occupation and other basic rights.[43] The second pattern of legislation grants the government powers similar in essence to the power granted to it—by force of sections 38–39 of Basic Law: The Government—to enact emergency regulations, in the sense that in both cases, the legislature authorizes the executive branch to regulate an area without stipulating in primary legislation the principles that are meant to guide and limit the executive's judgment. Below I will describe some of the limits the Court has placed on the powers granted to the government by force of the two abovementioned patterns of primary legislation.

As noted, the Supervision of Commodities and Services Law granted ministers authorized by the government the power to arrange dealings in products and services. The primary limit on this power lies in section 3, which states that "A minister will not use his authority according to this law, unless he has a reasonable basis that it is needed to carry out a vital action." A "vital action" is defined, among other things, as an action that the minister considers to be vital to the defense of the country, public safety, and so on.[44] In the past, the Court adopted an expansive interpretation of the term "vital action," and even granted ministers broad discretion in choosing the means that might promote the goals they consider vital. However, since the beginning of the 1990s, and especially since the passing of Basic Law: Freedom of Occupation, the Court has changed its approach. It stated that the term "vital" should be interpreted narrowly, "to be close to something where life is dependent on it . . ." The Court also stated that a narrow interpretation should be given to the expression "'*needed* to carry out a vital action' . . . Meaning, it is very likely that without it the vital action would not take place . . ."[45] Another erosion, led by the Court, of the powers granted to the government by force of the Supervision Law regarded the status of regulations enacted on that basis. For many years, the regulations enacted by force of the Supervision Law enjoyed the status of supremacy over contradictory primary legislation. In the wake of harsh criticism of the Supreme Court,[46] the law was amended in 1990, and the power of ministers to enact regulations contrary to law was revoked.[47]

As for the Detention Law: this law empowers the Minister of Defense to authorize the detention of an individual for a period of up to six months, without requiring proof of that person's guilt of any crimes. The use of this power seriously harms the right to freedom and to due process, a fact that explains the many limitations the Court imposed on the use of this authority. The Court stated, inter alia, that this authority can only be used if it is proven that the security of the state and the safety of the public cannot be ensured by means of the normal criminal justice route,[48] or, at the very least, via alternatives less harmful than arrest, such as banning the entry to a particular area or house arrest, the authority for which is established by the Defense Regulations (Emergency Period).[49] However, I should note that despite the critical approach of the Court on this matter, the cases where it actually ordered the revocation of an order of administrative detention are fairly rare.[50]

3. Emergency Period Instructions in Regular Laws

As opposed to the previous category, in which the validity of the entire law is conditional on the declaration of a state of emergency, the present category involves regular laws whose validity is not conditional on the existence of a state of emergency, but that contain instructions allowing deviation from the established basic principles in times of emergency. Thus, Annual Vacation Law, 1951, establishes the right of the worker to a vacation but allows, in section 32 of the law, the Minister of Labor and Welfare to issue an order delaying the date of vacation regarding all workers in a period in which the country is in a state of emergency.

III. The New Model

Until the first decade of the twenty-first century, activity in the defense area was primarily based on arrangements established by the executive branch, almost without intervention by the legislature—whether by force of the authority granted the government in the Defense Regulations or via emergency regulations. Indeed, as I noted above, some of these matters were also regulated in primary legislation; however, these were largely extensions of existing emergency regulations, or laws that granted the government general authority, without stating the principles guiding or limiting its action (such as the Supervision of Commodities and Services Law). In recent years, there has been a clear change in the pattern of legal coping with defense needs, which is expressed by three primary elements: the center of gravity has shifted to primary legislation,[51] which goes into detail and does not suffice with general arrangements, and it is not conditional on the existence of a state of emergency.[52] For instance, in 2002, the Imprisonment of Illegal Combatants Law and the General Security Services Law were passed; in 2003, the Citizenship and Entry into Israel (Temporary Provision) Law was passed; and in 2005, the Terror Funding Prohibition Law was passed.[53] The peak of this pattern was undoubtedly the Combatting Terrorism Law in 2016, whose preparation began in 2010. This law carried out an extensive reform by which many arrangements were repealed, and others changed and unified under one roof.

What led the Israeli legislators to get into the thick of things and to start regulating these matters in detailed primary legislation?[54] What caused them to cut the Gordian knot between security legislation and the declaration of a state of emergency? We will offer a number of possible explanations below.

1. A MISMATCH BETWEEN THE EMERGENCY MODEL AND ONGOING REALITY

As was explained at the beginning of this chapter, emergency laws, as their name implies, are supposed to regulate the legal situation in times that are not "normal." Accordingly, they are supposed to be temporary, in the sense that once the state of emergency is over, they are meant to expire, allowing the system to return to operating based on routine rules. In addition to making emergency laws dependent on the existence of a state of emergency, these laws are characterized by the legislators as granting legislative and executive discretion to the executive branch, an action justified in light of the urgency of the emergency situation and the uncertainty it involves. The model of emergency legislation is inappropriate for regulating an ongoing situation, to say nothing of a permanent one. The ongoing nature of the state of emergency removes its abnormality, and makes the threats the state has to deal with into part of the normal state of affairs. Therefore, even if it turns out that the threats the state faces and has to deal with require taking drastic measures—including harm to human rights, to the extent that the justification of taking these measures has become routine—it is natural that the powers the state should be allowed to use and the tools it should be allowed to wield be anchored in detailed primary legislation, whose validity is independent of the existence of a state of emergency. The emerging move in Israel from a pattern of enacting emergency legislation to a pattern of enacting regular legislation can therefore be explained in the growing unease in Israel from the mismatch between the pattern of handling security challenges and reality.

This explanation of the change in legislative power is sound, but it fails to explain why the change happened precisely at that point in time. After all, the model of emergency legislation of the executive branch, whose validity is conditional on the declaration of a state of emergency, has been the dominant one for at least fifty years, from the establishment of the state until the beginning of the 2000s. What led the Knesset to start preferring the pattern of detailed primary legislation, whose validity is unconditional on the aforementioned declaration, only then, and not long before? It would seem that this is due to the petition against the continued declaration of a state of emergency submitted in 1999. First, during the thirteen years in which the petition was pending, the Court demanded and received ongoing updates from the state regarding the legislative activities that it was taking to cut the connection between security legislation and the declaration of a state of emergency.[55] Second, it is true that the petition was ultimately rejected, but in its decision to reject the petition, the Court repeatedly stressed that "we must not make peace with the use made over the years in declaring a state of emergency in situations when it was necessary to arrive at updated and balanced legislation, which is not emergency legislation."[56] Finally, the decision to reject the petition was justified by the Court based on the aforementioned process, among other things, in the framework of which the Knesset was gradually anchoring emergency laws in primary legislation, while detaching them from a declaration of a state of emergency.[57]

2. THE STRENGTHENING OF JUDICIAL OPPOSITION TO THE SWEEPING DELEGATION OF AUTHORITY

According to the first explanation, the gradual change in the pattern of regulating security matters should be attributed to the pressure applied by the Court on the political system in the direction of canceling the declaration of the state of emergency.

The following two explanations (which are not contrary to the first one) focus more on the two additional characteristics of the new arrangement pattern: anchoring the arrangements in Knesset primary legislation that delves into details.

In the first part of the book, I stressed the increased power of the Court in recent decades, against the background of the legislation of Basic Laws regarding human rights, and the interpretation given them by the Court. We primarily focused on the authority the Court arrogated to itself to review the constitutionality of primary legislation. However, alongside the addition of primary legislation to the realm of review, the declaration of the constitutional revolution also led to the upgrading of two additional principles: the demand for explicit authorization from the legislators, as a condition for government harm to human rights; and the demand for anchoring primary arrangements in primary legislation, while reducing the legislative authority of the executive branch to secondary arrangements only. According to the explanation I will propose, this upgrading significantly reduced the ability of the government to rely on the model of declaring a state of emergency, which transfers much authority from the legislative to the executive branch, thereby "forced" the legislators to anchor the arrangements in detailed primary legislation. We will describe these two principles, and how the Court used them in the security context below.

The demand for explicit authorization: as was described in Chapter 1, the Supreme Court developed tools to protect human rights from the moment it was established, many years before the constitutional revolution was declared. One of these tools was the demand that harm to human rights by the executive branch must be explicitly authorized by the legislature. This demand was upgraded in 1992, when it was anchored in the two Basic Laws regarding human rights. In practice, the Court did not always enforce the aforementioned demand. However, in 1999, the Court signaled that it intended to give it teeth, in its ruling in the matter of *Public Committee Against Torture in Israel*.

In this case, the methods of interrogation—which deviate from those acceptable in normal criminal cases—used by the General Security Service against people suspected of terror activity were reviewed. The petitioners argued (among other things) that the state is not authorized to use these interrogation techniques, while the state, for its part, pointed to the source of its authority as being based on section 32 of Basic Law: The Government, which grants the government the authority to carry out "any action the execution of which is not legally obligated of another authority." The Court rejected the state's position, and stated that "we cannot conclude from this instruction authority for interrogation in the sense we are dealing with in these petitions . . . the government's 'vestigial' authority is not a source of authority to harm the freedom of the individual . . . harm to this freedom requires a special instruction."[58]

The ruling in the *Public Committee Against Torture* case aroused public criticism, but the rule it established was quickly absorbed. Shortly after it was published, the Knesset passed the General Security Service Law, 2002, which regulated the powers of the General Security Service in a detailed manner.[59] It is clear that the Court's decision in the *Public Committee* affair was what led to the primary legislation in an area that for years had been the domain of the executive branch, by force of merely general authorization by the legislators.

The demand to establish primary arrangements in primary legislation—the prohibition to delegate authority in primary matters from the legislative to the executive branch (henceforth: the non-delegation doctrine, or the doctrine) is a constitutional principle in a number of countries.[60] In Israel, it enjoys the status of an interpretive rebuttable presumption. The rule appears in various forms in Supreme Court rulings from the state's early years.[61] However, in the country's early decades, it still expressed the desirable state of affairs without having practical significance.[62] The applicability of the rule was also limited, dealing primarily with the prohibition of establishing arrangements based on religious arguments or with the aim of protecting religious sensibilities.[63] In recent decades, the power of the doctrine, in terms of both the readiness of the Supreme Court to use it and the extent of its reach, has been expanded. The Court applies an interpretive presumption, according to which the legislature does not intend to authorize the executive branch to establish primary arrangements, and does everything within its power to interpret the authority granted the executive by the legislature in a narrow manner, which would not allow the executive to make its own decisions regarding important social issues or matters that involve harm to basic freedoms.[64] One of the prominent cases in which the Court used this interpretive presumption is the *Rubinstein* case of 1998,[65] where the Court rejected the long-standing policy arrived at by the Minister of Defense in deferring the service of yeshiva students who study full-time.

The Security Service Law [Consolidated Version], 1986, establishes the obligation of service in the defense forces. Alongside the imposition of the obligation, the law grants the Minister of Defense the authority to defer such obligations or to exempt people from it. Section 36 of the law states that the minister is permitted to do so "for reasons related to the size of the regular forces or the reserve forces of the Israel Defense Forces, or for reasons related to educational needs, defense settlement or the national economy, or for reasons of family or for other reasons." Over many years, the Minister of Defense deferred the defense service of yeshiva students whose "Torah is their craft," basing his authority on the grounds of the "other reasons" clause. In the *Rubinstein* affair, the Court used the non-delegation doctrine as a tool to disqualify the minister's policy.[66] The Court stated that reading section 36 in light of the doctrine requires a narrow interpretation of the power granted the

Minister of Defense by the legislators, in a manner denying him the authority to establish a principled arrangement in the matter of all yeshiva students. In the wake of the Court's ruling, the Knesset was "forced" to arrange the matter in detailed primary legislation.

The strengthening of the non-delegation doctrine has direct relevance for emergency arrangements in Israel. The more these arrangements are anchored in secondary legislation by force of general authorization from the legislators, the more they are exposed to being repealed by the Court without even addressing their content, on the grounds that this is a primary arrangement that cannot be delegated from the legislators to the executive. The *Rubinstein* ruling therefore marked the path that the political system must take in order to regulate security affairs, meaning that they must move from sweeping delegation of judgment to the executive branch to detailed arrangement in primary legislation.

3. EXPANSION OF JUDICIAL INTERVENTION IN JUDGMENT IN SECURITY AFFAIRS

The previous explanation pegged the change to the strengthening of judicial enforcement of constitutional principles that require anchoring in primary arrangements, especially those that harm human rights, in detailed primary legislation. However, alongside the expansion of judicial intervention on the matter of *authority*, in recent decades the Court has demonstrated an increasing readiness to also intervene in the *content* of government decisions concerning security affairs.[67] Accordingly, the explanation I will now propose for a gradual move to the regulation of security issues in detailed primary legislation pegs it to the desire to strengthen the arrangements in light of the increasing "threat" to their content on the part of the Court.

A good example of the connection between the expansion of substantive judicial oversight in the area of security and the trend of anchoring powers in this area in primary legislation can be found in the circumstances of the passing of the Imprisonment of Illegal Combatants Law, 2002. This law was passed after the Supreme Court ruled that the Minister of Defense lacks the authority to detain Lebanese civilians as "bargaining chips," and that people can be detained administratively only when they themselves pose a danger to the security of the state.[68] Section 7 of the law grants the state the authority taken away by the Supreme Court, stating a presumption that a person who was part of a force carrying out acts of terror against the State of Israel, or who took part in the terror acts of that force, will be perceived as one whose release will harm the security of the state, so long as the terror attacks of that force against the State of Israel have not ended, and all this so long as this has not been proven otherwise.[69]

However, this explanation is insufficient, as with the declaration of the constitutional revolution, the Court arrogated to itself the power to also repeal primary legislation to the extent that it believes that its content disproportionately harms human rights. It therefore turns out that following the constitutional revolution, the anchoring in primary legislation ceased to serve as a shield against judicial intervention, which places the aforementioned move in doubt. A good example of the weakness of this explanation can be seen in the Supreme Court ruling regarding yeshiva students in 2012. As was explained above, in 1998 the Court rejected the arrangement of exemption for yeshiva students from being drafted into the IDF after ruling that the Minister of Defense was not authorized to establish a principled arrangement in the matter. We also explained that in the wake of the Supreme Court's ruling, the Knesset was "forced" to regulate the matter in detailed primary legislation. However, a decade after the arrangement had been anchored in primary legislation, the Court once again disqualified it, this time on substantive grounds, after stating that the law disproportionately harmed the right to equality. This ruling forced the legislators to adopt a new arrangement, which significantly limited the extent of draft exemptions given to yeshiva students.[70]

The law regarding the drafting of yeshiva students is not the only security-related piece of legislation the Supreme Court has repealed. In one case, the Court disqualified section 5 to the Criminal Procedure Law (Detainee Suspected of Security Crime) (Temporary Provision, which authorizes the Court—given certain conditions—to deliberate on the extension of the detention of a suspect of security crimes without that suspect being present. The Court stated that the goal of this law is proper, but that it disproportionately harms the suspect's right to a fair trial, including the right of the suspect to be present during court-related arrest proceedings.[71] In another case, the Court disqualified the Civil Wrongs Law (Liability of the State) (amendment no. 7), 2005, which exempted the state of responsibility for damage caused in a conflict area due to an action taken by security forces.[72] This ruling is very relevant for our subject, since much like the ruling in the matter of drafting yeshiva students, the law in question was passed by the Knesset, which was dissatisfied by the narrow interpretation granted by the Supreme Court to a similar exemption established by previous legislation.

The examples brought here ostensibly weaken the explanation I proposed for a gradual move to the new model. If the Court is undeterred when it comes to intervening (or continuing to intervene) in the decisions of the political system in security matters, even after they are anchored in primary legislation, what is the point of such an anchoring from the political system's perspective? There are two answers for this: First, even if the Court is willing to review Knesset laws, there is still logic from the Knesset's perspective in anchoring detailed authority in primary legislation, as it is reasonable to assume that the Court will act with more restraint when dealing with primary legislation, as opposed to an administrative arrangement.[73] Second, while moving from the old model to the new one, the legislators created a secondary model of legislation within the framework of the new model, whose validity may not be conditional on the declaration of a state of emergency, but which is nevertheless time-limited. The addition of the time limitation may lead the Court to be more restrained when reviewing legislation subject to such constraints. A good example of time-limited legislation is the Citizenship and Entry into Israel (Temporary Provision) Law, which limits the possibility of granting Israeli citizenship or residency status to Palestinians residing in Judea, Samaria, or the Gaza Strip, who are spouses of Israeli citizens.[74] We will deal with this law more extensively in Chapter 8 below. For our purposes, it is important to note that section 5 of the law limits its validity to a defined period, but allows the government, with the Knesset's approval, to issue an order extending its period, for a time of no longer than one year.

The addition of the limitation on the period of validity of security legislation into the model of permanent arrangement of security authorities in primary legislation is not unique to Israel. Other countries have also used this mechanism.[75] The choice of this mechanism seems logical, since even if we have abandoned the path of legislation conditional on a state of emergency (and perhaps because of this fact), it is still possible and proper to distinguish between threats whose end is not in the foreseeable future, and other matters, where there is reason to hope that there will be improvement rendering harm to human rights unnecessary. The use of this mechanism can also be based on the hope that this will moderate the extent of public and judicial criticism of this legislation.[76] Explicit support for the logic of this reason can be found, for instance, in the following written by Justice Cheshin in his opinion on the petition submitted against the constitutionality of the arrangement established by the Citizenship Law:

> the less we declare temporary laws void, the better . . . Security reasons are reasons that change from time to time, and determining that a law is a temporary law means a reduction in the harm caused by it merely to the areas where security reasons so demand.[77]

Note that even if the addition of the limitation on the period of the security legislation's validity weakens judicial criticism of the law's content, it cannot grant it immunity. Indeed, the Supreme Court has at least once repealed security legislation despite its formulation as a temporary order.[78] Moreover, the emerging practice in Israel is of repeated extensions of these kinds of laws. This practice fits with the de facto permanence of the declaration of a state of emergency, as well as the trend

I pointed to, of anchoring emergency period legislation, originally limited to three months, in law within the previous arrangement model I mentioned above. The fact that a significant amount of this legislation has remained in place over time, despite the existence of various mechanisms whose purpose was to limit the validity of security legislation, does not necessarily demonstrate dishonesty on the part of the legislators. We can attribute this phenomenon to the assessment of the political system that, unfortunately, the conditions justifying the legislation in question are still in place. Either way, the reality of repeated extension of time-limited legislation may reduce the weight the Court grants to the formally temporary nature of the law, or even ignore it and examine it as it would a permanent law, weakening the effectiveness of this model as a means to defend the permanent arrangements it establishes from judicial intervention.

Evidence of the weakening of the judicial avoidance of intervening in temporary legislation, with the extension of such legislation, can be found, again, in the Supreme Court's actions in the matter of the drafting of yeshiva students. In its aforementioned ruling from 2012, the Court repealed the law that arranged the drafting of yeshiva students. The validity of the law passed in 2002 was limited to five years, during which the Court rejected a petition against its validity. Afterwards, the validity of the law was extended for the same amount of time. During the extension period, another petition was submitted against the law, and this time the Court accepted the petition and repealed the law.[79]

4. THE STRENGTHENING OF PUBLIC COMMITMENT TO PROTECT HUMAN RIGHTS

According to the previous two explanations, the move to the new model can be seen as a confrontational move by the legislators, whose purpose is to fortify existing arrangements in the area of security from growing judicial critique of these arrangements. However, it may be that the process is more complicated than that, and that the wind blowing from the courts affects public opinion in Israel and strengthens the commitment of the Knesset to defending human rights, a fact expressed in the willingness of MKs to delve deep into security arrangements, and decide for themselves how to balance security needs and human rights. Take note: even according to this explanation, the agent of change is the Court, but as opposed to the previous two explanations, according to this explanation the move to a pattern of permanent and detailed arrangement in primary legislation is not a confrontational move, but rather one that aligns with the approach of the Court.

A complete demonstration of this argument requires going beyond what the present discussion will allow. I will therefore suffice here by pointing to a number of points that grant the argument a degree of support. First, in some of the cases, the move to the new model did not end in the mere anchoring of old model practices in primary legislation, but also involved the repeal and moderation of some of the authority granted to the executive branch within the framework of this model. A prominent example of such a move can be found in the Combatting Terrorism Law, which, as we noted, repealed and changed arrangements that were no longer necessary, or the sort that was sufficiently arranged in the law itself, but also arrangements that were found inappropriate in a democratic country. Second, the handling of the legislation of shaping arrangements within the framework of the new model is thorough and ongoing, and written and oral testimonies from the discussions in the relevant Knesset committees attest to a high level of awareness, and commitment to the need to balance security needs and human rights.[80] Finally, in some cases, the new legislation subjects the authority granted to the executive branch to periodic review by the legislators, on the manner in which this authority was used.[81] The adoption of this review mechanism may attest to a change in how the legislature views its role, from a body meant primarily to grant the executive the necessary authority to protect the security of the state and its citizens, to one that is also tasked with the responsibility to ensure that this authority will not be used excessively and unnecessarily.[82]

8

RELIGION AND STATE

I. Introduction

The Jewish religion holds a prominent place in legislation and public life in Israel. The reasons for this are varied. First, the Jewish religion has an all-encompassing character, which leads it to try and influence public life, as opposed to a religion such as Protestantism, whose ambitions are narrower. Second, the Jewish religious group in Israel is large and dominant, and therefore has more political power than religious groups in most of the countries of the West. Finally, even part of the non-religious Jewish public in Israel is interested in maintaining a degree of connection to religion, due to the unique connection between nation and religion in Judaism.

In the first decades of the state, relations between religion and state were anchored in a series of arrangements known as the "status quo."[1] There is a debate on the origins of the status quo. Some claim that most of the arrangements included in it were formed on the eve of the state's founding, in June 1947. According to this version, the arrangement was a compromise between the Zionist camp and the Haredi camp, which was meant to ensure that the Jewish community in the Land of Israel presented a united front before the UN Special Committee on Palestine, which was visiting the country to send the UN recommendations on its political future.[2] Others claim that the status quo arrangements were formed after the founding of the state, in the first years of its existence.[3]

Two reasons are given for the formation of the status quo at this time. One pegs this arrangement as being based on cost-benefit coalition calculations.[4] The second is that the arrangement was the conscious preference for a consensus solution to one involving deciding in favor of one side or the other.[5] Either way, the status quo was preserved over a number of decades, even if its arrangements changed somewhat from time to time. This situation has changed in the last two decades; the status quo has gradually weakened, and many arrangements once thought to be set in stone have been reopened for discussion.[6] A number of factors led to the crumbling of the status quo. One of these, perhaps the primary one, is the increasing intervention of the Supreme Court in value questions in general, and in matters of religion and state in particular.[7] In this chapter, I will describe the arrangement in force regarding three central subjects—the draft of yeshiva students into the IDF, marriage and divorce law, and Sabbath—and the changes that have occurred over the years in every one of them, with a focus on the role played by the Court in creating the change.

II. Drafting Yeshiva Students

The Security Service Law [Consolidated Version], 1987, states that, alongside the obligation of every citizen to serve in the security forces, the Minister of Defense has the authority to defer or exempt citizens from service for various reasons. For many long years, the Minister of Defense deferred the draft of yeshiva students whose "Torah is their craft". The historic background of the decision was the destruction of the yeshiva world of European Jewry in the Holocaust. The exemption for yeshiva students was seen as a lifesaver for a disappearing world, which had cultural and historical value for Jewish society.[8] In the state's first years, the extent of the deferral—which in the overwhelming majority of cases became a complete exemption within a few years—was very limited, involving a couple of hundred yeshiva students. Over the years, the extent of this exemption was expanded.[9]

Since the 1970s, the Supreme Court began to address this issue in response to petitions submitted to it on the matter. The first petition was filed in 1970.[10] The petitioner presented himself has having a personal interest in the matter, as he was a "student by profession and a reserve officer with the rank of lieutenant."[11] The court summarily rejected the petition on the grounds of non-justiciability and lack of standing.[12] The court's decision to base itself on the doctrines of the right of standing and of justiciability was well anchored in Supreme Court precedent. In accordance with the doctrine of standing, only an petitioner who was directly and personally harmed by the actions of the government authorities has the right to be heard.[13] According to the doctrine of justiciability, the court is only supposed to address petitions that raise issues whose dominant character is not political but legal, and can therefore be decided based on legal principles.

The next petition was filed in 1981. This petition was also summarily rejected.[14] Justice Cohen, who wrote the main opinion in the ruling, explained that the reasons given for rejecting the previous petition "have not become stale, and their taste has not expired."[15] Another petition, which was filed in 1982 by the same petitioner, was also rejected, but a third petition filed by the same petitioner, in the middle of the 1980s, marks a certain turning point in the court's approach to the subject.[16] The court did reject the petition, but this time it did so after deliberating on the petition itself, without summarily rejecting it. The rejection of the petition was based on the court's statement that the extent of the exemption for yeshiva students did not reach such dimensions as to require a ruling that it is not reasonable. Justice Barak explained:

> There is importance, in the end, to the number of yeshiva students whose draft has been deferred. There is a limit that the Minister of Defense may not pass. Quantity makes quality. In this matter, the petitioners have not taken on the burden they bear to show that the harm to security is not light.[17]

This ruling carried with it the seeds of a future change in how the Supreme Court would rule on the issue. This change occurred in the wake of a ruling handed down in the next petition on the subject, submitted at the end of the 1990s.[18] In this ruling, discussed at length in previous chapters,[19] the court came out, for the first time, against the exemption arrangement, and ruled it illegal. The court based its decision on the argument that the Minister of Defense was not granted the authority to exempt all the yeshiva students, but only to grant exemptions on an individual basis. This argument was based on the interpretive presumption that such arrangements ("primary arrangements") should be made by the legislature, and it is therefore unlikely that the legislator intended to delegate to the Minister of Defense the authority to decide to give a sweeping exemption to all yeshiva students. The court returned the question to be handled by the legislator, without stating if a possible decision of the Knesset to anchor the same arrangement in primary legislation would pass the test of constitutional review.

The court's ruling should have led to the immediate drafting of all yeshiva students, but the court suspended the validity of this ruling for a period of one year, to allow the political system to prepare and anchor an alternative arrangement in primary legislation. In the wake of this ruling, the government appointed a public committee to propose an appropriate arrangement. The committee deliberated, and ultimately recommended that the yeshiva students continue to receive exemption from military service, but after four years they will be able to leave the yeshiva for a "decision year" in which the student will decide his future: if he wishes to do so, he can go back to studying in yeshiva and not be drafted into the army, and if he wishes to leave the yeshiva, he will be drafted into shortened military or civilian service, after which he can look after his own affairs.[20] The Knesset adopted the committee's recommendations and anchored them in law (below: Deferral of Service Law).[21] The validity of the law was set for five years from the date of its publishing, and the Knesset was given the authority to extend its validity for another five years.

Shortly after the passing of the Deferral of Service Law, a number of petitions were filed against it, and were heard before an expanded panel of nine judges.[22] The petitioners argued that the Deferral of Service Law harms the right to equality, and that this harm does not meet the conditions of the limitation clause in Basic Law: Human Dignity and Freedom, which means that the law is not constitutional.

Contrary to previous times, this time the question of the constitutionality of primary legislation was on the agenda. Since the petitions were also based primarily on the claim of harm to equality, the court was first required to decide on the question of whether the right to equality was anchored in the new Basic Laws—even though it is not explicitly mentioned there, and was indeed omitted from the law by design—a question that was yet to be ruled on. Most of the judges ruled that the right to equality is included in the constitutional right to human dignity enumerated in Basic Law: Human Dignity and Freedom. The court ruled that the legal arrangements harm this right, in discriminating between those who serve in the army according to the normal rules, and yeshiva students, who are entitled to an exemption and deferral. Having ruled this, the court turned to the limitation clause to see if the harm to rights can be justified.

President Barak, who wrote the main opinion in the case, ruled that the Deferral of Service Law contains a number of proper purposes, including support for Torah study, based on the recognition of the value of these studies and the uniqueness of Haredi society, and the increase in equality in sharing the burden of military service in Israeli society, compared to the existing situation, where the overwhelming majority of Haredim do not serve at all. Barak went on from there to examine the question of proportionality. His central argument was that the picture emerging three years after the law went into force does not match the expectations in terms of the purposes noted above, a fact that places the law's meeting the first of the three proportionality tests—which examines if there is a rational connection between the purpose of the law and the means chosen to realize it—in serious question. But since this was a temporary law, whose goal was to examine processes over time, Barak preferred not to decide on the matter, and wait until the end of the five-year period. However, Barak stated that "alongside our decision that the petitions are rejected, as for now we cannot decide their non-constitutionality, we go on to state that if the trend continues, and there is no significant change in the state of affairs, there is a fear that the Deferral of Service Law will become unconstitutional."[23]

As noted, the validity of the Deferral of Service Law was limited to five years, but the Knesset was given the authority to extend this period, and it indeed used this authority and extended the law for another five years. Immediately afterwards, a number of petitions were submitted to the Supreme Court against the law.[24]

The central question that occupied the nine Justices on the panel and the representatives of both sides in the deliberation was whether or not the certain increase in the number of Haredim enlisting in the Israel Defense Forces (IDF) and national service was the "significant change" that the Supreme Court demanded in the above-quoted ruling.[25] The state argued that the slowness in implementing the law derived from the "non-introduction of appropriate tools" to implement it, in the first stage, but the state added that despite the difficulties, the increase in the number of those turning to service expressed a "dramatic change" that justified continuing to implement the law.

In September 2009, the Court decided once again to delay a decision on the matter for another fifteen months, and expressed displeasure at the slow implementation of the law.[26] The final ruling on the petition was handed down in February 2012. The Court ruled, by a majority vote of 6-3, that the Deferral of Service Law is not constitutional, and should therefore not be extended beyond its expected date of expiration in August 2012. The majority justices, headed by President Beinisch, stated that the data presented to the Court does not substantiate a connection between the means established by the law and the declared goal of increasing equality, and as such, the harm to equality embodied by the law's arrangements cannot be justified.[27] Justice Arbel, in a minority opinion joined by Justice Rivlin, believed that those charged with the implementation of the law should be given another extension to prove the aforementioned connection, and Justice Grunis, in his own minority opinion, repeated his opinion from previous rulings, that in light of the fact that the Deferral of Service Law was adopted by an entirely democratic procedure, with the agreement of the members of the secular majority group, there is no room for the intervention of the Supreme Court. Grunis further added that in his opinion, the repeated involvement of the Court in the matter, without real progress being achieved from judicial intervention, "certainly does not contribute to the status of the Supreme Court."[28]

In light of the Supreme Court ruling, the Knesset created a special committee to form an agreed arrangement, and after that committee finished its work, the Defense

Service Law was amended in 2014. The new arrangement established a two-stage process for integrating yeshiva students into military and civil service, which would take place over the course of nine years.[29] The arrangement was characterized by the move from a personal model of draft deferment to a collective model, in which the government was authorized to set draft targets for the entire Haredi community. The law set a minimal annual target of draftees for military and civilian service, obligating the government to increase this number every year. In the first stage, known as the "first adaptation period," it would be an entirely voluntary arrangement, lacking any element of coercing service. During this period, yeshiva students would be able to choose whether to enlist in regular military service, serve in civil service, or continue to learn in yeshiva. In the second stage, called the "second adaptation period", the draft targets would have practical significance. During this period, draft will be deferrable until age twenty-one, irrespective of the targets, but from that age a yeshiva student could receive another draft deferment only if that year's draft targets have been met. If they have not, a draft obligation to military or civilian service would apply to all yeshiva students—from age twenty-one, except for 1,800 yeshiva students—and economic and criminal sanctions would be imposed on those dodging the draft. The second adaptation period was set to end on June 30, 2023 (section 26b of that law), with the law not stating what would happen after that date.

A number of petitions were filed against the new arrangement, but before the ruling was handed down in the matter, the Knesset passed another amendment to the Defense Service Law, which softened the arrangement, and allowed the Minister of Defense to continue to grant draft exemptions in the second adaptation period, even if draft targets were not reached.[30] In the wake of the amendment, another petition was filed, and all the petitions were handled collectively. On September 2017, the Court nullified the aforementioned arrangement—by an 8-1 majority—after having found it to contain two primary flaws: "The first, the fact that even the new draft arrangement remains exclusively dependent on the goodwill of the executive branch and the yeshiva students and the Haredi community, as no practical sanctions have been determined in it . . . The second lies in the temporariness of the new draft arrangement, and the lack of any arrangement of a permanent solution on this matter."[31]

III. Marriage and Divorce

Looking at the legal state of marriage and divorce in various countries around the world reveals a range of options: at one end are states that do not even recognize religious marriages, and in which the only way to register for marriage and enjoy the associated benefits is civilian, and the same is true when dissolving marriage. In the middle of the spectrum are states where religious marriages are recognized by law as an equal alternative to civil marriage. At the other end of the spectrum are states where the only way to get married is in a religious ceremony. Most of the states in this last category are illiberal. Israel is the only liberal country belonging to this category, as it grants religious law exclusivity in the area of marriage. This exclusivity relates not only to Jews but also to citizens of other religions, who have to make use of their religious system (Muslim, Christian, or Druze) to get married.[32] We will focus below on Jewish marriages, but most of what is said here will also be relevant to non-Jews.

The religious monopoly in matters of personal status is the continuation of an arrangement that was in force in Mandatory Palestine, which is itself a continuation of the *millet* system applied by the Ottoman Empire in the nineteenth century. As part of the *millet* arrangement, religious courts were given official and exclusive judicial authority in matters regarding marriage and divorce, in an attempt to grant equal rights to the members of the various religious communities in the Empire.

With the foundation of the state, Israel had no interest in changing the arrangements that granted autonomy in matters of marriage and divorce to non-Jewish communities, but a debate took place when it came to Jewish marriage and divorce. Only in 1953 the arrangement set regarding marriage and divorce was made law, preserving the principle of the *millet* system (with minor changes), with an emphasis on the religious monopoly being vital to prevent a split in the Jewish People.[33]

Sections 1–2 of the Rabbinical Courts Jurisdiction Law, 1953 (henceforth: Jurisdiction Law), state as follows:

1. Matters of marriage and divorce of Jews in Israel who are citizens of the state or its residents will be under the exclusive jurisdiction of the rabbinical courts.
2. Marriage and divorce of Jews will be conducted in Israel according to Torah law.

The religious exclusivity in the field of marriage and divorce touches on two main levels: the law arranging marriage, which establishes who is fit to marry and what the mutual obligations of the couple are, and the ceremony in which the couple acquires the status of "married." This exclusivity leads to problems at two levels. Jewish Halacha has a patriarchal character, and if marriage laws are based on the Halacha, they will also be patriarchal, thus violating the obligation that Israel accepted upon itself to take "the appropriate steps to ensure equality of rights and obligations between the couple in the framework of marriage, during them and upon their dissolution."[34] Moreover, the Halacha imposes limits on the right to be married, which marks many people as "disqualified for marriage." It also does not allow marriage between a Jew and a non-Jew. These limitations do not sit with the right to marry as recognized in international human rights law.[35] Finally, the customary Orthodox marriage ceremony is clearly religious, and therefore Jews who wish to marry in Israel need to participate in a religious ceremony, an act that involves a violation of their conscience.[36]

If we described the situation in Israel only based on the law books, the conclusion would be that there is a serious conflict between the legal arrangement of marriage in Israel and basic liberal principles. However, when we turn our attention to the Supreme Court's rulings in these matters, a more complex picture emerges, the main outlines of which will be described below.

In the *Rogozinsky* case, handled by the Supreme Court in the beginning of the 1960s, the petitioners asked the Court to order the repeal of the religious monopoly on marriage and divorce, established by the Jurisdiction Law.[37] The petitioners argued that this arrangement harms the right to conscience, which was recognized in a previous ruling as one of the state's basic principles, and the commitment to which is included in the Declaration of Independence. The representative of the petitioners proposed that the Court learn from the example of the United States and nullify the problematic legal articles.

The Court rejected the comparison. Justice Berenzon, who wrote the main opinion on the case, stated as follows:

In the United States, when law and constitution faced each other, it was obvious that the constitution is superior, and the court only gave practical expression to this clear rule. By us, the question is a Knesset law against the Declaration of Independence, and the latter does not have the status of law, and certainly not the status of a constitution that overrides a normal law. When it is clear, beyond any doubt, that the will of the legislator is to hand over the affairs of marriage and divorce to the judgment of the Jewish religious courts and that these marriages and divorces be conducted according to Torah law... the court must respect this will and grant it validity, even if it does not align with the principle of freedom of conscience in the Declaration of Independence.[38]

As explained in Chapter 1 above, the refusal of the Court, in the *Rogozinsky* case, to intervene in the arrangements established by the Jurisdiction Law, fits the consistent line of the Supreme Court from the state's founding until the constitutional revolution, according to which it may not disqualify primary legislation without a constitution to rely on for doing so.[39] However, even after the revolution, the Court still came up short. First, as explained in Chapter 2, freedom of religion and conscience were not included in the Basic Laws passed in 1992, and this as part of the compromise that paved the way for the passing of these two Basic Laws.[40] The Court could overcome this hurdle by reading freedom of religion into the Basic Laws, as it did regarding the right to equality, which it used as the basis to disqualify the Deferral of Service Law. However, in the case of the Jurisdiction Law, the Court faces another hurdle in the form of section 10 of Basic Law: Human Dignity and Freedom, which entrenches "old" primary legislation, passed before 1992, and thus keeps it from being nullified.[41]

But even if the Court cannot nullify the Jurisdiction Law and the monopoly it grants to religion in the area of marriage and divorce, it can still operate in other ways—and so it has—to significantly moderate the harm to rights deriving from this monopoly.

In certain respects, the Halacha enjoys a monopoly—for instance, in terms of who is fit to be married—but in other aspects, primarily financial, it has no such monopoly, and in some cases it is even forbidden to follow it. This much was ruled in a revolutionary decision in 1994 regarding the *Bavli* case, in which the Supreme Court obligated the Rabbinical court to apply secular law to any subject not classified as "matters of personal status in the narrow sense," in a manner that would fit the principle of equality between the couple.[42]

We are left with three problems with the religious monopoly in matters of personal status: the denial of the right to be married, of those deemed unfit for this purpose according to the Halacha; the restriction of this right due to the inability to marry a non-Jew; and the harm to conscience involved in compelling participation in a religious marriage ceremony. Here the Supreme Court entered the picture and shaped two alternatives, which weaken the religious monopoly and the coercive element it contains. I will present these alternatives below, and see if they offer a reasonable solution to the problems.

1. RECOGNITION OF CIVIL MARRIAGE

From the standpoint of the written law, civil marriage is not available in Israel, but the Supreme Court rendered a precedent-setting decision in the 1960s, which opened the door to the recognition of such marriages.[43] Ms. Funk, a Christian resident in Israel, and Mr. Schlesinger, a Jewish citizen of Israel, obtained a civil marriage in Cyprus. When they returned to Israel, they applied to the Ministry of Interior to be registered as married. The Ministry rejected their application on the grounds that civil marriage is not available in Israel. The couple petitioned to the Supreme Court, and their petition was accepted in a majority decision, with the main justification being that the registration of personal status is meant only for statistical purposes, and takes no stand on whether the couple is "really" married or not.

At first glance, the Court's decision in this case has no practical significance, because it was said to apply only to mere registration—registration for statistical purposes only—yet it led to a revolution in the legal regulation of marriage in Israel. In practice, the ruling authorities—the housing administration, the social security administration, the military authorities, the tax administration, and others—determine marital status according to the official register, and do seek independent evidence to support it.[44] The result is that today, Israeli couples who got married in a civil marriage abroad enjoy all the rights and privileges of couples who get married through the Rabbinate, even when these are couples that the Rabbinate would have refused to wed.

For many years, the Supreme Court continued to claim that this registration implies no recognition of the validity of these marriages. More recently, however, the Court took an important step toward such recognition, relying on a revolutionary decision of the high Rabbinical Court in 2003. The decision concerned a couple who got married in Cyprus and then registered their marriage in the Israeli population register according to the *Funk-Schlesinger* precedent. Several years later, the husband decided to divorce his wife. Since Section 1 of the law on the jurisdiction of the Rabbinical Courts (1953) states that marriage and divorce between Jews in Israel are under the exclusive authority of the Rabbinical Court system, the husband approached his local Rabbinical Court to arrange the divorce proceedings. The Court agreed and announced the dissolution of the marriage. In contrast to the custom in other cases of divorce, the Court did not require the husband to give his wife a *get*, but considered this announcement of dissolution to be sufficient to allow each member of the couple to exit the marriage bond and remarry.

The divorced wife petitioned to the Supreme Court against the decision of the Rabbinical Court, and the Supreme Court asked the High Rabbinical Court to explain this decision. The Rabbinical Court started by explaining why no *get* was necessary in this case. The court said that if a Jewish couple chooses a civil marriage of their own free will, namely, in spite of the fact that it had the option of a religious marriage, it thereby explicitly rejects the Halacha, and expresses their desire *not* to get married according to Jewish law.

But now the following question arises: If the couple in question was never married according to the Halacha, then why did they need a divorce, and how could the local Rabbinic Court claim to have undone their marriage? The High Rabbinical Court based its answer on the halachic rules concerning marriage and divorce among *non-Jews*. That Jewish law includes such rules might seem bizarre, until one recalls that it does, in fact, include norms that apply to non-Jews as well, known as the Noahide

Laws.[45] For instance, according to Halacha, all human beings are subject to the prohibition against murder, theft and—directly relevant to the present context—adultery. Since the Halacha forbids adultery among non-Jews as well, it has to specify the ways by which non-Jews get married and divorced. Based on Maimonides, the court ruled that, according to Halacha, marriage and divorce between non-Jews is valid if performed in a way that is acceptable in a civilized society. A non-Jewish couple that gets married this way earns the halachic status of being married. If the couple wants to get divorced—we mean divorced according to the Halacha—it has to undergo the accepted procedure for divorce in that society. Thus a non-Jewish woman who was divorced in a civil court in Paris or Chicago would not be guilty of adultery if she married another man afterward, since her civil divorce is halachically valid.

But how is this religious law concerning *non*-Jews relevant to the marriage and divorce of *Jews*? This brings us to the revolutionary aspect of the Rabbinical Court decision. The court claimed that Jews can get married in one of two ways—either as Jews or as human beings (or as Noahides, to use the halachic term). The preferred way is the former, but the latter also has halachic validity. This means that a Jewish couple who obtains a civil marriage is halachically married, even though not "according to the law of Moses and Israel." And this means that the way to undo their marriage is not the one that applies to Jews who got married "according to the law of Moses and Israel," but the one that applies to Noahide-based marriages. That's why—to conclude—the lower Rabbinical Court that simply undid the marriage had full authority to do so. It treated the couple as having obtained a Noahide marriage, and accordingly applied the divorce procedure that applies to such a marriage, rather than the standard Jewish one.

Shortly after the High Rabbinical Court ruled this, the Supreme Court adopted this ruling enthusiastically, and used it to recognize the full validity of civil marriage between Jews conducted abroad.[46] This decision of the Court is indeed revolutionary, but its extent is limited. It recognized the complete validity of civil marriage of Israeli citizens who married abroad. However, it is limited to cases where both members of the couple are Jewish.

Additional progress in the gradual process of judicial recognition of the validity of civil marriage was registered in another ruling.[47] This time, the question regarded the validity of a civil marriage where only one member of the couple was Jewish. Jewish religious law does not recognize the possibility of inter-religious marriage, but the Court tended to the opinion that the personal, religious law applying to both members of the couple should not be applied here, but rather the laws of the state where the ceremony was conducted, and to recognize the validity of the marriage on that basis. However, at the end of the day, the Court limited its ruling to the specific context before it: the right of the widow to an inheritance. Israeli inheritance law grants the right of inheritance to the spouse of the deceased.[48] The Court ruled that the term "spouse" includes those who were married to a person in a marriage valid in the country where it was conducted. Despite this aforementioned limitation, this ruling contains a significant innovation, in the sense that it clearly shows a tendency to entirely reject religious law in the case of marriage conducted in a civil ceremony abroad, and that is valid according to that country's laws.

In sum, in the wake of the *Funk-Schlezinger* affair, Jews who are citizens of Israel and married in civil marriages abroad can be registered in Israel as married and enjoy all the rights of married couples. The revolutionary decision of the High Rabbinical Court, and the ruling of the Supreme Court handed down in its wake, strengthened this direction in granting a kind of official recognition to such marriages, and in the ruling that there is no need for a religious ceremony to dissolve them. Finally, the ruling in which the Supreme Court referred to the couple married civilly abroad as married for the purposes of inheritance, despite the fact that they cannot be married according to religious law, constituted another major step forward to full judicial recognition of civil marriages conducted abroad.

Despite this, it would appear that the aforementioned arrangement does not provide a satisfactory solution to the problems described above. Israeli citizens can get married and divorced on a track that is almost entirely "civil" (i.e., not religious), but the choice of the civil track requires going abroad. The need to go abroad to overcome the religious monopoly is problematic in two respects. First, this alternative is not available to all citizens equally, because using it requires means and knowledge not available to everyone. Second, if the religious monopoly is problematic, a state cannot avoid its obligation to respect the rights of its citizens by directing them to marriage arrangements offered in another country.

2. RECOGNIZING THE LEGAL STATUS OF COMMON-LAW SPOUSES

Another way in which the Court has reduced the religious monopoly in personal status matters is the institution of common-law unions. By that we refer to couples who live together, share a household, sometimes bring children into the world, and all this without officially marrying. The Supreme Court included these couples in the legal definition of "common-law spouses" [lit. in Hebrew: "known in public"], and has almost entirely equated their position with that of married couples. Other countries have also acknowledged this status, but in Israel, this recognition is particularly broad and deep.[49] For our purposes, Jewish couples in Israel who choose the common-law path do not get married, and sections 1–2 of the Jurisdiction Law do not apply to them at all. This means that the Rabbinical Court has no authority at all to handle their affairs, and religious law is also irrelevant for them.

I argued above that judicial recognition of the validity of civil marriage conducted abroad does not entirely settle the tension between Israeli marriage law and liberal values, but the flaws we found in the civil marriage arrangement are not relevant to the institution of the common-law partnership. First, the burden involved in acquiring the status of common-law partners, including the rights and obligations deriving from it, is not heavier than that involving getting married through the Rabbinate. There is therefore no room to argue that the Israeli arrangement coerces the secular Jew to get married in a religious manner because of the added burden involved in the alternative track. Second, the status of common-law partners is acquired in Israel without any need to make use of a foreign legal system. This institution can therefore ostensibly be assumed to offer a proper solution for the problems emanating from the religious monopoly in marital affairs.

Despite this, it seems that the alternative of the common-law partnership does not entirely settle the tension between the religious monopoly on marriage and divorce and the obligation to honor human rights. Specifically, this track does not provide a solution to the harm to the right to marry, anchored in international human rights charters[50] and some of the constitutions of democratic countries.[51] This right reflects a common approach that the status of "married" is very important to people, regardless of the specific benefits involved. Even in today's open and libertine society, most couples wish to be married, not just live together and get certain rights. In this state of affairs, the difference between a married couple and a common-law couple is of great importance. In light of all this, the requirement to participate in a religious ceremony as a condition for acquiring the status of being married amounts to coercion, harming conscience.

My conclusion is that despite the gradual weakening of the religious monopoly on marriage and divorce in Israel, it is still troubling in terms of liberal values. It would appear that the appropriate solution to the problem is the creation of a civil marriage track alongside the religious marriage one, in such a way that every couple can freely decide how to marry. This solution enjoys broad support among the Jewish population in Israel,[52] including some of the Rabbinic leadership.[53]

In recent years, several creative attempts have been made to improve the situation in the area of marriage, including promoting legislation that would institutionalize relations between a couple in the form of a "couple's covenant" without granting them the status of marriage. The use of the term "covenant" was meant to grant the relationship a serious and binding status even though it is not marriage. One of the attempts was even successful, when the Knesset passed the Spousal Association for Persons without a Religion Law, 2010 (henceforth: The Couple's Covenant Law), which allows two people who are not members of religions recognized in Israel (known as "devoid of religion") to enter a couple's covenant.[54] Does the couple's covenant offer a satisfactory solution for the problem of tension between the religious monopoly and liberal values? On the one hand, entering into a couple's covenant is a clear, public, and binding step, unlike the life of people in a common-law relationship, and in this sense it comes closer to the desired status of marriage. On the other hand, creating the new institution involves, in all its versions, an explicit rejection of the status of marriage from those who enter into it. It is therefore doubtful if this arrangement can be seen as a satisfactory alternative to the institution of marriage. By the way, after the Couple's Covenant Law was passed, a petition was filed to the Supreme Court to repeal it, on the grounds that it harms the constitutional right to family life and the constitutional right to equality. The Court rejected the petition, among other reasons because "this is a first legislative step, in a new and complex field, which may be accompanied by new legislative steps, and therefore would be worthy to be allowed to develop a bit before this court deals with it."[55]

IV. Work and Commerce on Sabbath

The issue of work and commerce on Sabbath has been accompanying the State of Israel throughout its existence, after already having precursors during the Mandatory period.[56] In the first two decades of the state, a political struggle was fought over the content of the arrangement to be anchored in law on this issue. On the one hand were the religious, who wished to pass a special Sabbath law that would protect the sanctity of Sabbath and its role as a national-cultural symbol, alongside the protection granted to the worker for a weekly day of rest. On the other hand was the ruling party in those years—Mapai (The Party of the Workers of the Land of Israel)—which stressed only the right of the worker to rest, which they wished to protect in a general law arranging the right of workers to rest.

The efforts to shape the public Sabbath in the State of Israel in legislation already had begun in the first government meeting of May 16, 1948, two days after the state was founded.[57] David Tzvi Pinkas, representative of the party that united all the Orthodox Jewish streams, offered to include in the first legislative act of the Provisional Council of State—the Law and Administration Ordinance—the unique status of Sabbath as a day of rest.[58]

The Proposed Days of Rest Ordinance, 1948, was submitted to the Provisional Council of State and accepted unanimously on June 3, 1948.[59] It was then integrated into section 18a of the Law and Administration Ordinance.[60] The validity of this article was retroactively determined from the eve of the state's founding.

Sabbath and the Jewish holidays—the two days of Rosh Hashanah, Yom Kippur, the first day and day of Shmini Atzeret of Sukkot, the first and seventh day of Pesach and the holiday of Shavu'ot—are the permanent rest days in the State of Israel. Those who are not Jews are permitted to have rest days on their Sabbaths and holidays. These holidays will be determined regarding each community according to a government decision to be published in the official record.[61]

The ordinance was—in the language of Minister of Justice Pinchas Rozen—an "ordinance of principles,"[62] lacking "teeth"[63] that would allow it to shape the image of Sabbath in the young state.[64] The declarative character of the ordinance led to dissatisfaction among the religious MKs, who insisted on passing a "Sabbath Law" with obligatory content.[65] Accordingly, the guideline agreement of the first government promised that "in a law that will establish the democratic and republican character of the State of Israel, Sabbath and the Jewish holidays will be the permanent rest days in the State of Israel."[66] The guideline agreement for the second government on this issue was much the same.[67]

Before the MKs of the religious parties could form a draft to the "Sabbath Law," a move aiming at shaping Sabbath in the State of Israel came from the opposite secular-socialist direction, in the framework of the Hours of Work and Rest Law, 1951, presented in the Knesset by Minister of Labour Golda Meir.[68] The law established the length of the workday and work week of the worker, and arranges work during overtime and compensation thereof. In addition, section 7 of the law establishes Sabbath as the rest day for Jewish workers, and allows workers who are not Jewish to choose another rest day—Friday or Sunday.

Those who held a religious or national view of Sabbath expressed disappointment at the "swallowing" of Sabbath into the Hours of Work and Rest Law. They saw it as proof that the drafters of the law did not intend to grant Sabbath a place as a day with its own value—religious or national-historical—but only use it to implement the general principle of a rest day.[69] The legal arrangements were also received with dissatisfaction. The law did not prohibit the opening of business on Sabbath, only the employment of Jews, and even this prohibition was not across the board, as the law only forbade *employing* Jewish workers, and it excluded freelancers and shared businesses from this prohibition. In addition, section 12 of the law granted the Minister of Labour the authority to grant work permits on the rest day "if he is convinced that stopping work for the weekly rest, for all or part of it, may harm the defense of the state or the bodily or monetary security, or cause great harm to the economy, the work process or the provision of some needs which are, in the Minister of Labor's opinion, vital for the public or part of it." According to the critics, this arrangement created a significant breach in the work prohibition established by the law.

This dissatisfaction led to the efforts to pass a Sabbath Law to remain energetic. For two decades, Mapai promised—in coalition agreements it formed with its coalition partner, the Religious National Party—time and again, to pass the Sabbath Law, but this promise was never kept. The only achievement the religious parties could point to was that in 1969, when an amendment to the law that imposed the prohibition of work on Sabbath on freelances and members of shared businesses was passed.[70] This amendment marked the end of the formative period of the legislative arrangement, and the arena of struggle for the shaping of Sabbath in the field of labor now moved to the courts.

Alongside the Hours of Work and Rest Law, the issue of work and commerce on Sabbath is also arranged via bylaws passed in most local authorities. The division of labor is as follows: The Hours of Work and Rest Law arranges the workers' rest on Sabbath, while the bylaws deal with the question of the opening (or closing) of the businesses themselves.

Until 1987, the legal basis for passing the bylaws arranging the opening and closing of businesses on Sabbath was contained within section 249(20) of the Municipalities Ordinance—legislation that originated in the Palestine Mandate—which stated as follows:

> [The municipality is authorized] to regulate the opening and closing of stores and workshops, restaurants, cafés, tea houses, drink houses, kiosks, cantinas and other establishments of this kind, and of cinema houses, theaters, and other places of public pleasure or of some form of them, and supervise their opening and closing, and determine—without harming the generality of the authority—the hours of their opening and closing on a given day.[71]

By force of this section, many local and regional authorities around the country passed bylaws that forbade opening businesses on Sabbath.[72] In 1987, the legal validity of these bylaws was put into question after then-Peace Court judge Ayala Procaccia ruled that the Jerusalem bylaw (opening businesses and closing them), 1955, which prohibited the opening of places of entertainment on Sabbath, cannot stand from a legal point of view. She ruled that the law authorized the local authorities to arrange the Sabbath rest, but not the preservation of Sabbath from a religious perspective. In light of this assumption, she turned to examine the bylaws, and found that the said bylaw was not meant "to ensure the person's welfare on the day of rest, but was entirely meant to shape the quality and content of the day of Sabbath in the spirit of the commandments of halakha."[73] This finding led the judge to conclude that the aforementioned prohibition was imposed without authority, and is therefore fundamentally invalid.

Procaccia's decision may not have obligated other courts at her level or above it, but those who supported the existing arrangement feared that additional judges would follow in her footsteps, and disqualify additional local bylaws. Against this background, the government passed an amendment to the Municipalities Ordinance in the Knesset, explicitly authorizing local authorities to pass bylaws that would order the closing of stores and businesses on Sabbath while relying on religious reasons.[74] The amendment, which became section 249(21) of the Ordinance, stated as follows:

> A municipality may use its authority based on passage (20) in the area of its jurisdiction or in part of it regarding the days of rest, in consideration of reasons of religious tradition.[75]

At the end of the 1960s, judicial involvement in various forms of Sabbath legislation began to emerge. Until the beginning of the 1990s, the discussion focused on the question of the validity of the bylaws passed on the basis of the Municipalities Ordinance and their interpretation, the interpretation of various sections in the Hours of Work and Rest Law, and the decisions made by the Minister of Labor by force of this law to grant work permits on Sabbath. In those years, jurisprudence demonstrated a clear tendency to minimize the extent of the prohibitions and expand the scope of the permits established in law. After the constitutional revolution, the court was also asked to examine the constitutionality of the arrangements established by the Hours of Work and Rest Law. A number of key milestones in the judicial involvement in this issue will be described below, separating between the rulings that dealt with the bylaws passed by force of the Municipalities Ordinance, and those that handled issues related to the Hours of Work and Rest Law.

1. OPENING AND CLOSING OF BUSINESSES

The Ramat Gan bylaw (opening businesses and clothing them), 1955, stated that "on rest days, a person will not open and will not allow the opening of a business or a place of entertainment." By force of this bylaw, the Ramat Gan municipality wished to fine a gas station that opened its gates on Sabbath. The Magistrate Court acquitted the station owner and canceled the fine. The District Court reversed the ruling, and the Supreme Court confirmed the decision of the first court by a majority decision.[76] Two arguments of the station owner were accepted: first, that it does not fall under the definition of a "store," as "if we go according to the common spoken language used by people . . . No one will call a gas station a store, just as no one will call a restaurant a store, even though it is managed in a structure that has the form of a store."[77] A second argument examined the bylaw through the lens of the "reasonable legislator": "In the present conditions of life, the gas station provides a vital service of the first order to the local population, and perhaps to a much broader population if it is on a main road. It is inconceivable that if they had considered it, they would equate the closing times of gas stations with those of normal businesses, a matter that would amount to preventing the supply of a particularly vital service from members of the public in those times."[78]

Another example of the role the Court played in providing a limiting interpretation of the Sabbath prohibitions in the bylaws can be seen in the case of the Hasharon mall in Netanyah from 1993. Section 3(d) of the Netanya bylaw (opening and closing businesses), 1957, stated as follows: "On rest days, aside from Yom Kippur and the eve of Tishav B'Av, no person will open and will not allow the opening of a place of entertainment, except for the purposes of cultural and educational activity."[79]

On 1989, Hasharon Mall was opened in Netanyah. The mall included movie theaters, and these began to operate on Sabbath nights as they did on weekdays. Two years after the mall was opened, the municipality decided to enforce the instructions of the bylaw, and ordered the cinema closed on Sabbath nights. The cinema petitioned to the Supreme Court, which accepted the petition after ruling that theater screenings are included in the category of "cultural and educational activities," which was removed from the prohibition established by the bylaw against the opening of places of entertainment on rest days.[80]

To protect the expansive interpretation given to "cultural and educational activities," President Shamgar had to overcome a significant hurdle: Section 1 of the bylaw, which defines the term "place of entertainment," explicitly included cinemas. According to a plain understanding of the text, if a cinema is a place of entertainment, then the routine activity therein—that is, the screening of movies—is prohibited, and its opening on Sabbath would be permitted only if it hosted a special activity of "culture and education"—of the sort that does not involve commercial screening of movies. President Shamgar dealt with this difficulty, and explained that when the bylaw instructs that "no person will open and will not allow the opening of a place of entertainment," this refers solely to the physical location and not to the content of the routine activity therein. Therefore, when the bylaw stated that a place of entertainment should not be opened, including cinemas, this does not mean the activity of screening movies, but rather the movie theater. Regarding the nature and content of activity taking place there, the law distinguishes between "cultural and educational activities" and other kinds of activities. If the location is hosting cultural activities, then the prohibition on the day of rest does not apply to it. The screening of a movie is a cultural activity, which takes place in a cinema, and is therefore permitted on Sabbath. Activities of other kinds, which may also take place in a cinema, are prohibited.

Shamgar's proposed interpretation of the bylaw is forced. Shamgar admitted as much, and explained that he chose it because "when some law comes to limit the right of the individual or harm it, it should not be interpreted in an expansive and sweeping manner. Its appropriate interpretation is limiting and precise."[81] For our purposes, the law's instruction does indeed come "to protect the interests of the religious public, to prevent harm to the character of the day of rest and its spirit, and especially to the population living nearby," but alongside this it involves "the limiting of the freedom of the individual, who wishes to seek out a form of cultural entertainment according to his taste, and sometimes precisely on the day of rest, in which he is free from his work." Therefore, it is appropriate that it be interpreted in a limiting fashion.

In 2017, the Court addressed the issue of the opening of businesses on Sabbath again, this time in the case of Tel Aviv. In recent years, Tel Aviv has seen the rapid expansion of a number of food chains that open their stores on Sabbath as well, contrary to the instructions of the municipal bylaw, which prohibited the opening of businesses on Sabbath. The municipality of Tel Aviv tended to impose fines on businesses violating this bylaw every Sabbath they opened their doors. The owners of small businesses petitioned to the Supreme Court against the municipality's choice to use this method of enforcement instead of others at its disposal. The petitioners argued that fines are not effective, and even harm the small businesses, since the large businesses can "absorb" the fine and still enjoy nice profits from sales on the day of rest, a luxury small businesses cannot afford.[82]

The Supreme Court accepted the petition.[83] Justice Naor, who wrote the primary opinion, stated that if it turns out that the means that the municipality uses to enforce the law are not effective, it must use other means at its disposal, including the option of appealing to the Court to issue an injunction against opening businesses that violate the bylaw.[84] Naor ruled that the municipality failed to show that, at the very least, it considered using this option, and thus violated its duties. Alongside the criticism of the non-enforcement of the bylaw, the Court explicitly stated that the municipality may change it:

> If the character of the Tel Aviv-Yafo requires, according to its leaders, who represent the population, not to close businesses like the respondents on Sabbath, the bylaw can be changed in the path established by law. However, so long as the bylaw has not been changed, the assumption is that it should be maintained.[85]

The municipality decided to amend the bylaw. The amended bylaw stated, among others, that stores for selling food can be opened on Sabbath and holidays, in accordance with a list of streets attached to the amendment, with each street having a quota, set by the municipality, of stores that can be opened. According to the Municipalities Ordinance, this change of a bylaw requires the approval of the Minister of Interior. The Minister used his authority and disqualified this arrangement. At the same time, the Minister approved another arrangement established by the bylaw, which allows the opening of businesses in a number of large commercial areas spread out throughout Tel Aviv. The Minister based his disqualification decision on a number of grounds. First, the Minister explained that the new arrangement effectively "adopts" the existing situation, and thus rewards businesses that operated against the law. In addition, the Minister stated that the arrangement harms the character of rest days and the national and social values they represent. The Minister explained that the arrangement is also in tension with the instructions of the Hours of Work and Rest Law, which prohibits the employment of Jews on rest days. Finally, the Minister pointed to the arrangement as leading to possible discrimination between small and large businesses.[86]

In light of the Minister's decision, the Tel Aviv-Yafo municipality adopted a different arrangement. This arrangement also ended the categorical prohibition on opening businesses on Sabbath, but adopted different permit criteria than those used in the disqualified amendment. The Minister of Interior, who was about to finish his tenure, did not disqualify the bylaw this time, but he did order the delay of the law's entry into force, leaving the final decision on the matter to his incoming replacement.

The Merchants Union petitioned to the Supreme Court against the municipality.[87] The petitioners claimed that the arrangements established by the new bylaw, in both its versions, were neither reasonable nor proportional. After the decision of the new Minister of Interior regarding the bylaw was slow in coming, the municipality also petitioned the Supreme Court, asking it to decide the status of this amendment.[88] The Court decided to wait, and instructed the Minister of Interior to decide at once. Such a decision did not come, with the incoming and outgoing Ministers of Interior tossing the hot potato to each other on various grounds.[89] At a certain stage, the authority to decide was transferred to the entire government, which also failed to reach a decision. During the scheduled deliberations on the petitions, the Court expressed its displeasure at the failure to honor its orders, but despite this, it granted more and more extensions for the government to make a decision.

Finally, the Court ran out of patience, and its decision on the petitions was published on April 2017.[90] The Court ruled that in light of the lengthy and ongoing avoidance of the Ministers of Interior to make a decision on the matter, this avoidance should be seen as a decision to disqualify the bylaw without justification. The Court ruled that such an unjustified decision cannot stand and is therefore invalid.

The Court then went on to reject the arguments raised by the Merchants Union. The Court ruled that "the limited scope of the areas and the businesses whose opening was permitted on Sabbath properly balances the overall consideration needed on the matter, while considering the status of Sabbath and the character of the city with its various neighborhoods and diverse population."[91]

2. HOURS OF WORK AND REST LAW

On November 2, 1969, the assembly of the Broadcast Authority decided to broadcast TV on Sabbath and Holidays, except on Yom Kippur, rejecting the government's recommendation to delay its decision to allow a discussion on the matter.[92] A few days later, the request of the Broadcast Authority to receive a permit for employing workers by force of section 12(a) of the Hours of Work and Rest Law was granted. The Chief Labor Inspector at the Ministry of Labor, who granted the request by force of the authority delegated to him by the Minister of Labor, noted that he had been convinced that "the cessation of work for a weekly rest, by the workers detailed in the permit, could lead to great harm in satisfying the needs, which are, in my opinion, vital to a significant part of the public, as stated in section 12(a) of the law."[93]

A petition against the Chief Labor Inspector's decision was filed by Simcha Miron, a religious man who was being trained as a television man. Miron's arguments were divided into two levels, personal and public. At the personal level, Miron claimed harm to his chances, as a religious person, to be accepted to work at the Broadcast Authority, due to the mismatch between his way of life and the new broadcast policy, which included Sabbath. Miron's personal argument was needed to establish his right of standing, in light of the Court's policy then, which required petitioners to prove a special personal interest as a precondition to hearing the petition.[94] At the public level, Miron claimed that "The public desecration of Sabbath, in the state framework of Israeli television, seriously harms the sensitivities of religious Jewry in Israel and in the diaspora—and the petitioner included."[95]

The Court summarily rejected the petition. It ruled that Miron had no right of standing, as he had yet to petition to the Broadcast Authority, asking to be accepted for work, and had not even finished his professional training, which was a prerequisite for even applying. In addition, the Court noted that the petition before it mixed questions of a clearly public nature, and repeated its known preference for avoiding such disputes, whose natural place of resolution was the political arena.[96]

A year after its decision in the Miron case, the Court deliberated on a similar petition filed by three members of the executive board of the Broadcast Authority.[97] The petitioners claimed that the permits for working in television on Sabbath were illegally issued, and that the operation of television on Sabbath negatively discriminated against workers (or potential workers) who observed the Sabbath. This petition was also rejected on the grounds of lack of standing, but it did contain a degree of innovation. The Court referred to the concept of "vital need," and ruled that "the question of whether continuous television broadcasts throughout all the days of the week are a vital or needless service, is not a legal question, but a public-political one, which has already been decided in the forum authorized to do so: the government and the Knesset."[98] A number of years later, the Attorney General published guidelines for interpreting the concept of "providing vital needs to the public," which fit the expansive interpretation provided by the Supreme Court.[99]

Until the beginning of the 1990s, the Supreme Court refused to deliberate on arguments against the constitutionality of Knesset laws, and judicial involvement in the Hours of Work and Rest Law focused solely on questions of interpretation. However, after the Basic Laws related to human rights were passed in 1992—and the statement by the Court that these engendered a "constitutional revolution" that would allow the judicial review of even primary legislation—attempts began to question the very constitutionality of the law. As I explained above, Basic Law: Human Dignity and Freedom included a "preservation of laws" section, which shielded older laws from judicial review, and the law could therefore not be attacked on the basis of the rights enumerated in this Basic Law.[100] By contrast, Basic Law: Freedom of Occupation grants no such immunity to older primary legislation, and the attempts to undermine the Hours of Work and Rest Law were based on claimed harm to freedom of occupation.

The Handyman company operated stores on Sabbath in a number of locations throughout the country, and employed Jewish workers. It was convicted in the Regional Labor Court of Tel Aviv of violating the Hours of Work and Rest Law. The company appealed to the National Labor Court, and claimed that the law was invalid due to the harm to freedom of occupation. The court agreed that the law harms freedom of occupation, but ruled that it meets the condition of the limitation clause of section 4 of the Basic Law, and therefore rejected the appeal. Handyman petitioned to the Supreme Court, which confirmed the decision of the National Labor Court.[101] Justice Dorner, who wrote the main opinion, ruled that the law meets the tests of the limitation clause: its twofold purpose—social and religious-national—is worthy, and the authority it grants the Minister to issue work permits on Sabbath allows it to meet the proportionality tests.

Two years later, in 2005, the Court once again confirmed the constitutionality of the Hours of Work and Rest Law. The Design 22 company operated its branches throughout the country on Sabbath, and employed Jews without requesting and receiving a permit for employing them on the day of rest. The company was hit with monetary fines due to violating the law, and to try and avoid further fines, it approached the authorities, asking for a permit according to section 12 of the law, but was refused. The company petitioned to the Supreme Court, and attacked both the administrative decision not to grant it the requested permit, and the law itself, on the grounds that it harms freedom of occupation, and does not meet the conditions of the limitation clause. The Court rejected the petition in both its facets.[102]

V. Discussion

In the first part of the book, the constitutional history of Israel was presented as divided into two periods. In the first period, from the founding of the state until 1992, Israel lacked a written constitution. As explained in Chapter 1, the Supreme Court already was acting in this period to protect human rights, whether by providing a limited interpretation of problematic legislation, or by disqualifying actions of the executive branch that the Court believed unjustifiably harmed those rights. However, lacking a written charter of human rights, the Supreme Court refused to examine the constitutionality of primary legislation, even if it believed that it unjustifiably harms human rights. The turning point came in 1992, with the passing of the two Basic Laws dealing with human rights (henceforth: The new Basic Laws). In the *Mizrachi Bank* ruling, the Court ruled that the passing of the new Basic Laws brought about a constitutional revolution, which granted all Basic Laws—the new ones as well as previous ones—the status of a constitution. From this point onward, the Court began to place even primary legislation within its purview. The conduct of the Court from 1992 onward was described in Chapter 3, with an emphasis on the Court's own role in creating this revolution.

Alongside the aforementioned division—which refers to the constitutional revolution of the beginning of the 1990s as the central turning point in Israeli constitutional history—scholars of Israeli constitutional law also point to another significant change, which occurred a decade earlier, in the 1980s, around the time the Supreme Court was experiencing a generational change. According to them, until the 1980s, the Supreme Court acted with restraint not only regarding primary legislation, but also in reference to the actions of the executive branch. The restrained approach made use of two main tools—the setting of high prerequisites for the hearing of petitions against the government, and a reticence to question the government's judgment. From this point on, the Court now began to intervene in matters that it used to avoid, increasing its intervention gradually.[103] According to this position, the declaration of the constitutional revolution was one expression of many of the activist approach that spread among the judges during the 1980s, and which, at the same time, added a powerful tool to the toolbox at the intervening Court's disposal.

These two descriptions do not contradict each other. True, according to the first description, the Court intervened in the activity of the executive branch even in the decades prior to the constitutional revolution; however, this does not contradict the statement that the degree and scope of the intervention increased and broadened in the 1980s. It is true that the second description points to the Court increasing its intervention during the 1980s, but it cannot be disputed that the readiness to disqualify primary legislation only formed in the 1990s, with the declaration of the constitutional revolution.

A survey of the developments in the three subjects from the area of relations between religion and state provides us with an opportunity to test the validity of both theses, and the contribution of both dramatic changes in the conduct of the Supreme Court to shaping the public face of the State of Israel.

The way the Court dealt with the issue of drafting yeshiva students fits both theses best. In the beginning, in the 1970s, the Court used the prerequisite of the right of standing and justiciability to entirely avoid dealing with the issue, fitting the description of the Court in this period as acting with restraint. Later, in the 1980s, it was the *Ressler* ruling, dealing with the drafting of yeshiva students, which served as the first precedent to almost entirely eliminate the two prerequisites, and open a wide berth for judicial intervention in issues that were controversial in terms of values and politics. However, in practice, more than a decade passed since *Ressler*, in which the Court agreed to deliberate on the issue itself, and the *Rubinstein* affair, in which the Court disqualified the exemption arrangement for yeshiva students, which had been in force for fifty years. Finally, it was again a ruling in the matter of the drafting of yeshiva students, from the beginning of the 2010s, which served as the first precedent for another dramatic constitutional development: the repeal of primary legislation because of claimed harm to unenumerated rights, which the Court read into the Basic Laws, in complete contrast to the intent of the legislator.

The conduct of the Court, when it comes to the religious monopoly on marriage and divorce, is excellent evidence in favor of the argument that the first generation of Supreme Court justices acted with judicial restraint, and the argument that this generation also came to the aid of human rights in cases where the harm to rights was palpable. The Court's ruling the *Funk-Schlezinger* case, handed down as early as the 1960s, led to the de facto recognition of civil marriage ceremonies that take place outside of Israel, and thus significantly reduced the harm to human rights deriving from the religious monopoly in this field. However, as we explained, in this case the Court avoided taking a clear stand on the political and value dispute, and presented its decision as being based solely on a formal reason.

The other significant development in this matter from the beginning of the 2000s, in which the Court recognized the validity of civil marriage conducted abroad, occurred almost incidentally, and was based on the surprising ruling of the Rabbinical Court. Ostensibly, there is nothing to learn from this ruling; however, additional reading shows that this development is also the result of pressure on the part of the Supreme Court. We cannot expand on this matter here, and we will only note that, as many explained, the reason for the Rabbinical Court's ruling was its fear that failure to recognize the validity of civil marriage would lead the Supreme Court, already ready and willing, to do so itself. Such recognition on the part of the Supreme Court, alongside a parallel refusal by the Rabbinical Court, would have been able to lead to another move, in which the Supreme Court would have arrogated the judicial powers related to matters of divorce in cases of civil marriage, on the grounds that in light of the Rabbinical Court's refusal to recognize the validity of civil marriage, the Jurisdiction Law, which grants Rabbinical Courts the unique authority to discuss questions of marriage and divorce of Jews in Israel, is not relevant to such marriages.[104]

Another fact, relevant for our case, is that this ruling and the following one, in which the Court recognized the particular validity of civil marriage between a couple with only one Jewish spouse, were both given within roughly the same time period, by Supreme Court President Aharon Barak, on the eve of his retirement from the bench. As many pointed out, Aharon Barak is the one who led the first revolution in the approach of the Court during the 1980s, as well as the constitutional revolution of the 1990s. These two rulings are therefore a fitting end to a career of an activist judge, who swept the entire Court along with him.

What of the Court's activity in the area of the public Sabbath? For two decades, from the end of the 1960s onward, the Court acted to reduce the scope of the prohibition laid down in law on work and commerce and on the opening of businesses on Sabbath. However, it would appear that a change has occurred in the character of arguments the justices used for their decisions. In the beginning, the Court based its decision on formal grounds, and later it turned to value-laden reasons. This change fits the argument that the Court underwent a change in the 1980s, from judicial restraint to activism.

This change is clear from a comparison between the *Izramax* ruling and the *Hasharon Mall* ruling. In the *Izramax* ruling, from the end of the 1960s, the Court excluded gas stations from the application of the legal prohibition contained in the bylaws by way of formalistic use of interpretive tools. The Court explained that daily speech and business logic supported a narrow interpretation of the term "store"— which the bylaw prohibited from opening—which does not include gas stations. The Court rejected a more far-reaching argument, based on a value-related argument, which aimed to entirely repeal the bylaw. Like the *Izramax* case, the *Hasharon Mall* case, decided in the beginning of the 1990s, also involved the Court accepting the petition based on a narrow interpretation of the bylaw, but it is the similarity to *Izramax* that also sharpens the difference between the two rulings. In *Izramax*, the Court interpreted the prohibition narrowly, based on formalistic considerations of interpretation—how a reasonable person would interpret the word "store." By contrast, in *Hasharon Mall*, the Court based its interpretation on a value-related consideration: the desire to reduce the extent of claimed harm to human rights.

All this regards the first three decades and the decades following that period. However, what of the relation between the years before and after the constitutional revolution? As described above, at two different opportunities after the constitutional revolution—the *Handyman* case and the *Design* case—the Court rejected the attempt to nullify the work prohibition on Sabbath, as laid out in the Hours of Work and Rest Law. These rulings, ostensibly, reflect not activism, but judicial restraint. Even the insistence of the Court in the *Tel Aviv* case on the use of effective means of enforcement for the Tel Aviv municipal bylaw paint a picture of a restrained court.

What possible explanation can there be for this trend of restraint? Why is the Court avoiding the use of its constitutional arsenal to further erode the legal prohibition to work on Sabbath? And why didn't it act to weaken the prohibition on opening businesses in Tel Aviv as it did in previous jurisprudence? Two possible explanations exist for this phenomenon. According to one explanation—the relevant one for the petitions against the validity of the Hours of Work and Rest Law—the fact that even before the constitutional revolution, the Court adopted an expansive interpretation of the term "vital need," the existence of which is a condition for the granting of a work permit on Sabbath, made the need to use the weapon of repealing the law to achieve the desired result unnecessary, at least in the eyes of the Court. As explained above, in *Handyman* and *Design*, the Court pegged its refusal to repeal the Hours of Work and Rest Law precisely on this basis: it is possible, within the framework of the existing law, to proportionately balance between the conflicting values. In this manner, the Court marked the path those in authority must take when it comes to granting permits, if they wish to protect the law from a possible future repeal. According to the second explanation—also relevant to the ruling in the matter of the bylaw—the surprising restraint on these matters lies in the difference between the matter under discussion in these cases and the ones that occupied the Court's time in previous cases. In the latter, activity coming under the heading of "leisure" (cinemas and television broadcasts), or the sort vital for ensuring freedom of movement (opening gas stations) were on the Court's agenda. By contrast, in *Handyman* and *Design*, as in the *Tel Aviv* case, the Court was dealing with commercial activity. There are many opponents of the existing legislation when it comes to work and the opening of businesses on Sabbath, including many secularists, who wish to distinguish between commerce and leisure, prohibiting the former and permitting the latter.[105] It may also be that the Supreme Court justices hold this view, or at the very least believe it to be within the realm of the reasonable.

Notes

1. *Official Gazette*: Number 1; Tel Aviv, 5 Iyar 5708, 14.5.1948, 1.

2. See Amnon Rubinstein and Barak Medina, *The Constitutional Law of the State of Israel* (6th edn. Tel Aviv: Schocken 2005), vol. 1, 42 [Heb.] (henceforth Rubinstein and Medina, *The Constitutional Law*).

3. See Zeev Scherff, *Three Days* (Tel Aviv: Am Oved 1959) [Heb.].

4. See Orit Rozin, *From "We" to "I": Individualism in Israeli Society in the Early 1950s* (Ph.D. diss. Tel Aviv University 2002), 31 [Heb.] (henceforth Rozin, *From "We" to "I"*).

5. Ibid, 32.

6. HCJ 7/48 *Al-Karbutali v. The Minister of Defense*, 2 PD 5, 25 (1949) (Isr.) (henceforth *Al-Karbutali*).

7. HCJ 10/1948 *Zvi Zeev v. the Acting District Commissioner of the Urban Area of Tel Aviv (Yehoshua Gubernik) and Another*, 1, 85 PD (1948) (Isr.). <http://elyon1.court.gov.il/files_eng/48/100/000/Z01/48000100.z01.pdf> (henceforth, references to online rulings are to the official English translations).

8. Ibid, 6. See also *Al-Karbutali*, (n. 6), 13 (we should not accept "the claim that this document is the constitution that should be used to test the legitimacy of laws, before the fundamental constitution, which the Declaration itself speaks of, has been framed by the Constitutional Assembly").

9. Rubinstein and Medina, *The Constitutional Law*, (n. 2), 41; Daphne Barak-Erez, *Key Trials: Landmarks in the Supreme Court* (Tel Aviv: Ministry of Defense 2003), 20 [Heb.] (henceforth Barak-Erez, *Key Trials*).

10. See, for example, Moshe Negbi, *Above the Law: The Crisis of the Rule of Law in Israel* (Tel Aviv: Am Oved 1987), 27 [Heb.] (henceforth Negbi, *Above the Law*); Miriam Ben-Porat, "A Constitution in Israel: Whether and When" (1985) 11 Iyyunei Mishpat 19 [Heb.]; Amnon Rubinstein, "On the Growth of Constitutional Law" in Aharon Barak et al. (eds), *Sefer Shamgar* (Tel Aviv: The Israel Bar 2003), vol. 1, 3 [Heb.]; Pnina Lahav, *Judgment in Jerusalem: Chief Justice Simon Agranat and the Zionist Century* (Berkeley: University of California Press 1997), 92.

11. However, see Aharon Barak, *Interpretation in Law* (Jerusalem: Nevo 1992), vol. 1,632 [Heb.] (henceforth Barak, *Interpretation in Law*). Barak implies that a missed opportunity here means that, had the Court taken such a step when Israel was established, the public would have agreed to it. In this understanding, the way the constitution is enacted does matter.

12. See, for example, Justice Agranat in HCJ 73/53 *Kol Ha'am v. Minister of the Interior*, 7 PD 871 (1953) (Isr.). <http://elyon1.court.gov.il/files_eng/53/730/000/Z01/53000730.z01.pdf>.

13. The Court's attitude began to change only at the end of the 1970s. See Menachem Mautner, *Law and the Culture of Israel* (Oxford: Oxford University Press 2011), 75–98 (henceforth Mautner, *Law and the Culture of Israel*). Some praise this change in the Court's attitude and others condemn it. See Ruth Gavison, Mordechai Kremnitzer, and Yoav Dotan, *Judicial Activism: For and Against* (Jerusalem: Magnes Press 2000) [Heb].

14. See the Proceedings of the Provisional Council of State, 1, Meeting 9, 12 (Isr.).

15. See Rozin, *From "We" to "I"*, (n. 4), 25.

16. At a later stage, MK David Bar-Rav-Hai of Mapai responded in the Knesset to the claim that his party's platform had promised to enact a constitution (*Divrei HaKnesset* 4, 728 (1950) (Isr.)): "Do not frighten us by stating that we promised a constitution . . . allow us to settle this issue with our voters." The United Religious Front also related to the constitution in its discussions: "The constitution of the state that the Constitutional Assembly will decide upon must be originally Israeli in its essence and content." See Archive of Religious-Zionism, Bar-Ilan University, files of the religious-Zionist faction in the Knesset, file 531.

17. Article 1 of the Transition Law, 5709-1949 (Isr.) states: "The Provisional Council of State will remain in office until the convocation of the Constitutional Assembly of the State of Israel; with the convocation of the Constitutional Assembly, the Provisional Council of State will dissolve and cease to exist."

18. Aharon Barak, Tana Spanic, and Shlomo Peretz (eds), *Uri Yadin: In Memoriam* (Tel Aviv: Bursei 1990), vol. 1, 80 [Heb].

19. This decision appeared suspicious to both the Right and the Left. MK Meir Vilner, from the Communist Party, and MK Menachem Begin, from Herut, expressed the view that this was part of a conspiracy to avoid the fulfillment of the obligation to draft a constitution. See Ruth Gavison, "The Controversy over Israel's Bill of Rights" (1985) 15 Israeli Yearbook of Human Rights 117 (henceforth Gavison, "The Controversy over Israel's Bill of Rights").

20. Provisional Council of State, 36th Meeting, January 13, 1949 (Isr.). See Zerah Warhaftig, *A Constitution for Israel: Religion and State* (Jerusalem: Mesilot 1988), 78 [Heb].

21. Article 1 of the Transition Law, 5709-1949 (Isr.).

22. For a review of the various claims for and against, see Gavison, "The Controversy over Israel's Bill of Rights", (n. 19). 147–150; Rozin, *From "We" to "I"*, (n. 4), 27–29.

23. Harari himself later expressed reservations about the description of his proposal as a compromise: "Compromise with whom? Let us not forget what the situation was then. The dispute hinged on the question of whether the State of Israel needs a constitution. The decision explicitly

states that a constitution is needed. On this, we made no compromise." *Sefer Barkatt: Symposia in Memory of Reuven Barkatt, Speaker of the Knesset* (Jerusalem: Israeli Association for Parliamentarism 1977), 121–122 [Heb.].

24. *Divrei HaKnesset* 5, 1743 (1950) (Isr.).

25. See, for example, the comment of Justice Berenson in *Haaretz*, December 13, 1993, B4: "What prevents the drafting of a constitution in Israel is the attitude of religious circles to the state, to the legislator, and to the law." For a similar view, see Ehud Sprinzak, *Illegalism in Israeli Society* (Tel Aviv: Sifriat Hapoalim 1986), 71–72 [Heb.]; Benjamin Neuberger, *The Constitution in Israel* (Tel Aviv: Open University 1997), 44 [Heb.] (henceforth Neuberger, *The Constitution in Israel*).

26. See Abraham Israel Sharir, "Compromise or Surrender" (2006) 25 Tsohar 69 [Heb.].

27. See, for example, *Divrei HaKnesset* 4, 725–746, 766–784 (1950) (Isr.) (discussion in the Knesset on the report of the Constitution, Law, and Justice Committee on the drafting of a constitution. The religious issue was raised by various Knesset members and discussed at length, as well as other issues touching on the enactment of the constitution and its character).

28. Shuki Friedman and Amihai Radzyner, *The Religious Community and the Constitution: What Can History Teach Us?* (Jerusalem: Israel Democracy Institute 2007) [Heb.] (henceforth Friedman and Radzyner, *The Religious Community and the Constitution*). See also Asher Cohen, *The Talit and the Flag: Religious Zionism and the Concept of a Torah State, 1947–1953* (Jerusalem: Yad Yitzhak Ben Zvi, 1998) 122–123 [Heb.].

29. See Ruth Gavison, "The Constitutional Revolution: A Description of Reality or a Self-Fulfilling Prophecy?" (1997) 28 Mishpatim 23, 66–67 [Heb.] (henceforth Gavison, "The Constitutional Revolution"): "The opposition, naturally, viewed the constitution as a way of protecting its rights and supported it. The coalition, naturally, did not want any limitation on its ruling powers." Giora Goldberg, "Religious-Zionism and the Framing of a Constitution for Israel" (1998) 3 Israel Studies 211: "At the start, immediately after the establishment of Israel, the religious parties were not opposed to framing a constitution. They changed their minds only after Ben-Gurion began to convey his opposition in public. The leaders of the religious parties understood that Ben-Gurion's opposition would stop the process and, therefore, preferred to join the opponents in order to present this to their voters as their own achievement." Daphna Sharfman, *Living without a Constitution: Civil Rights in Israel* (Armonk, NY: M.E. Sharpe 1993), 38–45; Michael Mandel, "Democracy and the New Constitutionalism in Israel" (1999) 33 Israel Law Review 274; Giora Goldberg, "'You Don't Need a Constitution to Plant Trees': On State-Building and Constitution-Framing" (1993) 38 State, Government and International Relations [Heb.] (henceforth Goldberg, "You Don't Need a Constitution"; Friedman and Radzyner, *The Religious Community and the Constitution*, (n. 28), 69.

30. Proceedings of the Constitution, Law and Justice Committee, First Knesset, 15th–24th Meetings (November 5, 1948–July 13, 1949) (Isr.).

31. For the presentation of this claim, and for a discussion of the reasons behind Ben-Gurion's opposition, see Rozin, *From "We" to "I"*, (n. 4), 34–36, 66; Goldberg, "You Don't Need a Constitution", (n. 29); Neuberger, *The Constitution in Israel*, (n. 25).

32. Negbi, *Above the Law*, (n. 10), ch. 2.

33. Jon Elster, "Forces and Mechanisms in the Constitution Making Process" (1995) 45 Duke Law Journal 395 (henceforth Elster, "Forces and Mechanisms").

34. For a description of developments, see Ruth Gavison, "The Constitutional Revolution", (n. 29).

35. Ibid, 78.

36. Ibid, 79.

37. See Benjamin Akzin, "Basic Laws and Entrenched Laws in Israel" in *Issues of Law and Statesmanship* (Jerusalem: Magnes Press 1966), 114 [Heb.]: "The Knesset's decision was worded as it was *not by taking into account legal considerations*, but by taking into account the parliamentary situation and seeking to ensure *maximal flexibility* regarding all aspects of the problem" (my emphasis); I. H. Klinghoffer, "The Establishment of the State of Israel: Constitutional History" in Yitzhak Zamir (ed.) *Klinghoffer Volume on Public Law* (Jerusalem: Hebrew University 1993), 100 [Heb.].

38. HCJ 98/69 *Bergman v. Minister of Finance*, 23(1) PD 693 (1969) (Isr.).

39. Ibid, 696.

40. David Kretzmer, "The Path to Judicial Review in Human Rights Cases: From *Bergman* and *Kol Ha'am* to *Bank Mizrahi*" (1997) 28 Mishpatim 362 [Heb.]. Yaakov S. Tsemah reached a similar decision in "The Manner of Creating the Power of Judicial Review (HC 231/73)" (1975) 29 Hapraklit 515 [Heb.]. See also Claude Klein, "The Constitutional Authority in Israel" (1970) 2 Mishpatim 51 [Heb.]; idem, "The Need for a Special Majority" (1972) 28 Hapraklit 563 [Heb.].

41. For a view that casts doubt on the possibility of the Knesset limiting itself through an ordinary law, see, for example, Barak, *Interpretation in Law*, (n. 11), vol. 1, 568–569; ibid., vol. 3, 274–276; CA 6821/93 *Bank Mizrahi v. Migdal Cooperative Village*, 49(4) PD 221 (1995) (Isr.) (henceforth *Bank Mizrahi*). <http://elyon1.court.gov.il/files_eng/93/210/068/z01/93068210. z01.pdf> para. 66 of President Barak's opinion, 212; Rubinstein and Medina, *The Constitutional Law of the State of Israel*, (n. 2), 65–66; Barak Medina, "The Limits of the Knesset's Power to Set Supra-Majority Rules" (2003) 6 Mishpat Umimshal 509 [Heb.].

42. Criminal Appeal 107/73 *Negev Car Service Station Ltd. v. The State of Israel*, 28(1) PD 640 (1974) (Isr.).

43. HCJ 148/73 *Kaniel v. Minister of Justice*, 27(1) PD 794 (1973) (Isr.).

44. Ibid.

45. See Ariel Bendor, "Entrenchment and Constitution: *Bergman* and the Constitutional Discourse in Israel" (2001) 31 Mishpatim 825 [Heb.].

46. HCJ 246/81, 260/81 *Agudat Derek Eretz et. al. v. Broadcasting Authority et. al.*, 35(4) PD 1 (1981) (Isr.). <http://elyon1.court.gov.il/files_eng/81/460/002/Z01/81002460.z01.pdf>; HCJ 141/82 *Rubinstein v. Speaker of the Knesset*, 37(3) PD 141 (1983) (Isr.). <http://elyon1.court.gov. il/files_eng/82/410/001/Z01/82001410.z01.pdf>; HCJ 142/89 *La'or Movement v. Speaker of the Knesset*, 44(3) PD 529 (1990) (Isr.) (henceforth *La'or*).

47. See, for example, Barak-Erez, *Key Trials*, (n. 19), 30; Menachem Hofnung, "Authority, Influence and Separation of Powers: Judicial Review in Israel in Comparative Perspective" (1997) 28 Mishpatim 226 [Heb.]; Martin Edelman, *Courts, Politics, and Culture in Israel* (Charlottesville: University Press of Virginia 1994), 13–25.

48. *Bank Mizrahi*, para. 35 of President Barak's opinion. Barak had already formulated this position in a previous ruling. See, for example, HCJ 761/86 *Miyari v. Speaker of the Knesset*, 42(4) PD 868, 873 (1989) (Isr.): "The Knesset has the power to enact any law it wishes, and only limitations imposed on it through the exercise of its power as a constitutive authority— limitations currently evident today mainly in entrenched Basic Laws—can prevent it from acting as it wishes." See also the statement of Justice Elon in para. 2 of his opinion in *La'or* (n. 46): "Unquestionably . . . the validity of Knesset legislation is usually not subject to judicial

review, barring one exception—when Knesset legislation contradicts the 'entrenchment' of a Basic Law. In the latter case, the validity of the legislation is subject to judicial review, and if it is found that the legislation failed to meet the entrenchment requirements, the Court will declare that the legislation was enacted illegally."

49. *Bank Mizrahi*, para. 1 of Justice Zamir's opinion.

50. Ibid 1. See also Gary Jeffrey Jacobsohn, *Apple of Gold: Constitutionalism in Israel and the United States* (Princeton, NJ: Princeton University Press 1993), 124.

51. Thus, for example, as a judge, Landau rejected the expansion of the Court's involvement in the activity of the Knesset. See his dissenting opinion in HCJ 306/81 *Plato Sharon v. Knesset House Committee*, 35(4) PD 118 (1981) (Isr.), and his article "Trends in the Decisions of the Supreme Court" (1982) 8 Iyyunei Mishpat 504 [Heb.]. Similarly, he strongly objected to the expanded use of the implausibility argument as a tool for examining the executive's actions. See the detailed discussion on this subject between him and Justice Barak in HCJ 389/80 *Golden Pages Ltd. v. Broadcasting Authority*, 35(1) PD 421 (1980) (Isr.).

52. Moshe Landau, "A Constitution as the Supreme Law of the State of Israel?" (1971) 27 Hapraklit 30 [Heb.].

53. Landau himself forcefully rejected the far-reaching meaning that was, at times, ascribed to his decision. See, for example, Moshe Landau, "Review of *Israel's Parliament: The Law of the Knesset* by Eliahu S. Likhovsky" (1972) 4 Mishpatim 214 [Heb.], 214. His view, however, was not accepted. See Ruth Gavison, "The Constitutional Revolution", (n. 29), 82; Aharon Barak, "The Constitutional Revolution: Bat Mitzvah" (2004) 1 Mishpat va-'Asakim 12 [Heb.].

54. See, for example, Mautner, *Law and the Culture of Israel*, (n. 13), 86–90 (in Israel's early decades, the Supreme Court functioned as a liberal institution, which made it an exception in the collectivist Israeli society). But see also Pnina Lahav, "The Formative Years of Israel's Supreme Court: 1948–1955" (1989) 14 Iyyunei Mishpat 497–499 [Heb.]: "In its first years, the Supreme Court showed self-restraint, that is, it refrained from essential examinations of the government's and the administration's discretionary actions. This restraint generally followed from the judges' identification with the policy of the government, and particularly with the collectivist views prevalent at the time."

55. See, for example, Amos Shapira, "The Status of Fundamental Individual Rights in the Absence of a Written Constitution" (1974) 9 Israel Law Review 497; Baruch Bracha, "The Protection of Human Rights in Israel" (1982) 12 Israel Yearbook of Human Rights 110; Amos Shapira, "Judicial Review without a Constitution: The Israeli Paradox" (1983) 56 Temple Law Quarterly 405; Asher Maoz, "Defending Civil Liberties without a Constitution: The Israeli Experience" (1988) 16 Melbourne University Law Review 815.

56. HCJ 1/49 *Bejerano v. The Minister of Police*, 2 PD 80, 83 (1949) (Isr.).

57. Ibid, 84.

58. HCJ 337/81 *Miterani v. The Minister of Transport*, 37(3) PD 337, para. 11 of Justice Shamgar's opinion (1983) (Isr.),

59. But see Oren Gazal, "Restriction of Basic Rights 'by Law' or as 'Prescribed by Law'" (1998) 4 Mishpat Umimshal 384–390, 396–412 [Heb.] (in the case law up to the legislation of the new Basic Laws, we find less restrictive approaches concerning the nature of the required agreement).

60. Article 5 of the *Penal Law Amendment (Bigamy) Law*, 5719 (1959), Book of Laws 144: "If Jewish law is the law that applies to the new marriage, a man will not be convicted for an offense according to Article 2 if the new marriage was performed after he had been granted a marriage

license according to a final decision of the rabbinic court, upheld by the two Chief Rabbis of Israel . . ." (the law was voided in a 1957 amendment).

61. HCJ 301/63 *Shtreit v. Israel Chief Rabbi*, 18(1) PD 598 (1964) (Isr.) (henceforth *Shtreit*).

62. Ibid, 612.

63. Ibid, 613.

64. See Pnina Lahav, "Freedom of Expression in the Decisions of the Supreme Court" (1972) 7 Mishpatim 388 [Heb.].

65. For a review of the Court's action in this regard, see David Kretzmer, "Forty Years of Public Law" (1989) 19 Mishpatim 555–561 [Heb.].

66. CA 450/70 *Rogozinsky v. The State of Israel*, 26(1) PD 129, 135 (1971) (Isr.) (Justice Berenson's opinion). See also HCJ 80/63 *Gurfinkel v. Minister of Interior*, 17 PD 2048, 2069 (1963) (Isr.); CA 228/63 *Ezuz v. Ezer*, 17 PD 2541, 2547 (1963) (Isr.); HCJ 356/83 *Lidor v. Minister of Housing*, 38(1) PD 602 (1984) (Isr.).

67. For a detailed description of the various initiatives, see *Bank Mizrahi*, paras. 24–29 of Justice Barak's opinion; Gavison, "The Constitutional Revolution", (n. 29), 75–95.

68. Elster, "Forces and Mechanisms", (n. 33), 370. See also Alfred Witkon, "Law in a Developing Country" in Haim Cohn (ed.), *Sefer Yovel le-Pinchas Rosen* (Jerusalem: Mif ' al ha-Shikhpul 1962), 75 [Heb.]; Gavison, "The Controversy over Israel's Bill of Rights", (n. 19), 152; Peter H. Russell, *Constitutional Odyssey: Can Canadians Become a Sovereign People?* (2nd edn. Toronto: University of Toronto Press 1993), 106.

69. For displays of pessimism concerning the chances of success, see Gavison, "The Controversy over Israel's Bill of Rights", (n. 19), 153–154; idem, "Forty Years of Constitutional Law" (1989) 19 Mishpatim 619 [Heb.]: "Both theoretically and practically, my view is that the advisable course is to focus on what happens to our constitutional law in the absence of a constitution, in the belief that this is the pattern of action and development that we can expect in the future as well."

70. See *La'or* (n. 46).

71. Ibid, para. 2 of Justice Elon's opinion. Justice Elon's view, as noted, is an excellent reflection of the Supreme Court's clear view until that time.

72. Ibid, para. 30 of Justice Barak's opinion. For a critical view of Barak's opinion from a jurisprudential perspective, see Adi Parush, "Judicial Activism, Legal Positivism, and Natural Law: Justice Barak and the Doctrine of the Omnipotent Knesset" in Ariel Porat (ed.), *Judicial Activism* (Tel Aviv: Ramot 1993), 247 [Heb].

73. See Gavison, "The Constitutional Revolution", (n. 29), 91 note 165: "In principle, he [Barak] also allows judicial review of the constitutional authority's action."

74. See Roei Amit, "Position(ing) of a Canon" (1997) 21 Iyyunei Mishpat 93 [Heb.].

75. The Israeli press did discuss the decision, but focused on the financial crisis threatening the political parties that had relied for their campaign financing on funds they would receive following the amendment of the law. See, for example, Menachem Rahat, Yosef Tsuri'el, and Tal Shahaf, "Commotion in the Parties: Everyone Took and No Way of Returning", (Maariv, July 2 1990) [Heb.]. Originally, some of the readers appeared to have overlooked the significant innovation entailed by Barak's statement. For example, in an article interpreting the ruling, Prof. Yitzhak Zamir is quoted as saying: "The question [in the ruling] was a technical issue of inter-pretation: does the requirement of a special majority at every stage of the legislation include the preliminary reading as well? The High Court of Justice answered in the affirmative . . . If the motion is tabled again in the Knesset, and passes with a special majority—at all stages of the

legislation, including the preliminary reading—the law will be valid even though it violates equality . . . Another question, at the public level, is whether it is proper for the Knesset to enact laws that contradict the principle of equality. The situation would be different if we had a constitution. *Since we do not have a constitution—a majority of sixty-one members can violate the principle of equality that the Knesset itself aspires to.*" Hayyim Shibi, "The Technical Flaw" (Yedi'ot Aharonot, July 2, 1990) [Heb.] (my emphasis). Zamir completely ignores Barak's suggestion that, even in the absence of a constitution, the Court can void primary legislation, including legislation enacted by a majority of Knesset members.

CHAPTER 2

1. Basic Law: Freedom of Occupation, L.S.I. 114 (1992) (Isr.); Basic Law: Human Dignity and Liberty, L.S.I. 150 (1992) (Isr.). For an English translation of Israel's Basic Laws, see <http://www.knesset.gov.il/description/eng/eng mimshal yesod1.htm>.

2. The limitation clause [Article 8 of Basic Law: Human Dignity and Liberty (1992) (Isr.)]; [Article 4 of Basic Law: Freedom of Occupation (1992) (Isr.)] forbids infringement of the declared rights, "except by a statute that befits the values of the State of Israel, for a worthy purpose, and not exceeding what is necessary." The Israeli limitation clause is framed in the model of the Canadian Charter of Rights and Freedoms, which is based on a European model and on one found in international human rights conventions. For documentation on the spread of this balancing formula in different constitutional systems, see, for example, Aharon Barak, *Proportionality: Constitutional Rights and Their Limitations* (Cambridge: Cambridge University Press 2012).

3. See, for example, Eli M. Salzberger, "The Constituent Assembly in Israel" (1996) 3 Mishpat Umimshal 679 [Heb.].

4. See, for example, the collection of articles in (1995) 19 Iyyunei Mishpat 3 [Heb.].

5. For a series of articles that discuss the effects of the Basic Laws in various legal areas in Israel, see Aharon Barak, "The Constitutional Revolution: Bat-Mitzvah" (2004) 1 Mishpat va-'Asakim notes 151–157 [Heb.] (henceforth Barak, "Bat-Mitzvah").

6. In an article published soon after the enactment of the Basic Laws, Claude Klein notes: "The paths of Israeli democracy and its legislators are strange. Is there any serious observer who, one year ago, would have risked anticipating the passage of those laws?" See Claude Klein, "Basic Law: Human Dignity and Liberty—An Initial Normative Assessment" (1993) 1 Hamishpat 123 [Heb.] (henceforth Klein, "Initial Normative Assessment").

7. Bruce Ackerman, *We the People* (Cambridge, MA: Harvard University Press 1991) (henceforth Ackerman, *We the People*). For the implementation of Ackerman's thesis in the United Kingdom, see Rivka Weill, "We the British People" (2004) 2 Public Law 380; idem, "Evolution vs. Revolution: Dueling Models of Dualism" (2006) 54 American Journal of Comparative Law 429.

8. For a similar description of the facts, see Richard A. Baker, "The United States Congress Responds to Judicial Review" in Eivind Smith (ed.), *Constitutional Justice under Old Constitutions* (The Hague: Kluwer Law International 1995), 62–71.

9. Prominent scholars of constitutional law in the United States strongly criticized Ackerman's theoretical claim about the 1936 reversal. See, for example, Larry Kramer, "What's a Constitution for Anyway? Of History and Theory, Bruce Ackerman and the New Deal" (1996) 46 Case Western Reserve Law Review 885; Lawrence Lessig, "Understanding Changed Readings: Fidelity and Theory" (1995) 47 Stanford Law Review 395; Kent Greenawalt, "Dualism and Its Status" (1994)

104 Ethics 480; Jennifer Nedelsky, "The Puzzle and Demands of Modern Constitutionalism" (1994) 104 Ethics 500; Michael J. Klarman, "Constitutional Fact/Constitutional Fiction: A Critique of Bruce Ackerman's Theory of Constitutional Moments" (1992) 44 Stanford Law Review 759.

10. Ackerman's theory attempts to settle a further difficulty, the countermajoritarian fallacy. As Marc Tushnet explains, "Ackerman's answer was that public deliberation during constitutional moments had special characteristics ... that gave constitutional innovations made during such moments normative priority over later decisions during periods of regular politics." See Mark Tushnet, "Misleading Metaphors in Comparative Constitutionalism: Moments and Enthusiasm" (2005) 3 International Journal of Constitutional Law 263.

11. Some scholars have questioned the normative validity of Ackerman's theory. In their view, without a constitutional amendment, an interpretation inconsistent with the original intent is not legitimate. See, for example, Steven Calabresi, "The President, the Supreme Court, and the Founding Fathers: A Reply to Professor Ackerman" (2006) 73 University of Chicago Law Review 476.

12. See the Barak and Shamgar rulings in CA 6821/93 *Bank Mizrahi v. Migdal Cooperative Village*, 49(4) PD 221 (1995) (Isr.). <http://elyon1.court.gov.il/files_eng/93/210/068/z01/93068210.z01.pdf>.

The thesis of constituent authority, which Barak relied upon, was first presented by Claude Klein after the *Bergman* ruling. See Claude Klein, "A New Era in Israel's Constitutional Law" (1971) 6 Israel Law Review 376; idem, "The Need for a Special Majority" (1972) 28 Hapraklit 563 [Heb.]. Note that Barak's reliance on this thesis is, itself, a deviation from the Court's traditional position. The Court had previously rejected this claim when it was presented relying on Klein's theory. See HCJ 60/77 *Ressler v. Chairman of Knesset Elections Committee*, 31(2) PD 556, 560 (1977) (Isr.); HCJ 148/73 *Kaniel v. Minister of Justice*, 27(1) PD 794 (1973) (Isr.); Crim A 107/73 *Negev v. State of Israel*, 28(1) PD 640 (1974) (Isr.).

13. For a focused attack on this thesis, see Justice Cheshin's ruling in *Bank Mizrahi*.

14. Basic Law: The Government, L.S.I. 1396 (1992) (Isr.). This move, as we know, turned out to be a dismal failure. For a presentation of the hybrid dimension in the model, see, for example, Reuven Hazan, "Non-parliamentary and Non-presidential: The Change in the Voting System and the Regime in Israel" (1998) 2 Politika 105–108 [Heb.]. For a critique of the model and an explanation of its failure see Yossi Beilin, "A Collision Known as Direct Election of the Prime Minister" in Gideon Doron (ed.), *The Electoral Revolution: Primaries and Direct Election of the Prime Minister* (Tel Aviv: Hakibbutz Hameuchad 1996), 199 [Heb.]; Gideon Doron, *A Presidential Regime for Israel* (Jerusalem: Carmel 2006), 45–122 [Heb.]; David Nachmias and Doron Navot, "The Electoral Reform and Broad Coalitions: The Sharon Government" in Asher Arian and Michal Shamir (eds), *The Elections in Israel 2001* (Jerusalem: Israel Democracy Institute 2002), 127.

15. For an explanation in this spirit, see Daphne Barak-Erez, "From an Unwritten to a Written Constitution: The Israeli Challenge in American Perspective" (1995) 26 Columbia Human Rights Law Review 351–352 (henceforth Barak-Erez, "From an Unwritten to a Written Constitution").

16. Ackerman, *We the People*, (n. 7), 266-277.

17. See, for example, Guy Bechor, *A Constitution for Israel* (Tel Aviv: Maariv 1996), 127–154 [Heb.].

18. Amnon Rubinstein, "The Knesset and Basic Laws on Human Rights" (2000) 5 Mishpat Umimshal 349 [Heb.] (henceforth Rubinstein, "The Knesset and Basic Laws"). In the weeks

following the passage of the laws, public law experts published several articles interpreting that passage. See Claude Klein, "The Quiet Constitutional Revolution" (Maariv, March 27, 1992) [Heb.]; Baruch Bracha, "From Rhetorics to the Language of Law" (Haaretz, April 2, 1992) [Heb.]; Amnon Rubinstein, "A Big Constitution Arrives" (Haaretz, 3 April 1992) [Heb.]. However, these articles actually point to the lack of public and media awareness concerning the far-reaching implications of the Basic Laws.

19. Basic Law: Human Dignity and Liberty, the more important of the two, was ratified in the Knesset in a third reading on March 17, 1992. Fifty-four MKs participated in the vote—32 voted for it, 21 against, and 1 abstained [*Divrei HaKnesset* 24, 3793 (1992) (Isr.)]. Basic Law: Freedom of Occupation was enacted with a majority of twenty-three MKs, without opposition or abstentions [*Divrei HaKnesset* 23, 3393 (1992) (Isr.)].

20. Ruth Gavison, "The Constitutional Revolution: A Description of Reality or a Self-Fulfilling Prophecy?" (1997) 28 Mishpatim 23, 96 note 177 [Heb.] (henceforth Gavison, "Self-Fulfilling Prophecy?"). Gavison refers to an interview conducted with Barak in the journal of the Israel Bar Association *Orekh Hadin*, where Barak said: "In March 1992, two Basic Laws are enacted in absolute silence. March passes, April, May—and nothing, nothing at all, and I read the two Basic Laws and I say to myself: this is our constitution. And then, in a brief lecture I gave, I spoke of a constitutional revolution." Barak generously credits Claude Klein with copyright on the term "constitutional revolution." See Barak, "Bat-Mitzvah", (n. 5), 5.

21. Aharon Barak, *Selected Writings*, (Haim Cohn and Yitzhak Zamir [eds], Jerusalem: Nevo 2000), vol. 1, 415–416 [Heb.].

22. See mainly Justice Cheshin's ruling in *Bank Mizrahi*.

23. Judith Karp, "Basic Law: Human Dignity and Liberty: A Biography of Power Struggles" (1993) 1 Mishpat Umimshal 338 [Heb.] (henceforth Karp, "Basic Law"); Rubinstein, "The Knesset and Basic Laws", (n. 18), 340.

24. See Rubinstein, "The Knesset and Basic Laws", (n. 18), 346.

25. Some authors have questioned the sincerity of the law's proponents concerning their willingness to compromise. See, for instance, Karp, "Basic Law", (n. 23), 358. But regardless of their degree of sincerity, members of the Israeli Supreme Court have clearly rendered the compromise meaningless. As will be described in the next chapter, the Court adopted a strategy that enables it to read into the language of the Basic Laws the rights that were deliberately omitted from them. The "validity of laws" Article has also lost most of its significance. The Court disregarded the deliberate omission of the passage requiring that extant laws be interpreted in the spirit of the Basic Law, and compelled the authorities to re-examine past interpretations of extant laws. See Criminal Further Hearing 2316/95 *Ganeimat v. The State of Israel*, 49(4) PD 589 (1995) (Isr.).

26. See above, Chapter 1, Section III2.

27. See below, Chapter 8.

28. The statements of MK Yitzhak Levi from the National Religious Party in a debate that preceded the first reading of a private bill submitted by Dan Meridor and Benjamin Begin, seeking to add an entrenchment provision to Basic Law: Human Dignity and Liberty, lend support to this explanation. Levi explained that, despite his party's support in the original legislation in 1992, his faction would oppose the new proposal because Barak had, in the interim, published an article clarifying his interpretation of the phrase "Jewish and democratic state," emptying the Jewish component from any content that is not also universal. See *Divrei HaKnesset* 7179–7180 (August 2, 1993) (Isr.).

29. This element of compromise was also rendered null by President Barak when he interpreted the term "Jewish" in a way that voids it of any value, at least from the religious parties' perspective. The position that Barak presented in his academic and judicial writing empties the expression "Jewish" from its halakhic meaning, and determines that the Jewish values of the State of Israel are only those that were born within Judaism and accepted by the enlightened nations of the world. See Aharon Barak, "The Constitutional Revolution: Protected Human Rights" (1992) 1 Mishpat Umimshal 29–30 [Heb.] (henceforth Barak, "The Constitutional Revolution"). Barak's remarks evoked resentment in the national-religious public, and perhaps on these grounds, Barak's later formulations are kinder to the Jewish component in the dual definition, at least rhetorically. See Aharon Barak, "The Values of the State of Israel as a Jewish and Democratic State" in Aharon Barak and Menashe Shava (eds), *Homage to Yitzhak: In Honor of Judge Yitzhak Shiloh* (Tel Aviv: Israel Bar Association 1999), 35–39 [Heb.]; idem, "The State of Israel as a Jewish and Democratic State" (2000) 24 Iyyunei Mishpat 10 [Heb.].

30. See, for instance, the following statements: "One day or, more precisely, one night, in perfectly ordinary circumstances, two laws were brought to the vote with less than half of the House members present ... Nobody mentioned that this was a constituent assembly, nobody spoke about a revolution, and nobody said that a constitutional change was under way. They voted. After a few months, the people were told that a revolution had taken place. Nu, the first revolution that took place without the public knowing about it. Only after the fact was it informed of the revolution ... those MKs who perhaps knew that this was a far-reaching step, deliberately concealed the information from the rest ... This is how you build a constitution? Why was it necessary to deceive the members of the Knesset?" MK Michael Eitan, *Divrei HaKnesset* 144a, 5246 (January 16, 1995) (Isr.). "In the previous Knesset, very very late at night, Basic Laws that should be passed in a plenum of 120 Knesset members—enacting a constitution is reason for celebration in a democracy—at a late hour, deliberately deceiving the religious and ultra-Orthodox public, whose consent they had required in the previous Knesset term ..." MK Aryeh Deri, *Divrei HaKnesset* 154, 4478 (February 12, 1996) (Isr.).

31. *Divrei HaKnesset* 125, 3783 (1992) (Isr.).

32. Ibid, at 3788.

33. See Moshe Landau, "Symposium: Three Years after Bank Mizrahi" (2000) 5 Hamishpat 254 [Heb.]: "The constitution depicted by Chief Justice Barak is the only one in the world to have been created by a judicial proclamation."

34. Gideon Sapir, "Religion and State in Israel: The Case for Reevaluation and Constitutional Entrenchment" (1999) 22 Hastings International and Comparative Law Review 657, note 134.

35. See above, Chapter 1, Section IV.

36. See Klein, "Initial Normative Assessment", (n. 6), 125: "For instance, if we were to adopt the view that has been accepted in Israel for many years, whereby non-entrenched Basic Laws enjoy no primacy whatsoever, the inevitable conclusion would be that any future legislation infringing a provision of Basic Law: Human Dignity and Liberty would supersede it."

37. Karp, "Basic Law", (n. 23), 361.

38. See, for example, Ehud Sprinzak and Larry Diamond (eds), *Israeli Democracy under Stress* (Boulder, CO: Lynne Rienner 1993) 20, note 1: "Although the law ... was adopted as a basic law, in contrast to the new Basic Law Freedom of Occupation, it was not entrenched ... Thus, although it is called a basic law, it does not include the element that grants this appellation practical meaning."

39. See Barak, "The Constitutional Revolution" (n. 29), where he expresses hope that discussions on the special status of Basic Law: Human Dignity and Liberty, which contains a non-entrenched limitation clause, will become redundant when this law too is entrenched; Aharon Barak, "Protected Human Rights and Private Law" in Yitzhak Zamir (ed.), *Klinghoffer Volume on Public Law* (Jerusalem: Hebrew University 1993b), 167 [Heb.]. Note that Barak's expansive interpretation was supported by other academic scholars. See, for example, David Kretzmer, "The New Basic Laws on Human Rights: A Mini-Revolution in Israeli Constitutional Law?" (1992) 26 Israel Law Review 246; idem, "The New Basic Laws on Human Rights: A Mini-Revolution in Israeli Constitutional Law?" (1996) 14 Netherlands Quarterly of Human Rights 177–178; Barak-Erez, "From an Unwritten to a Written Constitution", (n. 15), 334–335.

40. See Roei Amit, "Positioning of a Canon" (1997) 21 Iyyunei Mishpat 118 [Heb.]. In his article, Amit describes additional methods through which Barak succeeds in endowing the positions he presents with canonical status, even when they represent innovations and deviations from previous positions. One method is the recourse to *obiter dictum*, which is later quoted as part of the ruling. Awareness of Barak's uses of this technique has spread even to the United States. See Richard A. Posner, "Enlightened Despot" (April 23, 2007) The New Republic.

41. See below, Chapter 3, Sections II–III.

42. Rubinstein, "The Knesset and Basic Laws", (n. 18), 350.

43. Ibid, 341.

44. Ibid, 350. Barak too praises Levi for his key role in the success of enacting the Basic Law. Barak, "Bat-Mitzvah", (n. 5), 10.

45. See also Levi's statements in the Constitution, Law, and Justice Committee: "Should the Marriage and Divorce Law confront this Law, it could be claimed that it is unsuitable for a democratic state. If I were a judge and if I were not a believing man, I would say that to forbid a man who is a *cohen* [having priestly ancestry] to marry a divorced woman is unsuited to a democratic state. The issue will be brought before a panel of nine judges, and this will undermine things we view as foundations of a Jewish state, even if it is a secular state of law. We tread a fine line. We have some laws that fit a Jewish state and Israel is a democratic state, we always move along two courses—a Jewish state and a democratic state" [Minutes of the Constitution, Law, and Justice Committee, 12th Knesset, 15 (July 1, 1992) (Isr.)].

46. For a description of developments in this regard, see Rubinstein, "The Knesset and Basic Laws", (n. 18), 347.

47. Yoav Dotan, "A Constitution for the State of Israel: The Constitutional Dialogue after the 'Constitutional Revolution'" (1997) 28 Mishpatim 166–167 [Heb.].

48. Minutes of the Constitution, Law and Justice Committee, 12th Knesset, 32 (February 5, 1992) (Isr.) (my emphasis). None of the members of the Committee bothered to relate to these comments. In a conversation I had with Levi on October 9, 2007, he argued that he had understood at the start that the two Basic Laws would allow the Supreme Court to engage in judicial review of primary legislation, and that he even consulted on this matter with Justice Elon. This report is incompatible with his statements as cited here.

49. Rubinstein, "The Knesset and Basic Laws", (n. 18), 350, note 7.

50. See Uriel Lynn, "Basic Laws as Part of Israel's Written Constitution" (2000) 5 Hamishpat 277 [Heb.]. In an article that Lynn published soon after the enactment of the Basic Laws, he does not refer to the deception claim, apparently because it had not yet been raised. See Uriel Lynn, "A Foundation for a Written Constitution in Israel" (1993) 1 Hamishpat 81 [Heb.].

51. This conclusion is warranted by the context. Lynn first voiced his position, as quoted in the body of the text, in the deliberations of the Constitution Committee in response to the proposal of MK Ravitz to include an explicit provision in the Basic Law, stating it would not affect arrangements bearing on marriage and divorce, as well as on the Sabbath and religious holidays. Lynn replied that this motion was negotiable, but "it must be remembered that the big difference between this Basic Law and the other laws that you considered is the establishment of the Supreme Court as a constitutional court. In those bills, the Supreme Court was given power to repeal laws. Here we are not dealing with this subject, here we are not giving this power to the Supreme Court" (Minutes of the Constitution, Law and Justice Committee, 12th Knesset, 34 (March 9, 1992) (Isr.)). Through these comments, Lynn obviously attempts to appease Ravitz, and to explain why legislation dealing with the Sabbath and personal status, extant or future, could not be harmed by the Court. If all Lynn was saying is that the Supreme Court would not be vested with exclusive authority, his comments would not have answered Ravitz's concerns.

52. See the opinion of Justice Cheshin in *Bank Mizrahi*.

53. Elon's comments here are somewhat laconic, but they can be understood in this manner. See Menachem Elon, "Basic Laws: Their Enactment and Their Interpretation: From Where and to Where?" (1996) 12 Mehkarei Mishpat: Bar-Ilan Law Studies 256 [Heb.]: "In my view, there are no grounds nor any basis for assuming that the Basic Laws have taken away from the legislature, in our parliamentary regime, its status at the head of the three branches pyramid: the legislative, the executive, and the judiciary. It still preserves its status / . . . "

54. Moshe Landau, "Reflections on the Constitutional Revolution" (1996) 26 Mishpatim 419 [Heb.]; idem, "The Supreme Court as Constitution Maker for Israel" (1996) 3 *Mishpat Umimshal* 697 [Heb.].

55. Gavison, "Self-Fulfilling Prophecy?," (n. 20); Ruth Gavison, "Constitutions and Political Reconstruction? Israel's Quest for a Constitution" (2003) 18 International Sociology 62–67 (although the enactment of the Basic Laws relating to human rights was declared a "Constitutional Revolution" by some, Israel's constitutional history shows that such a declaration is mistaken).

56. Barak, "Bat-Mitzvah", (n. 5), 14.

57. The best proof of the link between the MKs' awareness of the Basic Laws' importance and the rate of their participation in the voting is the high participation rate in later votes, on 1994, dealing with their amendment. But see Ariel Bendor, "Defects in the Enactment of Basic Laws" (1994) 2 Mishpat Umimshal 445–447 [Heb.] (The 1994 amendment of Basic Law: Freedom of Occupation passed hastily. Many of its most important provisions were not included in the original draft and appeared only in the second and third readings, with MKs unaware of their change of content. Some MKs wrongly assumed that they were voting for a statute prohibiting the importation of non-kosher meat rather than for the Basic Law).

58. *Divrei HaKnesset* 124, 2596 (1992) (Isr.).

59. Klein, "Initial Normative Assessment", (n. 6), 123. The 1992 Basic Laws were enacted three months before general elections were held.

60. Aharon Barak, "The Law of Israel: Past, Present, and Future" (1997) 43 Hapraklit 5 [Heb.].

61. Barak, "Bat-Mitzvah", (n. 5), 19.

62. MK Aryeh Deri goes even further and argues that the enactment of the two Basic Laws was coordinated a priori with the Supreme Court: "I have no doubt that Basic Law: Human Dignity and Liberty was arranged with the Supreme Court. I say this and I stand behind this statement.

The wording of the law was arranged with them and they, through the eye of this needle, have passed whatever they wanted." [*Divrei HaKnesset* 360 (1996) (Isr.)].

63. From the late 1970s, the hegemony of the Labor Party that had ruled until then in the *Yishuv* and in the state began to crack. The 1977 elections, when the Labor Party first lost its majority, marked a clear transition to a post-hegemonic era, characterized by the split of political power among various parties, none of which enjoys hegemonic status. For a description of the collapse of the Labor movement's hegemony, see Menachem Mautner, "The Eighties: The Years of Anxiety" (2003) 26 Iyyunei Mishpat 645 [Heb.] (henceforth Mautner, "The Eighties").

64. An interesting instance of a politician's strategic move, when aware he may soon lose power, is the behavior of François Mitterrand. Alec Stone notes that in 1986, confronting growing signs of the Socialists' expected failure in the coming elections, Mitterrand prepared himself to be in the opposition by appointing his Minister of Justice as President of the Supreme Constitutional Court. See Alec Stone, *The Birth of Judicial Politics in France: The Constitutional Council in Comparative Perspective* (New York: Oxford University Press 1992) 47, 86.

65. Such as Shas (representing traditional Mizrahi Jews), Israel be-Aliyah and Israel Beitenu (representing immigrants from the Former Soviet Union), and various parties that represent the Arab minority.

66. See, for example, Martin Edelman, *Courts, Politics, and Culture in Israel* (Charlottesville: University Press of Virginia 1994), 34: "By established practice, appointments to the Supreme Court require an affirmative vote of all three justices on the panel." Moshe Ben-Zeev, who served as attorney general in 1963–1968, wrote: "No appointment to judicial office is possible, and certainly not to the Supreme Court, if all three Supreme Court judges in the Committee are against it. I had hoped that this was the unwritten practice, but if this is not the case, my view is it [the practice] should be anchored in law." See Moshe Ben-Zeev, "Politics in the Appointment of Judges" (May 27, 1981) Orekh Hadin 13 [Heb.]. For additional sources, see Mordechai Haller, "The Court That Packed Itself" (1999) 8 Azure 73–77. Over the last few years, this practice has begun to evoke resistance, and Supreme Court justices have increasingly been confronting Ministers of Justice unwilling to accept it. On the mechanism of judicial appointments, see below, Chapter 4, Section II3.

67. The recent amendment, requiring a majority of seven out of the nine members of the committee as a condition for selecting a candidate, only strengthened the status of the Supreme Court by turning them into a bloc with veto powers. See Ariel L. Bendor and Zeev Segal, *The Hat Maker: Discussions with Justice Aharon Barak* (Or Yehuda: Kinneret, Zmora-Bitan 2009), 66 [Heb.], where Barak says: "The amendment in my view has only one advantage—it grants veto power to the three Supreme Court judges who are members of the committee." The law's declared aim had been different. See the explanatory note of the Bill on the Judiciary (amendment No. 51) (special majority for the appointment of a Supreme Court judge), 1984, Knesset Bill 354 (Isr.).

68. For a similar argument see Mautner, "The Eighties", (n. 63), who argues that the loss of hegemony and the incipient struggle over the character of the State of Israel evoked anxiety among the old elites, leading them to increasingly resort to the Supreme Court and to acquiesce without any criticism to the changes in Supreme Court rulings during the 1980s.

69. See, for example, Ran Hirschl, "The Struggle for Hegemony: Understanding Judicial Empowerment through Constitutionalization in Culturally Divided Polities" (2000) 36 Stanford Journal of International Law 87; idem, "The Political Origins of Judicial Empowerment through Constitutionalization: Lessons from Four Constitutional Revolutions" (2000) 25 Law and Social

Inquiry 91; idem, "Looking Sideways, Looking Backwards, Looking Forwards: Judicial Review vs. Democracy in Comparative Perspective" (2000) 34 University of Richmond Law Review 415; idem, *Towards Juristocracy: The Origins and Consequences of the New Constitutionalism* (Cambridge, MA: Harvard University Press 2004) 21–24, 50–74; idem, "Constitutional Courts vs. Religious Fundamentalism: Three Middle Eastern Tales" (2004) 82 Texas Law Review 1833–1847.

70. See Lisa Hilbink, "Beyond Manicheanism: Assessing the New Constitutionalism" (2006) 65 Maryland Law Review 17; Mark Tushnet, "Political Power and Judicial Power: Some Observations on Their Relation" (2006) 75 Fordham Law Review 764.

CHAPTER 3

1. See above, Chapter 1, Section IV.

2. Aharon Barak, "The Constitutional Revolution: Protected Human Rights" (1992) 1 Mishpat Umimshal 9 [Heb.].

3. Dan Meridor and Benjamin Begin did submit a private bill seeking to add a "rigidity clause" to Basic Law: Human Dignity and Liberty, but their motion was rejected. See Basic Law: Human Dignity and Liberty (Amendment—entrenchment of the law), Bill 287 5753-1993 (Isr.).

4. Family Agricultural Sector (Arrangements), Law 5752-1992 (Isr.). The Law was later amended through the Family Agricultural Sector (Arrangements) Law (Amendment) 5753-1993 (Isr.).

5. See Haim H. Cohn, "*Obiter* of Blessed Memory" (2000) 31 Mishpatim 415 [Heb.]: "The time has come to give a decent burial to the archaic ban on the *obiter*, which is for sure extinct, and recite a brief eulogy."

6. Eli Salzberger, "The Constituent Assembly in Israel" (1996) 3 Mishpat Umimshal 680 [Heb.].

7. CA 6821/93 *Bank Mizrahi v. Migdal Cooperative Village*, 49(4) PD 221 (1995) (Isr.) <http://elyon1.court.gov.il/files_eng/93/210/068/z01/93068210.z01.pdf>. (henceforth *Bank Mizrahi*), para. 64 of Pres. Barak's opinion. Several other justices in the panel joined Barak. Thus, for instance, Shamgar (ibid, para. 35 of his opinion); Bach (ibid, para. 3 of his opinion); Zamir (ibid, para. 2 of his opinion): Mazza (ibid, 421); Goldberg (ibid, 414).

8. Ibid, para. 63 of President Barak's opinion (my emphasis), 209–210.

9. In later decisions, the Court implemented this theoretical pronouncement in regard to several Basic Laws. Concerning Basic Law: The Knesset, see Elections Appeal 92/03 *Shaul Mofaz v. Chairman of the Central Elections Committee for the Sixteenth Knesset*, 57(3) PD 793 (2003). <http://elyon1.court.gov.il/files_eng/03/920/000/f06/03000920.f06.pdf> (henceforth *Mofaz*). Concerning Basic Law: The Judiciary, see HCJ 212/03 *Herut—The National Jewish Movement v. Justice Mishael Cheshin, Chairman of the Central Elections Committee for the Sixteenth Knesset*, 57(1) PD 750 (2003) (Isr.) <http://elyon1.court.gov.il/files_eng/03/120/002/A04/03002120.a04.pdf> (henceforth *Herut*); HCJ 3511/02 *Negev Coexistence Forum v. The Ministry of Infrastructure*, 57(2) PD 102 (2003) (Isr.) <http://elyon1.court.gov.il/files_eng/02/110/035/F11/02035110.f11.pdf>. Concerning Basic Law: The Government, see HCJ 1384/98 *Avni v. Prime Minister*, 52(5) PD 206 (1998) (Isr.).

10. *Herut*, (n. 9), para. 5 of President Barak's opinion.

11. Thus, for instance, the Japanese constitution states: "Amendments to this Constitution shall be initiated by the Diet, through a concurring vote of two thirds or more of all the members of

each House." The article defines who is allowed to propose an amendment to the constitution, who approves it, and what is the majority required for this purpose. See Japan Const. (1946) Art. 96.

12. See the remarks by MK Aryeh Deri, *Divrei HaKnesset* 360 (1992) (Isr.): "I say this openly ... even if you were to bring the Ten Commandments as a Basic Law of the Constitution Committee, I would vote against it ... I don't know what you and the Supreme Court judges are together conspiring to do to us." See also the comments of MK David Tal in the Minutes of Meeting No. 39 of the Constitution, Law, and Justice Committee, 15th Knesset (November 23, 1999) (Isr.).

13. *Bank Mizrahi*, (n. 7), para. 28 of President (ret.) Shamgar's opinion; ibid, para. 60 of President Barak's opinion.

14. Ibid, para. 61.

15. Ibid, para. 39 of Pres. (ret.) Shamgar's opinion.

16. Ibid, para. 64 of President Barak's opinion.

17. Ibid.

18. *Herut*, (n. 9), para. 4.

19. In support of this understanding of Barak's statement, see Aharon Barak, "The Constitutional Revolution: Bat Mitzvah" (2004) 1 Mishpat va-'Asakim note 134 [Heb.]: "In *Bank Mizrahi*, I left this as a question requiring further consideration ... In this, I was mistaken ... Barring an authorizing provision in the Basic Law—be it Basic Law: Human Dignity and Liberty or any other Basic Law—a regular law cannot infringe an arrangement determined in a Basic Law, even if the regular law explicitly states 'notwithstanding what is stated in the Basic Law.'" For a different understanding of Barak's comment, see Avigdor Klagsbald, "Amending and Offending against Basic Laws" (2006) 48 Hapraklit 293 [Heb.]: "Even if the Basic Law contains no provision explicitly authorizing its infringement through a regular law (that is, the Law is 'silent'), a regular law can still infringe it as long as it meets the conditions of the judicial limitation clause, which will be formulated according to the matter at stake."

20. *Herut* (n. 9).

21. *Bank Mizrahi*, (n. 7), para. 65 of Pres. Barak's opinion. For discussion, see Ariel Bendor, "Four Constitutional Revolutions?" (2003) 6 Mishpat Umimshal 307 [Heb.]: "Justifying an innovation such as this one with a laconic argument while misleadingly referring to a precedent is an unseemly act."

22. HCJ 3434/96 *Hofnung v. Knesset Chairman*, 50(3) PD 57, paras. 11–12 of Justice Zamir's opinion (1996) (Isr.). For a similar view, see *Mofaz*, (n. 9), para. 17 of Justice Mazza's opinion.

23. Ibid, President Barak's opinion.

24. *Bank Mizrahi*, (n. 7), Justice Tal's opinion: "There is a difference of opinion between President Shamgar and President Barak, and between the two of them and Justice Cheshin, regarding fundamental questions of the authority and status of the legislative branch. This difference of opinion is extremely important in terms of constitutional law. Nonetheless, I do not believe that these questions need to be decided upon in order to resolve the matter before us. I will therefore refrain from entering into the debate between these eminent jurists, and leave these questions to be decided at the appropriate time."

25. Ibid, para. 63 of Justice Cheshin's opinion.

26. For a description of Cheshin's opinion as "great," "instructive," and "courageous," see Joshua Segev, "Was It a Dream or Reality: Justice Cheshin on the Knesset Constituent Authority" (2007) 6 Moznei Mishpat 461 [Heb.].

27. *Bank Mizrahi*, (n. 7), para. 108 of Justice Cheshin's opinion.

28. Ibid, para. 91.

29. Ibid, para. 125.

30. Ibid, para. 132.

31. See above, Chapter 1, Section IV.4.

32. For a similar puzzlement about Cheshin's passivity after his opinion in *Bank Mizrahi*, see Ruth Gavison in an interview with Cheshin that was published in Aharon Barak, Yitzhak Zamir, and Yigal Marzel (eds), *Sefer Mishael Cheshin* (Tel Aviv: Israel Bar Association 2009), 88–89 [Heb.].

33. See Ariel Bendor, "Entrenchment and Constitution: *Bergman* and the Constitutional Discourse in Israel" (2001) 31 Mishpatim note 12 [Heb.].

34. HCJ 6055/95 *Tsemah v. Minister of Defense*, 53(5) PD 241 (1999) (Isr.) (henceforth *Tsemah*).

35. See, for example, Cheshin's opinions in HCJ 4542/02 *Kav Laoved Worker's Hotline v. Government of Israel*, 61(1) PD 346 (2006) (Isr.) <http://elyon1.court.gov.il/files_eng/02/420/045/028/02045420.028.pdf>. HCJ 11298/03 *Movement for Quality Government in Israel v. Knesset House Committee*, 59(5) PD 865 (2005) (Isr.); HCJ 5070/95 *Na'amat- Movement of Working Women and Volunteers v. Minister of Interior*, 56(2) PD 721 (2002) (Isr.) (henceforth *Na'amat*).

36. Cheshin is also silent in HCJ 1715/97 *Israel Investment Managers Association v. Minister of Finance*, 51(4) PD 367 (1997) (Isr.) (henceforth *Israel Investment Managers Association*), where the Court voided a statutory provision. As in *Tsemah*, (n. 34), here too Cheshin confined himself to the comment "I agree with the opinion of my colleague President Barak and have nothing to add."

37. HCJ 366/03 *Commitment to Peace and Social Justice v. Minister of Finance*, 60(3) PD 464, paras. 1–2 of Justice Cheshin's opinion (2005) (Isr.) (henceforth *Commitment to Peace and Social Justice*). <http://elyon1.court.gov.il/files_eng/03/660/003/a39/03003660.a39.pdf>.

38. See Yoram Shahar, "On the Structure of the Supreme Court of Israel" (2003) 19 Mehkarei Mishpat: Bar-Ilan Law Studies 411 [Heb.].

39. Ibid.

40. Ibid. Yoram Shahar develops and substantiates this thesis in "Solidarity and Inter-generational Dialectics in the Supreme Court: The Politics of Precedent" (2000) 16 Mehkarei Mishpat: Bar-Ilan Law Studies 161 [Heb.].

41. Justice Barak, for instance, had no problem subverting rulings he disagreed with, or at least casting doubt on them. See, for instance, his ruling in HCJ 1000/92 *Bavli v. High Rabbinic Court*, 48(2) PD 221 (1994) (Isr.).

42. See above, Chapter 1, Section VI.

43. HCJ 3267/97 *Rubinstein v. Minister of Defense*, 52(5) PD 255 (1998) (Isr.) (henceforth *Rubinstein*). <http://elyon1.court.gov.il/files_eng/97/670/032/A11/97032670.a11.pdf>.

44. For a discussion of this presumption, see Gideon Sapir, "Nondelegation" (2010) 32 Iyyunei Mishpat 5; Amnon Rubinstein and Barak Medina, *The Constitutional Law of the State of Israel* (6th edn. Tel Aviv: Schocken 2005), vol. 1 [Heb.].

45. *Rubinstein*, (n. 43), para. 15 of Justice Cheshin's opinion.

46. HCJ 6427/02 *Movement for Quality Government in Israel v. The Knesset*, 61(1) PD 619, para. 6 to the opinion of Deputy President Cheshin (2006) (Isr.) (henceforth *Movement for Quality*).

47. Ibid, paras. 73–74 of President Barak's opinion.

48. See Yuval Yoaz "Anyone Who Raises His Hand against the Supreme Court—I Will Cut Off His Hand" (Haaretz, February 8, 2007) [Heb.].

49. Mishael Cheshin, "Responses" (2007) 6 Moznei Mishpat 503 [Heb.].

50. See, for example, Civil Appeal 105/92 *Re'em Engineers v. Nazareth Illit Municipality*, 47(5) PD 189, 200 (1993) (Isr.): "Today we may derive freedom of speech from the protection granted to human dignity and liberty in Basic Law: Human Dignity and Liberty"; HCJ 5394/92 *Huppert v. Yad Vashem: Holocaust, Martyrs' and Heroes' Remembrance Authority*, 48(3) PD 353, 362 (1994) (Isr.): "Today the principle of equality may rest on Basic Law: Human Dignity and Liberty."

51. See Hillel Sommer, "The Non-enumerated Rights: On the Scope of the Constitutional Revolution" (1997) 28 Mishpatim 340 [Heb.] (henceforth Sommer, "The Non-enumerated Rights").

52. Two other possible sources of unenumerated rights, which were noted but quickly rejected, are Article 1A of Basic Law Human Dignity and Liberty (the "purpose clause")—which states: "The purpose of this Basic Law is to protect human dignity and liberty, in order to establish in a Basic Law the values of the State of Israel as a Jewish and democratic state"—and the right to liberty.

53. Judith Karp, "Basic Law: Human Dignity and Liberty—A Biography of Power Struggles" (1992) 1 Mishpat Umimshal 358 [Heb.].

54. Ibid, 359.

55. For a discussion, see Sommer, "The Non-enumerated Rights", (n. 51).

56. See, for instance, Moshe Landau, "The Supreme Court as Constitution Maker for Israel" (1996) 3 Mishpat Umimshal 701 [Heb.]: "I have allowed myself to say that you cannot bring in these rights into the Basic Laws through the window, after they had been taken out from the Basic Law through the door"; Sommer, "The Non-enumerated Rights", (n. 51), 340: "Our position can be summed up in a paraphrase of President Barak's comment, which stated: 'We must interpret Basic Law: Human Dignity and Liberty according to its purpose. This purpose is to protect the human rights set within it.' We hold that the opposite is also true: the purpose of Basic Law: Human Dignity and Liberty was not to protect human rights *that had not been set within it.*"

57. See, for instance, HCJ 355/79 *Catalan v. Israel Prison Service*, 34(3) PD 294 (1980) (Isr.).

58. HCJ 4541/94 *Miller v. Minister of Defense*, 49(4) PD 94 (1995) (Isr.) (henceforth *Miller*). <http://elyon1.court.gov.il/files_eng/94/410/045/Z01/94045410.z01.pdf>. (on the right to equality: "The legislative history of the Basic Law indicates that the omission of the general principle of equality was intentional ... In view of this background, I doubt whether it is possible—or at least, whether it is proper—to hold by means of construction that the purpose of the Basic Law is to provide constitutional protection to the principle of general equality"); PPA 4463/94 *Avi Hanania Golan v. Prisons Service*, 50(4) PD 136 (1996) (Isr.). <http://elyon1.court. gov.il/files_eng/94/630/044/Z01/94044630.z01.pdf>. (on freedom of speech: "Apparently, the national consensus required for enshrining freedom of speech in a Basic Law had not yet been reached, and the draft Basic Law: Freedom of Speech has not been enacted until today. In such circumstances, it seems doubtful to me whether it is possible, or at any rate appropriate, to confer super-legislative status on freedom of speech generally, by incorporating it in the right of dignity").

59. See Sommer, "The Non-enumerated Rights", (n. 51); Hillel Sommer, "From Childhood to Maturity: Outstanding Issues in the Implementation of the Constitutional Revolution" (2004)

1 Mishpat va-'Asakim 66–70 [Heb.]. For representative statements see, for instance, HCJ 2557/
05 *Majority Camp v. Israel Police*, 62(1) PD 200 (2006) (Isr.). <http://elyon1.court.gov.il/files_
eng/05/570/025/a19/05025570.a19.pdf>. para. 12 of President Barak's ruling: ". . . in a host of
judgments this court has held that the Basic Law also includes the freedom of speech, within the
framework of the rights and liberties protected by it, and it thereby gives the freedom of speech
the status of a constitutional right." In Leave for Civil Appeal 10520/03 *Ben Gevir v. Dankner* (12
November 2006), Nevo Legal Database (by subscription, in Hebrew) (Isr.), para. 10 of Justice
Rivlin's ruling: "Freedom of speech is no longer an unwritten basic right . . . we are speaking of a
protected constitutional right."

60. HCJ 6298/07 *Ressler v Knesset* (21 February 2012), Nevo Legal Database (by subscription)
(Isr.).

61. The Court gave the Knesset until August 1, 2012, to enact an alternative law that would
respect the religious needs of ultra-Orthodox Jews while not disproportionately infringing on the
others' right to equality, and a new law was enacted in March 2014. The law states that the number
of members of the ultra-Orthodox community serving either in the army or in the national serv
ice will rise gradually. In September 2017, the Court also rejected the new arrangement, after ruling that this arrangement also unjustifiably harms the right to equality [HCJ 1877/14 *Movement
for Quality of Government in Israel v. The Knesset* (12 September 2017) Nevo Legal Database (by
subscription) (Isr.). <http://elyon1.court.gov.il/files/14/770/018/c29/14018770.c29.htm>. For
more, see Chapter 8 below.

62. Aharon Barak, *Interpretation in Law* (Jerusalem: Nevo 1994), vol. 3, 413–418 [Heb.].

63. See, for example, Andrei Marmor, "Judicial Review in Israel" (1997) 4 Mishpat Umimshal
133 [Heb.]; Eli Salzberger and Alexander (Sandy) Kedar, "The Quiet Revolution: More on Judicial
Review According to the New Basic Laws" (1998) 4 Mishpat Umimshal 515 [Heb.]: "In the choice
of *Investment Consultants* as the object of the first successful judicial review and in the decision
itself," Justice Barak applied a "libertarian interpretation of Basic Law: Freedom of Occupation."

64. See, for instance, Leave for Civil Appeal 4905/98 *Gamzu v. Yeshayahu*, 55(3) PD 360, para.
19 of President Barak's opinion (2001) (Isr.): "Every person's right to minimal sustenance, including a person entitled to alimony following a judicial verdict, is an integral part of the constitutional protection granted by Basic Law: Human Dignity and Liberty."

65. See, for instance, *Commitment to Peace and Social Justice*, (n. 37), para. 15.

66. The change in Barak's stance on the matter is also evident in his public and academic pro-
nouncements. See, for instance, Aharon Barak, "Preface" in Aharon Barak and Hayyim Berenson
(eds), *Berenson Book* (Jerusalem: Nevo 2000), vol. 2, 10 [Heb.]: "Social rights should be properly
acknowledged . . . as rights possessing supra-legal constitutional status."

67. HCJ 10662/04 *Hassan v. National Insurance Institute* 65(1) PD 782 (2012) (Isr.). For an
in-depth analysis of the case, see Neta Ziv, "Constitutional Review of 'Eligibility Conditions' in
Social Rights Litigation" in Gideon Sapir, Daphne Barak-Erez, and Aharon Barak (eds), *Israeli
Constitutional Law in the Making* (Oxford: Hart Publishing 2013), 507.

68. See above Chapter 2, Section III.

69. HCJ 7339/15 *The Israeli GLBT Association v. Minister of Interior* (31 August 2017) Nevo
Legal Database (by subscription) (Isr.) (henceforth *the Israeli GLBT Association*).

70. For more, see Chapter 8 below.

71. *Divrei HaKnesset* 4 (17.3.1992) (Isr.).

72. *The Israeli GLBT Association*, (n. 69), para. 3 of Justice Baron's opinion.

73. Entry into Israel Law, 5712-1952 (Isr.).

74. HCJ 7803/06 *Abu Arfa v. Minister of Interior* (13 September 2017) Nevo Legal Database (by subscription), para. 67 to the opinion of Justice Fogelman (Isr.). <http://elyon1.court.gov.il/files/06/030/078/m42/06078030.m42.htm>.

75. Ibid, para. 37 to the opinion of Justice Hendel.

76. For example, article 79(3) of the Basic Law for the Federal Republic of Germany states: "Amendments to this Basic Law affecting the division of the Federation into Länder, their participation on principle in the legislative process, or the principles laid down in Articles 1 and 20 shall be inadmissible."

77. See, for example, Yaniv Roznai and Serkan Yolcu "An Unconstitutional Amendment—the Turkish Perspective: A Comment on the Turkish Constitutional Court's Headscarf Decision" (2012) 10 International Journal of Constitutional Law 175.

78. HCJ 142/89 *La'or Movement v. Speaker of the Knesset*, 44(3) PD 529 (1990) (Isr.) (henceforth *La'or*). For more, see Chapter 1, Section IV, above.

79. HCJ 4676/94 *Mitrael v. The Knesset*, 50(5) PD 15 (1996) (Isr.). For more, see Chapter 4, Section I below.

80. See, for example, CA 6821/93 *United Mizrahi Bank Ltd. v. Migdal Cooperative Village*, 49(4) PD 221, 394 (1995) (Isr.) for such a position.

81. HCJ 4908/10 *Knesset Member Bar-On v. The Knesset*, 64(3) PD 275 (2011) (Isr.). <http://elyon1.court.gov.il/files/10/080/049/n08/10049080.n08.htm>.

82. Basic Law: The State Economy for 2009–2010 (Special Instructions) (Temporary Provision) (Amendment) (5770-2010) (Isr.).

83. HCJ 8260/16 *Academic Ctr. of Law and Bus. v. The Knesset* (6 September 2017) Nevo Legal Database (by subscription) (Isr.) <http://elyon1.court.gov.il/files/16/600/082/t10/16082600.t10.htm>.

84. Ibid, para. 7 to the opinion of Justice Joubran.

85. By contrast, Justice Joubran and Justice Fogelman discussed the issue of an unconstitutional constitutional amendment at length, but ruled explicitly in paras. 5 and 9 to their opinions (respectively) that the doctrine of misuse is sufficient for this case.

86. Para. 11 to the opinion of Justice Rubinstein.

CHAPTER 4

1. On this matter, see Gideon Sapir, "Review of *Outlawed Pigs*, by Daphne Barak-Erez" (2008) 1 Mishpat Umimshal 611 [Heb.].

2. See, for instance, the remarks by MK Binyamin Elon of the Moledet faction in the discussion on the Bill on the Amendment of Basic Law: Freedom of Occupation, Amendment No. 2, second and third reading, March 18, 1998: "And Basic Law: Freedom of Occupation, that we are now seeking to amend . . . was enacted . . . with a vast majority, and no one thought it in any way problematic. No one understood then that social questions of tradition and dietary laws related to value decisions are now shifted to the Supreme Court . . ." See also the comments by Avraham Ravitz of Torah Judaism, Bill on the Amendment of the Basic Law: Freedom of Occupation, Amendment No. 3, first reading, March 3, 1998: "And I thought it only right that a society such as ours should have a law that would preclude the possibility of not employing individuals for immaterial reasons . . . Later, when it was enacted, this law reached the High Court of Justice, as

we know, through petitions to the Supreme Court, and the Supreme Court . . . greatly expanded [it], far beyond the legislator's intention. We never ever imagined that this law would take us into these realms, and that this law would facilitate the import of non-kosher meat to the State of Israel."

3. HCJ 2015/91 *Heirs of Jacob Falcon-Mitrael v. The Government of Israel* (24 May 1993) Nevo Legal Database (by subscription) (Isr.).

4. HCJ 3872/93 *Mitrael v. The Prime Minister*, 47(5) PD 485 (1993) (Isr.) (henceforth *Mitrael v. The Prime Minister*).

5. Ibid, para. 24 of his opinion: "Legislation conditioning the import of meat in compliance with dietary laws appears to limit freedom of occupation in ways that are not in accordance with the limitation clause."

6. See Article 4 of Basic Law: Freedom of Occupation (5752-1992) (Isr.) and Article 8 of Basic Law: Human Dignity and Liberty (5752-1992) (Isr.).

7. See Aharon Barak, "On the Amendments of Basic Law: Freedom of Occupation" (1994) 2 Mishpat Umimshal 545–551 [Heb.]. (Barak's letter to the Chairman of the Knesset's Constitution, Law, and Justice Committee, which includes comments on the Bill on Basic Law: Freedom of Occupation (Amendment). As the editor of the journal notes, "Justice Barak's comments resonate in the new version of the law," ibid.; Ariel L. Bendor and Zeev Segal, *The Hat Maker: Discussions with Justice Aharon Barak* (Or Yehuda: Kinneret, Zmora-Bitan 2009), 57 [Heb.] (henceforth Bendor and Segal, *The Hat Maker*), quoting Barak: "I was the one who advised adding this clause, the notwithstanding clause."

8. Article 33 of the Canadian Charter of Rights and Freedoms states: "(1) Parliament or the legislature of a province may expressly declare in an Act of Parliament or of the legislature, as the case may be, that the Act or a provision thereof shall operate notwithstanding a provision included in Article 2 or Articles 7 to 15 of this Charter. (2) An Act or a provision of an Act in respect of which a declaration made under this Article is in effect shall have such operation as it would have but for the provision of this Charter referred to in the declaration. (3) A declaration made under subArticle (1) shall cease to have effect five years after it comes into force or on such earlier date as may be specified in the declaration. (4) Parliament or a legislature of a province may re-enact a declaration made under subArticle (1). (5) SubArticle (3) applies in respect of a remade under subArticle (4)." Can. Const. (Constitution Act, 1982) pt. I (Canadian Charter of Rights and Freedoms), Act. 33.

9. For a claim in this spirit, see, for instance, the remarks of MK Naomi Chazan of Meretz, Bill on the Amendment of the Basic Law: Freedom of Occupation, first reading, *Divrei HaKnesset* 135, 4538 (1994) (Isr.): "If today we change Basic Law: Freedom of Occupation . . . we undermine the Basic Laws of the State of Israel . . . not for substantive reasons, but for pressing, manipulative, political reasons, in order to solve a coalition problem." See also the remarks of MK David Zucker, chairman of the Knesset's Constitution, Law and Justice Committee, against the notwithstanding clause, *Divrei HaKnesset* 136, 5365 (1994) (Isr.).

10. Article 2 of the law. The name of the law was later changed, and today it is called the Law of Meat and Meat Products, 5754-1994 (Isr.).

11. HCJ 4676/94 *Mitrael v. The Knesset*, 50(5) PD 15 (1996) (Isr.). (henceforth *Mitrael v. The Knesset*).

12. Ibid, para. 10 of President Barak's opinion.

13. Ibid, para. 16.

14. Elsewhere, Barak argued that, after the legislation of the new Basic Laws "it is no longer against 'legal conscience' to claim that, in a democratic society practiced in the separation of powers and the rule of law, the judicial power can legitimately void a law opposed to the system's basic principles." See Aharon Barak, *Interpretation in Law* (Jerusalem: Nevo 1992), vol. 1, 632 [Heb.].

15. See above, Chapter 1, Article 6.

16. Law on Local Authorities (Special Authorization) 5717-1956 (Isr.).

17. HCJ 953/01 *Solodkin v. Beit Shemesh Municipality*, 58(5) PD 595 (2004) (Isr.) <http://elyon1.court.gov.il/files_eng/01/530/009/A19/01009530.a19.pdf>. For a review of developments in this field from the beginning of the Zionist endeavor and until the Solodkin petition, see Daphne Barak-Erez, *Outlawed Pigs: Law, Religion, and Culture in Israel* (Madison: University of Wisconsin Press 2009).

18. Article 11 to the Law Forbidding Fraud Concerning Dietary Laws, 5743-1983 (Isr.).

19. HCJ 465/89 *Raskin v. Jerusalem Religious Council*, 44(2) PD 673 (1990) (Isr.).

20. HCJ 7120/07 7120/07 *Assif Yanuv Crops Ltd. v. Chief Rabbinate Council* (23 October 2007) Nevo Legal Database (by subscription), para. 3 of President Beinisch's opinion (Isr.).

21. For a review of the attack of religious and ultra-Orthodox sectors on the Supreme Court, see Asher Cohen and Bernard Susser, *Israel and the Politics of Jewish Identity: The Secular-Religious Impasse* (Baltimore, MD: Johns Hopkins University Press 2000), 85–86, 90–91 (henceforth Cohen and Susser, *Israel and the Politics of Jewish Identity*); Shahar Ilan, "The Duty of Hatred, the Duty of Contempt" (Haaretz, October 1, 1997) [Heb.]; Israel Harel, "The Battle Cry of the Vischnitz Admor" (Haaretz, November 29, 1996) [Heb.].

22. See, for instance, Aryeh Dayan, "Goodbye Old Rift, Hello New Rift" (Haaretz, July 30, 2000), [Heb.].

23. See, for instance, Shahar Ilan, "Hammer at the NRP Convention: The Religious Public Feels Persecuted by the Supreme Court" (Haaretz, September 20, 1994), A5 [Heb.]; idem, "Ginat's Bastille, Krauss' Calf" (Haaretz, January 11, 1999), A2 [Heb.]: "All interviewees for this feature agreed that large parts of the religious-national public have lost their faith in the Supreme Court."

24. At this time, both the religious and the ultra-Orthodox press were highly concerned with the issue. See, for instance, Eliezer Schohat, "Why I Went to the Rally" (Hatsofeh, December 16, 1999), 9 [Heb.]: "Could someone remind me of a Supreme Court ruling in recent years in favor of a religious or a right-wing public? . . . I therefore found myself most naturally and genuinely siding with the minority"; B. Rabinowitz, "R. Gafni in a Letter to PM Netanyahu: The Religious and the Ultra-Orthodox Public Feel Choked and Impotent Facing a Dictatorial and Unelected System" (Yated Ne'eman, February 3, 1999) [Heb.]: "In recent years, courts of all instances, but particularly the Supreme Court, intervene in intolerable fashion in non-legal issues . . . stating one-sided and unequivocal positions on conversion, the Sabbath, yeshiva students, religious councils, and granting legitimation to all the filth and vileness diametrically opposed to the Torah and to Judaism." For a discussion of the demonstration and its implications, see Ran Hirschl, "The Political Origins of Judicial Empowerment through Constitutionalization: Lessons from Four Constitutional Revolutions" (2000) 25 Law and Social Inquiry 91.

25. Cohen and Susser, *Israel and the Politics of Jewish Identity*, (n. 21), 93–94; Shahar Ilan, "Controversy in the NRP: The Rabbis Call Upon the Religious-National Public to Participate in the Rally; The Ministers Are Against" (Haaretz, February 11, 1999) [Heb.].

26. Menachem Mautner, "Israeli Law in a Multicultural Society" in Eyal Yinon (ed.), *The Rule of Law in a Polarized Society: Proceedings of the Conference (February 17, 1998)* (Jerusalem: Ministry of Justice 1999), 43 [Heb.].

27. This was Begin's response to the 1979 decision of the High Court of Justice, which rejected the establishment of a settlement in its original location. He thereby conveyed his support for the Supreme Court and its decision, even though he opposed it. See Giddy Weitz, "What a Man, Review of *Begin 1913–1992*, by Avi Shilon" (Haaretz, December 21, 2007) [Heb.].

28. *Divrei HaKnesset* 168, 5799 (1998) (Isr.).

29. HCJ 1661/05 *Gaza Coast Regional Council v. The Knesset*, 59(2) PD 481 (2005) (Isr.) (henceforth *Gaza Coast*).

30. For general statistical data see Guy Zeidman, "Expanded Panels in the Israeli Supreme Court" (2003–2004) 3 Netanya Academic College Law Review 3, 226, note 262 [Heb.] (henceforth Zeidman, "Expanded Panels").

31. Ibid, 182.

32. See Haim Cohn, "Deportation According to Law" (1992) 1 Mishpat Umimshal 471 [Heb.]: "Our legal system—as opposed to the continental system—is that each judge speaks for himself, in his own style and taste."

33. See Guy Zeidman and Hillel Sommer, "The Supreme Court and the Disengagement" (2006) 9 Mishpat Umimshal 592 [Heb].

34. *Gaza Coast*, (n. 29), 570, 572–573, 575.

35. For a description and evaluation, see Daphne Barak-Erez, "The Justiciability Revolution: An Evaluation" (2008) 50 Hapraklit 3 [Heb.].

36. *Gaza Coast*, (n. 29), 578–579.

37. See Rivlin's speech at a conference that the Israel Democracy Institute held at the President's house on May 22, 2003, as reported by Efrat Weiss and Ilan Marciano, "Rivlin Threatens the Court and the Balance of Powers" (Ynet, May 22, 2003). <www.ynet.co.il/articles/1,7340,L-2630459,00.html> [Heb.].

38. Criminal File (Tel Aviv Magistrate Court) 4696/01 *The State of Israel v. Handelman* (April 14, 2003), Nevo Legal Database (by subscription) (Isr.).

39. For instance, Barak and Rivlin met on April 18, 2002, at the initiative of then President Moshe Katsav. See Eyal Reuveni, "Rivlin at a Reconciliation Meeting with Justice Barak" (Ynet, April 18, 2002). <www.ynet.co.il/articles/0,7340,L-2904179,00.html> [Heb.].

40. See Moshe Gorali, "The New Supreme Court: Less Briliant, but No Less Efficient" (Haaretz, April 16, 2002), Article 2 [Heb.]: "Under Barak's leadership, the Supreme Court has been drawn into harsh confrontations with the Bar, with the academia, and mainly with politicians."

41. HCJ 4908/10 *Knesset Member Bar-On v. The Knesset*, 64(3) PD 275, para. 8 of Justice Rubinstein's opinion (2011) (Isr.).

42. For instance, a sharp controversy erupted in the United States concerning the Supreme Court decision in *Roe v. Wade*, 410 U.S. 113 (1973), where the Court recognized a woman's right to have an abortion as derived from the right to privacy. This interpretation was claimed to exceed the bounds of legitimacy. See, for instance, Robert H. Bork, *The Tempting of America: The Political Seduction of the Law* (New York: Free Press 1990), 111–117; idem, *Slouching towards Gomorrah: Modern Liberalism and American Decline* (New York: Regan Books 1996), 103.

43. See, for instance, David Kretzmer, "The Path to Judicial Review in Human Rights Cases: From *Bergman* and *Kol ha'am* to *Bank Mizrahi*" (1997) 28 Mishpatim 385 [Heb.]. Ariel

Bendor notes: "Much has been written . . . praising the effect of the new basic legislation and the subsequent constitutional revolution on the protection of fundamental human rights." Bendor emphasizes that his article, which pointed to several flaws in the actions of the Knesset as a constitutional authority, in no way detracts from his praise. See Ariel Bendor, "Flaws in the Enactment of the Basic Laws" (1994) 2 Mishpat Umimshal 443 [Heb.].

44. Ruth Gavison, "The Constitutional Revolution: A Description of Reality or a Self-Fulfilling Prophecy?" (1997) 28 Mishpatim 23 [Heb.].

45. See Moshe Landau, "Symposium: Three Years after *Bank Mizrahi*" (2000) 5 Hamishpat 254 [Heb.]; idem, "Reflections on the Constitutional Revolution" (1996) 26 Mishpatim 419 [Heb.]; idem, "The Supreme Court as Constitution Maker for Israel" (1996) 3 Mishpat Umimshal 697 [Heb.].

46. Note that transcending group interests is difficult for all camps. It is a plausible assumption that, were the Court to act according to the ideology of the other sector, the members of the latter would have also refrained from action, even though intellectual integrity would require them to be critical.

47. Ruth Gavison, "The Constitutional Revolution: A Description of Reality or a Self-Fulfilling Prophecy?" (1997) 28 Mishpatim 23, 23–26 [Heb.] (henceforth Gavison, "The Constitutional Revolution").

48. It is worth noting that the apology was not accepted. Gavison, as is well known, became persona non grata to taste arbiters in the group of former hegemons. See, for instance, Yuval Yoaz, "Barak Opposes Gavison's Appointment: Her Agenda Is Unworthy" (Haaretz, November 13, 2005) [Heb.].

49. See Bendor and Segal, *The Hat Maker*, (n. 7), quoting Barak, 139: "In the past . . . criticism came from the margins of Israeli society. I think that what has happened in recent years is that the critique of the Court's jurisprudence comes not only from the margins."

50. And yet, despite the changed attitude to the Court in the former hegemons' camp, we are definitely not speaking of a full reversal. Key spokespersons from academia persist in their passionate defense of the Court. See, for instance, Mordechai Kremnitzer, "The Recent Supreme Court and the Civil Interest" (2008) 33 Alpayim 103 [Heb.].

51. Menachem Mautner, "The Decline of Formalism and the Rise in Values in Israeli Law" (1993) 17 Iyyunei Mishpat 503 [Heb.]. This article also appears as ch. 4 of his *Law and the Culture of Israel* (New York: Oxford University Press 2011), 75–98.

52. Menachem Mautner, "Appointment of Judges to the Supreme Court in a Multicultural Society" (2003) 19 Mehkarei Mishpat: Bar-Ilan Law Studies 423 [Heb.].

53. See, for instance, Uri Paz, "The Church of Justice" (Makor Rishon, November 4, 2007) [Heb.]; Uri Paz, "The Last Liberal" (Makor Rishon, August 15, 2008), [Heb.]. These articles argued that Mautner had been critical of the constitutional revolution from the start. As the quotations above show, this claim is incorrect.

54. See, for instance, Menachem Mautner, *Law and the Culture of Israel* (New York: Oxford University Press 2011), 178–180 (henceforth Mautner, *Law and the Culture of Israel*): "It should be borne in mind that Israel does *not* have a written constitution . . . The rhetoric of 'a constitutional revolution,' so goes the argument, is simply a ruse to provide the Court and its supporters with powers vis-à-vis the Knesset and the government that the Knesset never intended to grant . . . The two Basic Laws of 1992 are thin statutes that refer to only a few (and not necessarily the most important) of the basic constitutional rights that citizens in a liberal democracy enjoy . . . If Israel wishes to have a constitution, no 'shortcuts' are available."

55. Friedmann proposed, inter alia, a change in the composition of the Judicial Appointments Committee, including lowering the number of Supreme Court justices in the Committee from three to two, and adding to the Committee three members who are not part of the executive. See Memorandum on Basic Law: The Judiciary (Amendment—Composition of the Judicial Appointments Committee), 5768-2008 (Isr.) and Memorandum on the Courts' Law (Amendment—Members of the Judicial Appointments Committee 5768-2008) (Isr.); reserving authority for voiding laws to the Supreme Court, and expanding the panel allowed to perform this review (Memorandum on Bill on Basic Law: Legislation, Article 24), and adding a general exception clause to apply in every case of law annulment (ibid, Article 11). For a review of Friedmann's initiatives, see Zeev Segal, "Hurt All You Can" (Haaretz, January 7, 2008) [Heb.].

56. This is Barak's view. See Bendor and Segal, *The Hat Maker*, (n. 7), quoting Barak, 139: "An attack coming from the Minister of Justice himself, Daniel Friedmann, made all attacks legitimate."

57. Mautner, *Law and the Culture of Israel*, (n. 54), 161 (emphasis in original). Mautner's sensitivity to the change in the attitude to the Supreme Court within the former hegemonic camp is not a trivial matter. Several of the writers who claim to understand and analyze the prevailing moods of the Israeli public have failed to detect this change. See, for instance, Gadi Taub, "Israeliness—That Isn't Us". <http://acheret.co.il/en/?cmd=articles.323&act=read&id=2042> [Heb.].

58. Mautner, *Law and the Culture of Israel*, (n. 54), 162. For a similar view, see Eyal Benvenisti, "No Sword, No Wallet, No Friends" (Haaretz, May 9, 2008) [Heb.].

59. See, for instance, Amnon Rubinstein, "Legal Crisis" (Maariv, June 8, 2007) [Heb.]: "The Knesset must settle, once and for all, the matter of judicial review of Knesset laws through a Basic Law explicitly stating that only the Supreme Court is allowed to void a law opposed to a Basic Law—when at least nine judges sit on the bench and issue a decision agreed by a two-thirds majority." See also the Bill of NRP MK Zevulun Orlev, Constitutional Court 5766-2006. From the explanatory note of the Bill: "Since the Supreme Court views Basic Law: Human Dignity and Liberty and Basic Law: Freedom of Occupation as a constitutional revolution, and in its view these Basic Laws are a constitution, we face a new situation whereby the Supreme Court might void Knesset legislation. It is thus proper that a special constitutional court be established, as is the case in most countries in the world, which will specialize in the examination of a contradiction, if any, between a Knesset law and the Basic Laws"; Bill of Ha-Yihud Ha-Leumi MK Eliezer Cohen, Bill on Basic Law: Constitutional Court, February 9, 2005; Bill on Basic Law: Constitutional Court by MK Yigal Bibi, January 2, 2002. Note that the proposal to concentrate authority in the Supreme Court was submitted before the constitutional revolution. See Bill on Basic Law: Legislation, 5736-1975, Bill 135 (Isr.); Bill on Basic Law: Legislation, Bill 5738-1977, 326 (Isr.).

60. See, for instance, Yoav Dotan, "Does Israel Need a Constitutional Court?" (2000) 5 Mishpat Umimshal 126 [Heb.] (henceforth Dotan, "Does Israel Need a Constitutional Court?"). Note that Dotan discusses this claim in order to reject it.

61. Aharon Barak, "Judicial Review of the Constitutionality of Statutes: Centralism vs. Decentralism" (2005) 8 Mishpat Umimshal 21–22 [Heb.]. Note that Barak supported concentrating authority within the Supreme Court when he was still the Attorney General, although then he relied on a different reason. See Aharon Barak, "The Foundations of Judicial Review in Knesset Legislation" in *Sefer Barkatt: Symposia in Memory of Reuven Barkatt, Speaker of the Knesset* (Jerusalem: Israeli Association for Parliamentarism 1977), 291 [Heb.]: concentrating authority will

ensure that "constitutional questions will be decided by the supreme organ, that there will be no contradictory decisions in lower instances, and that we will save the judicial time of lower courts." Zeev Segal conveyed a similar view in "The Way to Judicial Review on the Constitutionality of Statutes: The Authority to Disqualify Acts—To Whom?" (1997) 28 Mishpatim 239 [Heb.]; Yitzhak Zamir, "Judicial Review of Statutes" (1992) 1 Mishpat Umimshal 395 [Heb.].

62. See, for instance, Dotan, "Does Israel Need a Constitutional Court?", (n. 60), 123; Oren Sofer and Gabriela Fishman, "Judicial Review in a Polarized Society" (2001) 24 Iyyunei Mishpat 693 [Heb.]. For the presentation and rejection of this argument, see Aharon Barak, "The Supreme Court as a Constitutional Court" (2003) 6 Mishpat Umimshal 322–323 [Heb.] (henceforth Barak, "The Supreme Court as a Constitutional Court").

63. Barak wonders "why would parties representing a minority of the population strive to realize this ideal, whereby their members will always be a minority" (n. 62), 321. In this volume of *Mishpat Umimshal*, the CEO of "Adalah" (an organization that deals with the rights of the Arab minority in Israel) indeed supports the continuation of the current situation. See Hassan Jabareen, "The Politics of Legal Professionalism in Constitutional Cases" (2003) 6 Mishpat Umimshal 329 [Heb.].

64. For a description of the two models and the differences between them, see Mauro Cappelletti, *The Judicial Process in Comparative Perspective* (Oxford: Clarendon Press 1989), 132–148; Allan R. Brewer-Carias, *Judicial Review in Comparative Law* (Cambridge: Cambridge University Press 1989), 125–135, 185–194 (henceforth Brewer-Carias, *Judicial Review*); Victor F. Comella, "The Consequences of Centralizing Constitutional Review in a Special Court: Some Thoughts on Judicial Activism" (2004) 82 Texas Law Review 1705.

65. Victor F. Comella, "The European Model of Constitutional Review of Legislation: Toward Decentralization?" (2004) 2 International Journal of Constitutional Law 468–470 (henceforth Comella, "The European Model").

66. Ibid, 465-468; Brewer-Carias, *Judicial Review*, (n. 64), 129.

67. Comella, "The European Model", (n. 65), 468.

68. Mauro Cappelletti and William Cohen, *Comparative Constitutional Law: Cases and Materials* (Indianapolis, IN: Bobbs-Merrill 1979), 81–83 (henceforth Cappelletti and Cohen, *Comparative Constitutional Law*).

69. See the Report of the Committee on the Structure of Regular Courts in Israel (1997, "Orr Committee"). For discussion, see Shahar Goldman, *The Proposed Reform of the Court System: Advantages vs. Risks* (Policy Paper 15, Jerusalem: Israel Democracy Institute 1999) [Heb].

70. In Canada, Supreme Court justices are selected by the executive power. In the United States, they are selected by both the legislature and the president working together.

71. For a description of the various ways and their development, see Cappelletti and Cohen, *Comparative Constitutional Law*, (n. 68), 86–90.

72. Comella, "The European Model", (n. 65), 472–474.

73. Ibid, 477–478.

74. Ibid.

75. The authority is based on Article 76 of the Law of the Courts [Combined Version], 5744-1984 (Isr.), which states: "If a matter is properly submitted to the court and a question incidentally arises that must be decided to clarify the matter at stake, the court is allowed to decide on it for the sake of that matter even if the issue in question is exclusively within the purview of another court or another religious court."

76. So far, only in a handful of cases has an Israeli trial court effectively struck down, *inter partes*, a statutory provision. See Criminal File (Tel Aviv Magistrate Court) 4696/01 *State of Israel v. Handelman* (April 14, 2003), Nevo Legal Database (by subscription) (Isr.); SC (PT) 940/07 *Taruf v. Iberia* (July 8, 2007), Nevo Legal Database (by subscription) (Isr.); SC (Ac) 1457/07 *Inbar v. Iberia* (November 20, 2007), Nevo Legal Database (by subscription) (Isr.); NI (Naz) 1822/09 *Yedinek v. National Insurance Institute* (January 7, 2010), Nevo Legal Database (by subscription) (Isr.).

77. For a similar claim, see Dotan, "Does Israel Need a Constitutional Court?", (n. 60), 128.

78. See, for instance, Article 15(1)(b) of the Bill on Basic Law: The Judiciary (Amendment No. 4) (Judicial Review of the Validity of Laws), Government Bill 5769-2009, 409 (Isr.): "A decision of the Supreme Court, according to subArticle 1, will be issued by a panel of nine judges or more, if the President of the Supreme Court has so decided, and by a majority of at least two-thirds of the justices in the panel." Bill on Basic Law: The Judiciary (Amendment—Voiding Laws by the Supreme Court of MK Ofir Pines-Paz (henceforth Pines Bill), Article 15 (1): "A judicial authority will not void a law, except for the Supreme Court in a panel of at least seven judges"); Bill on Basic Law: Legislation, 5752-January 1992 (Isr.). Article 35 stated that Basic Law: The Judiciary will be amended as follows: "The Supreme Court will also function as a constitutional court and, in this capacity, will include nine judges or a greater uneven number, as ordered by the President of the Supreme Court."

79. Pines Bill, Article 15(2)(5): "Should a concrete question be submitted to the judicial authority concerning a law's validity, and should the judicial authority find that the issue before it cannot be decided without deciding on the noted question of validity, and that it cannot dismiss the doubt and sustain the law's validity, it will submit the question to the Supreme Court; a question referred according to subArticle (2) will be submitted to the Supreme Court in a panel of three; should the Supreme Court determine that the law's validity is actually in question, and that a decision is required in this regard so as to rule on the issue pending before the referring authority, the question will be submitted to a panel of seven or more judges; should the Supreme Court determine that there is no room for discussing the question referred by the judicial authority, the latter will go on dealing with the matter according to the decision of the Supreme Court."

80. See the Israel Democracy Institute, "Constitution by Consensus" (henceforth *Constitution by Consensus Proposal*). <https://en.idi.org.il/media/6361/constitutionbyconsensus_draft.pdf>.

Article 163(a), p. 158, states: "The Supreme Court, and it alone, by a bench of no less than two-thirds of the body of Permanently Appointed Justices, may rule that a law is not valid because it is unconstitutional."

81. Article 26 of the Law of the Courts [Combined Version], 5744-1984 (Isr.).

82. See, for example, Zeev Segal, "Everything Depends on the Size of the Panel" (Haaretz, October 11, 2004), Article 2 [Heb.].

83. Bendor and Segal, *The Hat Maker*, (n. 7) 50: "On the question of religion and state, the panel will always include religious judges."

84. For a description based on internal information that casts doubt on Barak's claim of non-involvement in the size of the panel or its identity, see Naomi Levitsky, *The Supremes: Inside the Supreme Court* (Bnei Brak: Hakibbutz Hameuchad 2006), 334–339 [Heb.], describing Barak's actions in a case dealing with conversions, including the enlargement of the panel, seeking to ensure a solid majority for his own position. See also Meron Gross and Yoram Shahar, "Searching for Bench Selection Methods in Israel's Supreme Court: A Quantitative Analysis" (1998) 29

Mishpatim 567 [Heb.] (a study negating the claim of randomness in the assignment of justices to panels).

85. Gideon Sapir, "Law or Politics: Israeli Constitutional Adjudication as a Case Study" (2001) 6 UCLA Journal of International Law and Foreign Affairs 169. See also Daniel Statman and Gideon Sapir, "Freedom of Religion, Freedom from Religion, and the Protection of Religious Feelings" (2004) 21 Mehkarei Mishpat: Bar-Ilan Law Studies 71 [Heb.].

86. A similar situation prevails in the United States concerning exemptions for religious reasons. As Frederick Gedicks indicates, only a few cases reached the courts, and the religious lost in most of them. See Frederick Gedicks, "An Unfirm Foundation: The Regrettable Indefensibility of Religious Exemption" (1998) 20 University of Arkansas Law Journal 688.

87. The only cases where the Court accepted petitions on this basis were HCJ 1031/93 *Pessaro (Goldstein) v. Minister of Interior*, 49(4) PD 661 (1995) (Isr.) (henceforth *Pessaro-Goldstein*); HCJ 1438/98 *The Mesorti Movement v. The Minister of Religious Affairs*, 53(5) PD 337 (1999) (Isr.), and earlier in HCJ 262/62 *Peretz v. Kfar Shemariyahu*, 16 PD 2101 (1962) (Isr.). The first dealt with the validity of non-Orthodox conversion for registration in the Population Registry records, the second with the allocation of funds for the study of Torah in the Mesorti movement, and the third with the rights of Reform Jews to hire a public hall for prayer.

88. See, especially, the position of Justice England in Civil Appeal 6024/97 *Shavit v. Rishon Lezion Jewish Burial Society*, 53(3) PD 600 (1999) (Isr.) (henceforth *Shavit*). In HCJ 5016/96 *Horev v. Minister of Transportation*, 51(4) PD 1 (1997) (Isr.), Justice Tal accepted the claim concerning violation of freedom of religion, although this is not exactly clear. See para. 6 of the verdict.

89. Justice Elon in HCJ 47/82 *Fund of the Movement for Progressive Judaism v. Minister of Religion*, 43(2) PD 661 (1989) (Isr.); Justice Tal in *Pessaro-Goldstein*.

90. HCJ 5070/95 *Na'amat v. Minister of Interior*, 56(2) PD 721 (2002) (Isr.) (henceforth *Na'amat*); Justice Shamgar in *Pessaro-Goldstein*; Justice Shlomo Levin in *Fund of the Movement for Progressive Judaism*.

91. Indeed, in response to Barak's claim whereby "the Supreme Court will not issue an important decision on religion and state matters without having one of the religious judges in the panel," Zeev Segal said: "But the religious judge will always be in a minority." See Bendor and Segal, *The Hat Maker*, (n. 7), 146.

92. Article 20(b) of Basic Law: The Judiciary: "A rule laid down by the Supreme Court shall bind any court other than the Supreme Court."

93. Yoram Shahar, "On the Structure of the Supreme Court of Israel" (2003) 19 Mehkarei Mishpat: Bar-Ilan Law Studies 411 [Heb.]. See also idem, "Solidarity and Inter-generational Dialectics in the Supreme Court: The Politics of Precedent" (2000) 16 Mehkarei Mishpat: Bar-Ilan Law Studies 161 [Heb.].

94. Zeidman, "Expanded Panels", (n. 30). See also Suzie Navot, *The Constitutional Law of Israel* (The Hague: Kluwer Law International 2007), 139.

95. Zeidman, ibid.

96. According to a long-standing custom, the Knesset tends to choose to serve on the Judicial Appointments Committee one representative from coalition MKs and one from the opposition. This tradition was broken during the present Knesset. In the last elections to the Committee, held on July 22, 2015, a representative from the opposition was indeed elected, but on May 25, 2016, the party of that opposition member joined the coalition. In an appeal submitted to the Supreme Court in this matter, the appellants asked the Court to rule that the custom of electing an

opposition MK to the Judicial Selection Committee is a constitutionally binding one. The appeal was rejected on grounds of delay, but the Court did praise the custom, and recommended it be arranged in legislation, or at least in Knesset regulations. See: HCJ 9029/16 *Aviram v. Minister of Justice* (February 1, 2017), Nevo Legal Database (by subscription, in Hebrew) (Isr.). <http://elyon1.court.gov.il/files/16/290/090/z04/16090290.z04.htm>.

97. Mordechai Haller, "The Court That Packed Itself" (1999) 8 Azure 72–73.

98. Sammy Samuel, one of the Bar representatives on the Judicial Appointments Committee, argued: "The current composition of the Committee gives absolute control to the judges not only in all that concerns the appointment of new judges but also regarding promotions, so that every judge in the Magistrate and District Courts, when issuing a verdict, must take into account not to irritate the bosses. He knows that if he expresses an opinion that his bosses will not like, he can forget about a promotion. This undermines the foundations of the independence of the judge, who fears no one except the law." See Hadas Magen, "The Bar against the Zamir Commission" (Globes, January 10, 2002). <www.globes.co.il/news/docview.aspx?did=552679> [Heb.]; When he appeared as an advisor at the Constitution, Law, and Justice Committee of the Knesset, Nobel prize recipient Israel Aumann referred to the system as "institutionalized corruption," and explained it is not proper for judges to take part in the decision about the composition of the body they are part of. See Zvi Lavi, "Prof. Aumann: The Method for Choosing Judges Is Corrupt" (Ynet, June 17, 2008). <www.ynet.co.il/articles/0,7340,L-3556912,00.html> [Heb.].

99. For a comprehensive review, see Efrat Even, "The Participation of Public Representatives in Judicial Appointments Proceedings" (2003) 39 Parliament 4 [Heb.].

100. For a summary of the proposals until 2002, see Sarah Zvebner, "Appointing Judges: A Comparative Study" (2001) Knesset Research and Information Center [Heb.]. Many proposals for change have been submitted to the Knesset in recent years, too, but all have been rejected. See, for instance, MK David Tal, Bill on Basic Law: The Judiciary (Amendment—Appointing Judges to the Supreme Court), Bill 2006 87 (Isr.) (from the explanation to the bill: "It is proposed that the Judicial Appointments Committee present to the Knesset a list of candidates it considers appropriate for officiating at the Supreme Court, which will include up to three times and no less than twice the number of candidates required for the appointment. From the recommended list, in secret ballot, the legislative branch will choose the Supreme Court judges"); MK Zevulun Orlev—Bill on Basic Law: The Judiciary (Amendment—The Composition of the Judicial Appointments Committee), Bill 2006 920 (Isr.) (increasing the number of ministers and MKs at the Judicial Appointments Committee from two ministers to three and from two MKs to three). The latest change attempt, which resonated widely in the media, was that of the previous Minister of Justice, Daniel Friedmann. According to the proposal, the Committee will include eleven members. The number of Supreme Court representatives will decrease to two, and will be the same as the representatives of the government and the Knesset; the government will elect two representatives: a public figure and a retired judge. An additional representative will be appointed from the academia. See Aviram Zino, "Friedmann Launches a Revolution" (Ynet, January 2, 2008). <www.ynet.co.il/articles/1,7340,L-3489411,00.html> [Heb.].

101. Report of the Commission on the Judges' Selection Proceedings (2001, "Zamir Commission"), ch. 15: Summary, 85.

102. No evidence was cited for the first claim, whereas the second relied on a quote from the book by then Attorney General and later Supreme Court Justice Eliyakim Rubinstein, and on a quote from a book by a member of the Committee, Amnon Rubinstein—*The Constitutional*

Law of the State of Israel. Note that in the next edition of his book, published in 2005, Rubinstein cited the Commission in support of his statement. See Amnon Rubinstein and Barak Medina, *The Constitutional Law of the State of Israel* (Tel Aviv: Schocken 2005), vol. 1, 131, note 18 [Heb.] (henceforth Rubinstein and Medina, *The Constitutional Law of the State of Israel*). For a laconic, undocumented statement, see also Barak, "The Supreme Court as a Constitutional Court", (n. 62), 321: "The system for appointing judges in Israel is among the best in the world . . . The European legal systems are unhappy with the political character of judicial appointments to constitutional courts. Many look at our system with envy."

103. Report of the Zamir Commission, 86.

104. John Bell, *Judiciaries within Europe: A Comparative Review* (Cambridge: Cambridge University Press 2006), 28.

105. Ibid, 28–29.

106. A reform of English judicial appointments proceedings that took place in 2005 has brought them closer to the Israeli model. In the past, judges in England had been appointed by the Lord Chancellor, who is a member of the cabinet. Following the reform, some of the Lord Chancellor's powers to appoint judges have been transferred to a Judicial Appointments Commission comprising fifteen members, among them judges, lawyers, and representatives of the public. See Constitutional Reform Act 2005. As Yoav Dotan notes, however, "even after the new law, the Lord Chancellor retains a central role in the appointments proceedings" (Articles 82–83 of the law). See Yoav Dotan, "Judicial Review of Legislation: The Accountability Question" (2007) 10 Mishpat Umimshal 505, note 37 [Heb.].

107. Report of the Zamir Commission, ch. 12, "The Appointments Stage in the Judges Selection Committee", 76.

108. See Rubinstein and Medina, *The Constitutional Law of the State of Israel*, (n. 102), vol. 1, 131, note 17 (mention of a "practice, whereby all Supreme Court judges conducted an informal discussion about the candidates for the position of Supreme Court judge, meant to guide the judges who were members of the Committee").

109. See Hadas Magen, "Turkel Betrayed Us" (Globes, March 24, 2004) [Heb.]: "In the Supreme Court, they are very angry with Justice Yaakov Turkel. Turkel's vote yesterday in the Judicial Appointments Committee was diametrically opposed to the President's position, and inflicted a painful blow to his prestige. They say he will no longer have an easy time there."

110. Article 6a of the Law of the Courts [Combined Version], 5744-1984 (Isr.).

111. For a further example, see the Memorandum on Basic Law: Human Dignity and Liberty (Amendment—Citizenship, Residence, and Entry to Israel), 5768-2008 (Isr.), initiated by Minister Friedmann. The Memorandum stated, inter alia: "According to the proposal, claims stating that the Law of Return or any other law regulating citizenship, residence, or entry into Israel is unconstitutional will not be heard."

112. Constitution by Consensus Proposal, (n. 80), 158–159.

113. Ibid, 302.

114. See, for example, Yuval Yoaz, "Friedmann Proposes: The Thief Will Be Punished According to the Value of the Theft" (Haaretz, January 21, 2008) [Heb.] (citing Aharon Barak): "The proposals of Minister of Justice Daniel Friedmann could turn Israel into a third world country." Yuval Yoaz, "Shamgar Opposes Minister Friedmann's Initiative to Restrict the Powers of the High Court of Justice" (Haaretz, March 2, 2007) [Heb.] (citing former Supreme Court President, Meir Shamgar). Ruthi Abraham, "Beinisch: Friedmann Infringes the Court's Independence" (News

1, July 12, 2007) [Heb.] (citing Dorit Beinisch) Yuval Yoaz, Cheshin: "Friedmann Behaves Like a Wild African Elephant" (Haaretz, November 17, 2007) [Heb.] (citing former Supreme Court former Deputy President, Mishael Cheshin). Yuval Yoaz,"Mazuz: The Deliberations of the High Court of Justice on Legislation Should Not Be Restricted" (Haaretz, December 7, 2007) [Heb.] (citing Menny Mazuz, then retired Attorney General and today Supreme Court Justice).

115. On similar grounds, American scholars claim that, even if it were to emerge that, historically, the U.S. Constitution had not intended to grant the Supreme Court the authority to void laws, and even if originalism was to be adopted as the method of interpretation, it would no long er be possible to challenge the authority of the U.S. Supreme Court to void primary legislation in light of the long-standing practice of judicial review. See, for example, Michael J. Perry, *The Constitution in the Courts: Law or Politics?* (New York: Oxford University Press 1994), 26; Samuel Freeman, "Original Meaning, Democratic Interpretation, and the Constitution" 21 Philosophy and Public Affairs 7 (1992).

116. Gad Barzilai, Ephraim Yuchtman-Yaar, and Zeev Segal, *The Israeli Supreme Court and the Israeli Public* (Tel Aviv: Papyrus 1994) [Heb.].

117. In an article published in 1999, Zeev Segal, one of the authors of the survey that had been conducted in the early 1990s, argued that "even if there is a certain trend of decline in the enormous public trust in the Supreme Court, it seems to have retained the trust of a decisive majority of the Israeli public." See Zeev Segal, "The Supreme Court Sitting as a High Court of Justice: After Fifty Years" (1999) 5 Mishpat Umimshal 282–283 [Heb.]. Today, the trend of steep decline is no longer in doubt. See Yedidia Stern, "Opinion: The Crisis of Trust in the Court" (Yedi'ot Aharonot, June 11, 2008) [Heb.].

118. Moshe Landau, "A Constitution as the Supreme Law of the State of Israel?" (1971) 27 Hapraklit 30–41 [Heb.]. Note that Barzilai, Yuchtman-Yaar, and Segal, *The Israeli Supreme Court and the Israeli Public*, were much more optimistic than Landau. The popularity of the Court at the time they conducted their study led them to conclude that "the Supreme Court has the option of acting as a vanguard without jeopardizing its public legitimation . . . since it retains its strong public standing even when its rulings do not express political or social consensus." A similar position is presented in Moshe Negbi, "The Supreme Court in the Perception of Israeli Society" (1995) 3 Mishpat Umimshal 355–359 [Heb.]. This optimistic prognosis, as noted, has proved deceptive.

119. See, for example, Aharon Barak, "The Role of the Supreme Court in a Democracy" (1999) 33 Israel Law Review 1, 9 [Heb.].

120. Unfortunately, former Supreme Court President Dorit Beinisch did not seem to have recognized the gravity of the problem. In a speech she delivered to the Bar at the beginning of the legal year (September 18, 2007), she said the following: "Despite the various publications pointing to a decline in public trust in the Supreme Court, it is important to remember that, even to this day, the Supreme Court is the ruling institution enjoying the highest level of public trust, despite the media's continued attempts to diminish its standing, to discredit it, and to undermine the trust of the public in their judges, a trust that is vital to the functioning of the judiciary."

CHAPTER 5

1. For instance, the Canadian Charter of Rights and Freedoms, the American Constitution, and the German Basic Law. It should be noted that in some of these countries, the court derived the existence of social laws as derivative of enumerated laws. For instance, in Germany, the court

ruled (BVerfGE 125, 175 [2010] [Ger.]) that the right to a minimal dignified existence derived from the social character of the state (anchored in Article 20(1) of the Basic Law) with the right to dignity. For an English summary of the ruling, see: <http://www.bverfg.de/entscheidungen/ls20100209_1bvl000109en.html>. For a discussion of the ruling, see: Claudia Bittner, "Human Dignity as a Matter of Legislative Consistency in an Ideal World: The Fundamental Right to Guarantee a Subsistence Minimum in the German Federal Constitutional Court's Judgment of 9 February 2010" (2011) 12 German Law Journal 1941; Stefanie Egidy, "The Fundamental Right to the Guarantee of a Subsistence Minimum in the Hartz IV Decision of the German Federal Constitutional Court" (2011) 12 German Law Journal 1961. A similar proposal was raised in America, but was rejected. See, for example, Frank I. Michelman, "The Supreme Court, 1968 Term, Foreword: On Protecting the Poor through the Fourteenth Amendment" (1969) 83 Harvard Law Review 7; Frank I. Michelman, "In Pursuit of Constitutional Welfare Rights: One View of Rawls' Theory of Justice" (1973) 121 University of Pennsylvania Law Review 962.

2. South Africa is prominent on this list, as it enshrines a number of social rights in its constitution. For more, see: Sandra Liebenberg, "The Interpretation of Socio-Economic Rights", in Stu Woolman, Michael Bishop, and Jason Brickhill (eds), *Constitutional Law of South Africa* (2nd ed., 4th rev. Cape Town: Juta Legal and Academic Publishers 2012), chs. 1–33; Sandra Liebenberg, *Socio-Economic Rights: Adjudication under a Transformative Constitution* (Claremont: Juta Legal and Academic Publishers 2010).

3. This is the situation in the Indian constitution, for instance, which includes social principles in Part Four (India Cont. (1950) Arts. 36–51) (Directive Principles of State Policy). Article 37 of the constitution states as follows: "The provision contained in this Part shall not be enforceable by any court, but the principles therein laid down are nevertheless fundamental in the governance of the country and shall be the duty of the state to apply these principles in making laws." For a survey of the arrangements in various constitutions around the world, see: Lanse Minkler (ed.), *The State of Economic and Social Rights: A Global Overview* (New York: Cambridge University Press, 2013).

4. International Covenant on Civil and Political Rights (adopted on December 16, 1966, entered into force on March 23, 1973) 999 U.N.T.S. 171 (henceforth International Covenant on Civil and Political Rights); International Covenant on Economic, Social and Cultural Rights (adopted on December 19, 1966, entered into force on January 3, 1973) 993 UNTS. 3 (henceforth International Covenant on Economic, Social and Cultural Rights). In fact, the very split into two covenants derived from the dispute regarding the status of social rights.

5. Optional Protocol to the International Covenant on Civil and Political Rights, December 16, 1966, UN GA Res. 2200 A (XXI), GAOR, 21st Sess., Supp. No. 16 (A/6316 52, UN Doc. A/CONF. 32/4).

6. Since 1987, the periodical reports are examined by the UN Committee on Economic, Social, and Cultural Rights erected in 1985 (ECOSOC Res. 1985/17, UN Doc. E/1985/85 (1985)). For a description of the committee's work, authority, and influence, see: Matthew C.R. Craven, *The International Covenant on Economic, Social and Cultural Rights: Perspective on its Development* (Oxford: Oxford University Press 1995) (henceforth Craven, *The International Covenant*).

7. International Covenant on Civil and Political Rights, Art. 2(1).

8. These reservations are included in Article 2(1) of the Covenant, which is the framework article that encompasses all the rights noted in the covenant. For interpretation of these reservations, see Mary Dowell-Jones, *Contextualizing the International Covenant on Economic, Social*

and Cultural Rights: Assessing the Economic Deficit (2004). Some argue that the combination of all these reservations means that countries do not have any practical obligation, and that its importance is solely at the declarative level. See Henry H. Steiner et. al., *International Human Rights in Context* (3rd edn. New York: Oxford University Press 2008), 275.

9. Regarding the splitting of human rights into generations of rights, see Craven, *The International Covenant,* (n. 6), 8. Of course, one could argue that the entry of social rights into the rights discourse long after the entry of civil and social rights points to their normative inferiority. However, a no less logical explanation for this late entry is that until the twentieth century, the struggle for recognition of civil and political rights was fought by the property-owning middle and upper classes. See: M.R. Ishay, *The History of Human Rights: From Ancient Times to the Globalization Era* (Berkeley and Los Angeles: University of California Press 2008), 135ff.

10. In this context, it has been argued that civil and political rights impose negative duties on the state while social rights impose positive duties that are difficult to enforce, or that civil and political rights embody neutral rules of the game while social rights adopt a controversial position on the question of a just distribution of wealth.

11. In this context, it has been argued, for instance, that the Court has neither the expertise nor the tools to decide disputes regarding the extracting of social rights, or that the structure of discussion in court does not allow for the representation of all the interests involved in their enforcement, as is required.

12. For a description of the attempt to anchor social rights in the constitution, and an attempt to explain their failure, see Anat Maor, "A Lacuna in the Legal Code: A Basic Law Proposal: Social and Economic Rights—Chronicle of Legislation Failure" in Yoram Rabin and Yuval Shani (eds), *Economic, Social and Cultural Rights in Israel* (Ramot: Tel Aviv University 2004) [Heb.]; Uri Zilbersheid, *Social Equality? Not in Our Constitution! The Struggle over the Social Character of the Israeli Constitution from the Declaration of Independence to "A Constitution by Broad Consensus"* (Tel-Aviv: Schocken 2015) [Heb.].

13. Aharon Barak, *Interpretation in Law* (Jerusalem: Nevo 1994), vol. 3, 413–418 [Heb.].

14. HCJ 1554/95 *Friends of GILAT v. Ministry of Education, Culture and Sports* 50(3) PD 2, 24–26 (1996) (Isr.).

15. A request for a further hearing was rejected by the Supreme Court President, who stated: "in our case, no rule was set at the Supreme Court . . . The decision in the ruling on the appeal did not fall . . . on the basis of the position expressed by justice Orr regarding the existence or lack thereof of a right to education or other principled legal questions which arose during the discussion, but as a result of the decision of the Court not to intervene in the judgment of the Ministry of Education and Culture. In this matter there is no innovation or difficulty." FHHCJ 5456/96 *Itzhak v. Minister of Education* (November 27, 1996, unpublished) (Isr.).

16. Gershon Gontovnik, "Constitutional Law: Development in the Wake of the Constitutional Revolution" (1999) 22 Tel Aviv University Law Review. 129, 157–170 [Heb.]; Yoram Rabin, *The Right to Education* (Srigim-Lion: Nevo Publishing 2002), 341 [Heb.].

17. See, for example, Guy Mundlak, "Social Rights in the New Constitutional Discourse" in Aharon Barak et al. (eds), *Sefer Berenson* (Jerusalem: Nevo 2000), vol. 2, 183, 219 [Heb.]; Ran Hirschel, "The 'Constitutional Revolution' and the Emergence of a New Economic Order in Israel" (1997) 2 Israel Studies 136; Andri Marmor, "Judicial Review in Israel" (1997) 4 Mishpat Umimshal 60–133 [Heb.]; Eli Zaltzberger and Alexander Kedar, "The Silent Revolution—More on Judicial Review under the New Basic Laws" (1997–1998) 4 Mishpat Umimshal 489 [Heb.].

The argument regarding the libertarian bias of the Court is, to a great extent, the completion of another argument, according to which the constitutional revolution was meant primarily to protect the economic interests of the dominant class. See, for example, Menachem Mautner, *Law and Culture of Israel* (New York: Oxford University Press 2011), 179; Ran Hirschl, *Towards Juristocracy: The Origins and Consequences of the New Constitutionalism* (Cambridge, MA: Harvard University Press 2004), 22–24; idem, "The Political Origins of Judicial Empowerment through Constitutionalization: Lessons from Israel's Constitutional Revolution" (2001) 33 Comparative Political Studies 315. Other authors did not agree to label the Court as libertarian, but did criticize the Court for avoiding reading social rights into the Basic Laws. See, for example, Ruth Ben-Israel, "The Impact of Basic Laws on Labor Law and Industrial Relations" (1994) 4 Yearbook of Labor Law 21, 27 [Heb.]: "It's very strange and even odd, that Justice Barak, who is a knight defending human rights whenever it comes to human rights in the civil and political realm, did not include a single one of the social human rights in the framework of the fundamental beliefs of the enlightened public in Israel, according to which he directs the concept of human dignity and freedom in a Jewish and democratic state."

18. There was an almost complete consensus among academics writing on the matter. The only author who had reservations about the description of the Court as libertarian or as a force delaying the upgrading of social rights was Yoav Dotan. See Yoav Dotan, "The Supreme Court as the Defender of the Social Rights" in Yoram Rabin and Yuval Shani (eds), *Economic, Social and Cultural Rights in Israel* (Tel Aviv: Ramot, University 2004), 69 [Heb.].

19. The prominent ruling in this context is LTA 4905/98 *Gamzu v. Yeshayahu*, 55(3) PD 360, para. 19 to the opinion of President Barak (2001) (Isr.). The argument for the existence of a right to minimal means of subsistence as a part of the constitutional concept of human dignity was raised (and accepted) in this case by a man sued by his wife and daughter to pay an alimony debt to the execution office, after he avoided carrying out his duty for many years. This fact places the achievement of the ruling—the recognition of the constitutional right to minimum levels of subsistence—in doubt, for two reasons. First, the Court here protected merely the negative aspect of the right to minimal conditions of existence. Second, the cost of protecting Gamzu's right to minimal levels of existence was incurred by his wife and daughter, whose minimal levels of existence were supposed to be ensured by way of the alimony.

20. HCJ 366/03 *Commitment to Peace and Social Justice Movement v. The Minister of Finance*, 60(3) PD 464, 481–483 (2005) (Isr.). <http://elyon1.court.gov.il/files_eng/03/660/003/a39/03003660.a39.htm> (henceforth Commitment to Peace and Social Justice).

21. The change in Barak's position is also clear from his public and academic statements. See, for example, Aharon Barak, "Preface", in Aharon Barak et al. (eds), *Sefer Berenson* (Jerusalem: Nevo 2000), vol. 2, 9, 10 [Heb.]: "It would be proper to recognize social rights . . . as rights with a supra-legal constitutional status."

22. HCJ 5578/02 *Manor v. The Minister of Finance* 59(1) PD 729, 737 (2004) (Isr.).

23. The decision read as follows: "On the basis of these petitions brought today before this court, the court orders that a show cause order be issued to the respondents and which instructs them to present themselves and give reason why they should not establish a standard for dignified human living as required by Basic Law: Human Dignity and Freedom." (decision from January 5, 2004).

24. Knesset protocol (13 January 2004) (Isr.).

25. See *Commitment to Peace and Social Justice*, (n. 20), para. 31 to the decision of President Barak:

> The result is, therefore, that the petitions—on the basis of the succor requested—are to be struck down. This, because we have not been convinced that the amendment to the Income Supplement Law, in and of itself (not even with the cancelling of the associated reliefs), harms human dignity ... to arrive at this judicial conclusion, including an instruction to the state to right the wrong, we need an appropriate evidentiary basis. Such a basis was not brought before us in these petitions.

26. Avishai Benish and Michal Kremer, "Filling the Void: A Model for the Constitutional Right to Dignified Existence Based on the German Constitutional Law" (2015) 4 Work, Society and Law 263, 271 [Heb.] (henceforth Benish and Kremer, "Filling the Void").

27. See para. 31 to the opinion of President Barak: "Our ruling is not meant to put an end to petitions regarding the right of people to live in a dignified manner. This is a constitutional right, which should be maintained throughout public law. The courts are authorized to enforce it. Given a sufficiently pinpoint and established petition, it is their obligation to do so."

28. See Yuval Elbasan, *Strangers in the Realm of the Law: Access to Justice in Israel* (Tel Aviv: Hakibutz Hameuchad 2005), 128–164 [Heb.] (A discussion of the "failures of the court which revealed real impotence regarding the advancement of social rights," ibid, 128); Aeyal M. Gross and Daphne Barak-Erez, "Social Rights in Israel and the Struggle for Social Rights: Beyond the Right to Human Dignity" in Shulamit Almog and Yoad Nevo (eds), *Dalia Dorner Book* (Srigim-Lion: Nevo Publishing 2008), 189–217 [Heb.].

29. HCJ 10662/04 *Hassan v. National Insurance Institute* 65(1) PD 782 (2012) (henceforth *Hassan*).

30. Income Support Law, 5741-1980 (Isr.).

31. See *Hassan*, (n. 29), para. 68.

32. This was expressed at the end of the ruling, according to which: "The petitions before us were managed at the level of principle. We were not required as to the private matter of the petitioners, and thus we are not the appropriate venue for such an examination, which requires processes that begin both before the National Insurance Institute and before the authorized venues." Ibid, at para. 72 to the opinion of President Beinisch.

33. Ibid, at para. 36 to the opinion of President Beinisch (emphasis in original).

34. HCJ 1105/06 *Kav La'Oved v. Minister of Social Affairs* (June 6, 2014), Nevo Legal Database (by subscription) (Isr.) (henceforth *Kav La'Oved*).

35. Ibid, at para. 62 to the opinion of Justice Arbel.

36. Ibid, at paras. 90–91 to the opinion of Justice Arbel.

37. See *Commitment to Peace and Social Justice*, (n. 20), para. 14 to the opinion of President Barak.

38. Ibid. at para. 16 to the opinion of President Barak.

39. HCJ 5637/07 *Plonit v. Minister of Health*, (August 8, 2010), Nevo Legal Database (by subscription) para. 10 to the opinion of Justice Rubinstein (Isr.).

40. HCJ 3071/05 *Luzon v. Government of Israel*, (July 28, 2008) Nevo Legal Database (by subscription) para. 12 to the opinion of Justice Beinisch (Isr.). <http://elyon1.court.gov.il/files_eng/05/710/030/n12/05030710.n12.htm>.

41. *Hassan*, (n. 29), para. 35 to the opinion of Justice Beinisch.

42. Even the International Covenant on Economic, Social and Cultural Rights (n. 4) distinguishes between different levels of welfare and includes as part of the right to suitable living

standards anchored in Article 11 (a thin version of the minimal living conditions proposed therein being discussed here) only food, clothing, and housing.

43. For an approach to the right to education as part of the right to human dignity, see, for example, HCJ 7426/08 *Tebeka Advocacy for Equality and Justice for Ethiopian-Israelis v. The Ministry of Education*, (August 31, 2010), Nevo Legal Database (by subscription) para. 16 to the opinion of Justice Prokachia (Isr.): "The right to education constitutes, in and of itself, part of the right of people to human dignity in the constitutional context."

44. HCJ 3752/10 *Rubinstein v. The Knesset* (September 17, 2014), Nevo Legal Database (by subscription) (Isr.).

45. Ibid, at para. 18 to the opinion of President Grunis.

46. Ibid, paras. 20–22 to the opinion of President Grunis.

47. See notes 10–11 above.

48. See *Hassan*, (n. 29), para. 7 to the opinion of Justice Joubran.

49. For a referral to the ruling and a discussion of its significance, see the sources in note 1 above.

50. For a critique of the Israeli Court's approach in light of that of the Federal Constitutional Court, see Benish and Kremer, "Filling the Void", (n. 26), 275–277. For support for the development of a procedural review track in the spirit of the German approach, see the article of Supreme Court Justice Daphne Barak-Erez, "Social Rights in The Israeli Law: Direct Protection, Indirect Protection and Challenges Coming Next", in Ohad Gordon et al. (eds), *Edmond Levi Book* (Jerusalem: The Hebrew University of Jerusalem, 2017) 53 [Heb.].

51. National Insurance Law, 5755-1995 (Isr.), is the primary law arranging the activity of Israel's social security system. It regulates the activity of the National Insurance Institute, and determines the primary instructions regarding entitlement to stipends given by the Institute. In addition to this law, Israel passed other laws in the area of social security, which the National Insurance Institute is also responsible for implementing, including the Income Support Law, 5741-1980 (Isr.), a cut to which was the subject of deliberation in the *Commitment* case.

52. Article 3(a) of the National Health Insurance Law, 5754-1994 (Isr.) states: "Every resident shall be entitled to health services according to this law." The state's obligation to fund the basket of health services is anchored in Article 3(b) of the law. However, Article 14 of the law imposes an obligation on every resident to pay health insurance fees at a rate of 4.8 percent of their salary. This tax, along with other funding sources, serves as the basis for the funding of the health service. Article 2 of the Compulsory Education Law, 5709-1949 (Isr.), imposes an education obligation on all children aged 3–18. Article 6 of the law grants the right to free education in the official educational institutions of the state for anyone subject to the law. Thus, every child is entitled to fifteen years of free education in official institutions.

53. See *Commitment to Peace and Social Justice*, (n. 20), para. 1 to the opinion of Justice Levi. Levi's position on the location of the threshold fits the definition of the right as defined in Article 11 of the Covenant on social rights.

54. Ibid, at para. 15 to the opinion of President Barak.

55. An example of this can be seen in the field of public housing. While some 50 percent of all new housing was public housing in the first years of the state, the number dropped to 30 percent in the 1970s, and in the 2000s the construction of public housing was terminated altogether. For a survey and discussion, see Neta Ziv and Anat Rodnizky, "Disputed Public Housing: A critical Reading of Judicial Decisions regarding the 'Continuing Tenant' in Israeli Public Housing" (2014) 94 social security 99-134 [Heb.]. In other areas, the state expanded its responsibility. A prominent

example is the amendment to the Compulsory Education Law in 2007, which expanded the right to free education from thirteen to fifteen years.

56. Two prominent examples of this are in the fields of education and health. In the field of education, parents are required to pay for enrichment and reinforcement classes given in the framework of public education, a phenomenon known as "grey education." In the field of health, there is a prominent phenomenon regarding elderly care, which is not covered by law, and the development of private insurance services that complete the partial coverage given according to the Health Insurance Law, or which allow the receipt of superior medical treatment than that provided by the public system. See, for example, Daphne Barak-Erez, "The Israeli Welfare State: Between Legislation and Bureaucracy" (2002) 9 Labor, Society and Law [Heb.]. Sometimes the emergence of a private system is not due to a cut of an existing public service, but rather the avoidance of the state providing for a new need that did not exist before. See, for example, Daphne Barak-Erez, "Public Law of Privatization: Models, Norms and Challenges Privatization" (2008) 30 Iyunei Mishpat 461 [Heb.] (henceforth Barak-Eerz, "Public Law of Privatization").

57. Barak-Eerz, "Public Law of Privatization", (n. 56), 472–473.

58. See Barak-Eerz, "Public Law of Privatization", (n. 56), 478–491.

59. HCJ 2605/05 *Academic Ctr. of Law and Bus. v. Minister of Fin.* 63(2) PD 545, para. 21 to the opinion of Justice Levi (2009) (Isr.). <http://elyon1.court.gov.il/files_eng/05/050/026/n39/05026050.n39.htm>.

60. G. Rosenberg, *The Hollow Hope: Can Courts Bring About Social Change?* (Chicago: University of Chicago Press 1991) (henceforth Rosenberg, *The Hollow Hope*). In his book, Rosenberg examined the effect of such landmark rulings as *Brown v. Board of Education*, 347 U.S. 483 (1954) (finding racial segregation in schools to be unconstitutional) and *Roe v. Wade*, 410 U.S. 113 (1973) (finding limitations to the right to abortion in the first trimester to be unconstitutional). His conclusion was that *Brown* did not lead to better conditions when it came to racial segregation in southern schools, and that *Roe* did not really help advance abortion rights. The study was followed by a great deal of criticism, especially saying that it was a one-sided account that disregarded contrary evidence. See, for example, M. M. Feeley, "Hollow Hopes, Flypaper, and Metaphors" (1993) 17 Law and Social Inquiry 745; M. MacCann, "Reform Litigation on Trial" (2009) 17 Law and Social Inquiry 715. In the wake of the study, others appeared, arguing that appropriate times and conditions can see court rulings help promote social reforms. See, for example, C. E. Epp, *The Rights Revolution: Lawyers, Activists and Supreme Courts in Comparative Perspective* (Chicago: University of Chicago Press 1998); B. C. Canon and C. A. Johnson, *Judicial Policies: Implementation and Impact* (2nd edn, Washington, DC: CQ Press 1999); C. E. Epp, *Making Rights Real: Activists, Bureaucrats, and the Creation of the Legalistic State* (Chicago: University of Chicago Press 2010). By contrast, another source that examined the *Brown* case reached similar conclusions to Rosenberg's: M. Klarman, *From Jim Crow to Civil Rights: The Supreme Court and the Struggle for Racial Equality* (New York: Oxford University Press 2004).

61. Opinions on this issue are split as well; the classic source, arguing that the courts are not an effective vehicle for realizing social rights, is Tony Prosser, *Test Cases for the Poor: Legal Techniques in the Politics of Social welfare* (London: Child Poverty Action Group 1983) ("[I]n the Field of social welfare the courts alone are most unlikely to be a useful vehicle for achieving social rights." Ibid at 83). A more recent study of health rights litigation presents a more nuanced empirical record. See A. E. Yamin and S. Gloppen (eds), *Litigation Health Rights: Can Courts Bring More Justice to Health?* (Cambridge, MA: Harvard University Press 2011).

62. Special Education Law, 5748-1988 (Isr.).

63. HCJ 2599/00 *Yated—Association for Parents of Downs Syndrome Children v. The Ministry of Education*, 56(5) PD 834 (2002) (Isr.). <http://elyon1.court.gov.il/files_eng/00/990/025/L12/00025990.l12.htm>.

64. Special Education Law, 5762-2002 (as amended) (Isr.) (henceforth Special Education Law).

65. Draft Bill for Amending Special Education Law (as amended), 5762-2002 (Isr.).

66. HCJ 6973/03 *Marciano v. Minister of Finance* 58(2) PD 270, 272 (2003) (Isr.).

67. The state's request for a further hearing in the Marciano case was rejected on F.H.H.C.J. 247/04 *Minister of Finance v. Marciano* (May 10, 2004), Nevo Legal Database (by subscription) (Isr.). The Court ruled that the *Marciano* case had established no new rule, but merely "executed" the ruling of the *Yated* case and the amendment to the law.

68. HCJ 7443/03, 7448/03 *Yated—Association for Parents of Downs Syndrome Children v. The Ministry of Education* (June 2, 2004), Nevo Legal Database (by subscription) (Isr.).

69. HCJ 5989/07 *Alut—the Israeli Society for Autistic Children v. Minister of Education* (March 3, 2011), Nevo Legal Database (by subscription) (Isr.). (henceforth *Alut*).

70. Ibid, paras. 14–15.

71. Ibid, at para. 20.

72. Israel Comptroller General. 2013. Year Report, 63(3) at 1035–1100 (2013) (Isr.). <http://www.mevaker.gov.il/he/Reports/Report_114/a2ef9622-04ff-42b0-96a7-2fb083d6d5e8/7959.docx>.

73. For the negative aspect of social rights, see, for example, Frank I. Michelman, "The Constitution, Social Rights, and Liberal Political Justification" (2003) 1 International Journal of Constitutional Law 13, 17 (henceforth Michelman, "The Constitution, Social Rights") (noting that social rights can sometimes be "negatively protected" by comfortably kosher forms of judicial intervention). Regarding the positive aspect of civil and political rights, see, for example, Malcolm Langford, "The Justiciability of Social Rights: From Theory to Practice" in Malcolm Langford (ed.), *Social Rights Jurisprudence: Emerging Trends in International and Comparative Law* (New York: Cambridge University Press 2008), 30–31.

74. Mark Tushnet, *Weak Courts, Strong Rights: Judicial Review and Social Welfare Rights in Comparative Constitutional Law* (Princeton, NJ: Princeton University Press 2008), 234 (henceforth Tushnet, *Weak Courts, Strong Rights*) ("it is not that recognizing social and economic rights would have budgetary consequences, while recognizing other constitutional rights does not ... Protecting background private law rights and first-and second-generation constitutional rights is cheap, though not free. Protecting social and economic rights is expensive.")

75. See, for example, Mark Tushnet, *Taking the Constitution Away from the Courts* (Princeton, NJ: Princeton University Press 1999), 169 (argues that courts will have trouble giving precise content to vague rights of the sort of the right to food or housing).

76. For a presentation and discussion of various aspects of the argument, see, for example: Jeff King, *Judging Social Rights* (Cambridge: Cambridge University Press 2012), chs. 6–8.

77. *Alut*, (n. 69), para. 15. See also the opinion of Justice Cheshin in HCJ 240/98 *Adala v. Ministry of Religion*, 52(5) PD 167, 190 (1998) (Isr.).

78. *Government of the Republic of South Africa v. Grootboom* 2001 (1) SA 46 (CC).

79. Tushnet, *Weak Courts, Strong Rights*, (n. 74), 242–244; See also Cass R. Sunstein, *Designing Democracy: What Constitutions Do* (Oxford: Oxford University Press 2001), 233 (the Court had effectively "steer[ed] a middle course" between holding socioeconomic rights non-justiciable and holding them to "create an absolute duty" to provide housing or food or healthcare for everyone who needs it.)

80. See, for example, Theunis Roux, "Principle and Pragmatism on the Constitutional Court of South Africa" (2009) 7 International Journal of Constitutional Law 106; David Bilchitz, "Giving Socio-Economic Rights Teeth: The Minimum Core and Its Importance" (2002) 119 South African Law Journal 484; D. M. Davis, "Adjudicating the Socio-Economic Rights in the South African Constitution: Towards 'Deference Lite'" (2006) 22 South African Journal on Human Rights 301.

81. P. Joubert, "Grootboom Dies Homeless and Penniless" (Mail and Guardian, August 8, 2008), 35. <http://mg.co.za/article/2008-08-08-grootboomdies-homeless-and-penniless>.

82. Rosenberg, *The Hollow Hope*, (n. 61), 10–21.

CHAPTER 6

1. There are innumerable examples for this position in the Israeli Supreme Court decisions. See, for example, CFH 2401/*95 Ruti Nahmani v. Daniel Nahmani*, 50(4) PD 661, 750 (1996) (Isr.). <http://elyon1.court.gov.il/files_eng/95/010/024/Z01/95024010.z01.htm>: "The philosophy guiding this court argues that the rights recognized in our law are never 'absolute', but always relative." Thus, for instance, regarding freedom of expression: HCJ 73/*53 Kol Ha'am Ltd. v. Minister of Interior*, 7(1) PD 871, 879 (1952) (Isr.). <http://elyon1.court.gov.il/files_eng/53/730/000/Z01/53000730.z01.htm> (henceforth *Kol Ha'am*);t he right of protest and parade: HCJ 153/83 *Levi v. S. Dist. Police Commander*, 38(2) PD 393, 399 (1984) (Isr.). <http://elyon1.court.gov.il/files_eng/83/530/001/Z01/83001530.z01.htm>; freedom of occupation: CA 496/88 *Henfeld v. Ramat Hasharon Sports Association*, 42(3) PD 717, 721 (1988) (Isr.); and freedom of religion CA 2266/93 *John Doe v. Jane Doe*, 49(1) PD 221, 235 (1995) (Isr.).

2. The birth of the vertical test is usually attributed to the ruling of Justice Agranat in *Kol Ha'am*, (n. 1), in which the Court balanced the right of freedom of expression against national security. For the background to the ruling, see: Pnina Lahav, *Judgement in Jerusalem: Chief Justice Simon Agranat and the Zionist Century* (Berkeley: University of California Press 1997), ch. 5.

3. This test was used, for example, in HCJ 2481/93 *Dayan v. The Police Commissioner of Jerusalem*, 48(2) PD 456 (1994) (Isr.). <http://elyon1.court.gov.il/files_eng/93/810/024/Z01/93024810.z01.htm>, in which the conflict between the right to protest and the right to privacy was discussed.

4. Ibid, 475–476. It should be noted that the above-quoted passage shows that the decisive factor regarding the question of which test will be applied in the case was not the character of the value serving as justification for harming the right, whether as an interest or as a right, but rather the question whether the conflicting values are equal or different in weight. However, the Court usually tended to attribute equal weight to conflicting rights, and different weight to a right and interest conflicting with each other. Therefore, in most cases, the vertical balancing test was applied in a conflict between rights and interests, and the horizontal balancing test in a conflict between rights. For more, see: Aharon Barak, *The Judge in a Democracy* (Princeton: Princeton University Press, 2009), 169–172.

5. Yitzhak Zamir and Moshe Sobel, "Equality before the law" (1999) 8 Mishpat Umimshal 165, 215 [Heb.].

6. CA 105/92 *Reem Engineers Contractors Ltd v. Municipality of Upper Nazereth*, 47(5) PD 189, 204 (1993) (Isr.) (emphasis added).

7. The proportionality test originated in German public law. See Moshe Cohen-Eliya and Iddo Porat, *Proportionality and Constitutional Culture* (Cambridge: Cambridge University Press

2013), 24–32. The test then migrated to many other legal systems. See ibid, 10–14, and Aharon Barak, *Proportionality—Constitutional Rights and Their Limitations* (Cambridge: Cambridge University Press, 2012), ch. 7. (henceforth Barak, *Proportionality*).

8. See CA 6821/93 *Bank Mizrahi v. Migdal Cooperative Village*, 49(4) PD 221 (1995) (Isr.). <http://elyon1.court.gov.il/files_eng/93/210/068/z01/93068210.z01.pdf>. As support for the interpretation he gave for the requirement of proportionality, the court referred to the precedent-setting rulings in Germany: ("The Pharmacy Case" BVerfGE 7, 377 (1958) (Ger.), and in Canada: *R v. Oaks*, [1986] 1 S.C.R 103 (Can.); *R. v. Big M. Drug Mart. Ltd*, [1985] 1 S.C.R 295 (Can.); *Jones v. The Queen*, [1986] 2 S.C.R 284 (Can.)

9. See, for example, HCJ 5016/96 *Horev v. The Minister of Transport*, 51(4) PD 1, para. 54 to the opinion of Justice Barak (1997) (Isr.) (henceforth *Horev*). <http://elyon1.court.gov.il/files_eng/96/160/050/A01/96050160.a01.htm>. "Since the Knesset enacted the Basic Laws regarding human rights, we use their established criteria to interpret the governmental authority that was granted in legislation (primary or secondary), and this ... whether regarding harm to human rights 'covered' in the two Basic Laws regarding human rights, or regarding harm to human rights not 'covered' by these two basic laws."

10. See, for example, Justice Mazza's opinion in EA 92/03 *Mofaz v. Election Commissioner*, 57(3) PD 793, 811 (2003) (Isr.). <http://elyon1.court.gov.il/files_eng/03/920/000/f06/03000920.f06.htm>. "The triple structure of the aforementioned limitation clause is seen in our judicial consciousness as a proper tool for examining the constitutionality of a law. Once it became one of the fundamental principles of our constitutional system, the court may use it even in the absence of a limitation clause in the Basic Law in light of which the law is placed under its review."

11. See Dieter Grimm, "Proportionality in Canadian and German Constitutional Jurisprudence" (2007) 57 University of Toronto Law Journal 383 (henceforth Grimm, "Proportionality"). ("Usually, it is not too difficult to ascertain whether there are less intrusive means. It is much more difficult, however, to find out whether they would have the same or an equivalent effect").

12. Gideon Sapir, "Old to New—On Vertical Balancing and Proportionality" (2005) 22 Mehkarei Mishpat 471, 477 [Heb.]. I am aware that the accepted interpretation of this test differs in many countries from my own, and includes as part of this test only the means that realize the purpose in a manner identical to that chosen by the state. See, for example, Nicholas Emiliou, *The Principle of Proportionality in European Law* (London; Boston, MA: Kluwer Law International 1996), 30; Julian Rivers, "Proportionality and Variable Intensity of Review" (2006) 65 Cambridge Law Journal 174, 198; Barak, *Proportionality*, (n. 7), 320–323.

13. The distinction in question between the old balancing tests and the proportionality tests largely matches the distinction coined by American scholar Nimmer between a categorical balancing and an ad hoc balancing. A categorical balancing establishes a rule that the court will apply to succeeding cases without any need for further balancing. With ad hoc balancing, by contrast, the balance must be redone each time, based on the circumstances of each case. See: Melville B. Nimmer, "The Right to Speak from Time to Time: First Amendment Theory Applied to Libel and Misapplied to Privacy" (1968) 56 California Law Review 935, 942; Richard H. Fallon, "Individual Rights and the Powers of Government" (1993) 27 Georgia Law Review 343. According to Aharon Barak, "The main factor which differentiates between legal categorization and proportionality is proportionality *stricto sensu*" [Barak, *Proportionality*, (n. 7), 508]. In my opinion, the second

proportionality test also includes a significant component of ad hoc balancing, especially if one accepts the interpretation I propose for this test.

14. HCJ 2056/04 *Beit Sourik Village v. Government of Israel*, 58(5) PD 807 (2004) (Isr.). <http://elyon1.court.gov.il/files_eng/04/560/020/A28/04020560.a28.htm> (henceforth *Beit Sourik*).

15. HCJ 7052/03 *Adala v. Minister of Interior Affairs*, 58(5) PD 202 (2006) (Isr.). <http://elyon1.court.gov.il/files_eng/03/520/070/a47/03070520.a47.htm> (henceforth *Adala*).

16. *Beit Sourik*, (n. 14), para. 71 ("The security advantage achieved in the route established by the military commander in comparison to the alternative route is not at all balanced by the increased harm to the lives of the local residents.")

17. HCJ 8276/05 *Adalah v. Minister of Defense*, 62(1) PD 1 (2006) (Isr.). <http://elyon1.court.gov.il/files_eng/05/760/082/a13/05082760.a13.htm> (henceforth *Adala*).

18. For clarification of the two functions, see Barak, *Proportionality*, (n. 7), 350–356.

19. HCJ 358/88 *The Association for Civil Rights in Israel v. The Central District Commander*, 43(2) PD 529 (1989) (Isr.). <http://elyon1.court.gov.il/files_eng/88/580/003/Z01/88003580.z01.htm>.

20. Moshe Cohen-Eliya, "The Formal and the Substantive Meanings of Proportionality in the Supreme Court's Decision Regarding the Security Fence" (2005) 20 Hamishpat 54, 65 [Heb.], note 65 ("To the best of my knowledge, this is the first time a court in Israel or in the world refers to such an understanding of proportionality *stricto sensu*").

21. Aharon Barak, *Interpretation in Law* (Jerusalem: Nevo 1992), vol. 3,536 [Heb.] (henceforth Barak, *Interpretation in Law*).

22. HCJ 7146/12 *Adam v. the Knesset* (9 September 2013), Nevo Legal Database (by subscription) (Isr.) (henceforth *Adam*). <http://elyon1.court.gov.il/files_eng/12/460/071/b24/12071460.b24.htm>.

23. Prevention of Infiltration Law (Offences and Jurisdiction) (amendment and Temporary Provisions), 5772-2012 (Isr.).

24. *Adam*, (n. 22), para. 103 to the opinion of Justice Arbel.

25. For example, ibid, para. 25 to the opinion of Justice Fogelman.

26. Guy Davidov, "Separating Minimal Impairment from Balancing: A Comment on R. v. Sharpe (B.C.C.A)" (2000) 5 Review of Constitutional Studies 195 (henceforth Davidov, "Separating Minimal Impairment from Balancing"); idem, "The Principle of Proportionality in Labor Law" (2008) 31 Iyunei Mishpat 31 [Heb.].

27. This correct distinction between the two components of the proportionality tests—the technical component and the essential discretion component—is the reason I find David Beatty's argument, according to which the proportionality tests offer neutral constitutional interpretation test, odd, to say the least. See David M. Beatty, *The Ultimate Rule of Law* (Oxford: Oxford University Press, 2004), 161–162. For a criticism of Beatty's book in this spirit, see Moshe Cohen-Eliya, "Separation of Powers and Proportionality with Reference to David Beatty, The Ultimate Rule of Law" (2005) 9 Mishpat Umimshal 297 [Heb.]. See also Vicki C. Jackson, "The Ultimate Rule of Law (Book review)" (2004) 21 Constitutional Commentary 803. ("Taking up Beatty's implicit invitation to evaluate theories against criteria of existing practice, neutrality and determinacy, however, suggests that proportionality's . . . neutrality may be much more in the eyes of the beholder than Beatty allows." Jackson, supra, 813).

28. One of the few cases in which the Supreme Court used the second proportionality test to disqualify the barrier route was HCJ 2577/04 *Tahaa El-Hawaja v. Prime Minister of Israel*, para. 38 to the opinion of President Beinisch (July 19, 2007), Nevo Legal Database (by subscription)

(Isr.). In this case, President Beinisch focused on the fact that the army commander first determined a route that harmed the Palestinian residents less, and then changed his mind in a manner that increased the harm. As Gershon Gontovnick notes, "without the establishment of an alternative route by the authorized authorities, it is doubtful if President Beinisch would have reached the conclusion she did regarding the failure of the barrier to meet the proportionality standards of the second sub-test." Gershon Gontovnick, "Thoughts about Justiciability, Judicial Review and the Fear of Institutional Errors" in Aharon Barak et al. (eds), *Eliyahu Mazza Book* (Srigim-Lion: Nevo Publishing 2015), 219, 251 [Heb.].

29. See Barak Medina, *Human Rights Law in Israel* (2016), 203–204 [Heb.] (henceforth Medina, *Human Rights Law in Israel*). Davidov [Davidov, "Separating Minimal Impairment from Balancing", (n. 26), 198–200] claims that one can see a similar trend in Canadian jurisprudence: The court tends to rule on unconstitutionality within the framework of the second subtest on the grounds that there are alternatives that do not detract from the realization of the purpose, but these alternatives are clearly less effective than the option chosen in practice. This is also the opinion of Justice LeBel, in his minority opinion in *Alberta v. Hutterian Brethren of Wilson Colony* [2009] 2 S.C.R. 567, Article 198 (henceforth *Hutterian Brethren case*). This factual description is also accepted by the Chief Justice McLachlin in the majority opinion there. However, as opposed to LeBel, who proposes "whitewashing" this use of the second test, McLachlin prefers to sharpen the distinction between the second and third tests: "Rather than reading down the government's objective within the minimal impairment analysis, the court should acknowledge that no less drastic means are available and proceed to the final stage of *Oakes*." Ibid, Article 76).

30. HCJ 1715/97 *Israel Investment Managers Association v. Minister of Finance*, 51(4) PD 367 (1997) (Isr.) (henceforth *Israel Investment Managers*).

31. *Adala*, (n. 17).

32. One can say similar things on the *Hassan* ruling. There, the Court stated that the conclusive presumption anchored in legislation—anyone who owns a car cannot benefit from the income supplement stipend—disproportionately harmed the constitutional right to a dignified life. It stated this primarily because of the existence of other alternatives in the form of detailed income tests, which would achieve the proper purpose of providing the stipend only to those who need it to live. HCJ 10662/04 *Hassan v. National Insurance Institute*, 65(1) PD 782 (2012) (Isr.).

33. Aharon Barak, "The Constitutional Revolution: Protected Human Rights" (1992) 1 Mishpat Umimshal 253, 266 [Heb.] ("For the sake of balance between the human rights established in the Basic Law, the limitation clause does not apply.") CA 6601/96 *AES Sys. Inc. v. Sa'ar*, 54(3) PD 850, 861 (2000) (Isr.). <http://elyon1.court.gov.il/files_eng/96/010/066/a04/96066010.a04.htm>; HCJ 1514/01 *Gur-Aryeh v. Second Television and Radio Authority*, 55(4) PD 267, para. 6 to the opinion of Justice Dorner (2001) (Isr.). <http://elyon1.court.gov.il/files_eng/01/140/015/a06/01015140.a06.htm> (henceforth *Gur-Aryeh*). ("The criteria in the limitation clause, and especially the principle of proportionality, are not appropriate for the balance between two human rights.") For a different opinion, which aims to apply the limitation clause in balances between conflicting rights as well, see Justice Elon in CA 506/88 *Shefer v. State of Israel*, 48(1) PD 87, 105 (1993) (Isr.). <http://elyon1.court.gov.il/files_eng/88/060/005/z01/88005060.z01.htm> ("The aforementioned Article 8 deals with a case of a law that harms one of the rights in Basic Law: Human Dignity and Freedom, and does not address when such 'harm' arises in a conflict between two fundamental rights contained in the Basic Law itself... But there is no point and no logic in not expanding and applying the path laid down by the legislator in Basic Law: Human

Dignity and Freedom, in the case of harm to a fundamental right by force of another law, also to a case of harm and contradiction between two fundamental rights in the Basic Law itself.") HCJ 2911/05 *Elhanati v. Minister of the Treasury*, 62(4) PD 406, para. 12 to the opinion of Justice Procaccia (2008) (Isr.) ("The limitation clause does speak of the extent of the permitted harm of the law in reference to the Basic Law, but the analysis provided by the limitation clause for the purpose of achieving balance in this area, is similar in essence and character to those needed to achieve the internal balance between contradicting basic rights. Therefore, we can derive from the principles of the limitation clause, and especially the principles of the proper purpose and proportionality anchored therein, interpretive inspiration to realize the proper balance in a conflict between contrary rights.") HCJ 10203/03 *Hamiifkad Haleumi v. Attorney General*, 62(4) PD 715, para. 7 to the opinion of Justice Beinisch (2008) (Isr.). <http://elyon1.court.gov.il/files_eng/03/030/102/c22/03102030.c22.htm>. ("I tend toward the opinion that the limitation clause tests can serve to conduct horizontal balances between rights of equal standing.")

34. It appears that in his academic writing after stepping down from the bench, Barak has retreated from the position of rejecting the adaption of proportionality tests for cases of conflicts between rights. See: Barak, *Proportionality*, (n. 7), 534 ("the current prevailing approach—according to which a limitation on a constitutional right should be treated in the same manner whether it protects another constitutional right or furthers the public interest—is both justified and appropriate.")

35. See Grimm, "Proportionality", (n. 11), 8.

36. Ibid.

37. If I understand correctly, this is the path by which the Canadian court adapted the second proportionality test to the circumstances of balancing between conflicting rights. See Sujit Choudhry, "So What Is the Real Legacy of Oaks? Two Decades of Proportionality Case Analysis under the Canadian Charter's Article 1" (2006) 34 The Supreme Court Law Review 501, 514.

38. *Horev* (n. 9).

39. *Gur-Aryeh*, (n. 33).

40. Peter Hogg, *Constitutional Law of Canada* (5th edn, Ontario: Thomson Carswell 2007), vol. 2, 146. ("So far as I can tell . . . this step has never had any influence on the outcome of any case.") It is interesting to note that the situation in Germany is different; there, the third subtest is dominant. See Grimm, "Proportionality" (n. 11), 393 ("The most striking difference between the two jurisdictions [Canada and Germany; G.S.] is the high relevance of step 3 of the proportionality test in Germany and its more residual function in Canada".)

41. See Hogg, ibid, 153 ("an affirmative answer to the first step—sufficiently important objective—will always yield an affirmative answer to the fourth step—proportionate effect").

42. See Aharon Barak, "Proportional Effect—The Israeli Experience" (2007) 57 University of Toronto Law Journal 369. ("The objective chosen by the legislature might be proper. However, it might not suffice to ensure the constitutionality of the statute; not due to flaws in it, rather due to its severe effect upon human rights."); Barak, *Proportionality* (n. 7), 247–249. In the *Hutterian Brethren* case (n. 29), Chief Justice McLachlin used Barak's words above to reject Hogg's argument (ibid, paras. 75–76).

43. For support in this approach among academics in Israel, see: Barak Medina and Ilan Saban, "Human Rights and Risk-Taking: On Democracy, Ethnic-Profiling and the 'Limitation Clause' (following the Decision on the Validity of the Citizenship and Entry into Israel Law)" (2008) 39 Mishpatim 47 [Heb.]; Barak Medina, "On 'Infringements' of Human Rights and the 'Proper

Purpose' Requirement (following Aharon Barak, Proportionality—Constitutional Rights and Their Limitations)" (2012) 15 IDC Law Review 281 [Heb.].

44. See, for example, HCJ 6427/02 *Movement for Quality of Government in Israel v. The Knesset*, 61(1) PD 619, para. 52 to the opinion of President Barak (2006) (Isr.) (henceforth *Movement for Quality of Government*).

45. HCJ 466/07 *Galon v. The Attorney General*, PD 65(2) 44, para. 23 to the opinion of Justice Levi (2012) (Isr.).

46. *Movement for Quality of Government*, (n. 44), para. 53 to the opinion of President Barak.

47. HCJ 951/06 *Stein v. Inspector General of Israel Police*, paras. 18–19 to the opinion of President Barak (April 30, 2006), Nevo Legal Database (by subscription) (Isr.) (henceforth *Stein*). See also Barak in *Horev*, (n. 9), 41.

48. After retiring from the bench, Barak retreated from his proposal to read the vertical balancing test into the proper purpose requirement. Instead, he proposed to consider its inclusion in the framework of the third proportionality test. See: Barak, *Proportionality*, (n. 7), 642–645. This proposal does not run into the same linguistic and conceptual obstacle the other proposal encounters, but in my opinion, it is also undesirable. Its weakness lies in replacing ad hoc balancing, sensitive to the specific circumstances of the case in question, with principled criteria, which cannot demonstrate such sensitivity.

49. If the proposal to read vertical balancing into the proper purpose test in the limitation clause is indeed based on a fear of unjustified harm to human rights, it can be seen as a softened version of a more rigid position, which entirely rejects the use of proportionality tests, on the grounds that if the protection of a constitutional right will be based on a process of ad hoc balancing, the court will prefer the public interest to the human right, especially in times of emergency. For a discussion of this criticism of the use of proportionality tests, see: Barak, *Proportionality*, (n. 7), 488–490.

50. For a similar opinion, see Moshe Cohen-Eliya and Gila Stopler, "Probability Thresholds as Deontological Constraints in Global Constitutionalism" (2011) 49 Columbia Journal of Transnational Law 75. <http://www.clb.ac.il/uploads/Cohen-Eliya_Thresholds.pdf>.

51. HCJ 2605/05 *The Human Rights Division, The Academic Center for Law and Business v. Minister of Finance*, 63(2) PD 545 (2009) (Isr.). <http://elyon1.court.gov.il/files_eng/05/050/026/n39/05026050.n39.htm>.

52. See, for example, ibid., para. 67 to the opinion of President Beinisch; ibid, para. 11 to the opinion of the dissenting Justice Edmund Levy: "Whereas judicial review cannot base itself on a weak assessment, my position is that we should set it aside for a proper time, and this is not the point in time we are in today."

53. *Stein*, (n. 47), para. 18 to the opinion of President Barak. For support for this position, see Medina, *Human Rights Law in Israel*, (n. 29), 178–181.

54. Ibid. In the *Stein* case (n. 47), the examination of the probability component within the proper purpose test referred only to the interest component, and not to the harmed right component. However, the use of this test in *Stein* was irrelevant, as the harm to the right from the order was certain and not merely probable.

55. *Israel Investment Managers*, (n. 30).

56. Ibid, paras. 4, 8 to the opinion of Justice Dorner.

57. HCJ 4541/94 *Miller v. Minister of Defense*, 49(4) PD 94 (1995) (Isr.). <http://elyon1.court.gov.il/files_eng/94/410/045/Z01/94045410.z01.htm>.

58. Ibid, para. 22 to the opinion of Justice Dorner.

59. HCJ 5239/11 *Avneri v. the Knesset* (15 April 2015), Nevo Legal Database (by subscription) (Isr.).

CHAPTER 7

1. Older constitutions usually did not include clear arrangements regarding states of emergency. For example, the U.S. Constitution does not deal with the matter except in U.S. Const. Art I, § 9, cl 2, which allows the suspension of a court habeas corpus order in crisis circumstances. For a discussion of the significance of this article as an emergency law, see, e.g., A. L. Tyler, "Suspension as an Emergency Power" (2009) 118 Yale Law Journal 600.

Constitutional arrangements of this kind were primarily created in the twentieth century, the most prominent example of this being Article 48 of the Weimar Constitution. For a description and explanation of the failure of the German arrangement, see F. M. Watkins, *The Failure of Constitutional Emergency Powers under the German Republic* (Cambridge, MA: Harvard University Press 1939); Arthur J. Jacobson and Bernhard Schlink (eds), *Weimar: A Jurisprudence of Crisis* (Berkeley, CA: University of California Press 2000).

This failure led to the exclusion of this emergency mechanism in the German Basic Law of 1949, but in 1968, the law was amended and articles arranging the matter in fine-grain detail were added: a115 and 80a115.

2. The Indian constitution, for instance, defines a state of emergency as "war, external aggression, armed rebellion, failure of constitutional machinery and a threat to financial stability," and Articles 352, 356, and 360 to the constitution deal with each one of these three situations [India Cont. (1950) Art. 352, 356, 360]. A state of emergency deriving from a natural disaster is arranged in a separate Indian law, the Disaster Management Act 2005. For a survey and discussion, see Rahul Sagar, "Emergency Powers" in Sujit Choudhry, Madhav Khosla, and Pratap Bhanu Mehta eds., *The Oxford Handbook of the Indian Constitution* (New York: Oxford University Press 2016), 213–218.

3. Contrary to conventional wisdom, according to which Israel's emergency regime has no parallel among Western liberal democracies See, e.g., Menachem Hofnung, *Democracy, Law and National Security in Israel* (Aldershot: Dartmouth 1996) 51 (henceforth Hufnung, *Democracy, Law and National Security*). The reality is that this is a common phenomenon in which "emergency regimes tend to perpetuate themselves." See Oren Gross and Fionnuala Ni-Aolain, *Law in Times of Crisis: Emergency Powers in Theory and Practice* (Cambridge: Cambridge University Press 2006), 175. Some argue that the tendency of emergency arrangements to become permanent is not a common abnormality, but rather the rule. See, e.g., Mark Neocleous, "The Problem with Normality: Taking Exception to 'Permanent Emergency'" (2006) 31 Alternatives: Global, Local Political 191, 204 (Historically, "either the state of Emergency is constantly re-enacted, or it remains in place by virtue of not being explicitly repealed or it is eventually placed on the statute books as part of 'ordinary' legislation."); Mary L. Volcansek and John F. Stack Jr. (eds), *Courts and Terrorism: Nine Nations Balance Rights and Security* (New York: Cambridge University Press 2011), 231 ("perhaps the most striking and potentially disturbing lesson repeated throughout this book is the tendency for [emergency] policies that are temporary to be transformed into permanent ones.")

4. Law and Administration Ordinance, 5708-1948 (Isr.).

5. A temporary legislature that created the ordinance, and was dispersed after the elections for the Constituent Assembly, which also became the first Knesset. For more, see Chapter 1 above.

6. Basic Law: The Government, 5752-1992 (Isr.).

7. HCJ 3091/99 *Association for Civil Rights in Israel v. the Knesset* (May 8, 2012), Nevo Legal Database (by subscription) (Isr.) (henceforth *Declaration of Emergency*).

8. For a different opinion, which attributes little importance to the declaration of the existence of a state of emergency in terms of its influence on security arrangements and rulings in this matter in the State of Israel, see Adam Shinar, "Constitutions in Crisis: A Comparative Approach to Judicial Reasoning and Separation of Powers" (2008) 20 Florida Journal of International Law 115, 147 (henceforth Shinar, "Constitutions in Crisis").

9. Our discussion will focus on security legislation in areas where the Israeli law applies. I will not deal with arrangements in the territories of Judea and Samaria. For further discussion on that, see, Hufnung, *Democracy, Law and National Security*, (n. 3), part IV; David Kretzmer, *The Occupation of Justice: The Supreme Court of Israel and the Occupied Territories* (New York: State University New York Press 2002); David Kretzmer, "The Law of Belligerent Occupation in the Supreme Court of Israel" (2012) 94(885) International Review of the Red Cross 207; Guy Harpaz, "Being Unfaithful to One's Own Principles: The Israeli Supreme Court and House Demolitions in the Occupied Palestinian Territories" (2014) 37(4) Israel Law Review 401–431; Amichai Cohen, "Israel's Control of the Territories—An Emerging Legal Paradigm" (2016) 21(3) Palestine-Israel Journal of Politics, Economics and Culture 102–109.

10. For more, see Yoav Mehozay, *Between the Rule of Law and States of Emergency* (2016), 53–82 (henceforth Mehozay, *Between the Rule of Law*); Margit Cohn, "The Practice of 'Patching' in Emergency Legislation" (1998) 29 Mishpatim 623.

11. Defence (Emergency) Regulations, 5705-1945 (Isr.).

12. The regulations were presented in the *Palestine Gazette* with the following remark: "It is unfortunately the case . . . that in Palestine disorder has continued sporadically since 1944. In these circumstances, it is necessary to have legislation designed to assist the enforcement or restoration of law and order." British Government, Explanatory Note to the Defense Regulations (Emergency) 1945, 1442 Palestine Gazette 1105 (1945).

13. 3 Ha-Praklit, Journal of the Jewish Bar Association of Palestine 1 (1946) [Heb.]. See further, Claude Klein, "On the Three Floors of a Legislative Building: Israel's Legal Arsenal in Its Struggle against Terrorism" (2006) 27 Cardozo Law Review 2223, 2229.

14. For a survey of attempts made in the first decade of the state, see Menahem Hofnung, *Israel—State Security and the Rule of Law, 1948–1991* (1991), 79–87 [Heb.]; Mehozay, *Between the Rule of Law* (n. 10), 61–63.

15. Article 6(4) of the Palestine Order in Council, 1922–1947 (Isr.).

16. The reforms were carried out while other emergency laws were being passed. Thus, for instance, six emergency regulations were repealed. Article 4 to Supervision of Commodities and Services Law, 5718-1957 (Isr.) (henceforth Supervision of Commodities and Services Law).

17. Emergency Powers Law (Detention), 5739-1979 (Isr.).

18. See, for example, Alan Dershowitz, "Preventive Detention of Citizens during National Emergency—A Comparison between Israel and the United States" (1971) 1 Israel Yearbook on Human Rights 295–321.

19. Mara Rudman and Mazen Qupti, "The Emergency Powers (Detention) Law: Israel Courts Have a Mission—Should They Choose to Accept It?" (1990) 21 Columbia Human Rights Law

Review 469, 475 (Tamir's success constituted "a testament to what an individual committed to change can do").

20. See, for example, Harold Rudolph, "The Judicial Review of Administrative Detention Orders in Israel" (1984) 14 Israel Yearbook on Human Rights 148–181.

21. The IDF Chief of Staff is only left with the authority to arrest a person for forty-eight hours based on their order; a person who is so arrested shall be released after that time, unless the Minister of Defense also orders the arrest; See Article 2(b) of the Emergency Powers Law (Detention), 5739-1979 (Isr.).

22. Article 1 of the Emergency Powers Law (Detention), 5739-1979 (Isr.) ("This law will not apply except in a period in which a state of emergency exists in the country by force of a declaration according to Article 9 of the Law and Administration Ordinance, 5708-1948"). For more on the subject, as well as a comparative discussion of Israeli legislation regarding administrative detention, see Daphne Barak-Erez and Matthew C. Waxman, "Secret Evidence and the Due Process of Terrorist Detentions" (2009) 48 Columbia Journal of Transnational Law 3 (henceforth Barak-Erez and Waxman, "Secret Evidence").

23. Combatting Terrorism Law, 5776-2016 (Isr.).

24. On these grounds, for instance, most of part 13(a) of the Defense Regulations, which arranged the marking of vehicles and the prevention of deception regarding their possession.

25. On these grounds, for instance, most of Article 61 of the Defense Regulations, which granted the Minister of Defense the authority to limit the wearing of a cutting article of clothing or object, establishing a criminal penalty for violating such a limitation.

26. For this reason, for instance, Article 10 of the Defense Regulations, which subjected the Israeli Police "to the control of the Chief of Staff" in a categorical and sweeping formulation—including as regards everything related to "maintaining the public order."

27. On these grounds, for instance, regulations 84–85 of the Defense Regulations, granting the Minister of Defense the authority to declare an "unpermitted organization," were canceled, instead arranging the declaration in question, and replacing it with chapter two of the Combatting Terrorism Law.

28. On these grounds, for instance, a significant portion of part eight of the Defense Regulations, arranging the authorities of the military censor, was canceled.

29. HCJ 5/48 *Lion v. Gubernick,* 1 PD 58 (1948) (Isr.). <http://elyon1.court.gov.il/files_eng/48/050/000/Z01/48000050.z01.htm>.

For a similar issue, which was decided in an identical manner shortly afterward, see HCJ 10/48 *Ziv v. Gubernick,* 1 PD 85 (1948) (Isr.). <http://elyon1.court.gov.il/files_eng/48/100/000/Z01/48000100.z01.htm>.

30. Ibid, 66.

31. Ibid, 69.

32. Ibid, 69–70.

33. See Mehozay, *Between the Rule of Law* (n. 10), 61.

34. For a survey of the development of jurisprudence in the field, see Shinar, "Constitutions in Crisis", (n. 8), 151–153.

35. HCJ 680/88 *Schnitzer v. Chief Military Censor,* 42(4) PD 617, 628 (1989) (Isr.). <http://elyon1.court.gov.il/files_eng/88/800/006/Z01/88006800.z01.htm>.

36. Basic Law: The Government, 5752-1992 (Isr.). This change was repealed after a few years, and the 2001 Basic Law: The Government, 5761-2001 (Isr.) readopted the parliamentary model.

37. A prime example is that the Covenant on Civil and Political Rights with its rights, as identified in Article 4, cannot be derogated.

38. For instance, Emergency Regulations (Security Zones) were extended by laws from 1949 to 1972; Emergency Regulations (Carrying and Presenting of an ID Card) were extended from 1956 to 1981. For more examples, see Mehozay, *Between the Rule of Law,* (n. 10), 66.

39. HCJ 2994/90 *Poraz v. Government of Israel,* 44(3) PD 317, 322 (1990) (Isr.).

40. HCJ 6971/98 *Paritzky v. Government of Israel,* 53(1) PD 763, 781–782 (1999) (Isr.). Justice Mishael Cheshin argued, in a minority opinion, that the government should be obligated to act in an expedited process of legislation, and that only if this process fails can it enact emergency period regulations. Ibid, 789–796.

41. Several such laws were extended annually for decades. For instance, Emergency Regulations (Security Zones) 5079-1949 (Isr.), which established the areas subject to the Military Administration, were extended many times over a period of twenty-three years, until their validity expired and was not renewed in 1972.

42. See HCJ 243/52 *Bialer v. Minister of Finance,* 7 PD 429, 429 (1953) (Isr.) ("it is clear that once the Knesset renews, by law, the duration of emergency regulations … it asserts that … for the duration of their renewal, they receive the validity of a primary law").

43. Supervision of Commodities and Services Law, 5718-1957 (Isr.). For a survey of the legislative history of the Supervision Law, see HCJ 2740/96 *Chancy v. Diamond Supervisor,* 51(4) PD 481, 497–500 (1997) (Isr.) (henceforth *Chancy*).

44. Article 1 of the Supervision of Commodities and Services Law, 5718-1957 (Isr.).

45. See *Chancy,* (n. 43), 510–511.

46. HCJ 256/88 *Medinvest Ltd. v. The Director-General of the Ministry of Health,* 44(1) PD 19, 40–46, 50–51 (1989) (Isr.).

47. Article 46 of the Supervision of Commodities and Services Law, 5718-1957 (Isr.).

48. ADA 2/82 *Lerner v. The Minister of Defense,* 42(3) PD 529, 531 (1882) (Isr.).

49. See, for example, ADA 8607/04 *Fahima v. State of Israel,* 59(3) PD 258 (2004) (Isr.).

50. For an example where the court revoked an arrest order, on the grounds that even if the prisoner committed a crime, they can be tried by a normal criminal process, see ADA 4/96 *Ginzburg v. the Minister of Defense and the Prime Minister,* 50(3) PD 221 (1996) (Isr.).

51. For a description of the gradual move of the center of gravity from the executive branch to the legislative, see, for example, Chen Friedberg and Reuven Y. Hazan, "Israel's Prolonged War against Terror: From Executive Domination to Executive-Legislative Dialogue" (2009) 15 The Journal of Legislative Studies 257. (henceforth Friedberg and Hazan, "Israel's Prolonged War against Terror").

52. The two arrangement models described here largely fit the two archetypal models established by Daphna Barak-Erez: The Executive Model and the Legislative Model. See Daphne Barak-Erez, "Terrorism Law between the Executive and Legislative Models" (2009) 57 American Journal of Comparative Law 877 (henceforth Barak-Erez, "Terrorism Law").

53. The law was repealed in 2016, and its primary arrangements were integrated into the Combatting Terrorism Law.

54. We are not arguing that this pattern was only created in Israel at the beginning of the 2000s, only that an increasing use thereof can be seen from this period onward. For a different opinion, according to which security issues in Israel were always arranged primarily according to the Legislative Mode, see Barak-Erez, "Terrorism Law", (n. 52); Daphne Barak-Erez, "Terrorism

Law: Past, Present and Future" in V. V. Ramraj, M. Hor, K. Roach, and G. Williams (eds), *Global Anti-terrorism Law and Policy* (2nd edn. New York: Cambridge University Press 2012) 597, 599.

55. *Declaration of Emergency,* (n. 7), para 10 ("In the framework of this petition, twelve deliberations and more than thirty decisions were given, which led the respondents to come back and provide answers regarding the progress of the legislative process and the rearrangement of the subject").

56. Ibid, para. 12.

57. Ibid, para. 16.

58. HCJ 5100/94 *Public Committee against Torture in Israel v. State of Israel,* 53(4) PD 817, 832 (1999) (Isr.). <http://elyon1.court.gov.il/files_eng/94/000/051/a09/94051000.a09.htm>.

59. While preparing the bill, the option of including explicit authorization to using abnormal interrogation techniques was considered, but it was ultimately decided to avoid doing so, and Article 8 of the law granted GSS agents powers similar to those of police officers.

60. For differing positions on the question of whether the prohibition on delegation is included in the U.S. Constitution, see, for example, Eric A. Posner and Adrian Vermeule, "Interring the Nondelegation Doctrine" (2002) 69 University of Chicago Law Review 1721; Larry Alexander and Saikrishna Prakash, "Reports of the Nondelegation Doctrine's Death Are Greatly Exaggerated" (2003) 70 University of Chicago Law Review 1297; Gary Lawson, "Delegation and Original Meaning" (2002) 88 Virginia Law Review 327, 335–353. In Germany, the principle is anchored in the constitution and enforced by the constitutional court. See: David P. Currie, *The Constitution of the Federal Republic of Germany* (1994), 125–134.

61. See, for example, HCJ 113/52 *Zaks v. Minister of Trade and Industry,* 6 PD 696 (1952) (Isr.).

62. Amnon Rubinstein and Barak Medina, *The Constitutional Law of the State of Israel* (Tel Aviv: Schocken 2005), vol. 1, 165 [Heb.].

63. See, for example, HCJ 122/54 *Axel v. Mayor of Netanya, Members of Its Municipal Council and the People of Netanya Region,* 8(2) PD 1524 (1954) (Isr.); HCJ 155/60 *Elazar v. Mayor of Bat yam, Members of Its Municipal Council and the People of Bat Yam Region,* 14 PD 1511 (1960) (Isr.).

64. Evidence of the strengthening of the status of this rule can be found in the increasing frequency of its being mentioned by the Court. A Nevo search conducted in May 2017 revealed seventy mentions of the term "initial arrangements" in cases ruled from 1994 onward, as opposed to only eighteen such references from the state's establishment until 1994. See here for a recent such case, HCJ 4491/13 *College of Law and Business v. Government of Israel,* para. 8 to the opinion of Justice Rubinstein (July 2, 2014), Nevo Legal Database (by subscription) (Isr.) ("The interpretive presumption is that the legislator did not intend to authorize the executive branch to determine initial arrangements for itself . . . We are not dealing with a presumption that cannot be contradicted, but in order to refute it, explicit consent is required—in law—to the government for determining initial arrangements, consent which needs to be clear prima facie").

65. HCJ 3267/97 *Rubinstein v. The Minister of Defense* PD 52(5) 481 (1998) (Isr.). <http://elyon1.court.gov.il/files_eng/97/670/032/A11/97032670.a11.htm> (henceforth *Rubinstein*).

66. Ibid.

67. See, for example, Yoav Dotan, "Legalising the Unlegaliseable: Terrorism, Secret Services and Judicial Review in Israel 1970–2001" in M. Hertogh and S. Halliday (eds), *Judicial Review and Bureaucratic Impact: International and Interdisciplinary Perspectives* (Cambridge, Cambridge University Press 2004), 190; Yigal Mersel, "Judicial Review of Counter-Terrorism Measures: The

Israeli Model for the Role of the Judiciary during the Terror Era" (2005) 38 N.Y.U. Journal of International Law and Policy 67.

68. CrimFH 7048/97 *John Does v Ministry of Defence*, 54(1) PD 721 (2000) (Isr.). <http://elyon1.court.gov.il/files_eng/97/480/070/a09/97070480.a09.htm>.

69. The constitutionality of this law was first reviewed by the Supreme Court in June 2008, CA 6659/06 *Anonymous v. The State of Israel*, 62(4) PD 329 (2008) (Isr.). <http://elyon1.court.gov.il/files_eng/06/590/066/n04/06066590.n04.htm>.

This case involved the petition of residents of the Gaza Strip who were arrested by law due to their affiliation with Hezbollah. Supreme Court President Dorit Beinisch ruled that the law meets the limitation clause of Basic Law: Human Dignity and Freedom, and that there are therefore no grounds for the Court to intervene.

70. Combatting Terrorism Law, 5776-2016 (Isr.).

71. CHR 8823/07 *John Doe (Anon) v. State of Israel* (February 11, 2010), Nevo Legal Database (by subscription) (Isr.). <http://elyon1.court.gov.il/files_eng/07/230/088/p25/07088230.p25.htm>.

72. HCJ 8276/05 *Adalah Legal Center for Arab Minority Rights in Israel v. Minister of Defense*, 62(1) PD 1 (2006) (Isr.). <http://elyon1.court.gov.il/files_eng/05/760/082/a13/05082760.a13.htm> (henceforth *Adalah*).

73. Daphna Barak-Erez presents this assumption as a general consideration in evaluating the two models. See Barak-Erez, "Terrorism Law", (n. 52), 893.

74. Citizenship and Entry into Israel (Temporary Provision) Law, 5763-2003 (Isr.).

75. See, for example, Articles 224, 115 of The USA Patriot Act, Pub. L. No. 107-56 Stat. 272 (2001); Anti-Terrorism Act, S.C. 2001, s 83.32 (Can.); Article 3 of the Prevention of Terrorism Act 2005 (Eng.). For a survey, see Kyle Welch, "The Patriot Act and Crisis Legislation: The Unintended Consequences of Disaster Lawmaking" (2015) 43 Capital University Law Review 481, 485–502; George F. Bohrer, "Information Law since September 9/11: The USA PATRIOT ACT and Other Government Limitations of Expression Rights" in Charles H. Sides (ed.), *Freedom of Information in a Post 9-11 World* (London: Routledge 2017); Amanda Spitzig, "Terrorism and Anti-terrorism Legislation in Canada" (2016) 1 Legal Studies Undergraduate Journal 13, 16–17; Wilhelm Mirow, *Strategic Culture, Securitization and the Use of Force: Post-9/11 Security Practices of Liberal Democracies* (London: Routledge 2016), 105–133, 200–221.

76. For a presentation and discussion of the possible advantages of this mechanism in general, particularly in the context of security legislation, see J. E. Finn, "Sunset Clauses and Democratic Deliberation: Assessing the Significance of Sunset Provision in Antiterrorism Legislation" (2010) 48 Columbia Journal of Transnational Law 442.

77. HCJ 7052/03 *Adalah v. Minister of Interior*, 61(2) PD 202, para. 118 to the opinion of the Deputy President Cheshin (2006) (Isr.). See also paras. 9, 11 to the opinion of Justice Edmund Levy. <http://elyon1.court.gov.il/files_eng/03/520/070/a47/03070520.a47.htm>.

78. See *John Doe (Anon)*, (n. 71).

79. An additional testimony of this can be found in the ruling on the second petition against the Family Unification Law. The petition was rejected, but some of the justices expressed dissatisfaction with the repeated extensions of the law. HCJ 466/07 *Gal-on v. Attorney General*, 65(2) PD 44 (2012) (Isr.).

80. The Combatting Terrorism Law can serve as a good example on this point. See HCJ 3091/99 *Association for Civil Rights in Israel v. the Knesset*, para. 7 (May 8, 2012), Nevo Legal Database

(by subscription) (Isr.) (A description of the repeated appeals of the relevant Knesset committee to the government asking for reports on the progress of legislative work meant to repeal or change legislation the validity of which is dependent on a state of emergency.)

81. Article 47(3) of the Prohibition on Terrorist Financing Law, 5765-2005 (Isr.).

This Article states that regulations, orders, and permits to a nonspecific public according to this law will be enacted with the approval of the Knesset Constitution, Law, and Justice Committee.

Article 5 of the Citizenship and Entry into Israel Law, 5763-2003 (Isr.).

According to this Article, the declaration of a military action or war that was approved will remain in force for three months, after which the government will require the approval of the Knesset Foreign Affairs and Defense Committee to extend its validity.

Article 10a of the Incarceration of Unlawful Combatants Law, 5762-2002 (Isr.).

This Article states that the law will remain valid until June 30, 2017, and the government may, with the Knesset's approval, extend its validity via an order that will last for no more than one year for each extension.

82. For scholarship pointing to a growing awareness and commitment on the part of the Israeli legislature regarding its role as overseer of the authorities of the executive branch in the field of security, see Friedberg, as well as Friedberg and Hazan, "Israel's Prolonged War against Terror", (n. 51) ("Until the 1980s, Knesset oversight of successive governments' anti-terrorist and national security policies was practically non-existent . . . Since then, oversight has evolved from non-existence towards greater effectiveness and accountability." Ibid, 273).

CHAPTER 8

1. For general background on the status quo, see, for example, Charles S. Liebman and Eliezer Don-Yehiya, *Religion and Politics in Israel* (Bloomington: Indiana University Press 1984), ch. 3.

2. Moshe Prager, "A History of the Status Quo" (Summer 1964) 62–63 *Beit Yaakov* 18–22 [Heb.].

3. Menachem Friedman, "The Chronicle of the Status-Quo: Religion and State in Israel" in Varda Pilowski (ed.), *Transition from "Yishuv" to State 1947–1949: Continuity and Change* (Haifa: University of Haifa 1990), 47 [Heb.].

4. Zvi Zameret, "Ben-Gurion in the Early Years of the State and His Attitude to Religious Zionism and the Ultra-orthodox" in N. Ilan (ed.), *Ein Tova: Dialogue and Controversy in Israeli Culture* (Tel-Aviv: Hakibbutz Hameuchad 1998), 349–370 [Heb.].

5. Eliezer Don-Yehiya, "Conflict Management of Religious Issues: The Israeli Case in a Comparative Perspective" in Reuven Y. Hazan and Moshe Maor (eds), *Parties, Elections and Cleavages: Israel in Comparative and Theoretical Perspective* (London and Portland, OR: Frank Cass 2000) 85–108.

6. For a description of the erosion of the status quo, see, for example, Daphne Barak-Erez, "Law and Religion under the Status Quo Model: Between Past Compromises and Constant Change" (2009) 30 Cardozo Law Review 2495–2508; Reuven Y. Hazan, "Religion and Politics in Israel: The Rise and Fall of the Consociational Model" in Reuven Y. Hazan and Moshe Maor (eds), *Parties, Elections and Cleavages: Israel in Comparative and Theoretical Perspective* (London and Portland, OR: Frank Cass 2000) 109–140.

7. For an explanation along these lines, see, for example, Asher Cohen and Bernard Susser, *Israel and the Politics of Jewish Identity: The Secular-Religious Impasse.* (Baltimore: The Johns Hopkins

University Press 2000); Gideon Sapir, "Religion and State in Israel: The Case for Reevaluation and Constitutional Entrenchment" (1999) 22 Hastings International and Comparative Law Review 617–666. For other explanations, see, for example, Guy Ben-Porat, *Between State and Synagogue: The Secularization of Contemporary Israel* (New York: Cambridge University Press 2013) (focuses on the role of the economy and the consumer culture in the erosion of the status quo).

8. See Ben Gurion's words in *Divrei HaKnesset*, 25 I, 13 (13/10/1958) (Isr.): "With the founding of the state, one of the greats of Judaism Rabbi Maimon and also Rabbi Yitzhak Meir Levin came to me to speak about the yeshiva students. They said: Since all the places of Torah in the exile were destroyed and this is the only country where yeshivas remained and the students are few, they should be released from military service. Their words were acceptable to me. It seemed to me that they are right, and I gave the order to release the yeshiva students."

9. For a description of the history of the arrangements in this field, see Daphne Barak-Erez, "The Military Service of Yeshiva Students: Between the Citizenship and Justiciability Dilemma" (2006) 22 Mehkarei Mishpat: Bar-Ilan Law Studies 227, 236–246 [Heb.].

10. HCJ 40/70 *Becker v. The Minister of Defense*, 24(1) PD 238, 246 (1970) (Isr.).

11. Ibid, 241.

12. Ibid, 247.

13. Zeev Segal, *Standing before the Supreme Court Sitting as a High Court of Justice* (2nd edn. Tel Aviv: Papyrus 1993), 77–105 [Heb.].

14. HCJ 448/81 *Ressler v. The Minister of Defense*, 36(1) PD 81 (1981) (Isr.). An appeal for a further hearing on this ruling was rejected by Supreme Court President Moshe Landau. FA 2/82 *Ressler v. Defense Minister*, 36(1) PD 708 (1982) (Isr.).

15. Ibid, 84.

16. HCJ 910/86 *Ressler v. The Minister of Defense*, 42(2) PD 441 (1988) (Isr.) (henceforth *Ressler*). <http://elyon1.court.gov.il/files_eng/86/100/009/Z01/86009100.z01.htm>.

17. Ibid, 505.

18. HCJ 3267/97 *Rubinstein v. The Minister of Defense*, PD 52(5) 481 (1998) (Isr.). <http://elyon1.court.gov.il/files_eng/97/670/032/A11/97032670.a11.htm> (henceforth *Rubinstein*).

19. See above, Chapter 7, Section III2.

20. Report—the Committee to Formulate the Proper Arrangement Regarding the Recruitment of Yeshiva Students to the IDF (2000) (Isr.).

21. Deferral of Service for Yeshiva Students Law, 5762-2002 (Isr.).

22. HCJ 6427/02 *Movement for Quality of Government in Israel v. The Knesset*, 61(1) PD 619 (2006) (Isr.) (henceforth *Movement for Quality of Government*).

23. *Ibid*, para. 28 of President Barak.

24. HCJ 6298/07 *Ressler v. The Minister of Defense* (February 21, 2012), Nevo Legal Database (by subscription) (Isr.). <http://elyon1.court.gov.il/files_eng/07/980/062/n18/07062980.n18.htm>.

25. Ibid, para. 6 of Justice Hayut's opinion.

26. Ibid, para. 9 of Justice Hayut's opinion.

27. Ibid, paras. 62–64 of President Beinisch's opinion. For a survey of reasons for the failure of the Deferral of Military Service Law in fulfilling its aim of integrating the ultra-Orthodox sector into the army, see Etta Bick, "Tal Law: A Missed Opportunity for Bridging Social Capital in Israel" (2010) 52 Journal of Church and State 298–322.

28. *Ressler v. The Minister of Defense*, (n. 24), para. 2 of Justice Grunis's opinion.

29. The Defense Service Law (Amendment No. 19), 5764-2014 (Isr.).

30. The Defense Service Law (Amendment No. 21), 5765-2015 (Isr.). Article 26 18(3) of the amended law states that the Minister can defer the calling up of a draft candidate in these circumstances, "considering the security needs and the scope of the regular forces," and that he will decide how many draft deferment orders will be given, "with attention to the overall annual target for the draft."

31. HCJ 1877/14 *Movement for Quality of Government in Israel v. The Knesset* (September 12, 2017) (Isr.). <http://elyon1.court.gov.il/files/14/770/018/c29/14018770.c29.htm>.

32. Regarding Muslims and Christians, see Articles 52 and 54 of the Palestine Order in Council, 1922–1947 (Isr.). Regarding Druze, see: The Druze Religious Courts Law, 5723-1962 (Isr.).

33. For instance, during the Knesset deliberations prior to the passing of the Rabbinical Courts Jurisdiction Law, Deputy Minister of Religion Zerach Warhaftig said the following: "There is nothing that is more important for the unity of the people as a uniform law of marriage and divorce . . . The Jewish law on marriage and divorce is binding, and any deviation from it means serious harm to the unity of the nation and could lead to its dissolution." *Divrei HaKnesset* 14, 1410 (1951) (Isr.).

34. Article 23(4) of The International Covenant on Civil and Political Rights, 2004; See further, Ruth Halperin-Kaddari, *Women in Israel: A State of Their Own* (Philadelphia: University of Pennsylvania Press 2004), ch. 11.

35. Article 16 of the Universal Declaration of Human Rights (UDHR), adopted by the United Nations General Assembly on December 10, 1948, and confirmed by the State of Israel, states that: "Men and women of full age, without any limitation due to race, nationality or religion, have the right to marry and to found a family." For a description and a discussion of Israel's failure to meet this obligation, see Yuval Merin, "The Right to Family Life and Civil Marriage under International Law and Its Implementation in the State of Israel" (2005) 28 Boston College International and Comparative Law Review 79–148.

36. See Daniel Statman and Gideon Sapir, "Religious Marriage in a Liberal State" in Michel Rosenfeld and Susanna Mancini (eds), *Constitutional Secularism in an Age of Religious Revival* (Oxford: Oxford University Press 2014), 269–282.

37. Civil Appeal 450/70 *Rogozinsky v. State of Israel*, 26(1) PD 129 (1971) (Isr.) (henceforth *Rogozinsky*).

38. Ibid, 136.

39. See above, Chapter 1, Section V4.

40. See above, Chapter 2, Section III.

41. This Article, headed "Preservation of Laws," states: "This Basic Law shall not affect the validity of any law that existed before prior to the inception of the Basic Law."

42. HCJ 1000/92 *Bavli v. Great Rabbinical Court*, 48(2) PD 221 (1994) (Isr.).

43. HCJ 143/62 *Funk Shlezinger v. Minister of the Interior*, 17 PD 225 (1963) (Isr.).

44. See Eitan Levontin, "A Tower Floating in the Air: *Funk-Schlesinger* and the Law of the Population Register" (2007) 11 Mishpat Umimshal 129.

45. The source lies in the Babylonian Talmud, Tractate Sanhedrin 56a: "Our Rabbis taught: seven precepts were the sons of Noah commanded: social laws; to refrain from blasphemy, idolatry; adultery; bloodshed; robbery; and eating flesh cut from a living animal."

46. HCJ 2232/03 *Ploni (anonymous) v. Tel-Aviv-Jaffa Regional Rabbinical Court*, 61(3) PD 496 (2006) (Isr.). <http://elyon1.court.gov.il/files_eng/03/320/022/a16/03022320.a16.htm>.

47. LFA 9607/03 *Ploni v. Plonit*, 61(3) PD 726 (2006) (Isr.).

48. Article 11 of The Inheritance Law, 5725-1965 (Isr.).

49. See Shahar Lifshitz, "Married against Their Will? Toward a Pluralist Regulation of Spousal Relationships" (2009) 66 Washington and Lee Law Review 1565–1634.

50. See above, note 35, and also Article 9 of the Charter of Fundamental Rights of the EU, which became legally binding on the EU with the entry into force of the Treaty of Lisbon in December 2009. As for the question of whether Israel recognizes this right, see the discussion from para. 24 to the opinion of President Barak at HCJ7052/03 *Adala v. Minister of Interior Affairs*, PD 61(2) 202 (2006).

51. For example, Spain Const. (1978) Art 32; Portugal Const. (1976) Art 36. The United States Supreme Court has also recognized the right to marriage as being a constitutional right. See *Loving v. Virginia*, 388 U.S. 1 (1967).

52. A survey of the Israel Central Bureau of Statistics published in April 2011 showed that 90 percent of secularists, 60 percent of nonreligious traditionalists, 39 percent of religious traditionalists, 20 percent of religious Jews, and 3 percent of Haredi Jews support civil marriage. See Central Bureau of Statistics, Israel statistical yearbook (2010). <www.cbs.gov.il/shnaton61/st08_19.pdf>.

53. See Rabbi Eliyahu Bakshi-Doron, "Marriage and Divorce Law" (2005) 27 Techumin 99–107 [Heb.]; Rabbi Yuval Scherlow "Civil Union to begin With" (Ynet, February 19, 2009). <www.ynet.co.il/articles/0,7340,L-3674199,00.html> [Heb.].

54. The Spousal Association for Persons without a Religion Law, 5770-2010 (Isr.).

55. HCJ 1143/11 *The Jerusalem Institute for Justice v. The Knesset and the Ministry of Justice* (October 18, 2012) Nevo Legal Database (by subscription) (Isr.).

56. Legislation on the matter began with bylaws passed by the municipality of Tel Aviv in the 1920s. For a description of events from Tel Aviv's founding until the founding of the state, see Anat Helman, "Religion and the Public Sphere in Mandatory Tel Aviv" (2002) 105 *Qatedrah* 85 [Heb.].

57. For a firsthand survey of Sabbath legislation in the first decades of the state, see Zerah Warhaftig, *A Constitution for Israel: Religion and State* (Jerusalem: Mesilot 1988), 262–280 [Heb.] (henceforth Warhaftig).

58. First session of the Provisional Council of State, vol. A, 12–13 (Isr.).

59. Third session of the Provisional Council of State, vol. A, 26, 33 (Isr.) (henceforth Provisional Council of State, vol. A, third session).

60. For an argument pointing to the Law and Administration Ordinance as having a decisive impact on shaping the status quo in religious matters in Israel, see Amichai Radzyner, "Forgotten Basic Elements in 'The Law and Administration Ordinance', and the Covert Struggle over Religion and State in Israel" (2010) 136 Qatedrah 121–150 [Heb.]; Ron Harris, "Absent-Minded Misses and Historical Opportunities: Jewish Law, Israeli Law and the Establishment of the State of Israel" in Mordechai Bar-on and Zvi Tsameret (eds), *On Both Sides of the Bridge: Religion and State in the Early Years of Israel* (Jerusalem: Yad Yitshak Ben-Tsvi 2002), 21–55 [Heb.].

61. Proposed Days of Rest Ordinance, 5748-1948 (Isr.).

62. Provisional Council of State, vol. A, third session, (n. 59), 26.

63. An earlier version of the law proposal included an article giving the Minister of Religion authority for carrying out the law, but this version was rejected by secular ministers. See Aviad Hacohen, "The State of Israel: This Is a Holy Place! Forming a Jewish Public Domain in the State

of Israel" in Mordechai Bar-on and Zvi Tsameret (eds), *On Both Sides of the Bridge: Religion and State in the Early Years of Israel* (Jerusalem: Yad Yitshak Ben-Tsvi 2002), 144, 158 [Heb.].

64. A similar description was given thirty years later by Justice Haim Cohen: "The instruction of Article 18a(a) regarding days of rest is nothing more than a framework instruction, in the sense of a declaration of rest days that has no legal consequence, so long as the norms of behavior on that rest day have not been determined in other legislation." CA 858/79 *Ron Lapid v. State of Israel*, 34(3) PD 386, para. 3 to the opinion of Justice Cohen (1980) (Isr.).

65. For instance, see the words of Rabbi Maimon from the Mizrahi party: "What is the rest of Sabbath and what is the punishment for a desecrator of Sabbath—no one knows. And after all, in the English constitution, there are thirty Articles explaining the day of rest on Sunday, what is rest and what is the punishment expected for those who violate it . . . I am willing to suffice with twenty Articles instead of thirty." See 23rd session of the Provisional Council of State, vol. B, 22 (Isr.).

66. *Divrei HaKnesset* 1, 55 (1949) (Isr.).

67. *Divrei HaKnesset* 7, 102 (2000) (Isr.).

68. The Hours of Work and Rest Law, 5711-1951 (Isr.) (henceforth Hours of Work and Rest Law).

69. See, for example, the words of MK Y. M. Levin of the United Religious Front in *Divrei HaKnesset* 6, 2591 (1949) (Isr.): "What is Sabbath for us? Sabbath is not just a day of rest. But, and primarily, a day of holiness! . . . This is the Sabbath that obligates Israel"; see also MK Yaakov Gil's words in *Divrei HaKnesset* 6, 2595 (1949) (Isr.): "Why embed such an important, ancient, historic, national value within the law . . . whose name is the Hours of Work and Rest Law?"

70. Article 9A of the Hours of Work and Rest Law (Isr.).

71. Article 249(20) of the Municipalities Ordinance (New Version), 5724-1964 (Isr.) (henceforth Municipalities Ordinance).

72. Bylaws restricting or prohibiting the opening of businesses on Sabbath were already enacted during the Mandate. Some eighteen such bylaws were in force when the state was established. Moshe Reich, "Bylaws for Saturday" in A. Goldrat and S. Daniel (eds), *The Religious Israel* (Tel-Aviv: Hasbarah 1953), 65 [Heb.]. For a survey of bylaws that exist today, see Gideon Zeira et al., "Enforcement of the Provisions Regarding the Opening and Closing of Business in the Days of Rest Day by the Local Authorities", Center of Research and Information of the Knesset (2014). <https://www.knesset.gov.il/mmm/data/pdf/m03360.pdf> [Heb.].

73. Crim.C (Jer.) 3471/87 *State of Israel v. Kaplan*, 1988(2) PM 265 (1987) (Isr.) (henceforth *Kaplan*).

74. Explanatory remarks for Proposed Local Authorities Law (Prohibition on opening and closing businesses on rest days), 5748-1988 (Isr.) PL 1872, 134: "In most local authorities, bylaws were enacted regarding the opening and closing of businesses, and among other things, instructions were laid down regarding the prohibition of opening businesses on Sabbath and Jewish holidays. Doubt has recently been raised regarding the authority of the local authorities to enact such instructions in the bylaws. The goal of the proposed law is to remove this doubt, and preserve the status quo in the matter under discussion. It is therefore proposed to grant local authorities the authority to arrange the prohibition on opening businesses on days of rest and ensure the continued validity of existing bylaws."

75. Article 249(21) of the Municipalities Ordinance (Isr.).

76. Crim.A 217/68 *Izramax Ltd. v. State of Israel*, 22(2) PD 343 (1968) (Isr.) (henceforth *Izramax*).

77. Ibid, 360.

78. Ibid, 363.

79. Article 3(d) of bylaw to Netanya (opening and closing businesses) 5717-1957 (Isr.).

80. HCJ 5073/91 *Israel Theatres v. Municipality of Netanya*, 47(3) PD 192, 209 (1993) (Isr.).

81. Ibid, 211.

82. Ido Efrati and Gabriela Davidovich-Weissberg, "Business Owners Profit up to 25% from the Financial Turnover at Weekends" (TheMarker, June 27, 2013). <http://www.themarker.com/consumer/1.2056697> [Heb.].

83. AA 2469/12 *Bremer v. Municipality of Tel Aviv-Yafo* (June 25, 2013) Nevo Legal Database (by subscription) (Isr.) (henceforth *Bremer*).

84. Article 264a of the Municipalities Ordinance states: "If the municipality enacted a bylaw according to Article 249(21), and a business was opened contrary to the instructions of the bylaw, the authorized court may discuss the violation of that law to order the owners, managers or the operators of the aforementioned business to avoid opening the business on rest days, contrary to the instructions of the bylaw, if it was convinced that the business was opened contrary to the instructions of the bylaw."

85. *Bremer* (n. 83), para. 5 of Justice Naor's opinion.

86. Decision by Minister of Interior, "Bylaw for Tel Aviv-Jaffa" (opening and closing of businesses) (Amendment) (29/06/2014) (Isr.).

87. HCJ 6322/14 *The General Traders Association and the Self-Employed in Israel v. Minister of Interior* (April 19, 2017) Nevo Legal Database (by subscription) (Isr.) (henceforth *General Traders Association and the Self-Employed*).

88. HCJ 4558/15 *Tel Aviv-Yafo Municipality v. The Interior Minister* (June 30, 2015), Nevo Legal Database (by subscription) (Isr.).

89. Ilan Lior, "Likud Ministers Are avoiding Deciding on Opening Supermarkets in Tel Aviv on Saturday" (Haaretz, October 19, 2015). <http://www.haaretz.co.il/news/politi/1.2755016> [Heb.]. The last Minister of Interior who refused to deal with the matter is the Chairman of Shas, a party whose representatives all belong to the Haredi sector. See Yair Ettinger, "The Hot Potato of the Sabbath Is Rolling into Deri's Door" (Haaretz, January 15, 2016). <http://www.haaretz.co.il/news/politi/.premium-1.2822804> [Heb.].

90. *General Traders Association and the Self-Employed*, (n. 87).

91. Ibid, the opinion of Justice Hayut.

92. HCJ 287/69 *Miron v. Minister of Labor*, 24(1) PD 337, 341 (1970) (Isr.) (henceforth *Miron*).

93. Ibid.

94. Ibid, 343–345.

95. Ibid, 348.

96. Ibid, 355: "Just as some of the members of the public see the operation of Israeli television on Sabbath nights as a desecration of Sabbath, another part of the public sees it as providing a vital need to broaden their minds on the weekly day of rest . . ."

97. HCJ 80/70 *Elitzur v. Broadcasting Authority and Minister of Labor*, 24(2) PD 649 (1970) (Isr.) (henceforth *Elitzur*).

98. Ibid, 656.

99. Guideline No. 21.584 from October 1, 1973, at Itzhak Eliasuf, "Work at Weekly Rest Time" in Aharon Barak et al. (eds), *Goldberg Book* (Tel-Aviv: Sadan 2001) 115, 130. The instruction was given by Attorney General Meir Shamgar in the context of granting work permits on Sabbath to operate a bus for taking kids to cultural activities, social meetings, and trips. Mention in the *Kaplan* case, above, (n. 73).

100. Article 10 of Basic Law: Human Dignity and Liberty (Amendment—entrenchment of the law), Bill 287 5753-1993 (Isr.).

101. LCA 10687/02 *Handyman Do-It-Yourself v. State of Israel,* 57(3) PD 1 (2003) (Isr.).

102. HCJ 5026/04 *Design 22—Shark Deluxe Furniture LTS v. Head of Sabbath Work Permits Department, Ministry of Labor and Welfare,* 60(1) PD 38, 58 (2005) (Isr.).

103. For a description of the phenomenon and various explanations for it, see, for example, Menachem Mautner, "The Decline of Formalism and the Rise in Values in Israeli Law" (1993) 17 Iyyunei Mishpat 503 [Heb.]; idem, *Law & the Culture of Israel* (Oxford: Oxford University Press 2011) 99–126 (The change took place primarily due to the Labor Movement's loss of hegemony leading them to transfer their political efforts to the legal arena, which continued to be dominated by judges who were members of that formerly hegemonic group); Shay Mizrahi and Assaf Meydani, *Public policy between Society and Law* (Jerusalem: Carmel 2006) [Heb.] (The change occurred primarily due to the increase of the phenomenon of lack of governance, which increased the need to find solutions within the framework of the legal system).

104. For an explanation along these lines, see Amihai Radzyner, "Problematic Halakhic 'Creativity' in Israeli Rabbinical Court Rulings" (2013) 20 Jewish Law Annual 103, 154–175.

105. For instance, Israeli Prize winning author Amos Oz said, at a conference in February 2009, that "there is no reason that Sabbath should become a national day of shopping. We need to leave the malls and shopping centers closed, and perhaps search for another day when Israel will do its shopping." Kobi Nahshoni, "Amos Oz: Close Shopping Centers on Sabbath" (Ynet, February 15, 2009) [Heb.].

Bibliography

Ackerman, Bruce, *We the People: Foundations* (Cambridge, MA: Harvard University Press 1991).

Alexander, Larry and Saikrishna Prakash, "Reports of the Nondelegation Doctrine's Death Are Greatly Exaggerated" (2003) 70 University of Chicago Law Review 1297.

Amit, Roei, "Position(ing) of a Canon" (1997) 21 Iyyunei Mishpat 81 [Hebrew].

Baker, Richard A., "The United States Congress Responds to Judicial Review" In Eivind Smith (ed.), *Constitutional Justice under Old Constitutions* (The Hague: Kluwer Law International 1995) 51.

Bakshi-Doron, R. Eliyahu, "Marriage and Divorce Law" (2005) 27 Techumin 99 [Hebrew].

Barak, Aharon, "The Foundations of Judicial Review in Knesset Legislation" In *Sefer Barkatt: Symposia in Memory of Reuven Barkatt* (Jerusalem: Israeli Parliamentarism Association 1977) 291 [Hebrew].

Barak, Aharon, "The Constitutional Revolution: Protected Human Rights" (1992) 1 Mishpat Umimshal 9 [Hebrew].

Barak, Aharon, *Interpretation in Law*, vol. 3 (Jerusalem: Nevo 1994) [Hebrew].

Barak, Aharon, "Protected Human Rights and Private Law" In Yitzhak Zamir (ed.), *Klinghoffer Volume on Public Law* (Jerusalem: Hebrew University, 1993) 163 [Hebrew].

Barak, Aharon, "On the Amendments of Basic Law: Freedom of Occupation" (1994) 2 Mishpat Umimshal 173 [Hebrew].

Barak, Aharon, "The Law of Israel: Past, Present, and Future" (1997) 43 Hapraklit 5 [Hebrew].

Barak, Aharon, "The Role of the Supreme Court in a Democracy" (1999) 33 Israel Law Review 1.

Barak, Aharon, "The Values of the State of Israel as a Jewish and Democratic State" In Aharon Barak and Menashe Shava (eds), *Homage to Yitzhak: In Honor of Judge Yitzhak Shiloh* (Tel Aviv: Israel Bar Association 1999) 31 [Hebrew].

Barak, Aharon, "The State of Israel as a Jewish and Democratic State" (2000) 24 Iyyunei Mishpat 9 [Hebrew].

Barak, Aharon, "Preface" In Aharon Barak and Hayyim Berenson (eds), *Sefer Berenson*, vol. 2. (Jerusalem: Nevo 2000) 3 [Hebrew].

Barak, Aharon, "On Law, Judgment, and Judicial Activism" In Haim Cohn and Yitzhak Zamir (eds), *Aharon Barak: Selected Writings* (Jerusalem: Nevo 2000) 695 [Hebrew].

Barak, Aharon, "The Supreme Court as a Constitutional Court" (2003) 6 Mishpat Umimshal 315 [Hebrew].

Barak, Aharon, "The Constitutional Revolution: Bat Mitzvah" (2004) 1 Mishpat va-'Asakim 3 [Hebrew].

Barak, Aharon, *The Judge in a Democratic Society* (Haifa: University of Haifa Press 2004) [Hebrew].

Barak, Aharon, "Judicial Review of the Constitutionality of Statutes: Centralism vs. Decentralism" (2005) 8 Mishpat Umimshal 13 [Hebrew].

Barak, Aharon, "Proportional Effect—The Israeli Experience" (2007) 57 University of Toronto Law Journal 369.

Barak, Aharon, *Proportionality: Constitutional Rights and Their Limitations* (Cambridge: Cambridge University Press 2012).

Barak, Aharon, Tana Spanic, and Shlomo Peretz (eds), *Uri Yadin: In Memoriam* Vol. 1. (Tel Aviv: Bursei 1990) [Hebrew].

Barak, Aharon, Yitzhak Zamir, and Yigal Marzel (eds), *Sefer Mishael Cheshin* (Tel Aviv: Israel Bar Association 2009) [Hebrew].

Barak-Erez, Daphne, "From an Unwritten to a Written Constitution: The Israeli Challenge in American Perspective" (1995) 26 Columbia Human Rights Law Review 309.

Barak-Erez, Daphne, "The Israeli Welfare State: Between Legislation and Bureaucracy" (2002) 9 Labor, Society and Law 175 [Hebrew].

Barak-Erez, Daphne, *Key Trials: Landmarks in the Supreme Court* (Tel Aviv: Ministry of Defense 2003) [Hebrew].

Barak-Erez, Daphne, "The Military Service of Yeshiva Students: Between the Citizenship and Justiciability Dilemma" (2006) 22 Mehkarei Mishpat: Bar-Ilan Law Studies 227 [Hebrew].

Barak-Erez, Daphne, "The Justiciability Revolution: An Evaluation" (2008) 50 Hapraklit 3 [Hebrew].

Barak-Erez, Daphne, "Public Law of Privatization: Models, Norms and Challenges Privatization" (2008) 30 Iyyunei Mishpat 461 [Hebrew].

Barak-Erez, Daphne, "Law and Religion under the Status Quo Model: Between Past Compromises and Constant Change" (2009) 30 Cardozo Law Review 2495.

Barak-Erez, Daphne, *Outlawed Pigs: Law, Religion, and Culture in Israel* (Madison: University of Wisconsin Press 2009).

Barak-Erez, Daphne, "Terrorism Law between the Executive and Legislative Models" (2009) 57 American Journal of Comparative Law 877.

Barak-Erez, Daphne, "Terrorism Law: Past, Present and Future" In V. V. Ramraj, M. Hor, K. Roach, and G. Williams (eds), *Global Anti-terrorism Law and Policy* (2nd edn, New-York: Cambridge University Press 2012) 597.

Barak-Erez, Daphne, "Social Rights in the Israeli Law: Direct Protection, Indirect Protection and Challenges Coming Next" In Ohad Gordon et al. (eds) *Edmond Levi Book* (Jerusalem: The Hebrew University of Jerusalem, 2017) 53 [Hebrew].

Barak-Erez, Daphne and Matthew C. Waxman, "Secret Evidence and the Due Process of Terrorist Detentions" (2009) 48 Columbia Journal of Transnational Law 3.

Barzilai, Gad, Ephraim Yuchtman-Yaar, and Zeev Segal, *The Israeli Supreme Court and the Israeli Public* (Tel Aviv: Papyrus 1994) [Hebrew].

Beatty, David M., *The Ultimate Rule of Law* (Oxford: Oxford University Press, 2004).

Bechor, Guy, *A Constitution for Israel* (Tel Aviv: Maariv 1996) [Hebrew].

Beilin, Yossi, "A Collision Known as Direct Election of the Prime Minister" In Gideon Doron (ed.), *the Electoral Revolution: Primaries and Direct Election of the Prime Minister* (Tel Aviv: Hakibbutz Hameuchad, 1996) 199 [Hebrew].

Benish, Avishai and Michal Kremer, "Filling the Void: A Model for the Constitutional Right to Dignified Existence Based on the German Constitutional Law" (2015) 4 Work, Society and Law 263 [Hebrew].

Bell, John, *Judiciaries within Europe* (Cambridge: Cambridge University Press 2006).

Ben Israel, Ruth, "The Impact of Basic Laws on Labor Law and Industrial Relations" (1994) 4 Yearbook of Labor Law 21 [Hebrew].

Bendor, Ariel, "Flaws in the Enactment of the Basic Laws" (1994) 2 Mishpat Umimshal 443 [Hebrew].

Bendor, Ariel, "Entrenchment and Constitution: *Bergman* and the Constitutional Discourse in Israel" (2001) 31 Mishpatim 821 [Hebrew].

Bendor, Ariel, "Four Constitutional Revolutions?" (2003) 6 Mishpat Umimshal 305 [Hebrew].

Bendor, Ariel, "The Limits of Justice Barak (Or, Does Judicial Discretion Really Exist)" (2005) 9 Mishpat Umimshal 261 [Hebrew].

Bendor, Ariel L., and Zeev Segal, *The Hat Maker: Discussions with Justice Aharon Barak* (Or Yehuda: Kinneret, Zmora-Bitan 2009) [Hebrew].

Ben-Porat, Guy, *Between State and Synagogue: The Secularization of Contemporary Israel* (New York: Cambridge University Press 2013).

Ben-Porat, Miriam, "A Constitution in Israel: Whether and When" (1985) 11 Iyyunei Mishpat 19 [Hebrew].

Ben-Zeev, Moshe, "Politics in the Appointment of Judges" (1981) May 27 Orekh Hadin 13 [Hebrew].

Berger, Raoul, *Government by Judiciary: The Transformation of the Fourteenth Amendment* (Cambridge, MA: Harvard University Press 1977).

Bick, Etta, "Tal Law: A Missed Opportunity for Bridging Social Capital in Israel" (2010) 52 Journal of Church and State 298.

Bilchitz, David, "Giving Socio-Economic Rights Teeth: The Minimum Core and Its Importance" (2002) 119 South African Law Journal 484.

Bittner, Claudia, "Human Dignity as a Matter of Legislative Consistency in an Ideal World: The Fundamental Right to Guarantee a Subsistence Minimum in the German Federal Constitutional Court's Judgment of 9 February 2010" (2011) 12 German Law Journal 1941.

Bork, Robert H., *The Tempting of America: The Political Seduction of the Law* (New York: Free Press 1990).

Bork, Robert H., *Slouching towards Gomorrah: Modern Liberalism and American Decline* (New York: Regan Books 1996).

Bracha, Baruch, "The Protection of Human Rights in Israel" (1982) 12 Israel Yearbook of Human Rights 110.

Brewer-Carias, Allan R., *Judicial Review in Comparative Law* (Cambridge: Cambridge University Press 1989).

Canon, B. C. and C. A. Johnson, *Judicial Policies: Implementation and Impact* (Washington, DC: CQ Press 1999).

Calabresi, Steven, "The President, the Supreme Court, and the Founding Fathers: A Reply to Professor Ackerman" (2006) 73 University of Chicago Law Review 469.

Cappelletti, Mauro, *The Judicial Process in Comparative Perspective* (Oxford: Clarendon Press 1989).

Cappelletti, Mauro and William Cohen, *Comparative Constitutional Law: Cases and Materials* (Indianapolis, IN: Bobbs-Merrill 1979).

Cheshin, Mishael, "Responses" (2007) 6 Moznei Mishpat 503 [Hebrew].

Choudhry, Sujit, "So, What Is the Real Legacy of Oaks? Two Decades of Proportionality Case Analysis under the Canadian Charter's Section 1" (2006) 34 Supreme Court Law Review 514.

Cohen, Amichai, "Israel's Control of the Territories—An Emerging Legal Paradigm" (2016) 21(3) Palestine—Israel Journal of Politics, Economics and Culture 102.

Cohen, Asher, *The Talit and the Flag: Religious Zionism and the Concept of a Torah State, 1947–1953* (Jerusalem: Yad Yitzhak Ben Zvi 1998) [Hebrew].

Cohen, Asher and Bernard Susser, *Israel and the Politics of Jewish Identity: The Secular-Religious Impasse* (Baltimore: Johns Hopkins University Press 2000).

Cohen-Eliya, Moshe, "The Formal and the Substantive Meanings of Proportionality in the Supreme Court's Decision Regarding the Security Fence" (2005) 20 Hamishpat 65 [Hebrew].

Cohen-Eliya, Moshe, "Separation of Powers and Proportionality with Reference to David Beatty, The Ultimate Rule of Law" (2005) 9 Mishpat Umimshal 297 [Hebrew].

Cohen-Eliya, Moshe and Iddo Porat, *Proportionality and Constitutional Culture* (Cambridge: Cambridge University Press 2013).

Cohen-Eliya, Moshe and Gila Stopler, "Probability Thresholds as Deontological Constraints in Global Constitutionalism" (2011) 49 Columbia Journal of Transnational Law 75.

Cohn, Haim, "Deportation According to Law" (1992) 1 Mishpat Umimshal 471 [Hebrew].

Cohn, Haim, "*Obiter* of Blessed Memory" (2000) 31 Mishpatim 415 [Hebrew].

Cohn, Margit, "The Practice of 'Patching' in Emergency Legislation" (1998) 29 Mishpatim 623 [Hebrew].

Comella, Victor F., "The Consequences of Centralizing Constitutional Review in a Special Court: Some Thoughts on Judicial Activism" (2004) 82 Texas Law Review 1705.

Comella, Victor F., "The European Model of Constitutional Review of Legislation: Toward Decentralization?" (2004) 2 International Journal of Constitutional Law 461.

Craven, Matthew C.R., *The International Covenant on Economics, Social and Cultural Rights: Perspective on Its Development* (Oxford: Oxford University Press 1995).

Currie, David P., *The Constitution of the Federal Republic of Germany* (Chicago: University of Chicago Press 1994).

Davidov, Guy, "Separating Minimal Impairment from Balancing: A Comment on *R. v. Sharpe* (B.C.C.A)" (2000) 5 Review of Constitutional Studies 195.

Davidov, Guy, "The Principle of Proportionality in Labor Law" (2008) 31 Iyyunei Mishpat 31 [Hebrew].

Davis, Dennis M., "Adjudicating the Socio-economic Rights in the South African Constitution: Towards 'Deference Lite'" (2006) 22 South African Journal on Human Rights 301.

Dershowitz, Alan, "Preventive Detention of Citizens during National Emergency—A Comparison between Israel and the United States" (1971) 1 Israel Yearbook on Human Rights 295.

Don-Yehiya, Eliezer, "Conflict Management of Religious Issues: The Israeli Case in a Comparative Perspective" In Reuven Y. Hazan and Moshe Maor (eds), *Parties, Elections and Cleavages: Israel in Comparative and Theoretical Perspective* (London and Portland, OR: Frank Cass 2000) 85.

Doron, Gideon, *A Presidential Regime for Israel* (Jerusalem: Carmel 2006) [Hebrew].

Dotan, Yoav, "A Constitution for the State of Israel: The Constitutional Dialogue after the 'Constitutional Revolution'" (1997) 28 Mishpatim 149 [Hebrew].

Dotan, Yoav, "Does Israel Need a Constitutional Court?" (2000) 5 Mishpat Umimshal 117 [Hebrew].

Dotan, Yoav, "The Supreme Court as the Defender of the Social Rights" In Yoram Rabin and Yuval Shani (eds), *Economic, Social and Cultural Rights in Israel* (Tel Aviv: Ramot 2004) 69 [Hebrew].

Dotan, Yoav, "Legalising the Unlegaliseable: Terrorism, Secret Services and Judicial Review in Israel 1970–2001" In M. Hertogh and S. Halliday (eds), *Judicial Review and Bureaucratic Impact: International and Interdisciplinary Perspectives* (Cambridge: Cambridge University Press 2004) 190.

Dotan, Yoav, "Judicial Review of Legislation: The Accountability Question" (2007) 10 Mishpat Umimshal 489 [Hebrew].

Dowell-Jones, Mary, *Contextualizing the International Covenant on Economic, Social and Cultural Rights: Assessing the Economic Deficit* (Leiden: Martinus Nijhoff Publishers 2004).

Edelman, Martin, *Courts, Politics and Culture in Israel* (Charlottesville: University Press of Virginia 1994).

Egidy, Stefanie, "The Fundamental Right to the Guarantee of a Subsistence Minimum in the Hartz IV Decision of the German Federal Constitutional Court" (2001) 12 German Law Journal 1961.

Elbasan, Yuval, *Strangers in the Realm of the Law: Access to Justice in Israel* (Tel Aviv: Hakibutz Hameuchad 2005) [Hebrew].

Eliasuf, Itzhak, "Work at Weekly Rest Time" In Aharon Barak et al. (eds) *Goldberg Book* (Tel-Aviv: Sadan, 2001) 115 [Hebrew].

Elon, Menachem, "Basic Laws: Their Enactment and Their Interpretation: From Where and to Where?" (1996) 12 Mehkarei Mishpat: Bar-Ilan Law Studies 253 [Hebrew].

Elster, Jon, "Forces and Mechanisms in the Constitution Making Process" (1995) 45 Duke Law Journal 364.

Emiliou, Nicholas, *The Principle of Proportionality in European Law* (London; Boston, Mass: Kluwer Law International 1996).

Epp, Charles R., *The Rights Revolution: Lawyers, Activists and Supreme Courts in Comparative Perspective* (Chicago: University of Chicago Press 1998).

Epp, Charles R., *Making Rights Real: Activists, Bureaucrats, and the Creation of the Legalistic State* (Chicago: University of Chicago Press 2010).

Even, Efrat, "The Participation of Public Representatives in Judicial Appointments Proceedings" (2003) 39 Parliament 4 [Hebrew].

Ewing, K. D., *Bonfire of the Liberties: New Labor, Human Rights and the Rule of Law* (Oxford: Oxford University Press 2010).

Fallon, Richard H., "Individual Rights and the Powers of Government" (1993) 27 Garman Law Review 343.

Feeley, Malcom M., "Hollow Hopes, Flypaper, and Metaphors" (1993) 17 Law and Social Inquiry 745.

Finn, J. E., "Sunset Clauses and Democratic Deliberation: Assessing the Significance of Sunset Provision in Antiterrorism Legislation" (2010) 48 Columbia Journal of Transnational Law 442.

Freeman, Samuel, "Original Meaning, Democratic Interpretation, and the Constitution" (1992) 21 Philosophy and Public Affairs 3.

Freeman, Samuel, "The Constitution, Social Rights, and Liberal Political Justification" (2003) 1 International Journal of Constitutional Law 13.

Friedberg, Chen and Reuven Y. Hazan, "Israel's Prolonged War against Terror: From Executive Domination to Executive-Legislative Dialogue" (2009) 15 The Journal of Legislative Studies 257.

Friedman, Menachem, "The Chronicle of the *Status Quo*: Religion and State in Israel" In Varda Pilowsky (ed.), *Transition from "Yishuv" to State, 1947–1949* (Haifa: University of Haifa 1990) 47 [Hebrew].

Friedman, Shuki, and Amihai Radzyner, *The Religious Community and the Constitution: What Can History Teach Us?* (Jerusalem: Israel Democracy Institute 2007) [Hebrew].

Gavison, Ruth, "The Controversy over Israel's Bill of Rights" (1985) 15 Israeli Yearbook of Human Rights 113.

Gavison, Ruth, "Forty Years of Constitutional Law" (1989) 19 Mishpatim 617 [Hebrew].

Gavison, Ruth, "A Jewish and Democratic State: Political Identity, Ideology, and Law" (1995) 19 Iyyunei Mishpat 631 [Hebrew].

Gavison, Ruth, "The Constitutional Revolution: A Description of Reality or a Self-Fulfilling Prophecy?" (1997) 28 Mishpatim 23 [Hebrew].

Gavison, Ruth, "Constitutions and Political Reconstruction? Israel's Quest for a Constitution" (2003) 18 International Sociology 55.

Gavison, Ruth, "On the Relationships between Civil-Political Rights and Social-Economic Rights" In Yoram Rabin and Yuval Shany (eds), *Economic, Social, and Cultural Rights in Israel* (Tel Aviv: Ramot 2004) 25 [Hebrew].

Gavison, Ruth, Mordechai Kremnitzer, and Yoav Dotan, *Judicial Activism: For and Against* (Jerusalem: Magnes Press 2000) [Hebrew].

Gazal, Oren, "Restriction of Basic Rights 'by Law' or as 'Prescribed by Law'" (1998) 4 Mishpat Umimshal 384 [Hebrew].

Gedicks, Frederick, "An Unfirm Foundation: The Regrettable Indefensibility of Religious Exemption" (1998) 20 University of Arkansas Law Journal 555.

Gontovnick, Gershon, "Thoughts about Justiciability, Judicial Review and the Fear of Institutional Errors" In Aharon Barak et al. (eds), *Eliyahu Mazza Book* (Srigim-Lion : Nevo Publishing, 2015) 219 [Hebrew].

Gontovnick, Gershon, "Constitutional Law: Development in the Wake of the Constitutional Revolution" (1999) 23(1) Tel Aviv University Law Review 129 [Hebrew].

Goldberg, Giora, "'You Don't Need a Constitution to Plant Trees': On State-Building and Constitution-Framing" (1993) 38 State, Government and International Relations 29 [Hebrew].

Goldberg, Giora, "Religious-Zionism and the Framing of a Constitution for Israel" (1998) 3 Israel Studies 211.

Goldman, Shahar, *The Proposed Reform of the Court System: Advantages vs. Risks* Policy Paper 15 (Jerusalem: Israel Democracy Institute 1999) [Hebrew].

Greenawalt, Kent, "Dualism and Its Status" (1994) 104 Ethics 480.

Grimm, Dieter, "Proportionality in Canadian and German Constitutional Jurisprudence" (2007) 57 University of Toronto Law Journal 383.

Gross, Aeyal and Daphne Barak-Erez, "Social Rights in Israel and the Struggle for Social Rights: Beyond the Right to Human Dignity" In Dalia Dorner, Shulamit Almog and Yaad Rotem (eds), *Dalia Dorner Book* (Srigim-Lion: Nevo Publishing 2008) 189 [Hebrew].

Gross, Oren and Fionnuala Ni-Aolain, *Law in Times of Crisis: Emergency Powers in Theory and Practice* (Cambridge University Press 2006).

Gross, Meron, and Yoram Shahar, "Searching for Bench Selection Methods in Israel's Supreme Court: A Quantitative Analysis" (1998) 29 Mishpatim 567 [Hebrew].

Hacohen, Aviad, "The State of Israel: This Is a Holy Place! Forming a Jewish Public Domain in the State of Israel" In Mordechai Bar-on and Zvi Tsameret (eds), *On Both Sides of the Bridge: Religion and State in the Early Years of Israel* (Jerusalem: Yad Yitshak Ben-Tsvi 2002) 144 [Hebrew].

Haller, Mordechai, "The Court That Packed Itself" (1999) 8 Azure 64.

Halperin-Kaddari, Ruth, *Women in Israel: A State of Their Own* (Philadelphia: University of Pennsylvania Press 2004).

Harpaz, Guy, "Being Unfaithful to One's Own Principles: The Israeli Supreme Court and House Demolitions in the Occupied Palestinian Territories" (2014) 47(3) Israel Law Review 401.

Harris, Ron, "Absent-Minded Misses and Historical Opportunities" In Mordechai Bar-On and Zvi Zameret (eds), *On Both Sides of the Bridge: Religion and State in the Early Years of Israel* (Jerusalem: Yad Yitzhak Ben Zvi 2002) 21 [Hebrew].

Hazan, Reuven Y., "Non-parliamentary and Non-presidential: The Change in the Voting System and the Regime in Israel" (1998) 2 Politika 105 [Hebrew].

Hazan, Reuven Y., "Religion and Politics in Israel: The Rise and Fall of the Consociational Model" In Reuven Y. Hazan and Moshe Maor (eds), *Parties, Elections and Cleavages: Israel in Comparative and Theoretical Perspective* (London and Portland, OR: Frank Cass 2000) 109.

Helman, Anat, "Religion and the Public Sphere in Mandatory Tel Aviv" (2002) 105 Qatedrah 85 [Hebrew].

Hilbink, Lisa, "Beyond Manicheanism: Assessing the New Constitutionalism" (2006) 65 Maryland Law Review 15.

Hirschl, Ran, "The 'Constitutional Revolution' and the Emergence of a New Economic Order in Israel" (1997) 2 Israel Studies 136.

Hirschl, Ran, "Looking Sideways, Looking Backwards, Looking Forwards: Judicial Review vs. Democracy in Comparative Perspective" (2000) 34 University of Richmond Law Review 415.

Hirschl, Ran, "The Political Origins of Judicial Empowerment through Constitutionalization: Lessons from Four Constitutional Revolutions" (2000) 25 Law and Social Inquiry 91.

Hirschl, Ran, "The Struggle for Hegemony: Understanding Judicial Empowerment through Constitutionalization in Culturally Divided Polities" (2000) 36 Stanford Journal of International Law 73.

Hirschl, Ran, "Constitutional Courts vs. Religious Fundamentalism: Three Middle Eastern Tales" (2004) 82 Texas Law Review 1819.

Hirschl, Ran, *Towards Juristocracy: The Origins and Consequences of the New Constitutionalism* (Cambridge, MA: Harvard University Press 2004).

Hofnung, Menachem, *Israel—State Security and The Rule of Law 1948–1991* (Aldershot: Dartmouth 1991) [Hebrew].

Hofnung, Menachem, *Democracy, Law and National Security in Israel* (Aldershot; Brookfield, USA: Dartmouth 1996).

Hofnung, Menachem, "Authority, Influence and Separation of Powers: Judicial Review in Israel in Comparative Perspective" (1997) 28 Mishpatim 211 [Hebrew].

Hogg, Peter, *Constitutional Law of Canada*, vol. 2 (5th edn, Ontario: Thomson Carswell 2007).

Holmes, Stephen, "Gag Rules or the Politics of Omission" In Jon Elster and Rune Slagstad (eds), *Constitutionalism and Democracy* (Cambridge: Cambridge University Press 1988) 19.

Ishay, Micheline R., *The History of Human Rights: From Ancient Times to the Globalization Era* (Berkeley and Los Angeles: : University of California Press, 2008).

Jabareen, Hassan, "The Politics of Legal Professionalism in Constitutional Cases" (2003) 6 Mishpat Umimshal 315 [Hebrew].

Jackson, Vicki C, "The Ultimate Rule of Law" (Book review) (2004) 21 Constitutional Commentary 803.

Jacobson, Arthur J. and Bernhard Schlink (eds), *Weimar: A Jurisprudence of Crisis* (Berkeley: University of California Press 2000).

Jacobsohn, Gary Jeffrey, *Apple of Gold: Constitutionalism in Israel and the United States* (Princeton, NJ: Princeton University Press 1993).

Karp, Judith, "Basic Law: Human Dignity and Liberty—A Biography of Power Struggles" (1992) 1 Mishpat Umimshal 323 [Hebrew].

King, Jeff, *Judging Social Rights* (Cambridge: Cambridge University Press 2012).

Klagsbald, Avigdor, "Amending and Offending against Basic Laws" (2006) 48 Hapraklit 293 [Hebrew].

Klarman, Michael J., "Constitutional Fact/Constitutional Fiction: A Critique of Bruce Ackerman's Theory of Constitutional Moments" (1992) 44 Stanford Law Review 759.

Klarman, Michael J., *From Jim Crow to Civil Rights: The Supreme Court and the Struggle for Racial Equality* (New York: Oxford University Press 2004).

Klein, Claude, "The Constitutional Authority in Israel" (1970) 2 Mishpatim 51 [Hebrew].

Klein, Claude, "A New Era in Israel's Constitutional Law" (1971) 6 Israel Law Review 376.

Klein, Claude, "The Need for a Special Majority" (1972) 28 Hapraklit 563 [Hebrew].

Klein, Claude, "Basic Law: Human Dignity and Liberty—An Initial Normative Assessment" (1993) 1 Hamishpat 123 [Hebrew].

Klein, Claude, "On the Three Floors of a Legislative Building: Israel's Legal Arsenal in Its Struggle against Terrorism" (2006) 27 Cardozo Law Review 2223.

Klinghoffer, I. H., "The Establishment of the State of Israel: Constitutional History" In Yitzhak Zamir (ed.), *Klinghoffer Volume on Public Law* (Jerusalem: Hebrew University 1993) 53 [Hebrew].

Kramer, Larry, "What's a Constitution for Anyway? Of History and Theory, Bruce Ackerman and the New Deal" (1996) 46 Case Western Reserve Law Review 885.

Kremnitzer, Mordechai, "The Recent Supreme Court and the Civil Interest" (2008) 33 Alpayim 103 [Hebrew].

Kretzmer, David, "Forty Years of Public Law" (1989) 19 Mishpatim 551 [Hebrew].

Kretzmer, David, "The New Basic Laws on Human Rights: A Mini-revolution in Israeli Constitutional Law?" (1992) 26 Israel Law Review 238.

Kretzmer, David, "The New Basic Laws on Human Rights: A Mini-revolution in Israeli Constitutional Law?" (1996) 14.2 Netherlands Quarterly of Human Rights 173.

Kretzmer, David, "The Path to Judicial Review in Human Rights Cases: From *Bergman* and *Kol Ha'am* to *Bank Mizrahi*" (1997) 28 Mishpatim 359 [Hebrew].

Kretzmer, David, *The Occupation of Justice: The Supreme Court of Israel and the Occupied Territories* (New York: State University of New York Press 2002).

Kretzmer, David, "The Law of Belligerent Occupation in the Supreme Court of Israel" (2012) 94(885) International Review Red Cross 207.

Lahav, Pnina, "Freedom of Expression in the Decisions of the Supreme Court" (1972) 7 Mishpatim 375 [Hebrew].

Lahav, Pnina, "The Formative Years of Israel's Supreme Court: 1948–1955" (1989) 14 Iyyunei Mishpat 479 [Hebrew].

Lahav, Pnina, *Judgment in Jerusalem: Chief Justice Simon Agranat and the Zionist Century* (Berkeley: University of California Press 1997).

Landau, Moshe, "A Constitution as the Supreme Law of the State of Israel?" (1971) 27 Hapraklit 30 [Hebrew].

Landau, Moshe, "Review of Israel's Parliament: The Law of the Knesset" (1972) 4 Mishpatim 213 [Hebrew].

Landau, Moshe, "Reflections on the Constitutional Revolution" (1996) 26 Mishpatim 419 [Hebrew].

Landau, Moshe, "The Supreme Court as Constitution Maker for Israel" (1996) 3 Mishpat Umimshal 697 [Hebrew].

Landau, Moshe, "Symposium: Three Years after *Bank Mizrahi*" (2000) 5 Hamishpat 249 [Hebrew].

Landau, Moshe, "Trends in the Decisions of the Supreme Court" (1982) 8 Iyyunei Mishpat 504 [Hebrew].

Langford, Malcolm, "The Justiciability of Social Rights: From Theory to Practice" In Malcolm Langford (ed.), *Social Rights Jurisprudence: Emerging Trends in International and Comparative Law* (New York: Cambridge University Press 2008) 30.

Lawson, Gary, "Delegation and Original Meaning" (2002) 88 Virginia Law Review 327.

Lessig, Lawrence, "Understanding Changed Readings: Fidelity and Theory" (1995) 47 Stanford Law Review 395.

Levitsky, Naomi, *The Supremes: Inside the Supreme Court* (Bnei Brak: Hakibbutz Hameuchad 2006) [Hebrew].

Levontin, Eitan, "A Tower Floating in the Air: *Funk-Schlesinger* and the Law of the Population Register" (2007) 11 Mishpat Umimshal 129.

Liebenberg, Sandra, *Socio-economic Rights: Adjudication under a Transformative Constitution* (Clzaremont: Juta Legal and Academic Publishers 2010).

Liebenberg, Sandra, "The Interpretation of Socio-economic Rights" In Stu Woolman, Michael Bishop, and Jason Brickhill (eds), *Constitutional Law of South Africa* (2nd edn., 4th rev. Cape Town: Juta Legal and Academic Publishers 2012), ch. 3.

Liebman, Charles S. and Eliezer Don-Yehiya, *Religion and Politics in Israel* (Bloomington: Indiana University Press 1984).

Lifshitz, Shahar, "Married against Their Will? Toward a Pluralist Regulation of Spousal Relationships" (2009) 66 Washington and Lee Law Review 1565.

Lowi, Theodore J., *The End of Liberalism: Ideology, Policy, and the Crisis of Public Authority* (New York: Norton 1969).

Lynn, Uriel, "A Foundation for a Written Constitution in Israel" (1993) 1 Hamishpat 81 [Hebrew].

Lynn, Uriel, "Basic Laws as Part of Israel's Written Constitution" (2000) 5 Hamishpat 267 [Hebrew].

MacCann, Michael W., "Reform Litigation on Trial" (2009) 17 Law and Social Inquiry 715.

Mandel, Michael, "Democracy and the New Constitutionalism in Israel" (1999) 33 Israel Law Review 259.

Maor, Anat, "A Lacuna in the Legal Code: A Basic Law Proposal: Social and Economic Rights— Chronicle of Legislation Failure" In Yoram Rabin & Yuval Shani (eds), *Economic, Social and Cultural Rights in Israel* (Tel Aviv, Ramot, University 2004) 195 [Hebrew].

Maoz, Asher, "Defending Civil Liberties without a Constitution: The Israeli Experience" (1988) 16 Melbourne University Law Review 815.

Marmor, Andrei, "Judicial Review in Israel" (1997) 4 Mishpat Umimshal 133 [Hebrew].

Mautner, Menachem, "The Decline of Formalism and the Rise in Values in Israeli Law" (1993) 17 Iyyunei Mishpat 503 [Hebrew].

Mautner, Menachem, "Israeli Law in a Multicultural Society" In Eyal Yinon (ed.), *The Rule of Law in a Polarized Society: Proceedings of the Conference on February 17, 1998* (Jerusalem: Ministry of Justice 1999) 27 [Hebrew].

Mautner, Menachem, "Appointment of Judges to the Supreme Court in a Multicultural Society" (2003) 19 Mehkarei Mishpat: Bar-Ilan Law Studies 423 [Hebrew].

Mautner, Menachem, "The Eighties: The Years of Anxiety" (2003) 26 Iyyunei Mishpat 646 [Hebrew].

Mautner, Menachem, *Law and the Culture of Israel* (New York: Oxford University Press 2011).

Medina, Barak, "The Limits of the Knesset's Power to Set Supra-majority Rules" (2003) 6 Mishpat Umimshal 509 [Hebrew].

Medina, Barak, "On 'Infringements' of Human Rights and the 'Proper Purpose' Requirement (following Aharon Barak, Proportionality—Constitutional Rights and Their Limitations)" (2012) 15 Mishpat va'Asakim 281 [Hebrew].

Medina, Barak, *Human Rights Law in Israel* (published on Nevo and Sacher, 2016) [Hebrew].

Medina, Barak and Ilan Saban, "Human Rights and Risk-Taking: On Democracy, Ethnic-Profiling and the 'Limitation Clause' (following the Decision on the Validity of the Citizenship and Entry into Israel Law)" (2008) 39 Mishpatim 47 [Hebrew].

Mehozay, Yoav, *Between the Rule of Law and States of Emergency* (Albany: State University of New York Press 2016).

Merin, Yuval, "The Right to Family Life and Civil Marriage under International Law and Its Implementation in the State of Israel" (2005) 28 Boston College International and Comparative Law Review 79.

Mersel, Yigal, "Judicial Review of Counter-Terrorism Measures: The Israeli Model for the Role of the Judiciary during the Terror Era" (2005) 38 New York University Journal of International Law and Politics 67.

Michelman, Frank I., "The Supreme Court, 1968 Term, Foreword: On Protecting the Poor through the Fourteenth Amendment" (1969) 83 Harvard Law Review 7.

Michelman, Frank I., "In Pursuit of Constitutional Welfare Rights: One View of Rawls' Theory of Justice" (1973) 121 University of Pennsylvania Law Review 962.

Michels, Robert, *Political Parties: A Sociological Study of the Oligarchical Tendencies of Modern Democracy* (New York: Collier Books 1962).

Mirow, Wilhelm, *Strategic Culture, Securitization and the Use of Force: Post-9/11 Security Practices of Liberal Democracies* (London: Routledge 2016).

Mizrahi, Shay and Assaf Meydani, *Public Policy between Society and Law* (Jerusalem: Carmel 2006) [Hebrew].

Mundlak, Guy, "Social-economic Rights in the New Constitutional Discourse" In Aharon Barak and Hayyim Berenson (eds), *Sefer Berenson*, vol. 2 (Jerusalem: Nevo 2000) 183 [Hebrew].

Nachmias, David and Doron Navot, "The Electoral Reform and Broad Coalitions: The Sharon Government" In Asher Arian and Michal Shamir (eds), *The Elections in Israel 2001* (Jerusalem: Israel Democracy Institute 2002) 135.

Navot, Suzie, *The Constitutional Law of Israel* (The Hague: Kluwer Law International 2007).

Nedelsky, Jennifer, "The Puzzle and Demands of Modern Constitutionalism" (1994) 104 Ethics 500.

Negbi, Moshe, *Above the Law: The Crisis of the Rule of Law in Israel* (Tel Aviv: Am Oved 1987) [Hebrew].

Negbi, Moshe, "The Supreme Court in the Perception of Israeli Society" (1995) 3 Mishpat Umimshal 355.

Neocleous, Mark, "The Problem with Normality: Taking Exception to 'Permanent Emergency'" (2006) 31 Alternatives: Global, Local Political 191.

Neuberger, Benjamin, *The Constitution in Israel* (Tel Aviv: Open University 1997) [Hebrew].

Nimmer, Melville B., "The Right to Speak from Time to Time: First Amendment Theory Applied to Libel and Misapplied to Privacy" (1968) 56 California Law Review 942.

Parush, Adi, "Judicial Activism, Legal Positivism, and Natural Law: Justice Barak and the Doctrine of the Omnipotent Knesset" In Ariel Porat (ed.), *Judicial Activism* (Tel Aviv: Ramot 1993) 717 [Hebrew].

Peretti, Terri Jennings, *In Defense of a Political Court* (Princeton, NJ: Princeton University Press 1999).

Perry, Michael J., *The Constitution in the Courts: Law or Politics?* (New York: Oxford University Press 1994).

Posner, Eric A. and Adrian Vermeule, "Interring the Nondelegation Doctrine" (2002) 69 University of Chicago Law Review 1721.

Posner, Richard A., "Enlightened Despot" (April 23, 2007) The New Republic 53.

Prager, Moshe, "A History of the Status Que" (1964) 62–63 Beit Yaakov 18 [Hebrew].

Prakash, Saikrishna B., "America's Aristocracy" Review of *Taking the Constitution Away from the Courts*, by Mark Tushnet (1999) 109 Yale Law Journal 549.

Prosser, Tony, *Test Cases for the Poor: Legal Techniques in the Politics of Social Welfare* (London: Child Poverty Action Group 1983).

Rabin, Yoram, *The Right to Education* (Srigim-Lion: Nevo Publishing 2002) [Hebrew].

Radzyner, Amichai, "Forgotten Basic Elements in 'The Law and Administration Ordinance' and the Covert Struggle over Religion and State in Israel" (2010) 136 Qatedrah 121 [Hebrew].

Radzyner, Amichai, "Problematic Halkhic 'Creativity' in Israeli Rabbinical Court Rulings" (2013) 20 Jewish Law Annual 103.

Reich, Moche, "Bylaws for Saturday" In A. Goldrat and S. Daniel (eds), *The Religious Israel* (Tel-Aviv: Hasbarah 1953), 65 [Hebrew].

Rivers, Julian, "Proportionality and Variable Intensity of Review" (2006) 65 Cambridge Law Review 198.

Rosenberg, Gerald, *The Hollow Hope: Can Courts Bring About Social Change?* (Chicago: University of Chicago Press 1991).

Roux, Theunis, "Principle and Pragmatism on the Constitutional Court of South Africa" (2009) 7 International Journal of Constitutional Law 106.

Rozin, Orit, "From 'We' to 'I': Individualism in Israeli Society in the Early 1950s" (Ph.D. dissertation, Tel Aviv University 2002) [Hebrew].

Roznai, Yaniv and Serkan Yolcu, "An Unconstitutional Amendment—the Turkish Perspective: A Comment on the Turkish Constitutional Court's Headscarf Decision" (2012) 10 International Journal of Constitutional Law 175.

Rubinstein, Amnon, "The Knesset and Basic Laws on Human Rights" (2000) 5 Mishpat Umimshal 351 [Hebrew].

Rubinstein, Amnon, "On the Growth of Constitutional Law" In Aharon Barak et al. (eds), *Sefer Shamgar* Vol. 1 Tel Aviv: The Israel Bar 2003) 3 [Hebrew].

Rubinstein, Amnon, *The Constitutional Law of the State of Israel* (6th edn. Tel Aviv: Schocken 2005) [Hebrew].

Rudman, Mara and Mazen Qupti, "The Emergency Powers (Detention) Law: Israel Courts Have a Mission—Should They Choose to Accept It?" (1990) 21 Columbia Human Rights Law Review 469.

Rudolph, Harold, "The Judicial Review of Administrative Detention Orders in Israel" (1984) 14 Israel Yearbook on Human Rights 148.

Russell, Peter H., *Constitutional Odyssey: Can Canadians Become a Sovereign People?* (2nd edn. Toronto: University of Toronto Press 1993).

Sagar, Rahul, *The Oxford Handbook of the Indian Constitution* (Sujit Choudhry, Madhav Khosla, and Pratap Bhanu Mehta (eds) (New York: Oxford University Press 2016).

Salzberger, Eli M., "The Constituent Assembly in Israel" (1996) 3 Mishpat Umimshal 679 [Hebrew].

Salzberger, Eli and Alexander (Sandy) Kedar, "The Quiet Revolution: More on Judicial Review According to the New Basic Laws" (1998) 4 Mishpat Umimshal 489 [Hebrew].

Sandel, Michael J., *Democracy's Discontent: America in Search of a Public Philosophy* (Cambridge, MA: Harvard University Press 1996).

Sapir, Gideon, "Religion and State in Israel: The Case for Reevaluation and Constitutional Entrenchment" (1999) 22 Hastings International and Comparative Law Review 617.

Sapir, Gideon, "Law or Politics: Israeli Constitutional Adjudication as a Case Study" (2001) 6 Journal of International Law and Foreign Affairs 169.

Sapir, Gideon, "Old to New—On Vertical Balancing and Proportionality" (2005) 22 Mehkarei Mishpat: Bar-Ilan Law Studies 477 [Hebrew].

Sapir, Gideon, "Review of *Outlawed Pigs*, by Daphne Barak-Erez" (2008) 11 Mishpat Umimshal 611 [Hebrew].

Scherff, Zeev, *Three Days* (Tel Aviv: Am Oved 1959) [Hebrew].

Segal, Zeev, *Standing before the Supreme Court Sitting as a High Court of Justice* (2nd edn., Tel Aviv: Papyrus 1993) [Hebrew].

Segal, Zeev, "The Way to Judicial Review on the Constitutionality of Statutes: The Authority to Disqualify Acts—To Whom?" (1997) 28 Mishpatim 239 [Hebrew].

Segal, Zeev, "The Supreme Court Sitting as a High Court of Justice: After Fifty Years" (1999) 5 Mishpat Umimshal 235 [Hebrew].

Segev, Joshua, "Was It a Dream or Reality: Justice Cheshin on the Knesset Constituent Authority" (2007) 6 Moznei Mishpat 461 [Hebrew].

Shahar, Yoram, "Solidarity and Inter-generational Dialectics in the Supreme Court: The Politics of Precedent" (2000) 16 Mehkarei Mishpat: Bar-Ilan Law Studies 161 [Hebrew].

Shahar, Yoram, "On the Structure of the Supreme Court of Israel" (2003) 19 Mehkarei Mishpat: Bar-Ilan Law Studies 397 [Hebrew].

Shapira, Amos, "The Status of Fundamental Individual Rights in the Absence of a Written Constitution" (1974) 9 Israel Law Review 497.

Shapira, Amos, "Judicial Review without a Constitution: The Israeli Paradox" (1983) 56 Temple Law Quarterly 405.

Sharfman, Daphna, *Living without a Constitution: Civil Rights in Israel* (Armonk, NY: M. E. Sharpe 1993).

Sharir, Abraham Israel, "Compromise or Surrender" (2006) 25 Tsohar 69 [Hebrew].

Shinar, Adam, "Constitutions in Crisis: A Comparative Approach to Judicial Reasoning and Separation of Powers" (2008) 20 Florida Journal of International Law 115.

Sofer, Oren and Gabriela Fishman, "Judicial Review in a Polarized Society" (2001) 24 Iyyunei Mishpat 663 [Hebrew].

Sommer, Hillel, "The Non-enumerated Rights: On the Scope of the Constitutional Revolution" (1997) 28 Mishpatim 257 [Hebrew].

Sommer, Hillel, "From Childhood to Maturity: Outstanding Issues in the Implementation of the Constitutional Revolution" (2004) 1 Mishpat va'Asakim 59 [Hebrew].

Spitzig, Amanda, "Terrorism and Anti-terrorism Legislation in Canada" (2016) 1 Legal Studies Undergraduate Journal 13.

Sprinzak, Ehud, *Illegalism in Israeli Society* (Tel Aviv: Sifriat Hapoalim 1986) [Hebrew].

Sprinzak, Ehud and Larry Diamond (eds), *Israeli Democracy under Stress* (Boulder, CO: L. Rienner 1993).

Statman, Daniel and Gideon Sapir, "Freedom of Religion, Freedom from Religion, and the Protection of Religious Feelings" (2004) 21 Mehkarei Mishpat: Bar-Ilan Law Studies 5 [Hebrew].

Statman, Daniel and Gideon Sapir, "Religious Marriage in a Liberal State" In Michel Rosenfeld and Susanna Mancini (eds), *Constitutional Secularism in an Age of Religious Revival* (Oxford: Oxford Univeristy Press 2014) 269.

Steiner, Henry H. et al, *International Human Rights in Context* (3rd edn., New York: Oxford University Press 2008).

Stone, Alec, *The Birth of Judicial Politics in France: The Constitutional Council in Comparative Perspective* (New York: Oxford University Press 1992).

Sunstein, Cass R., David Schkade, and Lisa Michelle Ellman, "Ideological Voting on Federal Courts of Appeals: A Preliminary Investigation" (2004) 90 Virginia Law Review 301.

Sunstein, Cass R., *Designing Democracy: What Constitutions Do* (Oxford: Oxford University Press 2001).

Tsemah, Yaakov S., "The Manner of Creating the Power of Judicial Review (HC 231/73)" (1975) 29 Hapraklit 515 [Hebrew].

Tushnet, Mark, *Taking the Constitution Away from the Courts* (Princeton, NJ: Princeton University Press 1999).

Tushnet, Mark, "Misleading Metaphors in Comparative Constitutionalism: Moments and Enthusiasm" (2005) 3 International Journal of Constitutional Law 262.

Tushnet, Mark, "Political Power and Judicial Power: Some Observations on Their Relation" (2006) 75 Fordham Law Review 755.

Tushnet, Mark, *Weak Courts, Strong Rights: Judicial Review and Social Welfare Rights in Comparative Constitutional Law* (Princeton, NJ: Princeton University Press 2008).

Tyler, A. L., "Suspension as an Emergency Power" (2009) 118 Yale Law Journal 600.

Vick, Douglas W., "The Human Rights Act and the British Constitution" (2002) 37 Texas International Law Journal 329.

Volcansek, Mary L. and John F. Stack Jr. (eds), *Courts and Terrorism: Nine Nations Balance Rights and Security* (New York: Cambridge University Press 2011).

Warhaftig, Zerah, *A Constitution for Israel: Religion and State* (Jerusalem: Mesilot 1988) [Hebrew].

Watkins, F. M., *The Failure of Constitutional Emergency Powers under the German Republic* (Cambridge, MA: Harvard University Press 1939).

Weill, Rivka, "We the British People" (2004) 2 Public Law 380.

Weill, Rivka, "Evolution vs. Revolution: Dueling Models of Dualism" (2006) 54 American Journal of Comparative Law 429.

Welch, Kyle, "The Patriot Act and Crisis Legislation: The Unintended Consequences of Disaster Lawmaking" (2015) 43 Capital University Law Review 481.

Witkon, Alfred, "Law in a Developing Country" In Haim Cohn (ed.), *Sefer Yovel le-Pinchas Rosen* (Jerusalem: Mif'al ha-Shikhpul 1962) 66 [Hebrew].

Yamin, A. E. and S. Gloppen (eds), *Litigation Health Rights: Can Courts Bring More Justice to Health?* (Cambridge, MA: Harvard University Press 2011).

Zaltzberger, Eli and Alexander Kedar, "The Silent Revolution—More on Judicial Review under the New Basic Laws" (1997–1998) 4 Mishpat Umimshal 489 [Hebrew].

Zameret, Zvi, "Ben-Gurion in the Early Years of the State and His Attitude to Religious Zionism and the Ultra-orthodox" In N. Ilan (ed.), *Ein Tova: Dialogue and Controversy in Israeli Culture* (Tel-Aviv: Hakibbutz Hameuchad 1998) 349 [Hebrew].

Zamir, Yitzhak, "Judicial Review of Statutes" (1992) 1 Mishpat Umimshal 395 [Hebrew].

Zamir, Yitzhak and Moshe Sobel, "Equality before the Law" (1999) 8 Mishpat Umimshal 215 [Hebrew].

Zeidman, Guy, "Expanded Panels in the Israeli Supreme Court" (2003–2004) 3 Netanya Academic College Law Review 155 [Hebrew].

Zeidman, Guy and Hillel Sommer, "The Supreme Court and the Disengagement" (2006) 9 Mishpat Umimshal 579 [Hebrew].

Ziv, Neta, "Constitutional Review of "Eligibility Conditions" in Social Rights Litigation" In Gideon Sapir, Daphne Barak-Erez, and Aharon Barak (eds), *Israeli Constitutional Law in the Making* (Oxford: Hart Publishing 2013) 349.

Ziv, Neta and Anat Rodnizky, "Disputed Public Housing: A Critical Reading of Judicial Decisions Regarding the "Continuing Tenant" in Israeli Public Housing" (2014) 94 Social Security 99 [Hebrew].

Zilbersheid, Uri, *Social Equality? Not in Our Constitution! The Struggle over the Social Character of the Israeli Constitution from the Declaration of Independence to "A Constitution by Broad Consensus"* (Tel-Aviv: Shocken 2015) [Hebrew].

Zvebner, Sarah, "Appointing Judges: A Comparative Study" (2001) Knesset Research and Information Center [Hebrew].

Index